Psychotherapy and the
Role of the Environment

PSYCHOTHERAPY AND THE ROLE OF THE ENVIRONMENT

By
HAROLD M. VOTH, M.D.
Department of Research
The Menninger Foundation
Topeka, Kansas

MARJORIE H. ORTH, M.S.W.

Formerly, Psychiatric Social
Worker, The Menninger Foundation,
Topeka, Kansas

Behavioral Publications   **New York**
1973

Library of Congress Catalog Card Number 72-13818
Standard Book Number 87705-102-X
Copyright © 1973 by Behavioral Publications

BEHAVIORAL PUBLICATIONS, 2852 Broadway—Morningside Heights,
New York, New York 10025

Printed in the United States of America
This printing   10   9   8   7   6   5   4   3   2   1

Library of Congress Cataloging in Publication Data

Voth, Harold M
    Psychotherapy and the role of the environment.

    Bibliography: p.
    1. Psychotherapy. 2. Man--Influence of environ-
ment. I. Orth, Marjorie H., joint author. II. Title.
[DNLM: 1. Environment. 2. Psychotherapy. WM 420
V971p 1973]
RC480.V68   616.8'914'08   72-13818
ISBN 0-87705-102-X

Contents

Acknowledgments

1. **The Place of Situational Variables in Psychotherapy Research**   1

2. **Definitions of Concepts and Measures of Changes**   8

3. **The Relationship of Environmental Factors to the Onset of Illness**   15

4. **A Reexamination of the Onset of Illness in the Light of Situational Variables**   26

5. **Summary of the Facts at Termination**   42

6. **A Conceptual Understanding of the Facts at Termination**   47

7. **Summary of Facts at Follow-up**   64

8. **A Conceptual Understanding of the Facts at Follow-up**   69

9. **Evaluation and Conclusions**   86

   References   92

   Appendix (Case Histories)   97

ACKNOWLEDGMENTS

This work is from the Psychotherapy Research Project of the Menninger Foundation. The investigation was supported by Public Health Service Research Grant MH 8308 from the National Institute of Mental Health, and earlier by the Foundations' Fund for Research in Psychiatry and the Ford Foundation.

Much credit is due Herbert Modlin, M.D. and Mrs. Mildred Faris, M.S.W. for their work during the early phases of the project. Special thanks are given Lolafaye Coyne, Ph.D. for the statistical analyses. The authors are deeply grateful for the secretarial support of Frances Gray, whose editing and typing of the drafts and final report was invaluable.

While the authors and the colleagues mentioned above were responsible for the collection of data pertaining to the environments of the patients studied in this project, this information could not have been used in a meaningful way without data pertaining to patient and treatment variables. Thus we owe a great deal to a large number of the professional staff of the Menninger Foundation. These include: Ann Appelbaum, M.D.; Stephen A. Appelbaum, Ph.D.; David Beale, M.D.; Francis Broucek, M.D.; Esther Burstein, Ph.D.; Donald Colson, Ph.D.; Gerald Ehrenreich, Ph.D.; Rudolf Ekstein, Ph.D.; Michelina Fabian, M.D.; Siebolt Frieswyk, Ph.D.; Helene Gerall, Ph.D.; Gerard Haigh, Ph.D.; Bernard H. Hall, M.D.; Leonard Horwitz, Ph.D.; Otto Kernberg, M.D.; Lester Luborsky, Ph.D.; T. W. Mathews, B.A.; Martin Mayman, Ph.D.; Karl Menninger, M.D.; Rowe Mortimer, Ph.D.; Gardner Murphy, Ph.D.; Ishak Ramzy, Ph.D.; Lewis Robbins, M D.; Irwin Rosen, Ph.D.; David Rosenstein, M.D.; Helen Sargent, Ph.D.; Richard Siegal, Ph.D.; Sydney Smith, Ph.D.; William Tarnower, M.D.; Ernst A. Ticho, Ph.D.; Gertrude R. Ticho, M.D.; and Robert Wallerstein, M.D.

In addition to the above, we also received a great deal of help from a number of consultants to the project. Included were: David Bakan, Ph.D.; John Benjamin, M.D.; Merton Gill, M.D.; Maxwell Gitelson, M.D.; Louis Guttman, Ph.D.;

Robert Holt, Ph.D.; Wayne Holtzman, Ph.D.; James Lingoes, Ph.D.; and Arnold Z. Pfeffer, M.D.

Drs. Holtzman and Coyne were particularly influential in our decision to organize the data in its present form. Dr. John Benjamin's observation that the most solid evidence regarding the efficacy of treatment is to be found in the way a patient lives his life after treatment served us well throughout the entire period of this project.

1. THE PLACE OF SITUATIONAL VARIABLES IN PSYCHOTHERAPY RESEARCH

Evidence exists in abundance which links environmental factors, including cultural influences, more immediate life situations, sudden and isolated events as well as continuous ones, to human adjustment and to psychiatric illness. Studies like those of Eaton & Weil (1955); Faris & Dunham (1939); Hollingshead & Redlich (1957); Leighton et al. (1963); and Langner & Michael (1963), to mention but a few, illustrate the effects of social and environmental influences on behavior and mental health.

The literature abounds with references citing the relationship of more specific life experiences to psychiatric illnesses. The relationship of loss to depression is well-known (Freud, 1917). Lindemann's study (1944) reveals the extensive effects of major losses. Paykel et al. (1969) demonstrated a significant relationship of several kinds of life events and depression.

Brown & Birley (1968) found a relationship between a variety of events similar to those described in our study and the onset of schizophrenia. Hilgard & Newman's study (1961) of anniversary reactions links recent events with earlier events and both to the onset of psychiatric illness. An excellent review by Burnham (1969) lists a number of life situations which appear to be linked with the onset of schizophrenia that are similar or identical to those detailed in our study. The work by Leff, Roatch & Bunney (1970) lists a number of situations similar to those mentioned by Burnham and ourselves that were related to the outbreak of psychiatric illness. They reported on a number of life events which triggered core conflicts, a concept which they found to be useful for the understanding of their findings. In a very comprehensive review Hocking (1970) has described the effects of stress on mental life and its significance for psychotherapy.

The work of Forrest, Fraser & Priest (1965), which is

1

a study demonstrating the illness-producing impact of the
environment, notes the distinction between environmental
effects which are additive and eventually overwhelming with
events which strike at a point of vulnerability within the
individual. Their work is especially relevant to the present
study in that they suggest, along with Lewis (1934), that
one of the functions of depression is to remove the individual from his noxious environment, thus allowing psychic
repair.

Despite the general awareness among professionals that
the environment has much to do with man's psychic equilibrium
and the onset of manifest illness, research in psychotherapy
has had difficulty incorporating the patient-environment
dimension. The complexities of the patient-environment interaction is rarely brought into sharp focus in research on the
treatment process; rather, the therapist-patient dimension
is nearly always the primary focus. This omission overlooks
the fact that people do not live in a vacuum before, during,
or after treatment. Events occur beyond the patient's control; he may bring about events in the environment which, in
turn, have a feedback on him. Many studies (probably most)
into the nature of the psychotherapy process ignore the
patient-environment dimension altogether. One is struck,
for instance, by the sparse attention paid the subject in
Research in Psychotherapy (edited by Strupp & Luborsky, 1962),
although one brief paragraph on page 324 refers to a consensus of opinion of the conferees that more attention must
be paid to social factors in psychotherapy research. They
note, however, that the ultimate test of the outcome of treatment "is the manner in which the patient actually changes
his way of living outside the treatment." This conclusion
is one with which we wholeheartedly agree, but we wish to
add that such changes can only be fully understood by a
thorough knowledge of environmental changes prior to, during
and after treatment within the life space of the patient, as
well as knowledge of the treatment process itself.

We wish to caution that any attempt to include the role
of environmental factors in the understanding of the onset
of a person's illness or of a patient's change during psychotherapy invites an oversimplified view of psychogenesis. One
can all too easily hold the environment directly or solely
responsible for both the patient's illness and for his improvement or failure to improve during treatment or, conversely, fail to recognize the vital role the environment may
have played in the patient's life.

On close inspection it will usually be discovered that

the environment, in ways which will be the focus in the body
of this work, bears a direct relationship to the onset of the
illness, its course, and its outcome. The findings of this
study strongly suggest that there exists a direct relationship between the extent and severity of manifest psychopathology and the nature of and intensity of the individual's
commitment to his environment, provided intrapsychic conditions exist which will permit an illness to develop and a
regressive process has been set into motion. Commitment to
one's environment refers to living out one's capabilities
where possible and living up to mature responsibilities.
Fewer unconscious conflicts and greater maturity permit a
more involved and committed life. Conversely, individuals
who live in a relative environmental vacuum tend to avoid
deeper involvement for potentially illness-producing intrapsychic reasons and thus avoid regression and illness. When
such persons attempt to intensify their involvement with
their environment in a mature way, signs of illness will
appear or old symptoms will become more exaggerated. On
the other hand, some mentally ill individuals may exhibit
a high degree of interaction with the environment but close
inspection will show that these interactions are highly
symptomatic in significance and are ways for avoiding a
mature involvement and commitment. For these persons, too,
attempting to commit themselves to life in a mature way
evokes even more exaggerated symptomatology, often of a more
autoplastic kind.

Behavioral and environmental data will be conceptualized in a way which gives psychoanalytic meaning to environ-
ment-patient interactions, thereby making it possible to
distinguish normal from abnormal involvements and the relationship of both kinds of interactions to the waxing and
waning of manifest psychopathology.

We think a number of psychoanalytic principles are
supported by the data and the work illustrates how vital a
role the environment plays in human adjustment, the appearance or disappearance of manifest illness, and the efficacy
of treatment.

A major problem in the study lay in the choice of the
measuring stick by which patient change was to be measured
and conceptualized, regardless of how well the empirical
data were understood. In studies on intrapsychic changes,
even if the design includes an analysis of the psychotherapy
process, the main reference point for assessing change is
the patient himself before treatment. In studies of a
patient's behavior in relation to the environment, the

faulty assumption is often made that the environment is stationary and, therefore, provides an invariant background against which the functioning of the patient is to be judged in before-treatment and after-treatment comparisons. The everchanging environment, especially in long-term treatments, and environmental events may play a major role in stimulating or inhibiting change in the patient and in the choice of modes he uses for adapting himself to his environment.

The research design is based on the view that the patient is in a continuous state of interaction with his environment, of which the psychotherapy is a highly specialized part. In Karl Menninger's words, "It is necessary to describe not only a changing individual living in that environment, but to describe the changing reactions of that (changed) individual to the environment, and vice versa" (1962). The task of the Situational Variables team in the Psychotherapy Research Project has been to record as accurately and objectively as possible the patient's condition and behavior and relevant environmental events at the beginning of treatment, at termination, and again two years later at follow-up. We defined the life space of the individual, and then conceptualized the raw data of the patient-environmental interaction so that both the patient and the environment had values or meaning in terms of each other. Thus considered, events in the patient's life which influenced him, and perhaps his treatment, either negatively or positively, became more evident and more understandable.

A detailed description of the overall design of the project and its rationale - that is, its theoretical underpinnings - can be found elsewhere (Luborsky & Sargent, 1956; Luborsky et al., 1958; Robbins & Wallerstein, 1956; Sargent, 1956a, 1956b; Sargent et al., 1958; Wallerstein & Robbins, 1956, 1958). However, in order for the reader to better understand the material presented and discussed in this work, it is necessary to give a brief sketch of the design.

Forty-two cases, half of whom were in psychoanalysis and the other half in various kinds of psychotherapy ranging from the supportive to expressive mode, were studied intensively prior to the onset of their treatments, at termination and two years later at follow-up. The study was naturalistic in that treatment was not influenced by the research team; in fact, neither the therapists nor the patients were aware of being included in the study until after treatment was completed. Treatments varied considerably; some were long-term psychoanalysis and others more short-term supportive treatment.

For the initial work-up the mass of data, which was taken from all possible sources (clinical history, social work history, psychological tests, correspondence, records from other hospitals, etc.), was ordered according to certain concepts and definitions into two major categories. These were referred to as Patient and Situational Variables. Patient Variables included Sex and Age, Anxiety and Symptoms, Nature of Conflict, Ego Factors and Defenses, Capacity Factors, Motivational Factors, Relationship Factors, and Reality Factors. Under these eight categories were subcategories, making a total of 28 variables. Situational Variables included statements regarding Relevance, Stress, Conflict Triggers, Need-congruence, Support, Opportunity, and Mutability.

Certain predictions were made by the Patient and Situational Variables teams about the patient's future life and behavior as a consequence of his treatment.

At the conclusion of treatment each case was again studied intensively by way of all clinical data available. These sources included hospital and treatment records, and psychotherapy and psychoanalytic process notes, if available. The patients were given a battery of psychological tests and they were interviewed by representatives of the Treatment and Situational Variables teams of researchers. Significant relatives and certain other persons, such as employers, were interviewed when possible. All of these data were sifted again and given conceptual meaning and recorded under the heading of three major categories of variables: Patient, Treatment, and Situational. Treatment variables, which could be defined only at termination and follow-up, included variables relevant to treatment modality, treatment arrangements and instructions, circumstances affecting treatment, techniques employed, content of material focused upon, the nature of treatment process, nature of termination, therapist's skills, supervision provided for therapist, and therapist's style. Predictions were again made independently about the patient's future functioning and condition by both teams.

Two years later, at follow-up, the patients were again interviewed and tested by the same battery of psychological tests and all other information that might have been collected was again - along with interview data from relatives or spouses - sifted and ordered under the three variables categories: Patient, Treatment and Situational. The data,

ordered in this way at the three points in time, provided
the basis for all research comparisons and analyses.

The information thus obtained was factual and gave a
longitudinal view of a segment of the patient's life. These
facts were recorded as such but were also restated concep-
tually. These conceptual meanings, treated as data realities,
became the mass of interacting variables, the understanding
of which has been the task of the various research teams. A
prediction study was included in order to test some of the
basic assumptions of psychoanalytic theory (Sargent et al.,
1968). Numerous other publications describe in detail the
various facets of the project (Hall & Wallerstein, 1960;
Sargent, 1960, 1961; Siegal, 1967; Siegal & Ehrenreich,
1962; Siegal & Rosen, 1962; Robbins & Wallerstein, 1959;
Wallerstein & Robbins, 1960; Watterson, 1954).

While the above sketches out in the barest way possible
the overall design of the project, a somewhat more detailed
account is now given of the work of the Situational Variables
team. It was the task of this team to describe as explicitly
as possible the nature of the patient's life adjustment
initially, at termination, and at follow-up. This team,
along with the other teams, was charged also with recording
the state of health the patient manifested at these three
points in time, as measured by the Health-Sickness Rating
Scale (Luborsky, 1962).

The data from all the clinical data available, and
from interviews of the patient and relatives and spouses,
provided the information regarding the following areas of
the patient's life: cultural background, his parental
family, marital family, friends and co-workers, community
and leisure and physical health. A case summary from the
situational point of view, was written for each patient at
the three points in time. The facts contained therein were
conceptualized according to the headings below.

The environmental factors which fell into each of the
above headings were redefined as to their significance as
Conflict Triggers, Stresses, Supports as to their Need-
congruence and as to the extent they provided an Opportunity
for growth and with regard to their Mutability. The definitions of these variables are found in the next section.
Thus each aspect of the patient's life, for instance his
marital family, was defined as to its stressful aspects,
its conflict-triggering aspects, and so on. The data were,
therefore, recorded in a clinically narrative form and in
outline form based on the above-mentioned concepts.

To put it as simply as possible, we have endeavored to discover whether or not environmental-patient interactions can be meaningfully conceptualized by the above concepts and whether a systematic longitudinal analysis of these inter-actions will shed light on the nature of patient change during and after treatment. We are impressed by the fact that while the ultimate basis for psychopathology is to be found within the individual psyche, environmental factors must be taken into account in order to enrich the under-standing of why an illness occurs when it does, of why and when it disappears with or without the benefits of treatment. This aspect of the study was based on the assumption that to make a reasonably accurate assessment of a person's psychic condition at any point in time, the environmental circum-stances must be known; that is, an illness may develop and be obvious under one set of environmental conditions but not in another. We based our study on the notion that the en-vironmental matrix in which a patient exists and through which he is passing and interacting must be understood, for it is this matrix which activates the illness or may permit it to recede, and may induce or retard recovery from illness and, finally, may further stimulate or retard maturation.

The research to be presented was carried out over a period of approximately ten years. What follows is an attempt to give an overview of the changes in the lives of the 42 cases and to give those changes conceptual meaning in situa-tional variables and a few central personality terms. This is essentially a clinical study. Our intimate knowledge of the patients permitted ordering the variables into groups which allowed for meaningful clinical comparisons. Statis-tical findings as regards the role of situational variables in outcome are described in detail elsewhere (Burstein et al., 1972).

2. DEFINITIONS OF CONCEPTS AND MEASURES OF CHANGES

Without giving some degree of abstract meaning to the data referred to as environmental factors, we would have nothing more than a mass of descriptions, unorganized and confused. Environmental factors can be defined as having an absolute value and yet at the same time have widely different meanings for different individuals. What is one man's meat may be another man's poison. One may be a round peg in a round hole, while another may be a square peg in that hole. After obtaining all of the facts from the various sources, it was the task of the Situational Variables team to define the various meanings of the environment, both usual and personal, for each of the 42 patients at initial study, at termination and at follow-up in the following way.

1. A statement was made regarding the life space of the patient with emphasis on the various degrees of relevance of the environment within that space. It was intended here to capture the degree to which the various aspects of the patient's environment impinged upon the patient; that is, the depth of the patient's commitment to or involvement with the elements in his environment. Some aspect of the person's background might be especially relevant (see Case Nos. 13, 22, 31). The nature of the patient's responsibilities, interests and involvement are spelled out in detail.

2. The environment with which the patient was involved was assessed as to its conflict-triggering impact on the patient. This variable rests on the assumption of the existence of unconscious forces which are defined as core conflicts. These unconscious forces may vary with respect to the degree to which they are triggered and activated by the environment and, therefore, to the degree to which they have a manifest effect upon the person at any given time. Those factors in the environment which trigger core conflicts are referred to as conflict triggers. These unconscious forces may themselves be defined in a variety of ways but, in the main, center around the libidinal and aggressive

8

drive organizations and associated object relationships
which characterize the various levels of psychosexual development. Conflict triggers, then, are simply those environmental factors in relation to which the person has some
investment and involvement and which, as a consequence,
trigger and activate his nuclear conflicts. The more intense the involvement with the environment, the greater will
be the conflict-triggering effect. Thus, environmental
factors, innocuous in their own right, can be conflict-
triggering and have an illness-producing effect. For example, commitment to a woman may be possible for one man
but difficult and illness-producing for another, not because
of the woman's inherent qualities as a person but because
she triggers unconscious conflict born out of his early
childhood experiences. A boss who in reality is a benevo-
lent man may be experienced as malevolent by a person who
has not resolved his unconscious conflicts revolving around
authority figures, and so on. If such a person is involved
with authority figures, his core conflicts will be activated and may produce neurotic distress and even more severe
psychopathology. If uninvolved, his conflicts may lie dormant to a greater extent, and there will be less evidence of
manifest psychopathology. The severity of the symptoms
bears a relationship to the intensity of the environmental
involvement, to the degree to which unconscious conflicts
are mobilized, and to the stability of the defensive organization. The essential point here is that the environment
is not the "cause" of the illness but merely the activator
of unconscious forces which are the true bases for the
illness.

Virtually any aspect of the environment may be conflict-
triggering. There are persons for whom the slightest
success activates unconscious conflicts which, in turn, produce symptomatic reactions. Even an intent to be successful
in some area of life, no matter how slight, may have a
similar effect in some. The illness-triggering effect of
the environment may be extremely subtle and tends to be
overlooked, and the assumption may easily be made that the
illness was "endogenous." A careful history will frequently
point to new or intensified environmental interactions
following which the person's behavior began to worsen. A
complete statement of the conflict trigger - core conflict
dimension requires, therefore, a statement of the nature of
the person's unconscious conflicts and those environmental
factors which trigger those conflicts.

The Patient Variables and the Situational Variables
teams independently assessed the nature of the core conflicts

for each patient. It was remarkable how parallel these assessments were. Conflict triggers were spelled out by the
Situational Variables team only.

3. The concept Stress refers to those environmental
factors which are noxious in their own right and, this being
so, would have a negative or harmful impact on anyone.
These factors are to be judged in terms of their common impact on anyone. Any or all of the external difficulties
which bedevil mankind may be considered here, from nagging
wives to heavy debts to high pressure jobs, and will refer
to continuing sources of strain and/or to single traumatic
events. We include in this category feedback stresses
brought upon the person by his own behavior.

The underlying assumption regarding stress is that
environmental factors which are sufficiently noxious may
weaken the defensive and adaptive organization of the ego.
Excessive fatigue, threat to life, excessive isolation,
continuing relationships with persons who are excessively
harsh or unpleasant are examples. This variable, unlike
environmental factors which are conflict-triggering, is
harmful in a direct sense. An environmental factor may be
both stressful and conflict-triggering, e.g., cancer, in
that fears of loss and castration anxiety may be awakened
by the disease. The death of a loved one is stressful and
may also be conflict-triggering in that the loss may repre-
sent a fulfillment of an infantile death wish or awaken
conflicts surrounding an earlier loss. Stresses may also
be conflict-triggering if core conflicts exist which bear a
meaningful relationship to the stress.

Even though stressful factors and factors which are
inherently innocuous but which trigger unconscious conflicts
both overwhelm the person's defensive organization, it is
important nevertheless to make the distinction because the
basic source of the assault on the ego is opposite. The
one, stress, exists in reality and its removal should have
rather immediate beneficial effects unless the person has
become excessively disorganized. Conflict triggers, however, activate unconscious forces, the assault is from within.
Therapeutic interventions require removal of the conflict
trigger or resolution of the unconscious conflicts, or both.
Once regressed, removal of the conflict trigger alone may
or may not reverse the regression.

4. The Support variable includes all factors which
were judged to be helpful, facilitating, or in any way beneficial to the patient. It should not be assumed that a

factor defined as supportive is necessarily supportive for
everyone. Financial support from parents may be nearly lifesaving for one person and serves to enhance another's dependence, resentment, or guilt, or may be helpful only to
infantalize later on. Supports have a positive and helpful
effect. This dimension refers to both material supports
and to people. Who does the person have pulling for him,
who stands by him through thick and thin, and how plentiful
are those persons? Other supports are less obvious and refer
to the kind of silent sustaining effect which comes from
being part of an organization such as one's work, church,
clubs, etc. To satisfy the requirements of this variable
it is necessary, therefore, to evaluate the amount and kind
of material support, on the one hand, and interpersonal
support on the other.

5. _Need-congruence_ of the environment refers to the
extent to which the individual is impinged upon by factors
which promote growth and maturation, and to the degree to
which the environment resonates harmoniously with established values, talents, skills, and interests.

The aspect of the need-congruence variable which is
most significant introduces a value system which pertains
to normality and gender identity. It is an underlying
assumption implicit in the concept of need-congruence - as
we have used it in the project - that the concepts of
normalcy, maturity, and gender identity can be defined as
psychological realities. This being so, the environment
must be assessed not only regarding its harmoniousness with
the individual's skills, talents, values, etc., but also to
the degree to which it promotes growth and maturation toward
normality and toward the full development and expression of
unmixed gender identity. Thus the environment can either
facilitate or inhibit the natural trend toward growth,
normality and unmixed gender identity, as well as thwart or
gratify skills, talents, values, etc. As an example, a
child is for a woman one of the most need-congruent factors
in the sense that the attainment of maturity and femininity
is facilitated by the experience. A shrewish, critical wife
is not need-congruent for a man attempting to achieve maturity and express his male identity.

6. _Opportunity_ refers to the extent to which the environment permits or invites the patient's expression of
his existing qualities and/or potential. The assessment
aims at defining how many options he has for constructively
developing and expressing what he is.

7. Mutability refers to the degree to which the environment can be changed. Some life circumstances can be easily and extensively altered while others are relatively fixed. An unmarried person, skilled and well-trained, can go most anywhere and do about anything he wishes to do. Another may be tied down by a large number of responsibilities and commitments. This variable is difficult to define but nonetheless important, for as patients change intrapsychically, the environment should be flexible anough to accommodate those changes. The burden on a person may be great when he might or has changed internally but lives in a rigid environment. A rigid environment tends to inhibit the extent to which the individual can change. Conversely, fortuitous changes in the environment may significantly facilitate, or even initiate, change in the person. A relatively unchanging environment which promotes maturation, in which the patient is fixed, may facilitate change within the patient by inducing him to mature and live up to his responsibilities. A patient in such an environment may take flight from treatment rather than change. If his environment is too mutable he may seek sick relationships and thereby avoid changing internally, or a mutuable environment may permit the finding of more mature relationships, etc. Mutability is closely related, therefore, to relevance. The facts to be established are: What are the life involvements, commitments and responsibilities, and how fixed or changeable are they?

Since the objective of the Psychotherapy Research Project was to investigate the relationship of personality change to patient, treatment and situational variables, the variables of these three categories required some degree of quantification. Similarly, scores reflecting patient change needed to be devised. In the beginning, rather than attempt to quantify the situational variables according to an absolute scale, the paired comparison method was used (Luborsky & Sargent, 1956; Robbins & Wallerstein, 1956; Sargent, 1956a, 1956b; and Wallerstein & Robbins, 1956). This method divided the 42 cases into seven overlapping groups of 12. The raters were required to judge which of each pair of patients possessed more of each of the situational variables. All patients were, as a consequence, ordered according to the number of times chosen for each variable and thus relative relationships only were established. This arduous task was undertaken primarily for the quantitative analyses (Burstein et al., 1972). An expectable by-product of this task was an intimate knowledge of each patient and his environment. These clinical data were easily refreshable by reading the written case summaries that were prepared at three points in time in which situational variables were described, making it possible for us to divide the patient groups for each variable for purposes of comparison at the three points in time. The groupings reflect the combined judgments of both authors. This task, which required a retrospective re- view of all cases, was undertaken near the conclusion of the data-gathering phase of the project.

This readily accessible information made it possible for us to do the outcome analyses in a way we had not antic- ipated doing until we were well along toward the end of the study. We found we could make much more meaningful analyses if we identified specific factors in the environment which were conflict-triggering. Similarly, the data became much more meaningful when we divided need-congruence into its two aspects. Thus we discovered that our clinical judgments (as recorded in our case write-ups) as regards "how much" of a given variable characterized a patient seemed to be more meaningful than quantitative scales. In short, we believed we could be more accurate in the analyses of the complex clinical data if we emphasized the clinical rather than the statistical aspects of the data. We therefore reread our case syntheses and upon reaching a consensus made clinically meaningful groupings which were used for compar- isons of various sorts.

Two independent scores of patient change were used in this study. They are (1) The Health-Sickness Rating Scale (Luborsky, 1962) as recorded at initial study, at termina- tion, and at follow-up by the Treatment Variables team, and (2) the Absolute Global Change score[1] which was devised by the Prediction Study team. In addition, there is a HSRS change score applicable at termination and follow-up. This is a residual score which takes into account the patient's original level on the HSRS points. It lacks an anchor point and is a relative score only. For a patient high in the scale initially, his amount of change is weighted more than a patient with the same amount of change who was low in the scale initially. The HSRS as determined by the Treatment Variables team scores and the Absolute Global Change scores which were made by the Prediction Study team for all 42 cases correlated .81 at termination and .82 at follow-up. It might be of interest to note that the Situational Vari- ables team's HSRS scores and the Treatment Variables team's HSRS scores correlated .99, .88, and .81 at the threesucces- sive points in time (initial, termination, and follow-up).

---

[1]Appelbaum, A. & Horwitz, L. Correlates of global change in psychotherapy. Unpublished manuscript.

In the analyses to follow, chi-square will be used with the Absolute Global Change score inasmuch as this score is not an equal-interval scale. Analysis of variance and t tests will be used with the HSRS scores.

3. THE RELATIONSHIP OF ENVIRONMENTAL FACTORS
    TO THE ONSET OF ILLNESS

The data which are to be presented in this section show
that psychiatric illness rarely, if ever, develops "spontaneously" and that while unconscious forces are clearly the
ultimate cause or source of the illness, the nature of the
individual's interaction, that is, involvement, with his
environment provides a clearer understanding of the illness
and why it developed at a particular time. The data to be
drawn upon to illustrate this illness-evoking impact of the
environment are taken from the case histories of the 42
patients.

The theoretical view around which these data are organ-
ized is that manifest illness occurs when unconscious forces
are no longer successfully bound by repression, other defenses and character traits. Under these conditions of dis-
equilibrium, the ego employs various defensive measures
which, when taken in the aggregate along with drive and
superego factors, form the symptom complex. It is obvious
that many persons successfully bind potentially pathogenic
unconscious forces and can function adequately so long as
their unconscious conflicts remain bound. They have established an equilibrium for themselves which may not permit a
full expression of the potentials within their personalities
but which is sufficiently adaptive and defensive to prevent
them from being classed as ill by most standards, or at
least to prevent them from seeking professional care.

Two closely related classes of forces which impinge on
individuals tend to upset a static equilibrium at any given
phase in their lives. These are, on the one hand, internal
maturational forces which "push" people toward maturity and,
on the other, there are social norms which must be fulfilled.
Stated in an overly simplified way, there are internal biologic forces which impel boys to become men and girls to
become women, alongside a psychological pressure to mature.
Every society has established norms which are typical for
men and women which each sex attempts to fulfill. Many of

15

the qualities of a masculine man are clearly defined and
distinct, as are many of the qualities of a feminine woman.
For instance, the role and identity of husband and father
are distinct and different from the role and identity of a
wife and mother. These identities and roles are not merely
idealizations but are operationally definable and achievable
by persons who live in a health-facilitating environment and
who are able, as a consequence, to successfully navigate
psychosexual development. Such persons, as adults, are
minimally burdened by repressed conflicts. They have resolved the Oedipus complex and other pregenital conflicts
and have established a character structure which reflects
a harmonious integration of introjects, identification objects, drives and those ego qualities which have been learned
and those which are constitutionally given. Such individuals will clearly bear a masculine or feminine identity and
will be able to discharge the responsibilities of their
respective gender within the limits of their talents, skills
and abilities and in accordance with social norms.

While it is true that the social roles of the sexes
are changing along with the norms for each sex, it is our
impression that many of these new values are heavy in unconscious meaning and conflict with the biologic thrust of
male and female. It is axiomatic to this study that male
and female roles and identities harmonize with biologically
distinct gender differences. Men and women in opposite roles
are in conflict within themselves.

The purpose of the above outline is to provide a conceptual basis for illustrating why those individuals who
are destined to become psychiatrically ill do so at certain
points in their lives. There are certain times when the
relationship to the environment changes in a very specific
way as one progresses through life. The individual, because
of internal maturational forces or because of a wish to fill
a social norm, or both, will seek to intensify or change his
involvement or commitment to his environment in a direction
which generally increases his adult responsibilities and
crystallizes his gender and initiates or intensifies his
relationship with the opposite sex. When such shifts take
place in relation to the environment, unconscious conflicts
become mobilized (where they exist) and illness may develop,
often to the extent that psychiatric help is required.
There are periods, such as adolescence, when many profound
internal changes are occurring but during these phases, too,
the person's relationship to his environment changes markedly. An exception to the illness-triggering effect of
increased involvement with the environment is when loss

occurrs, but here, too, the relationship to the environment
has changed in such a way as to trigger an illness-producing
conflict.

It may seem that we are implying that the environment
itself produces the illness. This is precisely what we do
not mean, although it is well known that there are environmental stresses which can overwhelm anyone - such as in
traumatic neurosis. Instead, we are suggesting that the
very process of deepening or attempting to deepen one's involvement with life, while adaptive in its aim, will activate
an illness where unconscious conflicts lie dormant and where
deepened life involvement disturbs character and adjustment
patterns which had successfully bound unconscious conflicts.
In the treatment situation, the phenomenon of transference
is an example of this principle. The patient's increasingly
deepened involvement with his doctor activates unconscious
forces which may produce new symptoms as well as transference distortions which also have symptomatic significance.

A detailed analysis was made of the case histories of
each of the 42 cases. Those life events which coincided
with the onset of symptoms and the period when the illness
finally required professional help were recorded for every
patient. The kinds of life circumstances at these two times
fell into the following categories: puberty, heterosexuality, marriage, parenthood, parents, work, school, object
loss, threat to life, and absent life involvement.

The facts which emerged clearly and unmistakably are
those which experienced clinicians will immediately recognize, namely, that certain kinds of attempts at commitment
to life coincide with the outbreak of illness, presumably,
as we have indicated, because of a disturbance of the intrapsychic equilibrium and mobilization of unconscious conflicts.
Many of the 42 patients had been symptomatic during childhood but most managed to pass successfully through early
childhood and the latency period without psychiatric help.

Nineteen of the 42 patients (Nos. 1, 2, 4, 6, 8, 11,
13, 14, 19, 23, 25, 27, 28, 29, 30, 32, 33, 38, 41) developed frank symptoms during puberty. Six of these (Nos. 14,
19, 27, 29, 32, 38) were at the time also making serious
efforts at establishing a heterosexual relationship, not
all of which were frankly sexual in nature. A case in
point is that of a young girl (No. 19) who, instead of
developing enduring and mature heterosexual contacts, fell
in love with a much older man as her first heterosexual
involvement and then took flight into polymorphous perverse

behavior and, finally, homosexuality as well as continued liaisons with much older men. She failed at school; worked, posing in the nude for a photographer, and eventually had to be hospitalized. Case No. 29 became rebellious at age 11 or 12 and eventually became virtually uncontrollable by the parents. She entered into a flurry of promiscuous heterosexuality, for several years failed in school, and ultimately took flight into overt homosexuality. Case No. 20 is that of a young man who was succeeding well in high school but his guilt over compulsive masturbation forced him to "take a rest" from school for awhile. His first serious symptom, that of excessive drinking, coincided with his first serious efforts at establishing a heterosexual relationship. These three cases illustrate the combined illness-producing effect of puberty and the effort to become involved with the opposite sex.

It should be repeated that in each of the 19 people puberty was the illness-activating force and that six of these patients were, at the same time, attempting to establish heterosexual contact of one sort or another. It is noteworthy that puberty alone (with minimal coincidental efforts to establish object relations) led to medical intervention in only four of the 19 cases (Nos. 14, 23, 25, 32), thus suggesting that while the intense internal instinctual forces of puberty cause much disturbance and even frank symptomatology, the psychic turmoil was not severe enough to require professional help except for four. The findings suggest that attempts to form heterosexual object relations are a significant factor for evoking psychopathology during puberty.

Heterosexuality (herein defined as an individual's attempt to establish an intimate and prolonged relationship short of marriage with a member of the opposite sex), irrespective of the age of the patient, triggered an illness in 15 cases (Nos. 5, 10, 14, 18, 19, 20, 21, 26, 27, 29, 32, 34, 36, 38, 39); of these, the illness appeared during puberty in six cases (see Nos. 14, 19, 27, 29, 32, 38). Another (No. 1) had a very difficult time establishing her feminine identity at puberty but she did not become manifestly ill. Ten of the 15 cases were past the puberty period when their illness erupted and thus forces other than heightened instinctual drives characteristic of puberty must be sought to account for the outbreak of the illness. It is our conclusion that it was primarily the attempt to form a relationship with the opposite sex that triggered unconscious forces which was the basis for the illnesses in these patients.

All 15 patients, including the six who were in the
puberty period, were making a serious effort to establish
a close heterosexual relationship. The other 27 of the 42
cases had managed to pass through puberty without developing noticeable symptoms and, similarly, their efforts to
establish heterosexual contact short of marriage did not
produce symptoms of much significance. Case No. 5 in the
group of 15 patients for whom heterosexual object relations
produced symptoms is that of a young woman who managed to
pass through puberty but who, after she began to date, became prudish to the point of slapping boys who tried to kiss
her. While in high school she was petting heavily with a
boy who ejaculated on her outer clothing. This experience
created much anxiety, she developed fears of pregnancy and
she had to be hospitalized briefly. Case No. 26 is that of
a young man whose eventually severe alcoholism began when
he first became engaged. Later, after marriage, his drinking became markedly worse. Case No. 18, who had been quite
attached to his mother, proposed marriage to an older girl
while still in high school. At age 26 he dated a woman
age 46. At the point when she asked him to kiss her he
developed gastrointestinal symptoms severe enough to require
medical attention. Subsequently he entered into many
affairs and a marriage failed. Case No. 32 first became ill
at age 15. She was dating a great deal and was acutely aware
of her sexual feelings. While at a party a boy kissed her,
an event for which she was severely criticized by the other
girls. She soon developed severe anxiety and was unable to
be alone.

The next step forward in heterosexual adjustment is
marriage. It is a reasonable assumption that a greater
degree of commitment and involvement with the opposite sex
characterizes marriage. Twenty of the 42 cases demonstrated
a relationship between the onset or worsening of some aspect
of their psychopathology and marriage (Nos. 1, 2, 3, 6, 7,
8, 9, 11, 18, 22, 26, 28, 30, 31, 32, 33, 36, 37, 40, 41).
It is of particular interest that the clinical history of
only five (Nos. 11, 18, 22, 32, 36) mentions symptoms associated with earlier heterosexual efforts severe enough to
be included in the case history. Nine (Nos. 1, 2, 6, 8,
28, 30, 32, 33, 41) of this group showed evidence of symptomatology at puberty sufficiently severe to be mentioned in
the clinical folder. It thus appears that an outbreak of
symptoms in association with puberty and early efforts
toward forming a heterosexual relationship may serve as a
prediction of a later illness when marriage is attempted.
Some are relatively unscathed by courtship alone but fall
ill when deeper commitment to the opposite sex is attempted

through marriage.

Of the 21 cases in whom illness onset or worsening of
illness coincided with marriage, formal treatment eventually
became necessary for eight (Nos. 3, 7, 11, 18, 30, 32, 33,
36). Case No. 7 is that of a woman who managed to adjust
successfully until she married, then symptoms of general
irresponsibility and alcoholism appeared and progressed in
severity with the birth of children. She finally lost her
entire family despite treatment efforts. Case No. 18 had
reacted symptomatically to courtship but managed, nonetheless, to attempt marriage to a woman he knew was not yet
legally divorced. Marked marital discord ensued, there was
sexual incompatibility and he sought psychiatric treatment
for the first time. Case No. 32 had had an earlier period
of treatment when she had first become interested in boys.
She improved and entered into a courtship which eventually
led to marriage. Initially she seemed to find strength in
this relationship for she functioned well for eight months.
Then she began to regress and finally became severely phobic.
Case No. 3 first married at age 18 and, while no symptomatology was reported, marked marital discord existed during
the 5-year period. The patient had one known extra-marital
affair and eventually divorced, then married another woman.
The second wife reported he became addicted to drugs during
the first year of their marriage.

A further step toward greater adult responsibilities
and one which generally stimulates intrapsychic change and
role definition, as well as intensification of the heterosexual relationship, is parenthood, especially for women.
Becoming a parent, like marrying, tends to crystalize gender
identity, intensifies the relationship to the opposite sex,
and to the infant. In 12 cases (Nos. 1, 5, 6, 7, 8, 9, 12,
28, 31, 33, 35, 36), the onset or worsening of the psychopathology bore a clear relationship to the new responsibilities of parenthood. Other cases suggested such a relationship but clear and definite evidence was lacking. Only two
of the 12 cases were men. They were already symptomatic
but their symptoms became worse after the birth of their
children. In seven of the 12 cases (Nos. 5, 7, 8, 9, 28,
35, 38), all women, the new child (born or adopted) or the
cumulative effect of children as their number increased,
led to the illness becoming sufficiently severe to require
medical assistance.

It appears that parenthood has a greater impact in its
illness-triggering effect on women than men. This is not
surprising since a good part of a man's responsibilities

lies outside the home while the woman's responsibility may
change markedly after the birth of a child, particularly
if she previously worked outside the home.

Case No. 5 is that of an infertile woman who went to
great lengths to adopt a child. Within a brief time after
the adoption the patient developed hostile obsessive thoughts
toward the infant and eventually had to return the child.
She required brief hospitalization. Years later, after a
long period of treatment, she was able to adopt a child,
but even then she became distressed to the extent that she
required drugs and supportive counsel from her priest.

Case No. 9 married at age 19 and soon became pregnant.
She was criminally aborted and divorced soon thereafter.
During her second marriage abdominal pain led to a bilateral
salpingectomy. After six years of a low-keyed marriage, a
child was adopted. From the very beginning the care of the
child fell to her husband. When the husband demanded she
do the housework and care for the child her symptoms became
worse. When the care of the child was relegated to someone
else she again felt better. Later the patient became
severely ill when her husband insisted she devote all her
energies to making a home, caring for the child, and give
up her lover.

Case No. 8 is that of a woman who had an obvious neurotic disposition most of her life. She had hoped marriage
would be the answer to her suffering, but instead her suffering increased. She was unable to care for her first child,
as well as the second, and by the time the children were
4 and 6 years of age she had become so ill that she required
hospitalization. The history is unmistakably clear with
respect to the illness-provoking aspects of marriage and
parenthood, particularly the latter.

Work, especially embarking on a career, was clearly
related to the outbreak of illness in ten cases (Nos. 2, 3,
16, 18, 22, 26, 30, 33, 35, 36), only one of whom was a
woman. Significantly, three of the ten were unmarried men,
and a close inspection of the development of their illness
shows that the responsibilities of work, while bearing a
relationship to the onset of the illness, was by no means
the only triggering factor. A typical case illustrating
the illness-producing impact of work is that of a single
man (No. 30) who was trying to follow in his father's footsteps. It was not until after he married that he finally
became ill. As his professional identity became more crystalized, and as he attempted to assume the duties of his

father's profession, his decompensation became progressively
worse to the extent that he required treatment. In this
case it appears that attempting to follow his father was
more illness-producing than work itself as illustrated by
the other cases cited above.

Patient No. 16 was a man who successfully increased
his responsibilities to the level of marriage and parenthood and was able to serve successfully in the military
service as an officer during World War II. He drank while
in the service but was never incapacitated. He did not
decompensate severely until he joined his father's firm and
began to be promoted rapidly with a view of assuming the
presidency of the company after his father's retirement.
His illness eventually caused him to be separated from the
company in order to receive psychiatric treatment.

Case No. 26 had already decompensated some after committing himself to a woman, first by engagement and then
by marriage. Self-destructive behavior and alcoholism were
the manifestations of his illness. When he attempted to
follow his father's professional footsteps he became markedly worse, to the extent of being incapacitated and in
need of hospitalization.

Case No. 22 was a man of obvious psychopathic tendencies; much of his behavior was clearly symptomatic in nature
but he managed not to run into conflict with the law or to
require treatment. He exaggerated his exploits to others
and found delight in wild living and seducing upper-class
women. It was not, however, until he entered his father's
business as a partner that he began to feel uneasy around
people and began to fail; and in the process he nearly bankrupt his father who had to assume the responsibility for
his financial dealings.

These cases illustrate a clear relationship between
work and the outbreak or worsening of illness, and show
that being a provider and/or attempting to follow the
father's footsteps triggered an illness sufficiently severe
so as to require hospitalization.

Going to school appears to have been an illness-triggering experience for four patients. Schoolwork, unlike other
responsibilities of life, did not emerge as clearly as an
illness-triggering life situation. This is not surprising
since being a student may provide a convenient escape from
adult responsibilities. Nevertheless, even success at
school and the responsibilities of being a student can

trigger illness or be a significant trigger among others
which all together activate illness. Three of the four
required psychiatric help while still students.

Case No. 20 was a medical student who first began
drinking heavily when exposed to women patients. He had
previously drunk heavily in association with his first
heterosexual efforts and therefore it might be supposed
that women, and not school as such, were the illness-
triggering factor. Data from the treatment process notes,
however, showed that being the "fair-haired boy" of his
professor of medicine created much anxiety in him. Later
follow-up data revealed his total inability to function as
a physician.

Case No. 13 was a very disturbed boy who had been so
much of his life. It was not, however, until he had to conform to school life and live up to the responsibilities of
a high school student that he broke down severely.

Parents were illness-triggering for 16 patients (Nos.
2, 13, 14, 15, 16, 19, 21, 23, 24, 25, 28, 29, 32, 38, 39,
41). The nature of the parental relationships varied but
the continued impact of the parent or parents on the patient
seemed to be a central factor in bringing on the illness.
This was more true among the unmarried patients, of whom
there were 12, than the married. The relationship with the
parents seems to have been sufficiently illness-producing
to the extent that psychiatric help became necessary in
four patients (Nos. 2, 24, 25, 41). In two instances where
a parent was illness-triggering, one patient (No. 2) was
a business associate of the father, and the other patient
(No. 16) was slated to take the presidency of a company, a
position held by the father. Patient No. 2 also had to
contend with a severely demanding mother.

Twelve of the 16 were unmarried patients who had not
yet emancipated themselves from their parents and were caught
up in close relationships with them. A few were attempting
to emancipate themselves, a process which itself contributed
materially to the outbreak of the illness.

Patient No. 21 was an only child who was unable to
leave home without great pangs of loneliness. His mother
infantilized him and his father (a weak, ineffectual man)
cried openly at each parting when he returned to college.
Compelled by an inner need to return home frequently, he
could not live without his parents (nor with them) nor
could he hold a girl friend.

Patient No. 15 was a man who was closely tied to his mother, the dominant one of the parents. He had longed for a close association with his father but never achieved it. Just prior to his death the father extracted a promise from the patient "that he would take care of his mother" just as the father had. Within three months after the father's death the patient had his first anxiety attack which, in retrospect, can be seen to have been the first sign of a slow but progressive decompensation. Interestingly, the patient never married until after his mother died - an event about which the patient made the comment, "It's all over now."

Patient No. 14 was a young woman who was sexually conflicted and alloplastically inclined, who openly revealed her avoidance of males and her preference for homosexual relationships. She did not decompensate to the point of requiring psychiatric assistance, however, until after her mother's death - an event which led to her having to assume many of her mother's former responsibilities. By this turn of events she was brought into a much closer association with her father. Under these conditions she became blatantly homosexual, she failed at school, and finally required psychiatric help.

Threatened or actual object loss was an environmental event which contributed to the activation of the illness in 13 patients (Nos. 6, 10, 12, 14, 15, 16, 17, 20, 25, 35, 39, 41, 42). In seven of these cases an object loss seems to have produced a decompensation severe enough to require psychiatric help.

Case No. 12 was a young, pregnant woman with two children whose husband died suddenly. The husband had been a good provider, but also was very supportive of the patient in a motherly way. He did many things for her around the home and, in addition, he stood between the patient and her very dominating mother. His loss was felt acutely but also threw the patient back into a closer relationship with her parents, particularly her mother. She soon became ill and then came for treatment.

Case No. 17 was a married man with a very sick wife who was in a psychiatric hospital. He was a meek, passive man but, nonetheless, he was able to work and at the same time take over most of his wife's home responsibilities. When the wife began to improve he became ill and required treatment. While this is not an uncommon finding in itself, his therapy revealed the fact that he feared his wife would

no longer need him if she recovered and, in fact, appeared
to be less dependent. Thus, it appears that the possibility of a loss contributed to his decompensation.

When Case No. 20 was a high school student he developed
neurocirculatory asthenia following his maternal grandfather's death. While in college he became depressed and
unable to continue in school after his paternal grandfather
died. Case No. 25 began to fail in school at age nine,
following his father's death. This patient had been deserted by his mother at age two.

Threat to life was illness-producing in one patient
(No. 14). This patient was a successful businessman who
developed carcinoma. He had withstood two operations and
radiation therapy. During the third operation the surgical
team suddenly left him alone (he was fully conscious of all
events) to attend to an emergency. Soon thereafter he
developed a severe progressive phobia which manifested itself as a fear of crowds and a fear of being alone. His
overriding fear was that he would die alone, unattended.

In summary, the findings of this retrospective study
suggest that clinicians might profitably renew their interest in the time-honored psychiatric concept referred to as
the "precipitating event." It appears that such events may
be stressful in their own right but more often they trigger
unconscious forces which are the ultimate basis for the
illness. By looking carefully at the environmental circumstances surrounding the patient at the time of the outbreak
of his illness important clues can be uncovered with respect
to the nature of the unconscious conflicts producing the
symptomatology. Unequivocally evident to us through out
detailed study of the histories and treatments of these 42
patients is the fact that increased responsibility, commitment to, and involvement in life, triggers unconscious conflicts which may previously have lain dormant. These life
circumstances are rarely exotic or unusual in nature but,
rather, they are the experiences, responsibilities, and
commitments of everyday life.

4. A REEXAMINATION OF THE ONSET OF ILLNESS
IN THE LIGHT OF SITUATIONAL VARIABLES

In the previous chapter we have outlined the life circumstances under which the manifest illness developed in
the 42 cases. We have said that while life circumstances
can have an illness-producing effect, it is not correct to
ascribe to the environment the primary source of the illness, except in cases of traumatic neurosis or instances
when the environmental stresses have weakened the personality to such an extent that the adaptive and defensive
structure of the person is overwhelmed. Under these conditions disorganization may also occur. An environment
which itself is not noxious may activate unconscious forces
which in turn produce illness. The defensive system loses
its effectiveness and unconscious forces which had hitherto
been held in check become "liberated" under conflict-triggering environmental conditions. These forces which are no
longer repressed or bound by other defenses or character
are the ultimate source of the manifest symptoms.

In our attempt to study the relationship of the environment to intrapsychic life of the individual - in particular
with regard to the onset of illness - we will reexamine the
facts presented in the preceding section, using the concepts
of the situational variables. This task requires us to
evaluate the environment in an absolute sense and also with
respect to personality variables, and to delineate those
factors, environmental and intrapsychic, the combined effects
of which produced an outbreak of the illness.

At first glance it might appear unconvincing to suggest
that such life events as dating, work, marriage, parenthood,
could lead to a mental breakdown even though a temporal
relationship was reported in the previous section between
these everyday events and responsibilities and the outbreak
of illness. How are these facts to be explained? An
obvious solution lies in uncovering the nature of the personality factors which rendered patients vulnerable to life
experiences which usually bring joy and fulfillment to others.

Stress: An obvious beginning to this analytic task is
to expose environmental factors which may have been overwhelming in their own right - that is, stressful - which
could have been expected to cause a mental breakdown in
anyone simply by virtue of their heavy noxious impact.
Turning to the stress variable we find, however, that only
12 patients were living under clearly stressful environmental conditions at the onset of their illness or at the
time of the initial study.

In only two of the 42 patients can we point to clear
stresses that seemed to bear a direct relationship to the
onset of their illness (Nos. 4, 12). There were ten other
patients (Nos. 2, 6, 7, 10, 14, 17, 26, 31, 33, 42) who
were experiencing one form of chronic stress or another,
but in no instance did the case evaluations point to a direct
overwhelming impact of these stresses on the patient and
to the outbreak of illness such as was seen in cases 4 and
12. In the ten patients, stresses ranged from a nagging,
diminishing wife or ne'er-do-well husband, to specific
work stress such as a heavy private medical practice or
physical disease. These stress factors were considered of
only peripheral significance in the genesis of the illness.
Even in the two cases who experienced acute stress, other
circumstances appear to have been weightier in their illness-producing effect.

Case No. 12 was a young pregnant mother of two children
whose husband unexpectedly burned to death. While the impact of death was direct and heavy and can, therefore, be
considered an illness-producing stress, her life was also
significantly changed. She was forced to live with her
parents again, a life circumstance which awakened unconscious
forces. Case No. 4 was temporarily deserted by a surgical
team while undergoing surgery, an event which was clearly
traumatic. Not to be overlooked, however, is the fact that
he was left alone while in an extremely helpless state, a
fact which also awakened archaic unconscious separation
fears as subsequent treatment revealed.

Support: If, then, environmental stress was not a
significant determinant for the outbreak of illness in the
42 cases, possibly the lack of environmental supports played
a central role. Examination of this variable also proved
to be disappointing in this respect. There were no patients
lacking in human support, although some had more than others,
and nearly all enjoyed plentiful material support. In fact,
some of the sickest patients were the most supported by
sympathetic marital and parental families. If any inference

were to be made about this variable, we suggest that less
support might have forced these patients out of their regressive positions. That is, despite the good intentions
of the supportive others, the sympathetic attitude may have
permitted the patient to cling to his sickness. It may
also be that what appeared as genuine support was, in fact,
not genuine. We cannot answer this question. One might
have predicted that persons who were more or less alone in
the world would be more vulnerable to illness-producing
forces than if surrounded by plentiful human and material
supports. This did not appear to be true, but our sample
shows that supports alone will not forestall the outbreak
of illness. For example, Case No. 23 is that of a young
woman whose parents were highly supportive. They gave her
almost anything she wanted, let her make her own choices
and remained constantly and steadfastly interested in her
future and welfare. Yet all of this support did not forestall the outbreak of her very serious illness. Case No.
38 was a young woman who enjoyed constant material and
parental support. Her illness nevertheless erupted under
the impact of puberty and her association with the opposite
sex. Case No. 32 was a young woman, an only child, who
received careful and constant support from her parents yet
when she came face to face with heterosexuality she became
severely ill.

Opportunity: It is reasonable to suppose that lack of
opportunity for work and expression of one's talents and
abilities might have led to chronic frustration which eventually led to a regressive withdrawal into illness. Nearly
every patient in the sample was considered to have had good
opportunities for personal expression and growth. Their
illnesses, however, prevented them from making good use of
their opportunities. Thus the environment cannot be blamed
for the illness by some limiting effect on the individual.

Conflict Trigger and Core Conflicts: Since we already
know from the material presented in the previous section
that heterosexual contact, marriage, parenthood, work - in
short, the various common responsibilities and commitments
which characterize maturity - bear a temporal relationship
to the onset of illness, as did loss to some extent, we now
turn to the dimension of conflict trigger and core conflict
in order to explain the illness of the 42 cases. It appears
that the bases for the illness were unconscious conflicts
for, as we have just seen, few external factors were sufficiently noxious in their own right to cause the patients to
decompensate. We could not test the hypothesis regarding
the absence of opportunities as an illness-producing factor.

Even for the two patients for whom external factors did play
an illness-producing role, unconscious forces were brought
to the surface by the traumatic, stressful events in their
lives.

With the definitions of "core conflict" and "conflict
trigger" in mind, a first order task is to make explicit
the nature of the major core conflicts in the 42 cases. The
hypothesis to be "tested" was that core conflicts repressed
in the unconscious or bound in character were the ultimate
bases for mental illness, and that environmental factors
which bore a temporal relationship to the illness had activated the unconscious conflicts. As we have indicated, this
triggering effect is most likely to occur when the individual
is attempting to commit himself or deepen his involvement
and commitment to the environment. This formulation implies
a direct relationship between the intensity or extent of
the involvement with or commitment to the environment and
the degree to which the unconscious conflicts are aroused
and hence the extent to which psychopathology erupts.

The following example taken from the preceding section
illustrates this principle. A man's casual relationship
with a woman may have only a minimal conflict-triggering
effect, while marriage to the same woman would more extensively arouse unconscious conflicts and produce symptoms.
Studying for a profession might cause no symptoms, while
assuming the responsibilities associated with the profession would trigger unconscious conflicts and produce symptoms.

Turning attention to the core conflicts which were
believed by both the Situational and Patient Variables teams
to exist in the 42 cases, we are immediately struck by the
fact that two levels of psychosexual fixation predominate
in these formulations.

Oral-dependency conflicts were considered to be central
and predominant in 37 of the 42 cases, and all 42 were believed to show evidence of phallic-oedipal conflicts. Fixation at the anal level or the partial instincts (exhibition-
ism, etc.) were represented only to a minimal degree. While
the form taken by these conflicts varied widely, the underlying conflictual meanings included both libidinal and
aggressive drive and the associated object relations of the
oral and phallic-oedipal phases. The assessments leading
to these conclusions came from an exhaustive study of all
the available clinical material, including an extensive
psychological test battery. Two research teams arrived at
the above-mentioned conclusions independently, and both

implicated the various aspects of the oral and phallic-
oedipal conflicts as being the primary unconscious conflicts.

Based on an equally careful clinical study which
spelled out the life circumstances in a detailed way for
each patient from birth to when he came for treatment, information was collected from which those external factors
which bore a direct temporal relationship to the onset of
symptoms and eventually the major illness could be identified. These were described in the previous section.

(a) Heterosexuality as a Conflict Trigger

This analysis suggested that heterosexual object seeking or attachments were conflict-triggering in all 22 unmarried patients. In the previous section we reported that
15 patients found this aspect of their life symptom-producing.
At the time of the initial study, all 22 unmarried patients
could be said to experience heterosexuality short of marriage
as conflict-triggering to some degree, but only 15 had
developed frank symptoms as a consequence of heterosexual
involvements alone. Four of these patients had tried marriage earlier but had divorced and were, therefore, classed
as unmarried at initial study. In all four, once married,
illness broke out - a fact clearly related to the marriage.
By the time of the initial research these four were again
unmarried and evidence clearly revealed that heterosexuality
had been conflict-triggering for them. The data showed
that oral-dependency and phallic-oedipal conflicts, primarily
the latter, which had lain relatively dormant, except during
puberty in some, had become mobilized in the 22 patients by
their efforts to establish heterosexual relationships. The
case material of the Appendix may be referred to for supporting evidence. Had these patients not tried to relate
to the opposite sex, and had they been prepared and able to
sublimate their drive energies, overt symptoms might never
have developed.

(b) Parents as Conflict Triggers

It is not surprising that virtually every one of the
22 unmarried patients found their parents conflict-triggering to some degree, and many became manifestly worse symptom-
wise and in their life adjustment if they remained in close
proximity to their parents. However, we considered parents
to be a major factor in causing the illness in only 12 of
the unmarried patients. The parents of only 11 (Nos. 2, 6,
7, 11, 16, 22, 26, 28, 30, 31, 32) of the 20 married patients
were conflict-triggering; that is, an intensification of the

relationship with parents produced a worsening in their behavior or symptoms. However, the parents in only four of
these can be said to have had a central role in triggering
the illness. That fewer of the parents of the 20 married
patients were conflict-triggering is due, to a large extent,
to the fact that some parents were dead, or were living far
away from the patients. It is remarkable how, even after
marriage, parents continued to have a conflict-arousing impact on this group of 11 patients. In the previous section
it was stated that parents were illness-triggering in 16
patients. This number is at variance with the figures just
cited. We wish to point out that there is a distinction
between the environmental factor which is clearly illness-
producing and one which simply activates conflict to some
degree. Furthermore, the life circumstances of these patients
had changed from the time of onset of illness to the time
of the initial research study.

(c) Marriage as Conflict Trigger

At the time of initial study 18 of the 20 married
patients found marriage conflict-triggering. Evidence
pointed to the fact that the close involvement with the
opposite sex mobilized conflicts which, in turn, led to
manifest symptoms. There were only two for whom heterosexual commitment, to the extent of marriage, did not arouse
conflicts (Nos. 4, 17). It should be recalled that of the
22 unmarried patients, six had been divorced earlier and one
was widowed. The clinical data make it unmistakably clear
that for all six patients marriage had failed because of
their own unconscious conflicts - conflicts mobilized by
the fact of having committed themselves to the opposite sex.

(d) Parenthood as Conflict Trigger

In the previous section we reported that 12 patients
became symptomatically worse or became ill for the first
time soon after becoming a parent. In a total of 16 patients,
however, becoming a parent was part of the overall environmental matrix in which the patient existed and which activated the illness. In the additional four patients, the
conflict-triggering effect of parenthood had less of a central significance than for the other 12. Women, as might
be expected, staggered more under the impact of parenthood
than did men. More is demanded of women at the onset of
parenthood than of men, a fact which again illustrates the
direct relationship between the degree of commitment to the
environment or extent of the environmental responsibility
and the degree to which unconscious conflicts will be

activated.

Patient No. 26 illustrates especially clearly how progressive commitment first to a woman, then to parenthood,
and, finally, to a life's work was paralleled by a progressive worsening of his illness. Case No. 33 fled from all of
his parental responsibilities in the course of becoming ill.
Later, after treatment, he became progressively involved in
life again. First he obtained work, then his wife rejoined
him, and finally his children rejoined the family one at a
time. Each of these steps provoked a progressive reaction
back into his old behavioral and symptom patterns, ending
in his death. It is especially noteworthy that his condition worsened significantly after each child rejoined the
family.

Patient No. 11 was able to marry and remained happily
married for about 16 months. Then without apparent cause
she questioned her husband on his premarital experiences.
When he confessed having had sexual relations with other
women she felt hurt, shaken, lonely, and let down; "it was
as if a beautiful and almost unreal dream had been shattered."
She became hostile and antagonistic toward her husband and
repeatedly brought up the issue, pressing him for details.
During her first pregnancy she felt well and untroubled, but
almost immediately following the delivery she suffered a
return of her hostility toward her husband; self-doubts
reappeared. After the birth of her second child her symptoms
worsened to the extent of requiring psychiatric hospitalization and eventually long-term psychotherapy. This case
illustrates especially clearly how marriage activated repressed oedipal conflicts which, in turn, were projected
onto the husband. The pressure of such powerful conflicts
moblized by marriage precluded a happy marriage and parenthood as well.

Cases 5 and 9 clearly illustrate how children proved
to be conflict-triggering. In both instances these women
were unable to carry out the mother's roles and functions.
One could not adopt the child and experienced intense thoughts
of killing it, and the other completely neglected the child
after she adopted it. It is interesting that patient No. 5,
who eventually was able to adopt a baby after treatment
ended, again became acutely disturbed during the adoption
proceedings but managed with the help of drugs and religious
counsel to keep the baby.

(e) Career as Conflict Trigger

Establishing one's self in a career, a business, or some form of life's work proved to be conflict-triggering in 14 patients. The responsibilities of work itself were not always a sufficiently strong trigger to be considered the sole illness-precipating factor, but in all 14 work had this effect to some degree.

Patient No. 16 was the heir apparent to his father's business and was being groomed for the presidency of the company. Each promotion brought a worsening of his symptoms. Patient No. 33 functioned well in his work while in the military service. Despite his initial success in private practice he ultimately failed completely. His father had been a private practitioner.

Patient No. 26 illustrates the conflict-triggering effect of a life's work, especially when the work follows the father's footsteps. This man's mother had wanted him to be an English teacher in a girls' school. He, instead, wished to follow his father's example but deviated from this course by studying for a Ph.D. degree in a related field. He finally entered medicine, functioned adequately in the military service, and aspired to join the staff where his father was a prominent physician. His symptomatic be- havior precluded this appointment; his behavior eventually deteriorated further, a fact which was due to the combined conflict-triggering effects of work, marriage and parenthood.

We have not presented detailed evidence to support the claim that the previously mentioned environmental facts were conflict-triggering. The case studies in the Appendix will provided fairly detailed data. Having repeatedly sifted the data and sought the truths embedded in it, we are com- pletely confident in our belief that the conflict triggers and, therefore, illness-producing forces include the usual responsibilities of mature commitments, or efforts to make commitments and assume new responsibilities. Simply put, it appears that the quest for maleness and femaleness, and the commitments and carrying out of responsibilities which are associated with these two gender identities, trigger and mobilize the unconscious childhood conflicts (repressed and unresolved); these, in turn, are the ultimate source of the illness. These conflicts, as mentioned earlier, were essentially two in kind. These are: (1) The repressed wishes and object ties and separation anxiety of the oral period. Thus the challenge to stand alone as an adult, independent, responsible, and giving to others, is pre- cluded by the unrelinquished wish to be cared for and the dread of separation from repressed early object attachments.

(2) To be adult, independent, responsible, and committed to
a member of the opposite sex is also precluded or made difficult by the fears and guilt associated with phallic-oedipal
wishes. Thus, to succeed as a man arouses castration anxiety
in association with the wish to possess the mother and replace the father; to succeed as a woman is to replace the
mother and win the father. To be a mother requires the
giving up of penis envy, overcoming of incestuous wishes,
etc., and represents a further crystalization of feminine
gender identity. The oral and phallic-oedipal conflicts may
be highly varied in their manifest form, but the essence was
the same for nearly all of the 42 cases. It should be noted
that anal core conflicts or conflicts derived from partial
instincts failed to emerge as significant factors in this
study.

Need-congruence: Further inquiry into the nature of
the environment at the time of initial study requires us to
examine the extent to which the environment was need-congruent
for the 42 patients. This variable will shed less light on
the causes for the outbreak of the illness although its
importance should not be underestimated. The usefulness of
this variable and its relationship to conflict triggers will
become apparent upon reading further into the text. Environments which are need-congruent tend also to be conflict-
triggering.

It should be recalled that need-congruence refers to
those environmental factors which harmonize with ego qualities which were never (or which no longer are) intimately
associated with intrapsychic conflict. For example, a person
whose artistic talents can find an outlet in the environment
can be said to be in a need-congruent environment in this
one respect. A person with learned skills will not find his
environment need-congruent if the opportunity to live out
those skills is unavailable. This variable covers a range
of constitutionally based or learned (that is, acquired)
character traits and skills which seek expression in the
environment. Where expression is not possible, the environment is low in need-congruence.

Need-congruence also refers to another quality of personality having to do with gender identity. Most theoretical
systems are based on one or more assumptions; our study is
no exception. It is an assumption of the authors that maleness and femaleness are distinct, that man is not biologically
bisexual, and that the qualities of maleness and femaleness
are definable. Analyzing the data of this project in accordance with these basic assumptions added much clarity to the

study. It is beyond the objective of this work to explore
extensively the myriad characteristics which distinguish
male from female. We ascribe to the view that there are
environmental factors and circumstances which facilitate
or inhibit the development and/or expression of what is the
biologically determined basis for gender identity. Psychologic bisexuality is a reality which is environmentally induced. Where such a condition exists, the individual is
necessarily in conflict within himself to some degree.

Although we based our assessments on the view that
biologic gender is not mixed, we assumed, further, that
biologic maleness and femaleness varies in strength. Where
the biologic force is weak, stronger environmental forces
may dilute or even seemingly submerge constitutionally
determined gender. Our assumptions are supported by current
research. Money (1967), Money, Hampson, & Hampson (1955),
and Stoller (1964) point to a biologic force which determines
gender identity and to the overwhelmingly significant effect
of attitudes and values early in life in contrast to hormonal
or anatomic factors which seem to have little if any effect
on the formation of gender identity. Rado (1956), for
instance, doubts the validity of the biologic bisexuality
concept, and states that there is no factual evidence to
support it and suggests how the concept has done harm by
leading to certain therapeutic nihilism in the face of
patients with mixed psychologic identities. Voth's analysis
(in press) of some aspects of the life and work of Freud
suggests that Freud clung to the concept of biologic bisexuality out of defensive need, the belief serving as a cover
for his identification with his mother and the consequent
feminine qualities in his personality.

The interplay of the environment and the biologically
determined gender is, indeed, highly complex and cannot be
examined in detail here. When a child is prevented by either
parent from developing and living out his biologically
determined gender, such parents are defined as need-incongruent. For example, a mother who failed to resolve her
penis envy and, as a consequence, hampers the development
of maleness in her male child is need-incongruent. Similarly, fathers who are femininely identified or passive and
cannot live out their maleness will not be able to help
their male child fully develop his own male gender or, if
it develops, fully express it. Such fathers are need-
incongruent for females as well. Men and women who bring
out the best, as regards gender, in their children and
spouses are need-congruent.

When assessing the environment of the 42 patients with
regard to its need-congruent aspects, we first assessed the
degree to which the environment was congruent with stable
nongender character traits, long-standing values and attitudes, talents and skills, and then with regard to the extent to which the environment permitted or encouraged the
patient either to develop or to express an already developed
gender. Need-congruent environmental factors as regards
gender are generally conflict-triggering for the following
reasons. Persons who have not resolved their unconscious
conflicts, particularly the phallic-oedipal ones, generally
show disturbances in either the degree to which their gender
identity was developed or, if developed, the degree to which
it could be expressed in daily life. Such persons tend to
make object choices with similar disturbances. For example,
an aggressive, somewhat masculinized woman will tend to
choose a passive and possibly even femininely identified
man. Such persons can be said to be need-incongruent and
not very conflict-triggering. However, since she is female,
she will always be conflict-triggering to some, even if
minimal, degree; the same applies to the man with regard to
his wife. Were such a man's maleness to be stimulated by
a more feminine and, therefore, need-congruent, woman,
oedipal conflicts would be activated simultaneously. For
a woman, her home, children, and her masculine husband will
stimulate the development of her feminine and maternal,
biologically rooted qualities. However, a passive husband
who maintains emotional distance from her, and who is unable
to express his maleness, is need-incongruent and, simultaneously, not much of a conflict-triggering influence. If
such a man changed because of treatment, or changed because
of less apparent reasons, and became able to find and express his gender with his family and thus press his wife
into a more feminine role and expect a greater intimacy
with her, he would then be classed as more need-congruent
and at the same time become more of a conflict-trigger for
his wife. Such is the nature of the interrelatedness of
need-congruence and the conflict trigger - core conflict
dimension. Thus it appears that the concepts of need-
congruence - conflict trigger satisfy the scientific demand
that concepts within a theoretical structure not disturb
the internal logic of the system.

Unconscious conflicts may remain dormant or relatively
so as long as the environment or internal factors do not
promote maturation, that is, remain relatively need-incongruent. Couples may have much in common as regards values,
interests, etc., and in this sense be mutually need-congruent,
yet possess few qualities which are need-congruent insofar

as a gender is concerned. The offspring of parents who are
need-incongruent with respect to each other are destined to
develop disturbed gender or some form of latent or manifest
psychopathology.

Only seven of the 42 patients had mates and/or a
family life which could be classed as need-congruent in the
sense of providing a good climate for the development and
expression of their gender identity. Twenty-seven patients
were nearly completely lacking in an environment which
facilitated or fostered growth in gender identity. Eight
were fortunate enough to live in circumstances that were
moderately conducive to such expression and growth. These
observations support the well-known clinical fact that the
personalities of patients tend to lead to object choices
and life commitments which reinforce illness rather than
promote growth. These need-incongruent environmental
factors tended to lock the patient in at a certain level of
development and impeded future growth and maturation.

The life circumstances of the 42 patients which had
little to do with gender identity were somewhat more need-
congruent. About half could be said to have had good stim-
ulation from their environment. Fifteen received little
from the environment that provided growth in skills, talents,
etc.

These conceptualizations are illustrated in the following case examples.

Patient No. 33 was a physician, father and husband,
and at first glance it might seem that his environment was
need-congruent. This was true of work because of his obvious
interest in his field, an interest which expressed his identification with his father. His children were need-congruent;
they stimulated him to be a man, a father, and a provider.
One might have presumed his wife to be need-congruent. This
woman was, however, highly unfeminine. Many of the mothering functions for the children fell by default to her
husband; she competed with him professionally; she encouraged
him to become interested in homosexuality and went so far
as to induce him to bring a homosexual lover into the home.
She eventually took all of their savings, soon after he had
begun his practice, relinquished all of her home responsibilities, which she never discharged adequately, and sought
specialty training of her own. They had few common interests. She did not provide a climate within the home and
in their marital relationship which enhanced the maleness
in him. Because of her own aggressive and "masculine"

qualities in her personality she also did not activate those
unconscious conflicts in her husband which were the primary
bases for his inability to be a successful man; that is,
she did not trigger his oedipal conflicts; rather, she
fostered a regressive solution (not resolution) by pushing
him into homosexuality. One could easily argue that she
created conflict for him by pushing him into a role which
was inconsistent with his (biologic) maleness. But she
made it easy for him to maintain his repression of his oedipal
conflicts which, if activated and resolved, would have
forced her to leave or change and become more need-congruent,
that is, feminine.

It was, therefore, work and parenthood that were the
main conflict triggers which activated his illness. Subsequent events in his life showed that he could live with his
wife if not burdened by the responsibilities of parenthood.
Inasmuch as she was need-incongruent, she did not activate
his unconscious conflicts as did work and being a parent.
After having been separated from his family early in treatment, he eventually began work. His wife rejoined him and
he managed reasonably well. When his children joined them
he progressively deteriorated. Thus it would appear that
the children were the main conflict triggers. His wife was
not a significant conflict trigger because she was not a
feminine woman; she demanded little of him as a man. Had
she been more need-congruent (that is, feminine and capable
of closeness with him), she would have been a conflict
trigger alongside the children and he might have gotten ill
sooner or recovered faster, depending on the balance of
health or sickness withim him and the effectiveness of
treatment.

Patient No. 32 illustrates the near reversal of roles
in a young married couple and the illness-stabilizing and
need-incongruent impact of both on each other. The patient
first became ill during puberty when she discovered her
interest in boys. It can be assumed that the biologic
forces in her were propelling her and the social norms were
pulling her toward the opposite sex, but it was also clear
that she eventually chose a mate for marriage who was not
manly nor very forceful. He had been her baby-sitter when
she was a child; he was a meek, passive male. The qualities
of the marriage were such that he was more of a mother than
a husband. Because of her severe phobias he eventually had
to give up his work in order to stay with her. Though kindly
and compassionate, this man was considered to be need-incongruent in the sense of stimulating maturation and a feminine
identity in the patient. This being so, he was not a

conflict-triggering husband either; he would have had to be
more of a man to have been so.

This patient eventually changed considerably as a result
of her treatment and in so doing she placed entirely different demands on her husband who, in turn, without treatment, became somewhat more manly and a great deal more
successful and also, therefore, more need-congruent. A
happy outcome. These fortunate changes in him promoted
further growth in the patient and, as might be expected,
his changes triggered her unconscious conflicts and new
symptoms appeared in her, all of which facilitated her treatment. She observed, for instance, how she resented his
successes and sometimes actively interfered with his studying; however, these newly activated conflicts were now more
subject to resolution. Thus both eventually became more
need-congruent for each other and the conflict-triggering
effects of this greater need-congruence diminished as their
unconscious conflicts were resolved. Such resolution was
observed during the patient's analysis but can only be
inferred in the husband who was never treated. They had
had many common interests and had been need-congruent in
this sense since the beginning of their relationship. Had
the man been unable to change along with his wife, he would
unquestionably have become intolerably need-incongruent and
inhibiting in his impact on her. Before her treatment he
was a mother substitute, a fact which sustained her even
though these very same qualities impeded her growth and
tended to reinforce her illness. As a consequence of her
treatment he changed along with her and became a husband.

The strengths and levels of health in the 42 cases
varied considerably, a fact which accounts for the variance
in the levels of achievement in terms of work and personal
life and degree to which gender identity had crystalized.
Some of the patients became frankly ill at their first
efforts at making heterosexual adjustments, others were able
to get quite far in achieving gender identity and were able
to find a relatively need-congruent environment but eventually succumbed to illness when the conflict triggers were
sufficiently great.

Case No. 42 is that of a married woman with two children
who had originally aspired to a professional career but who
married a man in the same profession. He was a strong man
whom she admired and in relation to whom she managed to
control her competiveness fairly well. Having such a strong
man, a home and a family was highly need-congruent and thus
provided the circumstances in which she could grow. Hers

was not a growth free from symptoms, however, for these same
circumstances kept her unconscious conflicts sufficiently
activated so that it was obvious to all in her family that
she discharged her womanly responsibilities always under
protest and sometimes shirked some of them. Her husband
went so far as to say that he thought she would have been
happier as a man. It was not until her son was preparing
to leave home that she became severely depressed. This
event, the major conflict trigger, induced a regression
because of its varied unconscious meanings, the main one
being a loss of a narcissistic extention of herself in her
son.

Another patient, No. 6, was surrounded by a reasonably
good environment insofar as its need-congruent aspects were
concerned. She had a husband, home, social position, and
children. Strong enough and healthy enough to accept this
environment she was, nonetheless, burdened by unconscious
conflicts which finally overwhelmed her when her fourth
child died. There had been signs of psychiatric disturbance
in her since age 13 due to the conflict-triggering impact
of heterosexuality, but despite that fact she had been able
to marry and have children. The death of her child, a
stress but also a conflict trigger, produced an illness
which rendered her unable to accept her reasonably need-
congruent environment.

Having evaluated the environment of our sample in
light of the situational variables, the following conclusions appear to be warranted. The environment, as such,
in our sample did not cause the outbreak of mental illness
by directly overwhelming these patients. This does not
imply that the environment had no part in the original formation of conflicts in these patients which later led to
illness, nor does it imply that environmental stresses,
such as loss, cannot directly lead to personality disorganization. The findings suggest, rather, that very ordinary
factors within the environment activate unconscious elements
which are the ultimate source of the illness. At the same
time, the environment can blend with those unconscious
elements and character derivatives thereof in such a way
as to reinforce the illness. The environment can, therefore, be conflict-triggering in that it activates unconscious conflicts, but it can also be need-congruent or
need-incongruent. Generally speaking, the more the environment is need-congruent, the more it will also be conflict-
triggering (where unconscious conflicts exist).

It now becomes clear why these patients became ill.

There appears to be in man a natural tendency to mature, and at the same time it is society's expectation that individuals increasingly commit themselves to the environment in a way which permits the full expression of gender in a mature and involved manner. And, furthermore, persons attempt to find environments which permit the expression of their natural talents and learned abilities, but there is also a tendency to seek out and relate to environmental factors which harmonize with the conflictually-based personality qualities. These environmental factors are need-incongruent. But since Nature will have us mature, and since society expects the same of us, individuals also tend more to seek out environmental factors which are need-congruent. If unconscious conflicts exist, these need-congruent factors simultaneously become conflict-triggering. Given a reasonably strong person who exists in a reasonably supportive environment, the chances of silent resolution of unconscious conflicts and growth are good. Where the balance of forces is toward sickness, for example where there are excessive unconscious conflicts, weak ego, or especially high environmental expectations for growth, the activation of unconscious conflicts will overwhelm the ego and produce manifest illness.

While we have not been able to show conclusively that Supports or Opportunity or Stress were especially significant factors in our sample, it is our impression that good environmental supports, the absence of too heavy stress, and the opportunity for self-expression favor illness resolution and growth.

5. SUMMARY OF THE FACTS AT TERMINATION

At the termination of treatment detailed assessments
of the patient, his life circumstances and his treatment
were made according to the outline presented earlier. The
patients in this project were, in the main, quite ill. The
mean number of hours for the patients treated by psychoanalysis was 835, and the mean number for those treated by
psychotherapy was 289 hours. Many had required hospitalization, all had character problems along with their manifest
symptomatology, both of which had significantly interfered
with their life adjustments. By the time of termination
most of the patients, with some notable exceptions, were
functioning better. The mean HSRS rating for the psychotherapy group had increased from 44 to 53. The mean HSRS
increased for those treated by psychoanalysis from 49 to 60.
There is a borderline significant difference ($p < .10$) over
the total of the two points in time between the psychoanalytic and psychotherapy groups in the direction of the
psychoanalytic patients being healthier at both the initial
study and termination study. In addition, there is a significant difference ($p < .001$) between the initial and
termination studies regardless of treatment modality in the
direction of improvement. However, the Groups by Time interaction is nonsignificant; this indicates that both the
psychoanalytic and the psychotherapy patients improved at
the same rate; that is, the differences in improvement between the psychoanalytic and psychotherapy patients are
due solely to chance.

Before exploring the basis for these improvements, we
will first describe the kinds of environmental changes and
new life adjustments that were achieved. What follows will
be an attempt to explain the changes in the patients and
an effort to relate these changes to those in the environment. A patient-environment context, as we have come to
discover, is essential for the task of assessing the extent,
depth, nature of and basis for changes within the patient.
Changes within the patient may all too easily be ascribed
to the treatment while, in fact, an altered environment,

42

not necessarily brought about by the patient himself, may have been the main force leading to those changes. On the other hand, essential intrapsychic change usually is reflected in the patient's environment and significant changes within the environment can, therefore, provide some of the best evidence for the efficacy of the treatment. Similarly, certain changes in the patient in a direction away from greater health, as in the case of acting out, may be reflected in marked alterations in the environment.

An overview of the events that took place in the lives of these patients shows that much happened during treatment.

Twenty of the 22 unmarried patients acquired new friends, 12 found new opposite sex attachments, and seven were married during treatment. A child was born to one patient. New attachments to the same sex occurred in three patients, although all three had been homosexual prior to treatment. Promiscuity developed or continued in four. Old friends were lost in six. There was a separation and a divorce among the seven who married during treatment. There were eight instances of parental death, nine patients moved closer to their families and five became more distant. Eleven of the patients were able to live alone when they had not been able to do so at the beginning of treatment. Two moved to foster homes, seven were able to increase their home responsibilities. Sixteen began new jobs and five lost old ones; four were promoted in their work. The financial situation improved in nine, worsened in five. Only a few became involved in new community or leisure activities. Little change was noted in physical health. A good number entered school, some continued, and a few completed school work.

Certain of these changes were clearly indicative of greater health; however, many cannot, in themselves, be taken as evidence of greater health. The overall impression gained, however, from these tabulated changes is that of improvement in life adjustment. This impression is consonant with the improved HSRS ratings. That nearly all of the patients acquired new friends is a positive sign although little was known at this point of the kinds of friends these were. Loss of friends might suggest the breaking of old neurotic friendships. New jobs and school accomplishments in 16 instances is further persuasive, even if presumptive, evidence of improvement in the patients. Seven were able to marry, but two of the marriages failed within the period of treatment. That patients became closer to their families in nine instances is significant in a positive sense.

The aforementioned facts all point to a deeper involvement in life by a good number of the patients.   The capacity
to live alone, to make new friends, to find a new job,
succeed at school, to be close to one's family, to marry,
are all positive signs and seem to reflect the good effects
of treatment.   The actual meaning of and causes for these
changes can only be known by knowing the patient and his
treatment in depth, and through understanding to what extent
outside influences initiated and/or supported positive intrapsychic changes induced by the treatment.

For instance, on the surface it might appear that the
seven marriages were indicative of greater health; that is,
were reflections of conflict resolution and greater maturity.
Actually, only three of these marriages (Nos. 18, 20, 38)
can be viewed in this positive way.   Two marriages (Nos.
10 and 19) were clearly acting out and both ultimately
failed.   Another marriage has continued despite many storms.
The man whom the patient chose was weak and hardly a need-
congruent object choice.   Such a marriage must be judged
as largely pathological, that is, acting out of unconscious
conflicts.

Further evidence which suggests unhealthy changes in
association with treatment are new homosexual object attachments (Nos. 14, 29, 39), and promiscuity (Nos. 3, 7, 9, 19,
27, 31, 33, 34).   Even some of the new interest in the
opposite sex may well have been displaced and acted out
transference - hardly an enduring or "healthy" basis for
the new relationships.   These facts are cited in order to
illustrate that mere environmental change in a patient's
life during treatment is not necessarily a sign of emerging
health.

Nonetheless, it is apparent that treatment had a rather
profound effect upon old homeostatic balances within the
patient and between patient and environment in nearly all
of the unmarried patients.   In general, the movement of
this group appears to have been in a positive direction,
that is, towards greater personal independence and, at the
same time, towards a deepened involvement with various aspects of the environment.   The new friends, new jobs, productive school work, closer and more mature ties with parental family, attempts at closer heterosexual relationships,
all constitute the supporting evidence for this judgment.
It should be noted, however, that only seven of the 21 were
able to marry, thus suggesting a limited treatment impact.

An immediate rejoinder to this observation, however, is that
patients in treatment should avoid making such a decision
during treatment; in fact, those in psychoanalysis are generally advised not to marry during treatment. Follow-up
data will provide the answer to whether or not treatment
may have been of greater help to the unmarried group than
appears to have been so at termination. Follow-up data will
also reveal to what extent the gains achieved during treatment have continued to hold up after the person of the
therapist was no longer a part of the ongoing life of the
patient.

An overview of the findings in the married group of
20 patients also reveals many changes. The most striking
fact is that eight patients (Nos. 8, 9, 11, 22, 26, 28,
30, 31) were divorced or separated during the treatment
period. In three instances (Nos. 9, 11, 30), it appears
as if making treatment arrangements crystallized the discontent of the spouse of the patient sufficiently for them
to initiate divorce. In all the rest, and even to some extent in these three cases, treatment seems to have contributed to the divorce. Four (Nos. 9, 26, 30, 31) of the
divorced patients married someone else during treatment. A
fifth (No. 36) had been married and divorced before treatment and married again during treatment. Of the 20 married
patients, only nine lived with their families during most
of the treatment period. The other 11 did not because of
hospitalization, separation or divorce.

Three women (Nos. 11, 28, 31) lived with their children
but not their husbands. All three had been divorced early
in treatment.

In summary, of the 20 married patients, nine (Nos. 2,
3, 4, 5, 16, 17, 32, 35, 42) remained married and lived with
their families, including spouse, during the major part or
entirety of treatment. Two more patients (Nos. 6, 33) rejoined families during treatment or near its conclusion.
Thus it can be seen that treatment planning and treatment
itself had a markedly unsettling effect on half of the
marriages. Follow-up data will reveal the ultimate outcomes
of these matches, including those which failed during
treatment.

New attachments to the opposite sex developed in seven
instances. Three of these patients eventually married their
newfound attachments. Promiscuity and perverse sexual behavior appeared or continued in five instances (Nos. 3, 7,
9, 31, 33).

Ten made new friends and two lost old friends; relatives died in six instances; three were closer to their parental families, and two were more distant. Children were born in five families (two of these marriages ended in divorce). Two patients lost their jobs but 12 found new ones after a period of unemployment. Nine experienced financial improvement - not always, however, because of their own efforts. Six showed a definite increase in acceptance of home responsibilities.

In summary, and without attempting to explain these many changes, it is to be noted that, as in the case of the unmarried patients, the period of treatment had a markedly unsettling effect on the lives of these patients. New jobs were begun, there were new marriages, children were born, new friends were made, promiscuity and perversity (in one instance) appeared in some, and there were eight divorces and four remarriages. For only ten patients were the marital and environmental arrangements about the same at the end of treatment as at the beginning, but even in two of these cases (Nos. 3, 22) the marriage collapsed near the end of treatment.

Like the unmarried patients, there is clearly some evidence of an overall intensification of the patient's involvement in or commitment to his environment. But it is also true that in a number of instances there was considerable disengagement from previous life commitments. An effort will be made in the next section to find meaning in these situational rearrangements.

6. A CONCEPTUAL UNDERSTANDING OF THE FACTS
AT TERMINATION

We will not attempt to account for all of the changes which occurred in the lives of the 42 patients. The extensive case studies written by Wallerstein,[1] and the more abbreviated ones that emphasized the role of the situational variables which are appended to this text, can be referred to by those interested in more details. The objective of this section is simply to sketch out patient-environment interactions and identify some of the major factors which appear to us to have caused some of the changes in the patients and in their environments.

If the assumption is accepted that a greater degree of commitment to or deepened involvement in life is indicative of greater health, then improvement in a patient can, to some extent, be judged objectively by assessing the changes in the extent and quality of his life commitments and involvements as well as by assessing the patient's intrapsychic condition.

The core conflicts, as mentioned earlier, most commonly and nearly exclusively represented in the patients were oral-dependent and phallic-oedipal. Since ratings of change in general showed improvement, it follows logically that significant core conflict resolution might account for these improvements. This appears, however, not to be true.

One situational variable, conflict trigger, relates most directly to the intrapsychic basis for psychopathology and to essential personality change as well as to symptom change. Because of the very central position of the conflict trigger - core conflict dimension, we will begin the analysis of the bases for the changes in the patients and their environments, as assessed at termination, by an

---

[1]Wallerstein, R. S. The Psychotherapy Research Project of the Menninger Foundation: 42 case studies. Unpublished manuscript.

47

examination of the fate of the core conflicts of the patients.

Among the unmarried patients there was no evidence to suggest that the core conflicts had been touched at all in 15 (Nos. 1, 10, 13, 14, 19, 21, 24, 25, 27, 29, 34, 36, 37, 39, 41). This group showed a mean increase of 7.5 HSRS points (mean HSRS change score of 32.1). HSRS change scores at termination ranged from 3.6 to 63.4. This is a relative score without a reference point. Rather extensive conflict resolution is believed to have occurred in one (No. 18), showing an HSRS increase of 2 points (HSRS change score of 38.0); rather complete resolution in another (No. 20) with an HSRS increase of 15 points (HSRS change score of 48.6); and partial resolution in five others (Nos. 12, 15, 23, 38, 40). The mean HSRS increase for these was 14 points (mean HSRS change score of 39.8). These scores simply show that extensive changes can occur in the absence of core conflict resolution. The patients in whom conflict resolution was greater were, with one exception, treated by psychoanalysis. The one exception was treated by long-term psychotherapy for a total of 718 hours.

Among the married group there appears to have been more extensive conflict resolution, but only one case (No. 26) appears to have rather thoroughly resolved his core conflicts, showing an HSRS increase of 39 points (HSRS change score of 63.4). Another (No. 32) resolved her core conflicts to a remarkable degree, showing an HSRS increase of 39 points (HSRS change score of 58.2); and eight others (Nos. 5, 6, 11, 17, 28, 30, 31, 35) can be said to have moderately altered their core conflicts, at least so it appeared at termination. The mean HSRS change at termination for these eight patients was 13 points (HSRS change score of 40.1). We wish to remind the reader that these judgments regarding the extent of conflict resolution were based on psychological test data, the therapist's view of the treatment, and a clinical appraisal of the patient. The core conflicts in ten (Nos. 2, 3, 4, 7, 8, 9, 16, 22, 33, 42) appear to have remained virtually untouched despite rather extensive treatment in several instances, showing a mean increase of 5 HSRS points (mean HSRS change score of 25.9).

Combining the married and the unmarried patients, there is a significant difference between those who had no conflict resolution (None) and those who had some conflict resolution (Some) on both the HSRS change score ($\underline{t}$ = 3.178, $\underline{p} <$ .005), and the Absolute Global Change score

$(X^2 = 14.357, \underline{p} < .001)$.

Since there are two aspects to the conflict trigger -
core conflict dimension, and since conflict resolution alone
occurred to an insufficient degree to account for the changes
in patients, we turn now to an inspection of the changes in
conflict triggers in order to discover other reasons for
symptomatic improvement.

Conflict Trigger: It should be recalled that at
initial study parents were considered conflict-triggering
for all of the 22 unmarried patients. At termination of
treatment parents were considered to be active conflict
triggers for only one of the 22 patients who were unmarried
at initial study. At first glance this fact might suggest
extensive intrapsychic change had occurred; however, our
best judgment, based on all the available facts collected
by the other research teams and ourselves, suggests that
at termination parents who were still living were potential
conflict triggers for many patients but had ceased having
this effect on their children simply by virtue of the geographic distance between parents and offspring. Simply
coming to Topeka, a move which separated parent from offspring, appears to have contributed to the achievement of
greater health for many of the patients by removing environmental factors which had more or less continuously kept
some elements of their unconscious conflicts activated. We
think there were a few patients (Nos. 1, 15, 18, 21, 23,
24, 38, 39, 40) who probably would have been able to better
tolerate their parents and not react symptomatically to them
were they again to have lived in their presence. We have
indirect evidence only for this statement, but visits with
parents seemed to go better for these nine patients.

Anticipating the final outcome, it is significant that
none of the unmarried patients returned to their parental
home after treatment. It can safely be assumed that treatment itself helped these patients break dependent parental
ties and in that sense contributed to the patient's growth,
but it also removed the parental conflict-triggering effect,
thus permitting unconscious conflicts to lie more dormant.

Parents were conflict-triggering in 11 instances among
the patients who were married at the time of initial study.
By termination, parents were actively conflict-triggering
for two patients (Nos. 2, 16) and somewhat triggering in
two others (Nos. 6, 32). Here, too, the lessened conflict-
triggering impact of parents at termination was due to geographic distance to a great extent. We have firm evidence

in only one case to show that the patient could live in
close proximity to his parents and not react symptomatically
again (No. 28). Several others reacted less symptomatically
(Nos. 6, 11, 26, 31, 32), but none of these patients lived
continuously near their parents. Part of the beneficial
effect of coming for treatment, as was the case for the
unmarried group, can be attributed to the removal of conflict triggers, in this instance the parents, thus permitting core conflicts to lie more dormant.

Some findings of special interest are those instances
where a parent had become less conflict-triggering by termination seemingly because the other parent had died, thus
changing the family constellation of which the patient had
been a part. Case No. 28, for example, was able to get
along much better with her mother by termination, a fact
which may well relate to the father's death during her treatment. It cannot be overlooked that when this patient later
formed a serious attachment to a man she again began to
get along less well with her mother. A triangle had been
created which triggered the repressed memories of the tri-
angular (oedipal) relationships of childhood.

Another patient (No. 39) began to get along better
with his father after his mother had died. He recalled how
his increasingly friendly feelings toward his father were
associated with the thought, "I have no bitch against him
now." The metaphoric reference to his mother is obvious
in this remark.

A clear statement illustrating the conflict-triggering
impact of parents was that of a woman who said, "Before
Father died, having a picture of him on the dresser was
like incest, but now I can have the picture of him displayed."
She regularly had severe anxiety attacks whenever he visited.
After his death his conflict-triggering impact on her lessened and the repressed infantile attachment to him presumably receded more deeply into her unconscious.

For both the unmarried and married patients, treatment
appears to have broken ongoing transactional dependent ties
with the parents and, once broken, unconscious conflicts
were also permitted to recede into the unconscious. Where
research evaluations revealed significant core conflict
resolution, patients regularly got along better with their
parents. Patients 26 and 40 are two examples. Not many
of the married patients had living parents. Some had one
parent and, as we have noted, the death of one parent often
appears to make possible a more harmonious relationship

with the remaining parent.

The possible role that escape from the conflict-triggering parents played in the improvements of all patients cannot be overlooked. The numerous instances where symptoms
became worse or reappeared when parents visited or when the
patient again lived closer to his parental family is weighty
evidence to suggest that some of the clinical improvement
at the time of termination can be accounted for by the
absence of these (parental) conflict triggers. Cases 14,
19, 23, 32, 37, and 41 illustrate especially well the
conflict-triggering effect of parents. The kinds of statements patients made about their parents suggest that parents
were still conflict-triggering for many of them after
treatment.

In order to illustrate further the significance of
the conflict trigger - core conflict dimension, and demonstrate its usefulness for assessing the nature of patient
change, we turn now to an inspection of the heterosexual
commitments of the patients before and after treatment.

In an earlier section we described in some detail how
attempts to form heterosexual relationships related directly
to the outbreak of illness in many of the patients. At
termination of treatment seven patients (Nos. 12, 15, 21,
25, 27, 34, 37) were sufficiently involved with the opposite
sex so as to render the opposite sex conflict-triggering.
Treatment had caused them to deepen their involvement with
the opposite sex but it had not resolved their core conflicts sufficiently to make such relationships rewarding
and without distress and pain. Eight other patients (Nos.
1, 13, 14, 24, 29, 39, 40, 41) were no more involved with
the opposite sex after treatment than before. One could
logically expect that core conflicts had not been resolved
by their treatment. This was so in every case. In the
seven cases who had become able to be somewhat involved
with the opposite sex, core conflicts were similarly
unresolved.

Why the one group became involved with the opposite
sex to some degree and the other did not is unclear. Since
involvement with the opposite sex during treatment can reflect acting out or be a new healthy adaptation, or both,
such involvement alone cannot be taken at face value to
reflect a beneficial effect of treatment. In fact, half
of those who did become involved were clearly acting out.
Of the eight who avoided the opposite sex, several were
young people who quite reasonably would have developed

interests in the opposite sex had their treatments been
more intensive and extensive; for example, see Case Nos.
14, 24, 29, 40.

Five of the unmarried patients married during treatment, a fact which suggests some resolution of core conflict
had occurred. This appears to have been true in three of
them (Nos. 18, 23, 38). One patient (No. 18) had to reenter treatment after his formal termination, a development
which is consistent with our judgment that he had only
partially resolved his core conflicts. His wife and child
were clearly still conflict triggers. The other patient
(No. 23) remained quite symptomatic after she married but
it appears that some resolution of conflict had given her
the freedom to marry again. Patient No. 38 improved clinically to a marked degree and this fact, along with her
ability to marry, is similarly consistent with evidence of
core conflict resolution as assessed by us and the other
teams. Two other patients (Nos. 10, 19) acted out during
treatment and married. Neither showed any evidence of
conflict resolution and it was no surprise that both
marriages failed. Taking on a mate further activated their
core conflicts.

The illustrations show how a deepened relationship
with the opposite sex is possible when the core conflicts
are partially resolved, but they also show that a subsequent
deepened commitment to the opposite sex results in further
activation of remaining core conflict. The patient then
may choose one of three courses. He may reenter treatment,
or take flight from the external trigger which activates
the core conflicts, or remain in a situation which causes
him continuous suffering, depending on the depth of his
involvement.

The pattern seems clear. Where treatment fails to
materially resolve the core conflicts, patients tend to
avoid the opposite sex. If the conflicts are somewhat resolved, patients tend to deepen their relationships with
the opposite sex. This involvement, in turn, further activates unconscious conflicts and unless treatment can effectively resolve internal conflicts, or unless spontaneous
resolution occurs, patients tend to shed their conflict
triggers by breaking off the relationship with the opposite
sex.

Barring the existence of reality circumstances which
preclude marriage, it appears that one of many indices of
the success of treatment, particularly in young people, is

the capacity to marry. In the unmarried group, five married but two of these marriages later failed. Six patients continued to find the opposite sex conflict-triggering and avoided marriage. Nine others (with one exception as subsequent facts revealed) avoided the opposite sex more or less entirely at termination. These levels of minimal or troubled involvements are congruent with the independently assessed state of their core conflicts. That conflict resolution occurred to a minimal degree is evident. The facts indicate the great difficulty in resolving their core conflicts by psychotherapy and psychoanalysis. Why this was so is not the purpose of our study although we will address ourselves to this fact in the final section.

One patient (No. 20) is of special interest. This man had become ill during his attempt to reach his life's goals in pursuit of a certain profession. His acute break came, however, when he was thrown into extremely intimate contact with women. It should be mentioned that much earlier he had been able to withstand the rigors and stresses of war but began drinking heavily when he was in contact with prostitutes while on leave. He married near the end of his treatment and it appeared at the time that his success in school and in marriage was due to conflict resolution by psychoanalysis. It seemed that women and work were no longer conflict-triggering. Subsequent events proved otherwise. After leaving treatment and upon having assumed the responsibilities of husband and physician, he decompensated severely in a way which clearly revealed that his core conflicts had not been resolved at all.

This case especially points to the importance of follow-up information for assessing the results of treatment, but in particular the importance of taking into account the life commitments the patient is able to make. Had he not made these commitments, that is, married and returned to his profession, he may well have remained more or less asymptomatic, and it would have appeared that psychoanalysis had resolved his core conflicts.

Further light can be shed on the core conflict - conflict trigger dimension by describing the changes, intrapsychic and external, that had occurred in the married patients by the termination of their treatment. In light of what has been said, we should want to know what happened to the marriages; did they continue; were they dissolved and if so, why; and, further, if the marriages continued, were they as conflict-triggering as before treatment?

The marriages of the following patients were not believed to be as conflict-triggering after treatment as they
were before treatment: Nos. 5, 6, 26, 30, 32, 35, 42.
This view coincides with the belief that their core conflicts were considerably resolved, but these statements
require some qualifications.

Two patients (Nos. 26 and 30) were divorced from their
first spouses during treatment and married different women
before their treatment ended. One man (No. 26) was treated
by extensive psychoanalysis before he remarried and evidence
suggests that his second wife was a much different person
from the first. This fact supports the belief that his
conflicts were resolved to a large extent; not only could
he tolerate marriage but he chose a better wife. The other
patient (No. 30) had been treated by supportive therapy
only. Here, too, the second wife was quite different from
the first. The second wife of patient No. 30 was less
feminine than the second wife of patient No. 26, a fact
which is congruent with greater conflict resolution in the
patient treated by psychoanalysis (No. 26).

Patient No. 6 was analyzed while away from home. After
returning to live with her family many of her symptoms returned. She was, therefore, also placed in the next group.
In the remainder of the patients there is a direct correspondence between the degree to which the marriage was
conflict-triggering and the extent to which core conflict
had not been resolved.

For another group (Nos. 2, 3, 6, 7, 16, 17, 31, 33,
36), despite extensive treatment in most instances, marriage
continued to be highly conflict-triggering and, as expected,
the core conflicts were believed not to have been significantly altered although, even in this group, the greater
the conflict resolution, even if minimal, the less the
marriage seemed to be conflict-triggering. Case No. 6 is
that of a woman who was analyzed while living away from
her family. Upon returning home after treatment many of
the old marital problems and symptoms reappeared, although
with less force.

Patient No. 31 was divorced early in her treatment
and married another man near its conclusion. For a time it
appeared as if the combination of conflict resolution and
a different man might make for a better marriage. This
marriage soon deteriorated after her treatment terminated
as did the psychological condition of the patient, facts
which confirmed an earlier assessment that the core conflicts

in this patient had not been materially altered. There
was some evidence to suggest that the core conflicts were
somewhat changed in this patient, but subsequent facts
showed they were insufficiently altered to permit succesful
marriage.

Several patients (Nos. 8, 9, 11, 22, 28) escaped from
the impact of unconscious pressures, rather than resolve
them in treatment, through divorce. Core conflicts were
essentially untouched in all of these patients; by removing
some of the conflict triggers their core conflicts troubled
them less. It is doubtful that any of these people could
live in a close heterosexual relationship without developing severe symptoms.

One patient (No. 28) was divorced early in her treatment. She was treated by psychoanalysis for over 1000 hours
and seemed to improve in many areas, but she never again
became involved with a man while in treatment. Her marked
obesity improved after treatment ended. Anticipating the
presentation of follow-up information, it can be revealed
here that this patient's symptoms reappeared in force when
she later planned to marry. The psychological test data
at that time revealed the fact that the total test picture
was much like the original test findings. These striking
facts suggest that not only was the analysis not complete
but that the stepwise removal of all men (father, husband,
and finally the analyst) from her life must be included
among those factors which permitted her to improve symptomatically but remain essentially unchanged. Obviously
her core conflicts might have been believed to have been
resolved but in fact had only receded into her unconscious
as the men in her life were removed. They were activated
again when she became seriously involved with a prospective
husband. Interestingly, her analyst, though bright, was a
passive man with an obese wife, factors which suggest that
his own makeup and countertransferences limited the results
of the analysis.

The effects of treatment for the married group of
patients insofar as living with the opposite sex is concerned, appears to have accomplished partial results; that
is, the core conflicts were not sufficiently resolved to
permit successful and happy and satisfying marriages for
most. Marriage did become tolerable for six patients;
however, it should be noted that only one of these cases
was believed to have been thoroughly analyzed. Three others
had not found marriage particularly difficult in the first
place; their conflict triggers were of another nature.

In the group for whom marriage was as triggering as
ever after treatment, several had had extensive treatment.
The ones who divorced (Nos. 8, 9, 11, 22, 28) seem to have
solved their problem by taking flight from the illness-
triggering environment. Another patient apparently committed suicide and thus, in a manner of speaking, shed all
his conflict triggers.

We have only focused on the heterosexual relationship
as an illustration of the concept "Conflict Trigger."
There are other environmental factors which are also conflict-triggering provided the patient commits himself to
them or becomes involved with them to some degree.

The next class of environmental involvement having
such an effect are the responsibilities of parenthood. It
should be recalled that there were two patients among the
unmarried group who had children who were conflict-triggering at the time of initial study. One would expect that
children should not be conflict-triggering at the conclusion of treatment had the core conflicts been significantly
altered. In one case (No. 1) there appears to have been
little change in the relationship to the children. The
mother had been divorced and also separated from her children before her treatment but during treatment managed to
find a house and bring her children into the home. She
terminated treatment when the positive transference had
become intense - a condition which repeated the original
conflict-triggering situation (husband, children, home).
She "divorsed" her analyst just as she had divorced her
husband earlier. While able to have the children with her,
she relegated their care to another woman and worked outside the home, thus shedding most of the home responsibilities.

The second patient (No. 12) was a bit more able to be
a mother to her children. She had been unable to take her
last child on her lap before treatment and after treatment
was able to do so for short periods of time only. Both of
her children had needed treatment themselves. She, too,
worked away from the home but some improvement in her relationship with her children coincided with other measures of
change which had suggested some alteration in her core conflicts. This patient remarried after the termination of
analysis and had to reenter treatment for several hundred
hours, a fact which supported the earlier assessment that
the core conflicts had been incompletely resolved. The new
husband and stepchildren had further activated her remaining core conflicts.

Turning now to the married group of patients, it should be recalled that at initial study children were considered to be conflict-triggering for 14 patients. Having had a child either marked the time of onset of the illness or the time it became significantly worse. At termination of treatment parenthood was considered conflict-triggering in eight cases (Nos. 2, 3, 6, 7, 17, 32, 33, 35) and, as could be expected, the core conflicts in the majority of these patients had not been altered to any significant degree.

For Patient No. 35 children appeared never to have been too much of a conflict trigger and with treatment they became somewhat more tolerable. For another (No. 32) considerable intrapsychic change appears to have occurred. This woman had a child during analysis and appears to have managed it well. For still another (No. 6), children were not as severely triggering, but still somewhat so.

Two patients (Nos. 26, 31) clearly showed greater tolerance for children and both received extensive treatment, one with apparent resolution of a major portion of his core neurosis and the other only partial.

Four patients lost their children by separation and eventual divorce (Nos. 8, 9, 11, 22). Intimate knowledge of the treatments of these four patients, along with assessments of the degree of resolution of core conflicts, leads us to suggest confidently that none of this group could again become parents and remain asymptomatic. One patient (No. 11) is able to care for one child but she works and thus is away from him much of the time; there is no man in her life.

One patient (No. 33) is of particular interest in that his history clearly illustrates the conflict-triggering impact of children. His analysis began while he was still a hospital patient. After a stormy course he settled down enough to be able to work and bring his family together again. He managed fairly well when living alone with his wife. With the return of each child he became significantly worse symptomatically. His treatment was terminated by death. All of his symptoms had returned with full force and the parallel between the conflict-triggering life circumstances at the time of his original decompensation with those at the time of his death were unmistakable. On both occasions he was living with his family and working as a physician. The presence of children and his work were major conflict triggers in his life, primarily the children inasmuch as he could work if living alone with his wife.

He was a strongly dependent man who was also deeply burdened by oedipal conflicts.

We suggested that part of the improvement of the patients could be accounted for by the absence of parents, who in most instances were considered to be conflict-triggering. It now appears that giving up marital and parental responsibilities contributed further and significantly to the improvement of some of the 42 cases. Conflict resolution occurred in some but not to a degree sufficient to account for the level of clinical improvement.

Additional facts to be taken into account in order to assess patient change is the ability of the patient to assume work and, in some instances, school responsibilities. At the time of initial study work was conflict-triggering for 14 patients (Nos. 2, 3, 13, 15, 16, 18, 20, 22, 25, 27, 30, 33, 36, 39). It should be noted that the list of cases for whom work was conflict-triggering at initial study does not fully coincide with the list illustrating how work played a significant part in the development of illness. Some of the patients were not working at the time of initial study and for this reason work could not be classed as a conflict trigger at that time even though it had been at the time of the outbreak of illness. For other cases, work became a conflict trigger during treatment.

Work continued to be conflict-triggering at termination as it had been at initial study for eight cases. Assessments for core conflict resolution showed none had occurred in any of these patients. Some of the patients found new jobs but ultimately failed, a fact which is congruent with the absence of core conflict resolution (see case Nos. 2, 3, 13, 16, 25, 27, 33, 39). Two others were able to work somewhat better but this ability was not related to conflict resolution. For one patient (No. 22) doing a different kind of work from that of his father seemed to make the difference. For five patients, work was definitely not as much a conflict trigger (Nos. 15, 18, 20, 26, 30) and in most instances this fact coincided with evidence of significant conflict resolution.

There is one apparent paradox. In Patient No. 30 no effort had been made to resolve his core conflicts; in fact, his therapist avoided making interpretations altogether. It is speculated that treatment supported him during a period of intrapsychic reorganization - which appeared manifestly as illness - thus making it possible for him to work when he had been unable to previously.

One patient (No. 20) is of special interest. Work
with women had had a major conflict-triggering and illness-
producing effect. Through treatment he had been able to
resume and successfully adjust to his work, facts which
were strong supporting evidence that his core conflicts had
been significantly altered. Some time later it was his
work which again triggered his illness - a fact which suggests that his core neurosis had not been resolved - and
like many patients he, in his desperation, gave up his
conflict-triggering responsibilities. After many months of
absence from work he again attempted to resume the same kind
of work. He promptly became ill again and a short time
later was found dead in his automobile, a presumptive
suicide.

We said earlier that new life involvement could be
taken as evidence of improvement. Acquiring new jobs meets
such a definition. It is interesting that of the 25 patients
who found new jobs seven, all men, failed at work. In contrast, ten were women and succeeded. Being able to work in
the case of a woman is evidence of improvement; however,
a number of these women patients had become ill under the
impact of marital and not work responsibilities. It
appears as if working outside the home provided a means
whereby they could escape from the conflict-triggering home
responsibilities (see case Nos. 5, 6, 9, 10, 12, 32).

For three women heterosexuality was clearly, in fact
overwhelmingly, still potentially conflict-tirggering (Nos.
14, 29, 41), and work fit into their pattern for avoiding
such commitments.

As a conflict trigger, work responsibilities were
many times more represented in men than in women, and therefore the capacity to work successfully appears to be a
more reliable criterion for determining the degree of conflict resolution for men than for women. Some of the
patients (Nos. 16, 26, 30, 33) were unable to follow their
father's footsteps prior to treatment. After treatment
only two (Nos. 26, 30) were able to succeed in the same work
as their fathers. Our impression is that work identical
to the father's work can become a greater conflict trigger
than other kinds of work. A second impression is that work
at a higher socioeconomic level similarly becomes a more
significant conflict trigger. It appears that a greater
demand is placed on the therapy to resolve core conflicts
in such cases as these.

We have traced the dimension conflict trigger - core

conflict during the period of treatment for these 42
patients. This was done with the view of giving meaning
to the many changes in the life circumstances of the patient
and to changes within the patient. Other situational variables will shed additional light on these changes. We
will next evaluate the effect of need-congruence.

Need-congruence: In order to assess the changes in
the patients and in their life circumstances at termination
in terms of the effect of need-congruent and need-incongruent
environmental factors, we will first briefly review the
definition of this variable.

Personality growth is stimulated when the environment
permits and stimulates the expression and development of
talents, values, abilities and skills. In the second place,
we consider the environment need-congruent when it evokes
and reinforces gender identity in a manner consistent with
biologic sex.

Successful treatment should result in the patient
surrounding himself with life circumstances after treatment
that are more need-congruent than before. It is reasonable
to expect that a healthier person would take on commitments
and surround himself generally with environmental factors
which would resonate positively with his newfound state of
greater health, and which by their own characteristics
would reflect the greater health of the patient. A corollary to this statement is that a sick person would tend to
make choices and commitments which would resonate harmoniously with the pathological aspects of his own personality
and which, therefore, would reflect the patient's illness.
Such environmental commitments would reinforce the illness
and tend to impede growth.

We will begin our analysis by examining the extent to
which patients were better able after treatment to live
out their talents, skills and abilities. The assumption
is that successful treatment should make it possible for
persons to find ways to more effectively live out their
potentialities and abilities. In the case of a professional person, for instance, whose illness prevented him
from practicing his profession, one could reasonably expect
that successful treatment should free him to resume his
professional work. Such a case is patient No. 26.

Of the 42 patients, the environments of 12 (Nos. 9, 17,
26, 28, 39, 30, 31, 32, 36, 38, 40, 41) were considered
significantly more need-congruent in the sense of permitting

the expression of skills, etc., and significantly less so
in eight others (Nos. 2, 3, 8, 11, 13, 16, 27, 39) at termination. For the remaining 22 patients, very little or no
change occurred in this dimension. Obviously something
went wrong for the eight patients whose environments became
less need-congruent, and it is reasonable to expect that
more should have happened in the treatments of the 22 cases
where no change occurred. The analysis of variance, using
HSRS change, shows a significant difference ($\underline{p} < .05$) among
the three groups, and individual mean comparisons, using
the Newman-Keuls test, show a borderline significant difference ($\underline{p} < .10$) between the "More Need-congruence" and
the "Same Amount of Need-congruence" groups, and a significant difference ($\underline{p} < .05$) between the "More Need-
congruence" and the "Less Need-congruence" groups; "Same"
and "Less" Need-congruence groups are not significantly
different. The chi-square test, using the Absolute Global
Change score, is also significant ($\underline{p} < .05$). The "Less"
group is quite small (8) which affects the chi-square.
This suggests that the greater the need-congruence, the
greater the improvement.

We now turn to what we consider to be the more essential aspect of the need-congruence variable - that which
favors the formation of unmixed psychologic gender. It is
reasonable to expect this aspect of need-congruence to be
a better indicator of essential personality change than
the one we have just considered. Helping a patient overcome conflicts and inhibitions which stood in the way of
his living out talents and abilities may reflect essential
intrapsychic changes but, as any experienced therapist
knows, suggestions, manipulation of the environment through
social work assistance, or just simple support, may lead
to such improvement. However, when a patient is able to
bring about change in the environment so as to reflect and
reinforce an unmixed and fully expressed psychologic gender
this, by definition, connotes essential personality change.

Patient environments were divided into four groups;
more need-congruent (Nos. 18, 20, 26, 30, 31, 32, 36, 38);
slightly more need-congruent (Nos. 1, 19, 21, 35, 37);
less need-congruent (Nos. 2, 3, 7, 8, 11, 13, 16, 22, 39);
and same as before (Nos. 4, 5, 6, 9, 10, 12, 14, 15, 17,
23, 24, 25, 27, 28, 29, 33, 34, 40, 41, 42). The analysis
of variance, using HSRS change, shows a significant difference ($\underline{p} < .05$)among the four groups. Newman-Keuls tests
show that the "More Need-congruence (Gender)" group is
significantly different ($\underline{p} < .05$) from the "Some Need-
congruence (Gender)," the "Same Amount of Need-congruence

(Gender)" and the "Less Need-congruence (Gender)" groups,
but the latter three groups do not differ significantly.
The assumptions for the chi-square, using the Absolute
Global Change, are not met. The TVG Change score of the
eight patients whose environments were considered to be
more need-congruent differed statistically from all the
rest. That the environments of so few patients were markedly more need-congruent supports the clinical impression
that few patients achieved thoroughgoing personality changes.

It is of especial interest for us to examine the fate
of the core conflicts in the group of patients whose environments were more need-congruent at termination. Seven of
these patients were believed to have extensively resolved
their core conflicts (Nos. 15, 18, 20, 26, 31, 32, 38).
All but one were treated by psychoanalysis. The exception
(No. 38) was treated by long-term expressive psychotherapy.
Two others, whose core conflicts were only slightly resolved
(Nos. 30, 36), showed marked shifts toward greater need-
congruence in their environments. Neither was treated by
psychoanalysis.

We believe these data having to do with core conflict
resolution, and those collected by the other teams, show
how very difficult it is to change people in an essential
way and, further, how upsetting treatment can be. Core
conflict resolution was not achieved in many, nor were the
environments of many significantly changed for the better
in the sense of greater need-congruence. The environments
of the majority remained unchanged or became less need-
congruent.

Stress: It might seem that stress in one's life would
necessarily have a hindering effect on the patient insofar
as achieving changes in his treatment. The converse might
be equally true; that is, a stressful life might serve as
an inducement to work harder in treatment. Furthermore, it
could be said that a goal of treatment is to add or remove
stressful factors in the patient's life. It seemed fruitful,
therefore, to group patients according to the presence or
absence of significant stress before and after treatment
and make outcome comparisons.

A first hypothesis suggests that persons living under
low stressful conditions, or whose lives lost their stressful qualities during the course of treatment, might have
changed for the better. There were 22 patients whose lives
were not stressful and 11 patients whose lives were highly
stressful initially but whose stresses were low at

termination. Adding these two groups together and comparing
them with a group whose lives were stressful throughout and
those whose lives became stressful during treatment - giving
a total sample of nine - we find a statistical difference
with one of the change scores (Absolute Global Change -
X^2 = 13.084, p < .005) in the hypothesized direction. The
HSRS change score failed to show a significant difference,
a finding for which we have no explanation.

Support: Another hypothesis is that persons for whom
human support was liberally available during their treatment should more readily achieve greater symptomatic and
essential change. Twenty-three of the 42 patients received
good human support during their treatment, and ten other
patients began treatment without much human support but in
time managed one way or another to surround themselves with
supports. Combining these two groups and comparing them
with the remainder of the sample, who had little support,
revealed a significant difference in the hypothesized
direction in the Absolute Global Change score (X^2 = 6.635,
p < .05), and a borderline significant difference with the
HSRS change score (t = 1.982, p < .10). Most of these
patients married during the course of treatment, a development which can be attributed directly to their treatment.
It thus appears that human support during treatment favors
good treatment results.

Opportunity: That persons with good opportunities for
growth and development should change more extensively is a
hypothesis which appears to be nearly self-evident. Stul-
tifying environmental circumstances could be expected to
nullify or inhibit the effects of therapy. Unfortunately,
the small number of patients who lacked such opportunities
precludes a comparison of treatment outcome with the high
opportunity group.

Mutability: Immutable environmental circumstances
could be expected to inhibit patient change. The environments of only four patients were classed as immutable,
making meaningful comparisons impossible.

7. SUMMARY OF THE FACTS AT FOLLOW-UP

It is generally accepted that the effects of psychiatric treatment may extend well beyond the termination date
of therapy, especially for patients in whom essential changes
occurred or in whom such changes were set into motion. An
obvious first step for assessing these changes or absence
thereof, and for identifying the factors which brought
them about or inhibited change, is to first detail the
changes in the lives of the patients from termination to
follow-up. With this objective in mind, we will now list
and classify the changes in the environments of the 42
patients.

As mnetioned in an earlier section, a rather reliable
criterion of health is a meaningful and nonsymptomatic involvement in life; that is, committed mature involvement in
people and things which permits the living out of one's
potentials. The life circumstances of the patient thus
not only provide objective criteria for assessing improvement but also for understanding the basis for these changes
and, therefore, for assessing the total effects of treatment. As we mentioned earlier, favorable and unfavorable
changes in the patient and his environment may unduly emphasize or minimize the importance of treatment and/or fail
to recognize the effects of fortuitous events in the patient's life.

The mean HSRS rating for the group treated by psychotherapy was 55.12 at follow-up. It was 43.7 initially and
52.78 at termination. The mean HSRS rating for the patients
treated by psychoanalysis was 49.57 at the time of initial
study and 62.21 at termination; by follow-up it was 61.47.

The simplest, and possibly superficial, kind of change,
and one which does not necessarily imply a deepened commitment to life but which may do so, is new friends. New
friends may simply reflect a change of residence, or may
reflect a degree of newfound health which leads to new
object choices. New friends may also reflect the acting

64

out of conflicts which treatment mobilized but failed to
deal with adequately. With these possible meanings in
mind, it should be noted that 20 of the 42 cases (Nos. 1,
3, 5, 9, 10, 11, 12, 16, 19, 21, 25, 27, 28, 29, 30, 31,
32, 35, 39, 41) made new friends during the follow-up
period.

For ten patients (Nos. 7, 9, 12, 13, 19, 25, 27, 28,
37, 41) new friends were classifiable also as new opposite
sex attachments. Of these ten, three (Nos. 7, 9, 28)
occurred in married patients and seven (Nos. 12, 13, 19,
25, 27, 37, 41) in the single patients. Thus one-third of
the unmarried group were able, to some degree, to form new
attachments to the opposite sex during the follow-up period.
Three of the unmarried patients (Nos. 14, 29, 39) formed
new homosexual attachments. Two of these (Nos. 14 and 29)
were young women who were very much on the fence at the
onset of treatment insofar as sexual identity and object
choice were concerned. After treatment they were exclusively homosexual. Such object attachments obviously do
not speak well for their treatment. A higher percentage
than the one-third who established new attachments to the
opposite sex might reasonably have been expected.

A mark of deeper commitment to the opposite sex is
marriage. At termination seven of the unmarried patients
had married (during treatment), and by follow-up one of
these (No. 19) was divorced, and another (No. 20) was
separated. It should be recalled that only three of the
patients out of the seven who married during treatment were
still married by follow-up. One of these had been married
before. By follow-up eight of the original unmarried group
of 20 patients were married; thus the effects of treatment
carried over into the follow-up period.

Divorce could reflect either a healthy development,
in that the person is freeing himself from a sick (need-
incongruent) relationship, or it could reflect a flight
from commitment. Of the married group of 22 patients
there were two (Nos. 7 and 8) who divorced, and one (No. 3)
who separated from his wife during the follow-up period.
It should be recalled that there were eight divorces and
separations during treatment and all of the separations
eventually ended in divorce. Thus, one-fourth of the
married patients were divorced by follow-up. Children were
lost to four women and one man as a consequence.

The divorces of the three who were married at the
time of the initial study were mainly flights from the

responsibilities of marriage. The marriages were by no
means ideal but they were tolerable and might have become
better had the patients been able to contribute more to
the marriage. One patient (No. 7) took flight into continued alcoholism and to a lover 20 years her junior;
another (No. 8) took flight into a state hospital; and a
third (No. 23) committed suicide. Two additional patients
(Nos. 19, 20) married during treatment; one later divorced
and the other separated from his spouse. In one instance
(No. 19), the marriage had been a clear acting out. Two
children were born of this pair before they divorced.
These two divorces can be viewed as healthy developments
in contrast to the other divorces.

Two of the three patients (Nos. 9, 26) who married
during treatment or follow-up were getting along satisfac-
torily at follow-up. The third (No. 31) was making a
marginal adjustment.

Nine patients (Nos. 5, 6, 12, 18, 19, 26, 30, 31, 38)
either became a parent for the first time during the follow-
up period or added to their families. Children born prior
to treatment were lost by five patients (Nos. 7, 8, 9, 11,
22).

New work commitments were found in 15 instances (Nos.
2, 7, 9, 13, 20, 21, 22, 27, 28, 29, 30, 34, 35, 36, 40).
In most, the new jobs reflected some growth in the patient
due to treatment. In several a pattern of job jumping
continued, and in one case a patient (No. 20) gave up his
life's work, that of physician, and took up farming, then
again tried to function as a physician but soon died - a
probable suicide.

Five patients (Nos. 1, 4, 17, 24, 39) received promotions at work, and in each instance personality growth
appears to have been a factor in bringing about the promotion. The financial situation improved in 16 cases (Nos.
1, 4, 5, 6, 14, 15, 17, 21, 25, 26, 27, 30, 35, 37, 39,
40). This change was largely due to the patient's own
efforts in 12 instances. Worsening of the financial picture
occurred in six cases (Nos. 3, 8, 9, 34, 36, 42).

Five patients entered school (Nos. 14, 23, 25, 32, 40),
and only one later dropped out. One patient who had been
very afraid of school obtained a Ph.D., and two others
graduated, one of whom subsequently went on to graduate
work.

Four patients (Nos. 11, 13, 25, 39) moved away from their parents. In all instances this appears to have been a function of greater personal strength. Parents died in five cases (Nos. 14, 15, 17, 25, 34).

Physical health worsened in two cases (Nos. 36 and 42), and five patients (Nos. 2, 3, 16, 20, 33) died in the termination to follow-up period, and another died during the post-follow-up period. One patient's health seemed to have improved due to weight loss (No. 28). Three of the deaths were clearly suicides, and the other three can be classed as unconscious suicides, and perhaps conscious ones.

Though there is some repetition in what follows, it will serve as a convenience to the reader to summarize some of the more salient changes which occurred over the entire research period. We will begin with the most striking facts.

Four patients were dead by follow-up. Two other patients died during the post-follow-up period.

Patient No. 16 was a man who was destined to inherit his father's position as president of a large company. Until he entered the father's company alcohol had not been a serious problem, but it soon became so. Treatment never touched this man despite the availability of hospitalization, psychoanalysis, and unlimited funds for treatment. Pneumonia and meningitis which developed during a prolonged drinking spree were the cause of death and marked the end of a long self-destructive life course. His brother's earlier accidental death had insured his being heir to his father's company.

Patient No. 3 was a young physician who could not shoulder the responsibilities of marriage, parenthood or work. His first marriage was an act of spite against his father; he could not manage the second, nor could he practice medicine without the support of drugs. Despite hospitalization and the availability of other forms of treatment, treatment failed to touch him. His death was a confirmed suicide.

Patient No. 33, a physician, had been successful during military service, a brief professorship, and initially in his private practice of medicine. As he became more successful, marital discord with his physician wife increased. He eventually decompensated severely, made some

gains during treatment when separated from his family, but
he went downhill again after being reunited with his family
and while engaged in the practice of his profession. He
died from alcohol and drugs and probable aspiration of
vomitus.

Patient No. 20 was a young physician who became ill
while still a student. He improved with treatment, graduated, married, but was unable to practice medicine without developing severe symptoms which included the use of
drugs. After a rest from work he reentered his practice
of medicine but soon thereafter was found dead in his car
with the engine running. All signs pointed to suicide although there was no positive proof. His treatment had
terminated by mutual agreement between doctor and patient.

Patient No. 2 was a chronic failure in business. He
eventually took flight from treatment and took his family
to Mexico where drugs were easily available and where his
inherited funds would stretch further. His death was
suicide from an overdose of drugs.

Case No. 23 was a young college student who prematurely
broke off her first efforts at treatment by entering into
a common-law arrangement with a young man. She reentered
treatment, married this man, and again ended treatment
prematurely. Her marriage was stormy, she competed with
her husband on a professional level, and eventually committed suicide about two years after the follow-up study
at a time when her husband was becoming more successful.

By follow-up, nine patients had divorced the spouse
to whom they were married at the time of initial study
(Nos. 7, 8, 9, 11, 22, 26, 28, 30, 31). Of this group,
four patients were remarried by the time of follow-up
(Nos. 9, 26, 30, 31).

Ten of the single patients were married by the time
of follow-up (Nos. 10, 12, 18, 20, 21, 23, 25, 36, 37, 38).
Three had been married prior to the initial study. One
single person (No. 19) married and divorced during treatment. She had not remarried by follow-up. Thus, fourteen
patients undertook marriage during the research period.

8. A CONCEPTUAL UNDERSTANDING OF THE FACTS
AT FOLLOW-UP

Earlier we outlined the way we assessed the degree
and nature of the changes in the patients at termination.
We also said that an index of change toward greater health
is a deeper and richer commitment to life. Implicit in
such commitment is the nonsymptomatic meaning of the behaviors which reflect the commitment. Intrapsychic change
can be assumed to have occurred if there is clear evidence
that great commitment to life no longer triggers and activates unconscious conflicts. For instance, if job promotions or marriage or children no longer evoke symptoms,
one can assume that core conflicts have been resolved to
some extent. However, this may not always be so. Through
supportive treatment the ego may have been strengthened so
as to adequately contain the patient's unconscious forces
when greater commitments are made. Therefore, assessments
of the patient, using other methods, must be made alongside
those which determine whether or not the environment con-
tinues to be conflict-triggering.

The core conflicts were untouched in the four patients
who were dead at follow-up. It is clear from the extent to
which symptoms had reappeared in the fifth patient who died,
probably by suicide, during the post-follow-up period
while attempting to reestablish his medical practice, that
the termination assessment of considerable conflict resolution was grossly wrong. The man had not been personally
examined, however, and all judgments were based on second-
hand information from his psychoanalyst. The sixth patient,
who died by suicide during the post-follow-up period, had
clearly failed to resolve her core conflicts to any significant degree. The turmoil in her life during the follow-up
period and her eventual suicide amply confirms the correct-
ness of this judgment. For the five suicides (without Case
No. 33 who had no follow-up scores), the mean decrease in
HSRS points is 7 (mean HSRS change score of 14.04). HSRS
change scores ranged at follow-up from 2.4 to 54.2. As
noted earlier, this score lacks a reference point.

The core conflicts were untouched in twenty other
patients (Nos. 1, 4, 7, 8, 9, 10, 11, 13, 14, 19, 21, 22,
24, 25, 29, 34, 36, 37, 39, 41), with a mean increase of
12 HSRS points (mean HSRS change score of 34.21), and only
slightly resolved in four others (Nos. 17, 27, 31, 42), with
a mean increase of 11 HSRS points (mean HSRS change score
of 34.50). Nine patients resolved their core conflicts to
a moderate degree (Nos. 5, 6, 12, 15, 28, 30, 35, 38, 40),
with a mean increase of 19 HSRS points (mean HSRS change
score of 44.32), and three others materially resolved their
core conflicts (Nos. 18, 26, 32), mean increase of 21 HSRS
points (mean HSRS change score of 47.47). There is a significant difference ($p < .01$) between those who had no conflict resolution and those who had some conflict resolution
on the HSRS change score. The Absolute Global Change score
failed to reach a significant difference.

It is apparent from these data that the improved clinical picture in these patients cannot be accounted for on
the basis of continued core conflict resolution alone during the follow-up period. Other factors which may account
for patient improvement outside those which are brought to
bear upon the patient for the purpose of conflict resolution
within the treatment situation are implicated.

As was done earlier, and in order to shed further
light on this question, we will begin by assessing the extent to which various environmental factors were conflict-
triggering. It should be recalled that the environment
can cease being conflict-triggering either because no meaningful contact exists between patient and the environment
or because core conflicts were resolved, thus permitting
meaningful involvement with the environment. Obviously,
in the latter instance meaningful contact with the environment will not cause the appearance of symptoms since core
conflicts are absent.

Conflict Triggers: Parents continued to be conflict-
triggering for two of the original group of unmarried patients
(Nos. 1, 24) at the time of follow-up. Parents were potentially conflict-triggering for 17 of the unmarried group
(Nos. 10, 12, 13, 14, 15, 19, 20, 21, 23, 25, 27, 29, 34,
37, 39, 40, 41), but were no longer so, largely because of
geographic distance between patient and parents. One patient
(No. 38) was actively involved with her parents and core
conflicts were not activated thereby, thus suggesting significant resolution of core conflicts. Another would probably have remained symptom free (No. 18) had he been
actively involved with his parents. The remaining unmarried

patients were not involved (some of the parents had died and
geographical distance separated the others) but, had they
been involved, evidence suggested that core conflicts
would have become activated and symptomatic behavior could
have been expected to reappear. Further validating evidence
is to be found in the assessment of the degree of resolution of core conflicts by the other research teams. None
of these cases were believed to have significantly altered
their core conflicts.

     Two unmarried patients are of special interest because
of the clarity with which they demonstrate the relationship of the environment to the unconscious.

     Following the death of the father of an unmarried
patient (No. 40), he clearly could get along better with
and do more for the mother. Similarly, following the death
of the father patient No. 38 could get along better with
the mother. While treatment was extensive for both parties, we are of the opinion that the improved relationship
with remaining parents would not have been achieved to as
great a degree had the other parent not died. The adult
triangle would have continued to activate the repressed
representations of the original oedipal situation.

     In the married group, parents were actively conflict-
triggering for only one man (No. 22). This patient was
divorced during treatment and had returned to his parental
home. Parents were potentially conflict-triggering for 13
patients (Nos. 2, 3, 5, 6, 7, 8, 11, 16, 30, 31, 32, 33,
42). For five others (Nos. 4, 17, 26, 28, 35), it seems
unlikely that parents would still trigger core conflicts.
Objective evidence for this assumption exists for only four
of the five. One of the parents had died in two instances
(Nos. 26, 28), a fact which may account to some degree for
the improved relationship between one patient, a woman
(No. 28), and her mother. Patients 9 and 36 had no parents
and no assessment can be made.

     Assessments of the extent of resolution of core con-
flicts of the 42 patients should be congruent with the
Situational Variables team assessments of the extent to
which parents were, or potentially were, or no longer were,
conflict-triggering. In no instance where parents were
rated as clearly conflict-triggering were the core conflicts
believed to be resolved. Four of the married patients for
whom the parents would probably not have been conflict-
triggering showed some degree of resolution of core conflict.
The fifth (No. 28) seemed at termination to have materially

resolved her neurosis, but her father had died during her treatment and she also had divorced, thus obscuring the basis for her improvement. Midway during the follow-up period she became seriously involved with a man and contemplated marrying him. Psychological test data, and the return of her old symptoms as she deepened a relationship with a man, provided strong evidence that her core conflicts had not been resolved. These facts make it seem unlikely that she could have had an ongoing relationship with both of her parents and remain symptom free. Here, again, the absence of the father broke up the adult triangle, which caused oedipal conflicts to recede.

We have suggested that geographic and greater emotional distance from parents can contribute to clinical improvement. We will next look into other areas of environmental involvement to see how these areas resonate with intrapsychic conflicts and the clinical condition of the 42 cases.

Assessment of the extent to which heterosexuality was conflict-triggering should be congruent with assessments of core conflicts. Since there were several marriages, divorces and remarriages, we will not separate the 42 cases into married-unmarried groups.

Seven cases (Nos. 13, 14, 19, 27, 28, 37, 40) experienced heterosexual involvement as actively conflict-triggering at follow-up, and we believe ten more (Nos. 1, 7, 8, 11, 22, 24, 29, 34, 39, 41) would have had they become involved with a member of the opposite sex. These assessments are congruent with assessments of the state of the core conflicts at follow-up. In no instance did a patient show evidence of a troubled relationship with the opposite sex when research evidence pointed to resolution of core conflict. The clinical data of the ten cases suggested that this group avoided the opposite sex because of the failure to have resolved core conflicts in their treatment.

Marriage continued to be conflict-triggering for nine patients (Nos. 2, 3, 8, 11, 16, 20, 22, 23, 33). Six of these were dead at follow-up and post-follow-up, a fact completely consonant with research assessments which showed little change in core conflicts in these six. The other three had been divorced by follow-up and were not involved with the opposite sex. None of these three married during treatment. All six of the dead patients had had or were having severe marital difficulties during the follow-up period. Five patients (Nos. 10, 12, 21, 31, 36) continued

to find marriage manageable but very difficult and clearly
conflict-triggering. In no instance was there evidence
that core conflicts had been resolved to any extent in these
five. We know of two separations in this group after the
follow-up study. Both of these patients had married during
treatment. These marriages were clearly symptomatic in
nature; that is, the marriages represented acting out during
treatment.

Marriage was assessed as being moderately conflict-
triggering for three at follow-up (Nos. 6, 35, 42). All
three showed some evidence of resolution of core conflicts.
Two had been in analysis and the other in long-term
psychotherapy.

Marriage continued to be mildly conflict-triggering
for ten patients (Nos. 4, 5, 9, 17, 18, 25, 26, 30, 32,
38). Significant changes in the core conflicts had occurred
in half of these as a result of their treatment. Interestingly, however, the other five were better able to adjust
to marriage (Nos. 4, 9, 17, 25, 30) although they had received only supportive therapy. These five cases merit a
few words of comment.

One (No. 30) was a divorced man who had become psychotic while married and on the brink of becoming a successful physician. It seems likely that some spontaneous resolution of unconscious conflicts occurred during his psychosis
within the protective bounds of hospitalization and long-
term supportive treatment. At the end of his treatment his
view of women and of his father had changed materially; he
was able to marry and had, indeed, picked a much more suitable and mature woman. Some signs of illness remained,
however.

Another man (No. 17) was treated supportively but
managed to become more manly and as a consequence achieved
a happier marriage.

Another (No. 4) emerged from an acute decompensation
and reestablished a preexisting happy marriage.

Another (No. 9) picked an entirely different kind of
man, a fact which clearly placed less demand on her and at
the same time permitted her to live out many of her interests, something she had been unable to do in her previous
marriage. She had lost her child in her divorce.

The fifth case (No. 25) was a very sick young man who

surprised the research team by his capacity to marry and
father children. Although unable to stick to gainful work
or school, he was devoted to his family and seemed to derive much benefit from them. However, post-follow-up
investigation has shown this marriage to have failed.

Parenthood continued to be severely conflict-triggering
for six patients (Nos. 1, 5, 6, 11, 12, 19). One of these
(No. 6) had apparently resolved her core conflicts to some
degree but treatment had been conducted while she lived
away from home. Upon terminating and returning to her home
all of her symptoms except a snake phobia returned. She
clearly experienced much difficulty resuming her responsibilities as a wife and mother. Her conflicts had been
altered only minimally, although in time she was better
able to adjust to marital life and parenthood.

After treatment had terminated, another patient (No.
12) married a man with children, but she soon developed
distress and required ·500 additional hours of treatment.
Family life activated conflicts which had not been resolved
in her analysis, which had been conducted while she was
single, working, and away from her home much of the day.

Another case (No. 5) had shown some conflict resolution by the time of follow-up. She subsequently adopted a
child and became quite symptomatic but managed to keep the
child, something she had been unable to do prior to her
treatment.

The other three were divorced women who kept their
children but relegated a major portion of their care to
others while they worked outside the home. None of these
altered their core conflicts during treatment.

Parenthood was moderately conflict-triggering at
follow-up for four patients (Nos. 30, 31, 32, 40). In the
main, the independent assessment of core conflict resolution is congruent with this degree of triggering effect of
parenthood. Case No. 40, a divorced man, had completely
ignored his child before treatment, and began taking an
interest in her after treatment although he did not live
under the same roof as his child. His analysis had only
partially resolved his core conflicts.

Case No. 30, while being pleased with his new baby,
also experienced excessive rage toward it and periodically
shook it because it wouldn't stop crying. This case was
cited as an apparent contradiction to the notion that core

conflicts must undergo change before more mature levels of
adjustment can be achieved. He had been treated only
supportively. It subsequently became apparent that part
of the basis for his having been able to marry successfully was the attention he got from his basically warm wife.
The coming of a child clearly stirred up conflicts which
were still very much there.

Both patients 31 and 32 showed more ability to adjust
to their children after treatment but not with complete
ease. Core conflicts had undergone considerable change in
these two.

Parenthood was not considered to be conflict-triggering for five patients (Nos. 4, 18, 25, 26, 38). Three of
these had undergone extensive treatment while two had not.
Case No. 25, paradoxically, found parenthood to be very
agreeable. This was a severely ill young man whose core
conflicts had not been dealt with in the treatment process.
Post-follow-up information revealed the marriage to have
failed, a fact which appears to bear a relationship to his
having established a family and the emergence of children
into the family constellation.

While no direct evidence is available for all patients,
it seems reasonable to predict that 23 of the patients would
have found parenthood conflict-triggering were they to have
married and had children, or had they reestablished their
families. The six deaths fall in this group.

One of these patients (No. 33) became progressively
more ill each time one of his five children rejoined him
and his wife. Three of these patients had never been able
to sustain their support of their families, and the fifth
had separated from his wife before his death. Symptoms in
four patients (Nos. 7, 8, 9, 22) significantly diminished
after leaving their children. Ten of the 23 had never
married, and no evidence was available to suggest parenthood would have been possible for them. Two others were
married during treatment but remained childless. The last
of the group was an older married woman whose two children
had left home. When she and her daughter were together
fights raged more or less continuously.

At the follow-up point, work - defined as occupation
for men and homemaking for women - was not considered to be
conflict-triggering for 18 patients (Nos. 1, 4, 9, 10, 12,
14, 17, 18, 21, 23, 24, 27, 28, 29, 30, 37, 38, 40). These
patients could work and there was no evidence that doing so

produced symptoms. Core conflicts, however, had not been resolved and were clearly evident in most of them. These facts show that environmental factors other than work were necessary to mobilize unconscious conflicts in these patients. As has been shown earlier, these were largely commitments to the opposite sex, children, and parents.

Work was mildly conflict-triggering for six patients (Nos. 5, 6, 11, 15, 35, 42). Evidence showed unresolved conflicts in these patients; work clearly produced distress or frank symptoms in all six. Work was moderately conflict-triggering in six (Nos. 7, 22, 26, 31, 32, 41). Again, evidence for inferring unresolved core conflicts was abundantly evident in all six. Attempting to work precipitated symptoms in all of them.

Work was severely conflict-triggering in eight cases (Nos. 8, 13, 19, 20, 25, 34, 36, 39). Core conflicts were unresolved in all eight of them, as might be expected.

Work was potentially conflict-triggering in four more cases, all of whom were dead. There was abundant evidence that work responsibilities had contributed to the mobilization of conflicts, leading to severe regression and to their deaths. It is clearly evident that more patients were able to work without becoming ill after treatment than before. It appears that progress can be made in the area of work with greater ease than in other areas of life adjustment. The effect of treatment insofar as improving and deepening heterosexual commitments was concerned was highly variable and was clearly more difficult to achieve.

Need-congruence: Having followed the course of core conflicts and conflict triggers through to the follow-up period, it will now be instructive to analyze the environment of the 42 cases as regards its need-congruence. Successful treatment should make it more possible for the person to surround himself with an environment which is more need-congruent. Such an environment should be less conflict-triggering; core conflicts should be diminished. In other words, an environment which is need-congruent, particularly as regards gender identity, will automatically be conflict-triggering if core conflicts exist. Therefore, assessment of the presence or absence of need-congruence in the environment provides a means for cross-validating the fate of the core conflicts and, therefore, the effects of treatment.

The environments of 13 patients (Nos. 5, 6, 12, 13, 15,

17, 19, 21, 25, 27, 33, 36, 37) were considered to be more
need-congruent at follow-up than at termination in the sense
of promoting growth.   Patient No. 33 was dead by follow-up
but it was clear that his environment, which was becoming
increasingly need-congruent, was at the same time highly
conflict-triggering.   He regressed, and died a probable
suicide.   Curiously, nine of these patients were believed
to have made no progress insofar as resolving their core
conflicts, yet all had made some progress in surrounding
themselves with more need-congruent factors.   This fact
suggests spontaneous maturation or more aftereffects from
the treatment than had been thought possible.

Four of the 13 patients were believed to have resolved
their core conflicts to some significant degree.   The four
cases could clearly tolerate maturity-stimulating environments which they had been unable to tolerate before treatment.   Patient No. 5 was able to adopt children.   She first
became seriously ill when she had tried years earlier to
adopt a baby.   After treatment, during the follow-up period,
she was able to adopt a child.   Patient No. 12 was able to
remarry and in so doing acquired several children.   That
she could surround herself with such an environment is consonant with some degree of resolution of core conflict,
but that she also had to return for further analysis after
she remarried is congruent with the evidence that not all
of her core conflicts had been resolved.

Patient No. 15 maried shortly after follow-up.   He
had been unable to tolerate a heterosexual relationship
prior to treatment.   Patient No. 6 was able to return to
her family and remain there despite the reappearance of
many of her old symptoms.   These cases illustrate how core
conflict resolution permits the patient to commit himself
to an environment which has a feedback maturing effect.

The patients who failed to resolve core conflicts are
of special interest for a variety of reasons.   Patient No.
19 had married during treatment, had two children, and then
divorced.   These children were considered to be need-
congruent factors despite the fact that much of their care
was relegated to hired help, but even so she did not give
them up and at times was able to associate with them.

Patient No. 27, surprisingly, had married by follow-up
but he picked a woman who, by his description, was by far
the stronger.   It is probable that her femininity was as
undeveloped as was his masculinity.   This case is an example
of an environmental commitment which has some need-congruent

aspects but which is also need-incongruent. His core
conflicts had been largely untouched by his treatment.

Patient No. 25 is a paradox. This man, who was married and had a family, could not work for any length of
time and supported his family on inherited funds. Research
findings indicated there had been no resolution of core
conflict. Some internal changes had apparently occurred
during this supportive treatment inasmuch as he had been
unmarried prior to treatment and by follow-up had a family
of his own.

Patient No. 17 stuck by his family through the wife's
treatment, and improvements in the wife and children were
tolerated by him.

Patient No. 37 married and it was clear that being
able to do so was a function of supportive therapy.

Patient No. 33 improved largely because of the supportive aspects of his treatment. As each child rejoined the
family he became progressively worse, and died of probable
suicide. This case reveals especially clearly the conflict-
triggering significance of a gender identity promoting
environment.

Patient No. 21 was in supportive therapy and, although
he married, his choice was a dominant woman who didn't
mind his impotence. It is clear that such a marriage is
not complete nor maximally need-congruent. Marriage was
somewhat need-congruent for this man; he was able to marry
and prior to treatment had been unable to sustain a relationship of any kind with a woman. The partial role reversal in the match was clear.

The remaining two (Nos. 13 and 36) were able to have
relationships with women. The first, a girl friend; and
the second married a somewhat boyish woman who did not
mind his complete impotence.

These findings are not striking and do not speak particularly well for the changes brought about by psychotherapy, for even those patients who deepened their heterosexual commitments had a troubled time as a consequence.

One patient (No. 20), whose environment was less need-
congruent at follow-up, was thought at termination to have
resolved his core conflicts. Subsequent events proved this
to be untrue. As he assumed the responsibilities of a

physician and husband he became ill and gave up his commitments. He found solace by leaving his wife and returning
to the farm of his boyhood. Upon attempting to resume a
medical practice he again became ill and was found dead
in his car - a probable suicide.

The environments of 13 patients (Nos. 3, 7, 8, 9, 10,
14, 16, 24, 29, 34, 39, 40, 41) remained devoid of need-
congruent elements which favor the formation of gender and
promotion of growth during the follow-up period. In general, treatment results were poor, particularly with regard
to the failure to resolve those conflicts which stood in
the way of a resumption or achievement of heterosexual
commitments. None of this group showed any evidence of
significant core conflict resolution by any of the criteria
used.

Patient No. 7 had been unable to adjust to marriage
and motherhood; she became ill, began treatment, but terminated prematurely. Failing again to adjust to marriage
after returning to her husband, she divorced. At follow-
up she was living with a very sick man 15 years her junior.

One patient (No. 40) improved in some areas of adjustment but his relationship to women was unchanged. Patient
No. 41 was no closer to heterosexual relationships despite
extensive treatment. Patient No. 8 lost her family.
Patient No. 3 was unable to respond to treatment, lost her
family, and committed suicide. Patient No. 10 married a
homosexual man but the marriage was not a success. Patient
No. 16, after a brief analysis, lost his family and died
of probable suicide. Patient No. 39, after having over a
thousand hours of analysis, continued to be homosexual and
alcoholic. Patient No. 34 was unable to marry and was as
sick as ever after extensive treatment. Patients 14 and
29, both young women, remained homosexual. The environments of all these 13 cases were grossly lacking in need-
congruence.

The environments of seven patients failed to change
for the better or worse but were considered to be moderately
need-congruent during treatment. Patient No. 1 was a
divorcee with two children, who took flight from her analysis. She continued to live with her children but did not
remarry, and she relegated much of the care of her children
to hired help. Had her treatment been a success, one could
reasonably have expected her to marry again. Her illness
had first appeared when children were born and she soon
took flight into illness, thus relinquishing her marital

responsibilities. That she could not surround herself with
a more need-congruent environment during follow-up is consistent with the failure to resolve her core conflicts as
well as the manner and timing of the termination of her
psychoanalysis. She took flight from her treatment after
bringing her children into her home and upon developing
romantic fantasies toward her analyst - a repetition of
the circumstances of her flight from her husband.

Patient No. 23 began living with a young man during
her treatment and eventually married him. He was a meek
fellow who accepted her many neurotic traits. For a time
the marriage seemed to succeed, but post-follow-up information revealed a breakdown of the marriage, with the
patient returning to treatment. Her core conflicts were
unresolved, by and large, and her inability to hold onto
her husband even though he was not very manly is entirely
consistent with this fact; that is, the failure of her
treatment. She eventually committed suicide.

Patient No. 28 is of particular interest. This woman
became ill under the conflict-triggering effect of marriage
and motherhood. Her analysis partially resolved her core
conflicts but by the time of termination the only need-
congruent aspect of her life was her small son. She had
divorced during treatment. Her psychological tests showed
considerable evidence of basic change, and indeed the clinical picture appeared much better. During the follow-up
period the patient met a man and seriously considered the
possibility of marriage. Many of her symptoms reappeared,
including her extreme obesity. The psychological tests
revealed a reappearance of most of the old signs which had
been seen at initial study. This case illustrates very
clearly the usefulness of using the need-congruent aspects
of the environment as an indicator of the intrapsychic
state and, therefore, as a means for assessing treatment
outcome.

Patient No. 2 failed to gain any benefit from treatment. He eventually committed suicide after several failures
at work. Though married and surrounded by many need-congruent elements, his wife was actually a shrew. It can be
presumed that her negative impact on the patient joined
forces with his own unconscious conflicts and contributed
to his destruction.

The treatment failure of Patient No. 22 is corroborated
by his loss of his wife and children. His wife was basically a good person who was devoted to him. His illness

precluded his holding on to these need-congruent aspects of
his life.

Unlike Patient No. 22, Patient No. 32 made good progress during treatment, as evidenced by her ability to remain married and have a family. No further change of
significance occurred during the follow-up period. Considerable change had occurred in her core conflicts. Had
they not been resolved, chances are she would have been
unable to hold onto her family.

Patient No. 11 had been advised to have treatment
despite the fact that treatment caused her to be separated
from her family. Her husband divorced her during treatment, and though she continued in treatment she failed to
resolve her neurosis and lived a lonely life with her
youngest child. That she never married again - that is,
again surrounded herself with a need-congruent environment -
is strong evidence of the failure of her treatment. While
not marrying cannot categorically be taken as evidence of
the presence of unconscious conflicts, failure to do so
was so in this case where other evidence clearly showed
the presence of unconscious conflicts.

Eight patients (Nos. 4, 18, 26, 30, 31, 35, 38, 42)
had been able, for the first time, to surround themselves
with, or had been able to retain, need-congruent environments. None of these eight gave up their pretreatment
commitments during the period from termination to follow-up,
a fact which suggests that their core conflicts had been
significantly altered if not resolved. Most of these
patients made significant changes in their core conflicts.

Combining those patients whose environments were more
need-congruent at follow-up than at termination (N = 13)
with those who were, for the first time, able to surround
themselves with a need-congruent environment (N = 8), and
comparing them with those patients whose environment became
less need-congruent (N = 13), some significant differences
were found as regards the change scores. The $\underline{t}$ test between
the High and Low need-congruence groups on HSRS change is
significant ($\underline{p} < .025$), as is the chi-square test on
Absolute Global Change ($\underline{p} < .01$). The chi-square has more
than 20% expected frequencies below 5 but none below 1.

The findings show the relationship between core conflict resolution, personality change and a need-congruent
environment. Thus, the environments of the majority of the
42 patients were still not very need-congruent in the

gender identity stimulating sense at follow-up. The ability to take on heterosexual commitments appears to bear no relationship to mode of treatment; as many were treated by psychoanalysis as had received supportive therapy.

The above data suggest that achieving internal change sufficient to permit heterosexual commitments which have a feedback, gender reinforcing, need-congruent effect does not come easily. The question immediately arises whether treatment can more easily produce changes which make possible greater commitments to need-congruent aspects in the environment in the second sense of the term; that is, to environmental factors which provide the opportunity for the individual to live out and develop his talents, skills, and abilities.

Eight patients (Nos. 1, 5, 12, 13, 17, 25, 27, 40) improved the need-congruent aspects of their environment in the second sense of the term during the period from termination to follow-up. Only two (Nos. 5 and 12) of these were believed to have significantly resolved their core conflicts; another two (Nos. 17 and 40) resolved their core conflicts to a slight degree, and the remainder, as well as the two just mentioned, received much support in their therapy. Obviously core conflict resolution is not the only means by which persons can achieve these treatment goals.

The environments of seven others (Nos. 2, 3, 7, 8, 19, 20, 39) remained poorly need-congruent or worsened. These patients were unable to live out their abilities, etc., in any improved way. Two died from probable suicide during the period between termination and follow-up. None had altered their core conflicts at all.

The environments of five others (Nos. 11, 16, 22, 28, 41) failed to change but were considered to be moderately need-congruent. One died from probable suicide. Only one (No. 28) altered her core conflicts to any significant degree.

The environments of 22 remained rather good in need-congruence. Twelve of these were women who found work to do outside the home. About half made significant changes in their core conflicts while the others did not.

Stress: The stress variable appears to have had little impact on the outcome of treatment during the period from termination to follow-up. Thirty-two of the patients were living under rather low stressful life circumstances. The

life of only one patient became stressful during the period
between termination and follow-up. The lives of four
others remained so, and the environments of five others
were highly stressful initially but became less so. Interestingly, three of the latter group died of probable suicide. For these three patients marriage had been highly
stressful and not need-congruent because of the characteristics of the spouse. The three cases do not permit drawing any conclusions as regards stress and treatment outcome.

Support: Inspection of the effects of human support
on patient change suggests a positive relationship between
these two variables. Comparing patients who were lacking
in human support with those who had such support revealed
significant differences. Using the HSRS change score, the
means for the high (N = 31) and the low (N = 10) Support
groups (one patient was dead at follow-up, there was little
support in his life) were significantly different using
the t test ($p <$ .025). Similarly, the chi-square test,
using the Absolute Global Change score, was significant
($p <$ .025). These findings do, indeed, suggest that human
support is an important factor in the achievement of greater
health. It should be noted that the human element in treatments where the emphasis is placed on uncovering unconscious
conflicts is receiving increasing recognition as being an
important factor, and perhaps decisive, for a good treatment outcome. It follows that good human supports from
family and friends should facilitate psychic repair and
maturation during treatment.

Opportunity: Opportunity for a successful life -
personal and vocational - should have a treatment-facilitating effect. Abundant opportunities should correlate
positively with favorable treatment results. At the same
time, the opportunities in a person's life may serve as
secondary indication of the person's level of health. Sick
people tend to place themselves in life circumstances which
are devoid of opportunities, and healthy persons surround
themselves with opportunities.

Of the three patients who had few opportunities in
their lives, none made basic change but all three made sym-
tomatic improvement. The environments of four patients
diminished in opportunity to a considerable extent during
the research period. None made basic change and only one
achieved moderate symptomatic improvement. It should be
noted that of the seven patients whose lives became devoid
of opportunity, six had, by and large, brought this state
of affairs on themselves. It would seem that few

opportunities in the immediate circumstances, like the presence or absence of need-congruent factors in a person's life, is some index of the severity of the sickness. Sick people tend to deprive themselves of a rewarding life or one that is potentially so.

Opportunities for three patients increased, and all three achieved symptomatic improvement but none made significant essential changes. Twenty-two of the group of 32 who had good opportunities in their life circumstances through the research period achieved good symptomatic results, and all seven who were rated as having made basic changes were found in this group. A closer inspection of the life circumstances of this group of 32 patients shows that most had opportunities available to them, but not of their own making. It is also clear that those who changed symptomatically and basically, or just symptomatically, behaved in ways which furthered their opportunities; that is, they did not throw away their opportunities. Eight of the ten patients who failed to improve also failed to make use of their opportunities even though they existed in their lives. The distribution of cases would not permit statistical analyses.

Mutability: An insufficient number of patients were living in immutable life circumstances to permit exploration of this variable with respect to symptomatic or basic change. Many who changed very little were by no means trapped by immutable life circumstances. It is true there often were environmental factors in the lives of the 42 patients which tended to retard changes within the patient.

The Usual Life Circumstances: A clinical comparison which captures some of the preceding findings is based on the well-known rule of thumb, to which most psychiatrists ascribe, that patients in therapy or analysis should be treated when living in their usual life circumstances. Just what "usual life circumstances" means may be difficult to define; however, the phrase generally refers to the commitments and responsibilities of the patient, particularly prior to and including the time he became ill. The rationale for this "rule of thumb" is that being in one's usual life circumstances provides a context for treatment and increases the patient's opportunities for better working through those conflicts which treatment exposes. This rule does not overlook the other clinical fact that if regression is severe, good treatment planning should include the removal of the patient from the circumstances which have overwhelmed him, irrespective of whether the environment was

stressful or conflict-triggering as herein defined. In
light of the present study, it appears that one's usual
life circumstances should facilitate treatment by activating
those unconscious conflicts which are the ultimate bases
for the illness, thus rendering them more accessible to the
treatment process.

It should be informative, therefore, to compare the
treatment results of those patients who left their commitments behind them when they came to Topeka for treatment
with those who brought their commitments with them or soon
took upon themselves the kinds of life commitments that
existed prior to the onset of treatment.

The 42 cases were separated into two groups, those who
were surrounded by their usual life commitments, and those
who were not. A statistical analysis was done comparing
the degree of patient change in these two groups. At termination the difference between the commitments group and
those without commitments was borderline significant
($p < .10$) on the HSRS change score, and not significant on
the Absolute Global Change score. However, at follow-up,
when the supportive effects of the therapist had been gone
for two years, the difference between the two groups was
significant for both the HSRS change score ($p < .005$) and
the Absolute Global Change score ($p < .025$) in the expected
direction.

The significantly greater improvement in those patients
who were surrounded by their commitments during the entire
research period can be attributed to several influences.
The supportive effects of the environment cannot be overlooked. Similarly, need-congruent factors which are powerful allies to the therapeutic process are present. Finally,
the conflict-triggering effect of the environment activates
unconscious conflicts, thus making them more available for
analysis and working through. All of these factors are
missing to a large degree when the patient is living more
or less in an environmental vacuum, particularly as regards
heterosexual commitments and parental responsibilities.

9. EVALUATION AND CONCLUSIONS

Without question the main, and most significant, finding of our study has to do with the absolute necessity,
when making personality assessments, for taking into account
the environmental circumstances of the patient, and the
nature and depth of the patient's involvement with and
commitment to his environment. This statement applies to
evaluations prior to treatment, assessments which are made
during treatment, and especially to evaluations in the
post-treatment period when the effects of treatment are to
be judged. We found a more or less direct correspondence
between the degree of manifest illness and the intensity
or depth of the patient's involvement with the environment,
provided there existed an unconscious basis for illness.

The retrospective data, compiled from an analysis of
the patient's involvement with his environment at the time
preceding the outbreak of his illness and during its outbreak, revealed a direct relationship to the depth of, or
ongoing deepening of, commitments to the environment, and
the outbreak or worsening of manifest psychopathology.
Conversely, the shedding of responsibilities and commitments
(which had triggered unconscious conflicts) as a consequence
of becoming ill, or by coming to Topeka, or as a consequence
of the effects of treatment, was regularly accompanied by
symptomatic improvement. The process of decreasing the
level or intensity of environmental commitments appears to
us to be the primary basis for the symptomatic improvements
of many of the patients. This is not to say that other
factors did not contribute to the symptomatic improvements.
Remaining relatively uninvolved (particularly with the
opposite sex) appears to have been, for many patients, a
means for avoiding psychic regression.

Resolution of core conflicts and the achievement of
essential intrapsychic change occurred in but a few patients.
Such changes were obviously (to us) very difficult to
achieve. Some patients modified their unconscious conflicts
but most were untouched and the patients unchanged in any
essential way by treatment. Symptomatic changes were

86

achieved by many but often, it seems, through changes in
the environment, the supportive effects of treatment and,
as indicated, by some core conflict resolution or modifi-
cation in a few.

When core conflicts were resolved or significantly
modified, patients were always able to become more involved
and more deeply committed to life in ways which appeared to
be devoid of symptomatic meanings. As expected, these
environmental involvements were classed as need-congruent.

It is not surprising to have found that the environment can be changed more easily to fit the personality of
the patient, including his pathology, or in a way which
will lead to the disappearance of symptoms (without basic
change having been achieved), than individuals can be
changed to meet the average expectations of a mature adjustment. As just indicated, we believe much of the clinical (symptomatic) improvement of many of the cases can be
attributed to a shift in environmental involvements (to
a lightened loan) and to the supportive effects of the therapeutic relationships which aided and abetted those shifts.
We refer to divorces, loss of children, relegating care of
children to hired help, avoidance of heterosexual commitment, geographical distance from parents, and changes in
work pattern.

Without assessing the nature of the patient's environment and his involvements with it at the time of personality
assessment, particularly when these assessments are to be
the bases for judging the effects of treatment, an accurate
picture of the patient's condition cannot be achieved.
Patients who have shed the bulk of their responsibilities
by the end of treatment may not show any signs of illness,
only to become ill again when resuming their responsibilities.
Conversely, no weightier evidence exists for basic personality change than the capacity to shoulder responsibilities,
especially those of an intimate heterosexual relationship
wherein no gender role reversal exists, as well as the
consequences (children, etc.) of such a relationship. When
such changes occur following treatment, treatment in all
probability can be said to have been conflict-resolving
and, therefore, to have brought about essential intrapsychic
change.

These comments relate directly to definitions of health.
When health is to be assessed one must ask the corollary
question, under what environmental conditions? Furthermore, the findings support the distinction between manifest

health and essential health. Treatment can be conducted
which reintegrates the ego, rearranges the environment,
often by removing conflict-triggering factors, so that
manifest health has improved while no basic changes have
been achieved at all. It can all too easily be assumed
that treatment resolved the illness when, in fact, the
patient shed those environmental commitments which had activated his unconscious conflicts. The final and most reliable test of essential change is the ability to live out
one's capacities and gender in relation to the environment
generally, and specifically in relation to a healthy
member of the opposite sex. A few of the patients passed,
or nearly passed, this test. Nearly all had worked extensively with their core conflicts in a variety of contexts
and appeared to have achieved considerable essential change.

It may well have been that some of the therapists were
aware of or sensed their patient's inability to achieve
basic changes, or at least they believed this to be so, and
may have knowingly entered into the process of assisting
the patient shed or avoid responsibilities and deeper
commitments and in this manner achieve a higher level of
manifest health. To do so may have been lifesaving.
Several of the deaths might have been avoided had the doctor
and patient been able to know and accept the fact that the
patient's solution for a relatively asymptomatic existence
depended on giving up marital, parental, and other higher
level responsibilities.

On the other hand, it appears that basic personality
change was achieved in too few patients in view of the therapeutic efforts expended in their behalf; that many of the
patients were not so ill as to preclude such changes. While
treatment cannot make purses from sows' ears, still, a
number of the patients were young enough or possessed sufficient personality and environmental resources to have changed
essentially more than they did. These results must be laid
squarely at the feet of the therapists and their supervisors and their conceptual understanding of the treatment
process.

We suspect that many clinicians tend to be unaware of
how powerful an ally the environment can be when one under-
takes to bring about essential change in his patient and,
conversely, how useful the shedding of environmental commitments can be when relief of symptoms without essential
changes is being sought. These impressions are supported
by the relative inattention the patient-environment dimension is given in psychotherapy research.

The principal author shared the same psychoanalytically-oriented view of the therapeutic process as most of the therapists in this study. These professionals, including the author, were trained in a tradition which focused heavily on the intrapsychic aspect of the patient's existence and the patient-therapist interactions. The primary foci during treatment are defensive processes, transference, resistance, dream analysis, interpretation, and reflection. This tradition relies heavily on understanding, and a tendency to believe that the patient's decisions and actions are the patient's responsibility and, in the mind's of some professionals, his free choice - even in the face of obvious unconscious motivations. This view, especially in treatment which aims at the achievement of insight, but even in supportive therapies, tends to permit symptomatic environmental involvements and/or flights from existing mature responsibilities and avoidance of new mature responsibilities, and from treatment itself. While this tradition includes the working through concept in the transference and external reality, there seems to be lacking a full and clear appreciation of how vital is the experiential aspect of a patient's life with regard to his interaction with his environment. The achievement of insight into personality and behavior is a necessary first step. Tracing these insights to their genetic roots is a second step. However, unless attitudes, feelings, symptoms and behavior change, unless the patient can assume reasonable environmental responsibilities, the insight, understanding, empathy, support, interpretation, etc., cannot be said to have resulted in essential change.

In addition to a treatment tradition which emphasizes the patient-therapist dimension, a second factor which appears to have clearly limited the extent to which many patients changed was that many of the patients in the project were necessarily removed from their usual environments simply by coming to Topeka for treatment. This fact placed a severe handicap on the therapists and precluded the achievement of more essential change; conflict triggers were reduced in number, and a meaningful environmental context was often missing for the very necessary working through process.

The data strongly support the well-known rule that for maximal essential change to occur in treatment the patient should be living in an environment which activates his unconscious conflicts, thus adding to the conflict-triggering effect of the therapeutic relationship, that is, the transference. Such conditions also provide a greater chance for working through and ultimately resolving unconscious conflicts. In order for these desirable effects to occur, the therapist must not permit the patient to take flight from those very experiences which increase personal discomfort by triggering unconscious conflicts. It is the resolution of these conflicts which will ultimately lead to greater health. These conflict-triggering factors are, as we pointed out earlier, usually need-congruent.

We believe many patients were not held to their adult responsibilities during treatment and were permitted to act out as well as take flight from mature adjustments and from treatment itself. For instance, two young women became consolidated in homosexual relationships instead of achieving a heterosexual outcome. These were outright treatment failures. There were unnecessary marriages which were based on acted out conflicts, events which cut treatment short and ultimately insured its failure. There was a divorce which need not, and should not, have occurred, thus depriving the patient of a treatment-facilitating environment as well as disrupting the lives of several persons. Some divorces, however, appear rather clearly to have reflected greater personal health in the patient at the conclusion of treatment; the divorce from a very sick spouse seemed like the only possible solution for a difficult and unhappy reality situation.

Too many of the patients left treatment prematurely. It seems reasonable to have expected more of the single patients to have been able to marry as a result of treatment, and that marriages would have been less conflict-triggering for those who did marry. Though all were seriously ill, the lives of the six who died might have gone differently had the impact of the environment on their lives been better understood and more effectively used.

It seems that manifest pathology bears a direct relationship to the degree to which the individual is attempting to or is involving himself with the environment, and to the extent to which unconscious conflicts have been mobilized thereby. The essential nature of the personality before or after treatment can only be assessed when the extent and quality of the environmental commitment is simultaneously assessed.

Therapy which aims at changing the environment to suit the patient appears to be much easier to conduct than treatment which aims at producing essential intrapsychic change so as to make the patient better able to live up to responsibilities commensurate with his abilities and interests. In order for essential change to occur, it seems the patient

must be treated in an environmental context which permits
meaningful, nonsymptomatic involvements and commitments.
These environmental factors will be simultaneously conflict-
triggering, need-congruent, and often supportive. Therapies
which fail to capitalize on the patient-environment dimension
are destined to produce limited results or to fail altogether.

An overview of the history of the psychoanalytic view
of the treatment process suggests that our conclusions about
the importance of the environment in treatment falls logically into a progression. In the early days, treatment
focused on unconscious content and - in the minds of some -
the deeper, the better. Then the id-ego dimension came
into focus; then ego processes themselves (character and
behavior). Yet to be developed is a full understanding of
the place of the environment in psychoanalytic theory generally and in the psychoanalytic theory of treatment.

While the behavior therapists have thrown out the baby
with the bath by denying the importance of unconscious forces
in symptomatic behavior and for treatment, their focus on
the person-environment dimension will, in all likelihood,
someday be viewed not as antithetical to psychoanalysis but
complementary to it. For instance, their gradual involvement of a patient with feared situations can be understood
as introducing the patient into a conflict-triggering situation. The behavior therapist fails to recognize the
presence of unconscious forces which emerge as a result of
his technique and misses the opportunity for rich interpretive work. The orthodox analyst avoids urging his patient to master the feared reality situation; instead, he
focuses excessively on the intrapsychic role of the patient's existence. Both behaviorist and psychoanalyst
should remember that Freud said that the phobic patient
must eventually face the feared situation. This bit of
advice contains a general principle which can guide the
treating person in his efforts for removal of the irrational
from the rational in his patient.

The results of our study have not only convinced us
of the vital importance of the patient-environment dimension
for successful treatment and for assessing the patient, but
also reemphasizes the importance of including the environment in psychoanalytic theory construction.

REFERENCES

Brown, G. W., & Birley, J. L. T. Crises and life changes
and the onset of schizophrenia. Journal of Health and
Social Behavior, 1968, 9, 203-214.

Burnham, D. C. Circumstances of onset of schizophrenia:
Relevance to faulty differentiation and integration.
In Schizophrenia and the need-fear dilemma. New York:
International Universities Press, 1969. Pp. 67-94.

Burstein, E. D., Coyne, L., Kernberg, O. F., & Voth, H. M.
The quantitative study of the psychotherapy research
project: Psychotherapy outcome. Bulletin of the Menninger
Clinic, 1972, 36, 3-85.

Eaton, J. W., & Weil, R. J. Culture and mental disorders,
an epidemiological approach. Glencoe, Ill.: Free Press,
1955.

Faris, R. E. L., & Dunham, H. W. Mental disorders in urban
areas: An ecological study of schizophrenia and other
psychoses. Chicago: University of Chicago Press, 1939.

Forrest, A. D., Fraser, R. H., & Priest, R. G. Environmental
factors in depressive illness. British Journal of Psychiatry, 1965, 111, 243-253.

Freud, S. (1917). Mourning and melancholia. In E. Jones
(Ed.), Collected papers. New York: Basic Books, 1959,
4, 152-170.

Hall, B. H., & Wallterstein, R. S. The psychotherapy
research project of the Menninger Foundation: Third report:
II: Termination studies. Bulletin of the Menninger Clinic,
1960, 24, 190-216.

Hilgard, J. R., & Newman, M. F. Evidence for functional genesis in mental illness: Schizophrenia, depressive psychoses and psychoneuroses. Journal of Nervous and Mental
Disease, 1961, 132, 3-16.

Hocking, F. H. Extreme environmental stress and its significance for psychopathology. American Journal of Psychotherapy, 1970, 24, 4-26.

Hollingshead, A. B., & Redlich, F. C. Social class and
mental illness. New York: John Wiley, 1957.

Langner, T. S., & Michael, S. T. Life stress and mental
health. New York: The Free Press of Glencoe, 1963.

Leff, M. J., Roatch, J. F., & Bunney, W. E., Jr. Environmental factors preceding the onset of severe depressions.
Psychiatry, 1970, 33, 293-311.

Leighton, D. C., Harding, J. S., Macklin, D. B., Hughes,
C. C., & Leighton, A. H. Psychiatric findings of the
Stirling County study. American Journal of Psychiatry,
1963, 119, 1021-1026.

Lewis, A. J. Melancholia: A clinical survey of depressive
states. Journal of Mental Science, 1934, 80, 277-378.

Lindemann, E. Symptomatology and management of acute grief.
American Journal of Psychiatry, 1944, 101, 141-148.

Luborsky, L. Clinicians' judgments of mental health: A
proposed scale. Archives of General Psychiatry, 1962,
7, 407-417.

Luborsky, L., Fabian, M., Hall, B. H., Ticho, E., & Ticho,
G. R. The psychotherapy research project of the Menninger
Foundation: Second report: II: Treatment variables.
Bulletin of the Menninger Clinic, 1958, 22, 126-147.

Luborsky, L., & Sargent, H. D. The psychotherapy research
project of the Menninger Foundation: First report: V:
Sample use of the method. Bulletin of the Menninger
Clinic, 1956, 20, 263-276.

Menninger, K. A. A manual for psychiatric case study. (Rev.
ed.) New York: Grune & Stratoon, 1962.

Money, J. Progress of knowledge and revision of the theory
of infantile sexuality. International Journal of Psychiatry, 1967, 4, 50-53.

Money, J., Hampson, J. G., & Hampson, J. L.   An examination
of some basic sexual concepts: The evidence of human
hermaphroiditism.   Bulletin of the Johns Hopkins Hospital,
1955, 97, 301-319.

Paykel, E. S., Myers, J. K., Dienelt, M. N., Klerman, G. L.,
Lindenthal, J. J., & Pepper, M. P.   Life events and depression.   American Journal of Psychiatry, 1969, 21, 753-760.

Rado, S.   Collected papers of Sandor Rado on psychoanalysis
of behavior.   New York: Grune & Stratton, 1956.

Robbins, L. L., & Wallerstein, R. S.   The psychotherapy research project of the Menninger Foundation: Rationale,
method and sample use: First report: I: Orientation.
Bulletin of the Menninger Clinic, 1956, 20, 223-225.

Robbins, L. L., & Wallerstein, R. S.   The research strategy
and tactics of the psychotherapy research project of the
Menninger Foundation' and the problem of controls.   In
E. A. Rubinstein, & M. B. Parloff (Eds.), Research in
Psychotherapy.   Washington, D.C.:   American Psychological
Association, 1959, 1, 27-43.

Sargent, H. D.   The psychotherapy research project of the
Menninger Foundation: First report: II: Rationale.
Bulletin of the Menninger Clinic, 1956a, 20, 226-233.

Sargent, H. D.   The psychotherapy research project of the
Menninger Foundation: First report: III: Design.
Bulletin of the Menninger Clinic, 1956b, 20, 234-238.

Sargent, H. D.   Methodological problems of follow-up studies
in psychotherapy research.   American Journal of Ortho-
psychiatry, 1960, 30, 495-596.

Sargent, H. D.   Intrapsychic change: Methodological problems in psychotherapy research.   Psychiatry, 1961, 24,
93-108.

Sargent, H. D., Horwitz, L., Wallerstein, R. S., & Appelbaum,
A.   Prediction in psychotherapy research: A method for
the transformation of clinical judgments into testable
hypotheses.   Psychological Issues, 1968, 6 (1, Mongr. No.
21).   New York: International Universities Press.

Sargent, H. D., Modlin, H. C., Faris, M. T., & Voth, H. M.
The psychotherapy research project of the Menninger
Foundation: Second report: III: Situational variables.
Bulletin of the Menninger Clinic, 1958, 22, 148-166.

Siegal, R. S. A psychological test study of personality
change. International Mental Health Research Newsletter,
1967, 9, 6-7.

Siegal, R. S., & Ehrenreich, G. A. Inferring repression
from psychological tests. Bulletin of the Menninger
Clinic, 1962, 26, 82-91.

Siegal, R. S., & Rosen, I. C. Character style and anxiety
tolerance: A study in intrapsychic change. In H. H.
Strupp, & L. Luborsky (Eds.), Research in Psychotherapy.
Washington, D. C.: American Psychological Association,
1962. Pp. 206-217.

Stoller, R. J. A contribution to the study of gender
identity. International Journal of Psycho-Analysis,
1964, 45, 220-226.

Strupp, H. H., & Luborsky, L. (Eds.). Research in psychotherapy. Washington, D. C.: American Psychological
Association, 1962.

Voth, H. M. Some effects of Freud's personality on psychoanalytic theory and technique. International Journal of
Psychiatry, in press.

Voth, H. M., Modlin, H. C., & Orth, M. H. Situational
variables in the assessment of psychotherapeutic results.
Bulletin of the Menninger Clinic, 1962, 26, 73-81.

Wallerstein, R. S., & Robbins, L. L. The psychotherapy
research project of the Menninger Foundation: First
report: IV: Concepts. Bulletin of the Menninger Clinic,
1956, 20, 239-262.

Wallerstein, R. S., & Robbins, L. L. The psychotherapy
research project of the Menninger Foundation: Second
report: I: Further notes on design and concepts.
Bulletin of the Menninger Clinic, 1958, 22, 117-125.

Wallerstein, R. S., & Robbins, L. L. The psychotherapy
research project of the Menninger Foundation: Operational
problems of psychotherapy research: Third report: I:
Initial studies. Bulletin of the Menninger Clinic, 1960,
24, 164-189.

Watterson, D. J.   Problems in the evaluation of psychotherapy. Bulletin of the Menninger Clinic, 1954, 18, 232-241.

APPENDIX

CASE HISTORIES

SYNTHESIS OF SITUATIONAL VARIABLES - CASE #1

1. Brief History

At the time of her initial evaluation this patient was in her mid-thirties, divorced, and the mother of two children. Her symptoms were anxiety, depression, and indecisiveness. She was the second eldest of four sibs. To the patient her father was a lovable, domineering man about whom there was no doubt regarding his headship in the family. She considered her mother kind, unselfish, and devoted, but her father more exciting, different, and less predictable. Allegedly, her sisters were all happily married. She recalled that she was a tomboy in her early years and that when it came time for her to make a shift and become a young woman she didn't want to make that change. The patient longed to play baseball, and was shy with boys. Shortly after puberty she decided to become a physician but she failed some of the prerequisite courses and eventually gave up a medical career. After a brief time in a sanitorium because of tuberculosis, she felt that she had to do something with her life and she began business school.

She met a man who was attractive to her because to her he seemed strong and everything was easy for him. After marrying him the patient became pregnant almost immediately. It was in connection with this pregnancy that she first noticed some anxiety, which she attributed to some advice she had gotten earlier about not having children because of her tuberculosis. Her anxiety was contributed to by her observation that her husband did not turn out to be the tower of strength she had perceived him to be and this seemingly required her to fall back on her own self-reliance and eventually on her family for emotional support. She found reasons to be separated from her husband. His irresponsibility was particularly irksome to her. However, the couple seemed to make a better marital adjustment and the patient became pregnant again. She noted that during this pregnancy her relationship with her husband became more strained and she felt deserted and alone. Following delivery

of the second child the patient developed an intense emotional reaction characterized by extreme mood swings and,
particularly, episodes of excitement. The patient believed
that she had never been the same after her second pregnancy.
Shortly after the second child was born her husband left her,
and she later divorced him and returned to her parental home
with her two small children. During the ensuing two years
she felt depressed most of the time and overwhelmed by excessive fatigue. In an effort to help her, the parents
bought her a small farm near their home. For a time she
became interested in running this farm and even entered into
some social life in a nearby small town. She said, however,
"something inside me stopped me," and she believed that
"something" was the fact that she was an outsider and a
divorced woman.

   During this period she met a married man who was estranged from his wife, and for about a year they enjoyed an
affair. The patient described this as the happiest time in
her life. She enthusiastically enjoyed the dining and dancing
but was less enthusiastic about the sexual aspects of the
relationship. Throughout she noted her indifference towards
sexual intercourse, both with her husband and during this
affair. When the man's wife intervened, the patient broke
off the relationship and had little to do with men thereafter.
Her continuing depression, anxiety, and "failure as a mother"
eventually brought her to psychiatric treatment.

2.   Summary of Situational Variables at the Time of the
     Initial Study

   The core conflict in this patient seemed to be phallic-
oedipal. She did not resolve her oedipal problems in the
usual direction. Rather, she was drawn into a masculine
identification with her father. As a consequence, she
evidently did not overcome her guilt regarding being feminine,
nor did she develop the values and skills of a woman which
would have made it possible for her to accept the responsibilities of marriage and motherhood. Evidence for this
formulation dates back to her tomboyishness and her reluctance
to become a young woman during the early adolescent period.
It is evident that the demands of marriage, which required
her to live intimately with a man and which demanded of her
the mothering role towards her children, were the conflict
triggers. Slowly but progressively this kind of involvement in life activated the neurosis in her and precipitated
a decompensation which remained more or less irreversible.

   It is noteworthy that she was extremely happy after the

divorce and was able to have some degree of intimacy with a
man who was quite unattainable. Not having a husband, she
was thrown into more intimate contact with her children and
with her own parents. The parents and children thus remained
conflict triggers in her life. By the time this woman came
for treatment she had even managed to "get rid of her children" so that by the time treatment actually began there
were very few conflict triggers in her life.

Her family was quite supporting throughout. They
offered her a home if she needed it, they bought her a farm,
and they helped take care of her children during this period
of turmoil in her life. There were no threats of financial
insecurity. The patient was a square peg in a round hole
insofar as finding a need-congruent environment was concerned.
Her obvious wishes for the achievement of a heterosexual
life were blocked by her own neurosis, and it was this very
neurosis which forced her to separate herself from those
aspects of the environment which would be congruent with the
feminine aspects of her personality. She did have the children, but her neurosis prevented her from taking care of
them. She no longer had a husband. Not having found outlets for her masculine tendencies she was, to a rather advanced degree, not blending with her environment. Her
opportunities for the future were rather good, however, at
this phase in her life by virtue of her age and attractiveness. In some respects her two children were a liability,
but she was young enough to marry again, provided her neurosis
could be cleared up. Nothing in her environment was immutable
although it would have been difficult for her to be rid of
her children permanently.

In summary, her illness was provoked by the conflict
triggers of marriage and motherhood. By the time she came
to treatment she had managed in one way or another to shed
most of these triggers. Her Health-Sickness Rating at the
time of beginning treatment was 65.

3. Summary of Situational Variables at the Time of Termination Study

This patient's psychoanalysis, consisting of 227 hours,
was not considered to be wholly successful. The duration of
this treatment was approximately one year. During this time
the patient obtained work, and eventually obtained a house
in anticipation of bringing her children to live with her.
Her psychoanalysis was stormy from the very beginning. She,
on the one hand, felt drawn positively to her analyst, but
yet could not cooperate, felt brainwashed, and eventually

left treatment.

It is of special interest to note that at the time the patient got her house she felt very inadequate and guilt-ridden, but at the same time was more and more troubled by an increasing positive transference. By the time she brought her children to Topeka (about a month and a half before she finally terminated treatment) she was experiencing an increased commitment to treatment and an intensification of the transference, and it seemed clear to the analyst that she was, in fantasy, relating to him as a husband.

Soon after the arrival of her children and the increasing intensification of her treatment, she began to withdraw from the treatment in one way or another. She began having somatic symptoms. She started missing hours, and then rather precipitously announced that she would be unable to go on with her treatment. In his discharge note the analyst, in essence, stated that the patient could not make the shift into full femininity and in this context face her affect life, and hence she fled from treatment as a defensive escape.

During those last few hours she drew heavily on her old contentiousness and argumentativeness and stubborn defiance. Assessment of the core conflict at the time of the interruption of her treatment indicated that little change had occurred. It is noteworthy, however, that her symptoms had subsided considerably during the treatment period, although they reappeared right at the time of termination. Her Health-Sickness Rating at termination was 75.

A marked shift had occurred in the conflict triggers, however, from the time of the beginning of her illness to the period of her treatment. She had, in fact, shed most of her conflict triggers. She was divorced, she was away from her children most of the time of her treatment, and she had begun working. It seems as though her self-concept had consolidated somewhat as a competent male, despite the efforts to find femininity within her treatment. As this effort increased and as she brought her children to live with her she had to get away from the man, in this instance the therapist. This repeats, in essence, what happened in her marriage. As her family enlarged she had to break up the family constellation by leaving her husband. She had, in addition, been able to extricate herself from her family somewhat, thus removing conflict triggers even more. She experienced remaining in Topeka as a defiance of her father. She had relegated the care of her children, in large part, to a housekeeper, thus avoiding the full impact of the maternal role. Under these conditions she could function. It seems reasonable to speculate that unconsciously she may have experienced herself as the man and the housekeeper as the wife.

There was some stress in her life in that she described the two boys as being quite a handful, particularly when they were together. Supports continued to be adequate. The family unquestionably was still silently behind her, she had a number of friends and co-workers, and a good job. It would seem that she had carved out an environment that was need-congruent in two aspects; there was enough of a heterosexual flavor in her life to satisfy the meagerly developed woman in her (this refers to homemaking and taking care of her two sons), and at the same time she satisfied the masculine aspects of her personality through working.

4. Summary of Situational Variables at Follow-up Study

This patient's life situation was essentially unchanged. She was relatively devoid of conflict triggers, those remaining were her children and her parents. She was still baffled by the maternal role, and the role of wife had been completely rejected and avoided. She continued to turn over most of the mothering functions of the children to her housekeeper and roomer and her own parents. There was no reason to assume that resolution of core conflict had occurred in light of this adjustment. Stresses were at a minimum, although there was some stress in this way of life. Supports were somewhat more abundant at follow-up than previously. The parental family continued to be definitely supportive; they visited three or four times a year, and she knew that she could turn to her parents during a crisis if she had to. Her friends and co-workers were abundant and supportive. She enjoyed her work. She had a comfortable home, a housekeeper who took care of the house and the boys, and a roomer who helped with the finances and provided some companionship. She still owned her farm and derived some income from it. Her main support was her work. Opportunity for growth seemed relatively fixed at this point although she could have expanded some in her job and, if her neurosis permitted, she could have married again. Need-congruence continued to be about the same. The work outlets provided congruence between her environment and the, by now, fixed masculine aspects of her character. Her minimal role with her own children provided some gratification for the meagerly developed woman in her.

5. Summary

Because of this patient's unresolved oedipal conflicts
and consequent characterologic developments, she was unable
to meet the demands of heterosexuality, specifically marriage
and motherhood. Involvement in and commitment to this kind
of life activated her core neurosis to such a degree that a
progressively developing decompensation took place as her
involvement in her marriage deepened. She shed these involvements and in so doing made it possible for her core neurosis
to be deactivated. Although she remained responsible for
her two sons, she was not, in fact, very deeply committed to
them or involved with them. In short, she ended up about
where she began - half woman, half man. Insofar as the
resolution of the basis for her illness was concerned, her
treatment is to be considered a failure. Insofar as helping
her recognize the disparate aspects of her personality and
carve out a way of life which blends with these divergent
qualities in her, her treatment may be considered to have
been helpful. Having shed her conflict triggers prior to
coming to treatment, a marked limitation was placed on the
extent to which treatment could change her in an essential
way. Had she been with her family and had her therapist
been sufficiently aware of the basis of her illness and himself a mature person, that is, one unconflicted about gender
identity, she might have been able to resolve her illness
and thereby preserve her family life.

SYNTHESIS OF SITUATIONAL VARIABLES - CASE #2

1. Brief History

    When this patient came for treatment he was a 42-year
old married, unemployed, salesman. His father, close to
death, was the successful owner of a fairly large business.
The mother was a very domineering, aggressive woman who had
run a business of her own for five years. She allegedly
was an alcoholic for a time but did not drink in later years.

    Evidence of illness dates back into the patient's college
years. He started drinking then, disqualified himself from
track (something his father admired very much) by pulling a
leg muscle. For reasons unknown he became unable to study
in school, almost failed, drank heavily, got into debt, and
eventually left the university. Subsequently, however, he
transferred to another university and graduated with a degree
in business administration. He then went to work in a branch
office of his father's business in another city. Apparently
he was quite successful. Later, because of the economic
depression, he worked as a laborer. He married and had two
children. This was a stormy marriage; he drank episodically;
the wife spent money excessively; they could not get along,
divorced and remarried once. Apparently the best period of
the marriage was during the years he worked as a laborer.

    The patient served as an officer during World War II;
during this time his drinking increased; he was often drunk
on duty and derelict in his responsibilities. Following
his military service he returned home to work for his father.
There were frequent quarrels and disagreements between the
patient and his wife, and it is evident that the wife was
the dominant one in this relationship. His drinking episodes
increased in intensity. His inability to work successfully
for his father became more manifest, and he was finally
brought to the Menninger Foundation after several brief
hospitalizations elsewhere.

2. Summary of Situational Variables at the Time of Initial
    Study

        At the time of the initial study the father was still
alive and in charge of his own business. The patient and
his family had moved to Topeka and the patient began treatment. The core neurotic problem was an oral one, anality
was indicated; however, it would seem that the phallic-
oedipal core neurosis was probably the predominant one. It
was evident that heterosexuality in both its narrow and broad
sense was difficult for the patient.

        He functioned best as a father when he was not working
in the same area of business as his own father, but rather
well as a laborer. And it is clear that trying to work with
his father or for his father materially contributed to his
illness. Both parents were marked conflict triggers. The
demands of being a father, husband, and breadwinner were
similarly conflict-triggering. Scanning back over his life
one can see that as he increased his responsibilities his
illness slowly but progressively increased in intensity. He
first became ill when he had an intense heterosexual relationship and got a girl pregnant. His first success in
college triggered an illness. However, he seemed to rally
from this and although he reattained a certain degree of
success for a time as he came more and more into father's
sphere and saw the possibility of taking over his father's
business he got progressively worse. It was noted, for instance, that the patient's periods of tension and excessive
drinking were always worse when he expected an inspection
of his father's business by company officials. Rather than
save his money and amass a fortune as his father had, he
squandered his money and, furthermore, was unable to stand
up to his wife and thus permitted her to squander it for
him, too.

        The patient's wife was a stressful factor. She was a
very neurotic woman, aggressive, and unable to permit intimacy with her husband in the broad sense of the word. She
spent money excessively. She avoided social contacts which
would have furthered their involvement in society.

        The patient's mother may be considered stressful to a
degree. She was dominating, jealous, friendless, and vin-
dictive. She continued to interfere in subtle ways with the
patient's life. For example, at the time of initial study
she did not accept the patient's wife at all.

        Despite these many conflict triggers and stressful factors,

there were adequate supports in his life. The father always
seemed to have a job for him and was willing to help the man
learn the family business; he paid him well. The father
helped him find psychiatric treatment and financed it. He
did not try to force the patient to follow in his footsteps,
although he indicated that he would be happy for him to do
so. There was some support in the marriage, including the
children. They made him feel worthwhile; they loved their
father and he loved them. Although the wife had been a cold
"bitchy" person who tried to destroy this man in her own
subtle ways, there was a narrow healthy streak in her which
made it possible for her to support the patient's attempt
to get psychiatric help.

Need-congruence was present. He had job opportunities,
and if the job situation did not have neurotic significance
for him he certainly would have made better use of this congruent environment which offered him many opportunities for
success. Being a father was need-congruent. The wife was
need-incongruent in that she resonated with the neurotic
elements in him, that is to say, with his passivity and
dependence. Opportunities for growth at work were abundant.
Opportunities for growth in the marriage were somewhat
limited by the wife's character.

3. Summary of Situational Variables at the Time of Termin-
    ation Study

There were two terminations. The first can quite properly be viewed as an acting out. The patient attempted to
convince the therapist that he was ready to leave treatment
by pointing out how well he was getting along in his marriage,
with his children, and by not drinking. He had just helped
his sister buy a business and managed this extremely well.
He was full of self-confidence and believed he could now get
on by himself. A fantasy of his in connection with the first
termination was that he would open his own business.

One week following this termination the patient's
father died. After the funeral the patient and his wife took
a trip to a neighboring country to consider living there.
While they were away their daughter attempted suicide. The
patient returned to Topeka and resumed psychotherapy. He
had gotten depressed again and recognized his need for
further treatment.

Following his father's death, the patient became manicky,
extravagant went on a car buying spree, purchasing two ex-
pensive cars. He became more aggressive with other women,

and had one extra-marital affair. However, the daughter's
suicide attempt provoked a marked depression in him and he
then contacted his former therapist and resumed treatment.

Soon after resuming treatment the patient realized he
had run away from treatment earlier but, interestingly enough,
managed to do this again. Shortly before terminating the
patient told his therapist that he was quitting treatment,
that he felt he would have to go the rest of the way by himself. The therapist did not encourage or discourage this,
and let him leave treatment again. Following this the patient
moved to a city on the coast.

At the time of termination a major conflict trigger had
been removed; this was the person of the father. It is
interesting to observe that this event seemed to have a lib-
erating effect on the patient for he became quite manicky
and expansive. However, the guilt engendered by the death
wish towards the father provoked self-defeat. The mother
remained a conflict trigger. The challenge to make a living,
be a breadwinner, father and husband remained. It is safe
to say that the core neurotic problem in this man had been
completely untouched by his psychotherapy.

The only difference between the conflict triggers at
the time of initial study and at termination was that the
patient's father was dead and that he was no longer trying
to work for the father. However, the challenge to take the
father's place may be considered to be even greater at the
time of termination. It was quite evident that he still had
difficulty in adapting to the role of father or husband or
head of the house.

The stresses were, by and large, the same. The patient's
mother continued to be silently manipulative and interfering. The patient's wife was unchanged and, of course, the
new stress of the daughter's attempted suicide was very
significant.

Supports were abundant. The inheritance from the father
was substantial; the mother, despite her aggressive, manipulative capacities, did stand behind the patient and, similarly, the wife stood by. The marriage continued to offer
some need-congruence. However, the wife was essentially
unchanged so that the marriage, in fact, was not particularly
need-congruent. The wife continued to interact with the
neurotic or sick elements within the patient. The opportunity
to be a father was there because of the two children. No
job openings were immediately available; however work

possibilities were more or less in abundance. All of these
possibilities provided opportunities and were need-congruent.
The man had demonstrated his salesman and organizational
capacities previously. The environment offered many opportunities. The marriage offered fewer opportunities because
of the wife's personality; however, it is not known whether
this wife might have changed had the patient been able to
change.

4.   Summary of Situational Variables at the Time of Follow-up
     Study

     After leaving Topeka upon termination of his psycho-
therapy, the patient went to another state and purchased a
business. The wife stated that he had already been drinking
and that he was able to go to his office for only one week
after making this purchase. The business lost money and
finally had to be sold. Because of increased alcohol intake
he again returned to the Menninger Hospital, where he remained one year. He left against medical advice and returned
to the coast. It is clear that the wife was in favor of his
leaving Topeka for she said that he could be sick elsewhere
as well as he could be sick here. He got a job of sorts and
went into therapy.

     He worked for a time for a company where he got along
well and was effective as a salesman, but he gave it up.
He then began selling for a business which was identical to
his father's and did very well at this; however, he soon
began getting migraine headaches, and he reacted adversely
to pressure from the sales management. Apparently when he
first returned to the coast he had been unemployed and during
this time he got along especially well. He played golf, he
got along well with his children, and he behaved well
socially. It is interesting to note, then, that when he
began to work he started going downhill again. While selling
he impulsively decided to consider another country as a
place to live, and he was supported in this plan by his wife.
He refused to heed the therapist's advice and persisted in
his plans to move to the other country.

     He made the move and under these new living circumstances
the wife controlled the various needs of the home. The
patient subsequently rebelled against this. The patient's
interests were varied and his projects were many, but he
felt incapable of succeeding in this new country. He was
interested in sports cars and mechanics, but in general
lived an ineffectual life. He began taking sleeping pills
for insomnia. He finally decided that he was going to set

up an export business. It is significant to note that it
was following this decision that his death came from an
overdose of sedatives.

The core neurotic problem in this man obviously continued to be unchanged, and the conflict triggers were those
of responsibility and the possibility of success. It is of
special interest that he was happy to function as a father
and a husband, and he was comfortable socially, during a
brief period on the coast when he was not working. With
complete regularity, illness always reappeared whenever he
attempted to work. The move to another country was obviously
a flight from responsibility and a relinquishing of his feeble
efforts to obtain manhood. His wife became even more dominant in this setting.

As far as need-congruence is concerned, this was a most
need-incongruent situation. Opportunities for growth and
maturity were limited, although the patient did find a possibility for himself insofar as an occupation was concerned.
He attempted to develop an export business, and it is significant that the wife looked the other way during these developments and let him get away with his self-destruction. In
the course of time this patient managed to progressively
reduce the number of opportunities for growth and maturation
and seek out an increasingly need-incongruent environment
for himself in which he could live out his neurosis. The
obvious conflict triggers were the demands of heterosexuality, maturity, fatherhood, being a husband.

5. Summary

This case illustrates very clearly the centrality of
the oedipal conflict in the genesis of neurosis. This patient could not accept success, parenthood, responsibility.
His illness was manifested in part by the submissive way he
related to his father but at the same time rebelled against
him. His illness was also manifested by the choice of woman
he took for his wife, by his alcoholic excesses, and overall
chronic failure. Treatment did not touch this patient for
in one way or another he managed to wiggle out from under
psychiatric control and intervention. His therapist failed
to grasp the fact that he had not changed the patient to any
significant degree and, therefore, did not realize that the
patient was bound to fail again. His life ended by suicide.

SYNTHESIS OF SITUATIONAL VARIABLES - CASE #3

1. Brief History

When he came to Topeka the patient was a 30-year-old
white, married physician who had been referred because of
drug addiction. His medical license had been suspended.
He was then married to his second wife and had two children
by her.

He was the younger of two sons born to a lower middle
class family. The most relevant aspect of the history was
that the father, although a constant worker, was a passive
man who drank and left the family for a period of about two
years. The patient's care fell largely to the mother, with
whom he developed a mutually dependent and highly intimate
relationship. It should be noted that the patient felt very
envious of, and perhaps threatened by, his brother's success
as an engineer. Although he showed considerable musical
talent with the violin, the mother had chosen medicine as a
career for him. When the father returned to the home after
a two-year absence the mother took to her bed as a chronic
hypochondriac. The patient's mother and father never had a
good marriage.

The patient was first married in the early forties.
This marriage lasted five years and there were two children.
The first wife was an active, aggressive woman, a year older
than the patient. The marriage was stormy and eventually
ended in divorce. While he was still married to this woman,
the patient began an affair with a woman he had known earlier,
and finally married her.

His behavior continued to deteriorate during the second
marriage but even so he sired two children. He had affairs
with other women, and one overt homosexual relationship
probably occurred. During his internship he had a grand mal
seizure, and the wife stated that he began taking drugs at
this time. He noted that the demands on him became more
difficult to handle, that fatigue and anxiety increased, he

110

developed migraine, visual disturbances, nausea, but he did
not have another seizure until he was in the Navy. Following this second seizure the intake of sedatives and narcotics
increased, and reached its zenith while he was attempting
to establish a practice. His drug intake resulted in a
period of treatment at a narcotics treatment center. Following this experience he took a psychiatric residency but
became worse and started taking narcotics again. He was
dismissed because of an affair and because of the narcotic
intake. This kind of behavior persisted, and finally he was
brought to Topeka for an evaluation and treatment.

2. Summary of Situational Variables at the Time of Initial
   Study

     At the time of initial study the patient had been dis-
charged from the hospital and had begun his psychotherapy.
His wife was in another city but soon joined him; she brought
the children soon afterwards.

     The core neurotic problem was defined as an extremely
infantile narcissistic character, with strong passive and
oral needs. A second area of conflict revolved around homosexuality. The oedipal problem was not defined in the research
records at the time of initial study, but in retrospect it
is perfectly clear that this was a major conflict.

     The wife, parenthood, fatherhood, success - all were
conflict-triggering. The illness began and worsened as he
attempted to be successful in these areas. After the original onslaught of symptoms he continued to regress up to
the time of his admission to the hospital. It is clear that
the first marriage was an acting out of his unconscious conflicts because he married "to spite his father," and in so
doing obviously wished to win the oedipal and oral nurturing
mother. He was frustrated in his oral and narcissistic
demandingness in his marital relationships, particularly so
when the children arrived. To be successful in his marriage
was forbidden to him. Two marriages ultimately failed. It
should be noted in this respect that the patient stated that
he wrecked his own life as revenge against his father for
leaving for two years. It seems rather clear that the deeper meaning of this statement is that the patient never
formed a good masculine identity. His revenge against the
father was in reaction to never having been "permitted" to
identify with him.

     Nearly all aspects of his existence were conflict-
triggering; the various facets of his life demanded that he

be giving and masterful, successful and responsible. At the time of initial study there were no actual stresses in his life other than the migraine and the epilepsy, although the epilepsy was not severe. For someone adequately prepared (psychologically and technically), being a physician is not stressful.

Support was moderate at best. The father had never been too willing to help him through college or medical school. The parents had lost their savings in the depression. The wife was somewhat more supportive, although there is more to be said about her in a moment. His work arrangement probably was the most supportive aspect of all. He was able to work at the hospital where he had been a patient and undoubtedly this must have increased his sense of security.

The work possibilities especially were probably the most need-congruent aspects in his life. At first glance it would seem that the marriage was need-congruent; that is to say, it offered an opportunity to be a father, a husband, and a breadwinner. This is undoubtedly true; however, the character makeup of his wife would indicate that she was more congruent with the neurotic aspects of his personality than with the healthy aspects. She was a very aggressive and dominating woman just like the patient's mother. She insisted that she take over the finances. She appropriated all of the funds that he earned, and one can speculate about this being her way of robbing his manhood. Curiously enough, she didn't seem to be too concerned about his numerous girl friends. It is quite clear that she was the dominant one in this marriage and if we hold to the value judgment that men should be men and women should be women, it would seem that the roles were reversed in this relationship, thus the marriage was need-incongruent. This being so, whatever maturational push there may have been in him to become a man met with resistance from the environment.

Opportunities were quite good provided the intrapsychic problems and the neurotic environmental entanglements could have been straightened out. The Health-Sickness Rating by one team's rating was about 35 at the time of the initial study.

3. Summary of Situational Variables at the Time of Termination Study

This patient began psychotherapy and terminated ten months later. His treatment accomplished very little.

The patient was unable to maintain work as an employed physician. He lied constantly to his therapist, he had many affairs, he took drugs, he drank, and he spent money recklessly. Although he had taken up residence in his home, he had been displaced to the basement by the fact that his wife's brother had moved in. Ostensibly this was so the wife would have more help around the house. The patient attempted suicide and had to be rehospitalized. It was clear that this first attempt was partly in the nature of a plea for help because he took pills while driving, got woozy and eventually ran into the back of a bus. At the time he entered the hospital his psychotherapy was terminated.

The core conflicts were considered to be essentially unchanged. He was still believed to be a demanding narcissistic character with marked dependence. Although the phallic-oedipal homosexual conflicts were not discussed, it is evident that this conflict existed and that it had been untouched. The conflict triggers at this period were essentially the same. The main trigger was the responsibility to the family as husband, breadwinner and father. Success was conflict-triggering. In short, the man had capitulated completely. The illness had a feedback stressful effect upon him in the nature of the turmoil he created in his environment, and also with respect to the intake of drugs. Drug intake reduced his ego functioning, which only made his illness worse. The research team rated the wife as somewhat stressful at the time of termination. She was a harsh woman, forced him to sleep in the basement, sometimes slapped him. Some of his friends might be considered stressful because of their own pathology. The wife was partially supportive because she did maintain a house, but it was hardly a home.

Opportunities were abundant. If he could have overcome his illness he might have made a success of himself professionally, and perhaps even in his marriage. The latter is somewhat open to question because of the need-incongruent aspects of the wife. Her character makeup blended with the neurotic character aspects of the patient. These two people were neurotically intertwined in a terribly destructive way.

This man was prevented from succeeding in life in any arena, primarily by his own internal conflicts (largely the phallic-oedipal one and, secondarily, the dependent one). The environment provided ample opportunity in the professional area. He was prevented from succeeding in his marriage, however, and quite significantly not only by his intrapsychic conflicts but, in addition, by the personality of his wife.

She was the dominant one; the one who said, "Perhaps this
will teach him a lesson," after his first serious suicide
attempt. For him to change intrapsychically would be difficult because of the kind of woman she was. For instance, in
addition to the many ways she hampered his changing, she
begrudged him the money for treatment. There had never been
any family activities in this marriage. After the patient
was rehospitalized, after his suicide attempt, this woman
had no common interests with other women; in fact, her prime
interest seemed to be the acquisition of money, which presumably gave her control over her environment and her husband.

4. Summary of Situational Variables at the Time of Follow-up
    Study

    Following his readmission to the hospital upon termi-
nation of his psychotherapy, he remained hospitalized for
approximately two years. During this time he made some
efforts to work. There was some continuing psychotherapy
but the patient finally committed suicide.

    The suicide notes very clearly revealed the extent and
intensity of his relationship to the mother. The provoca-
tion for the suicide apparently was the filing for a divorce
by his wife. It was clear in the notes to his parents, his
wife and his doctor that he recognized his dismal failure
as a husband, that without his wife he believed he was nothing
and that life would be meaningless. Thus, to lose his wife
appears to mean losing his mother and his own identity.
Loss of the wife also meant the loss of a love object that
he could not do without. The notes suggested that by dying
and having his wife collect the insurance he could give her
the good life a husband could give a woman, but only if he
were dead. It is interesting to note that one of the research
teams had the distinct impression that his suicide was
given additional impetus by the fact that the wife was dating another man. The patient stated that he thought that
she might not marry again if she had enough money to get
along on her own; thus he keeps his wife (mother) for himself even in death.

    Conflict triggers at the time of follow-up were the
continuing demands of maturity which resonated with the
phallic-oedipal, and the dependent narcissistic, conflict
which prevented him from making any kind of a successful
adjustment. The most significant conflict trigger, finally,
was the wife's rejection of him, which reawakened the early
separation anxiety, disturbed his identity (he was identified closely with the mother), and it represented an object

loss in the person of the mother with whom he could not do without. It is worth noting that shortly before his suicide it was discovered that he had impregnated another patient. This may have awakened his guilt even more.

5. Summary

This patient's illness and life course demonstrate the inability to accept the challenges of maturity, heterosexuality, and responsibility. Specifically, he could not work successfully as a physician, he could not be a husband or father. The underlying conflictual basis for this appears to revolve around the oral-dependent narcissistic conflict and the phallic-oedipal conflict. The man's character makeup was strongly passive, he was femininely identified. The irreconcilable forces within and around him finally forced him to suicide. These forces were the continuing demands of maturity, which he in no way could master, and the loss of the woman who, for him, represented the mother. The parents had, in the meantime, more or less withdrawn from him.

SYNTHESIS OF SITUATIONAL VARIABLES - CASE #4

1. Brief History

The patient was a man in his late forties who was referred for psychiatric treatment because of crippling anxiety
and severe phobias. He was the son of a successful businessman. The mother was a very active, energetic woman. The
parents were divorced whe the patient was entering puberty.
They were on good terms, however, and, although the family
was divided, the patient apparently saw both his mother and
father more or less continuously. He met his wife in college
and married her two years after he left school. When he
was referred for treatment they had a son in his early
twenties. The patient had been a successful businessman.
He originally was more interested in a profession but apparently because of his father's persuasion he joined the
family business. He never really liked this work although
he became successful at it. In the mid-forties he had
suddenly developed physical symptoms and subsequent inves-
tigations identified a carcinoma. He was operated on several
times and received X-ray therapy. It was in connection with
this illness that his psychologic decompensation began.

He was tolerating the surgery reasonably well but
during the third operation an emergency developed outside
the operating room and the operating team left him unattended
on the table. He had an acute panic attack and following
this developed the phobia of progressive severity. The
first anxiety attack occurred several months later in a
theater where he developed extreme claustrophobia and had
to leave. He became phobic in public places; he could not
tolerate close contacts at parties or board meetings; and
he relied increasingly on protection by his wife. He grew
very dependent upon her and at one point she had to take
him from a public place in a wheelchair. Along with his
dependence on his wife, he became increasingly critical of
her. His overriding fear was that he would die alone, unattended. He went into psychotherapy twice a week for less
than one hundred hours.

116

2.   Summary of Situational Variables at the Time of Initial
Study

The core neurotic conflict at the time of initial study
was thought to be the fear of the loss of the mother; that
is, infantile separation anxiety. A corollary to this main
central conflict was the ancient castration fear. The
obvious conflict triggers which aroused these two nascent
core conflicts were all of the events associated with the
carcinoma and being left while in the middle of surgery.
These core conflicts were expressed in the fear of dying
unattended, and they were also expressed by the increased
demandingness on his wife and his decrease in sexual potency.
The carcinoma and then the surgery for it, in addition to
being conflict-triggering, were considered to be a stress in
their own right. The business for which this man was responsible was considered a stress. During the course of
the illness a subsidiary company in which the patient was
interested got into difficulty because of the sudden absence
of the president of the company. These business problems
fell on the patient's shoulders.

The supports were abundant. First and foremost was
the patient's wife, who had been a very strong, loyal person
who tolerated the patient's illness extremely well. She
apparently reacted minimally to his increased demandingness,
his decreased potency, and so on. She remained reassuring
throughout. His position in the community, the fact that
he had a good business that paid him well, were supporting.
He found great pleasure in his friends and avocational
interests and undoubtedly derived a good deal of support
in these areas. Opportunities were good for this man; the
business had stablized, the marriage could improve as his
regression abated. The relationships within the patient's
situation were need-congruent. First and foremost was his
wife; however, the relationship with his father was probably
not the most need-congruent. The father was a man who
apparently found it difficult to let his son emancipate himself; he refused to retire and always stuck around the
business.

3.   Summary of Situational Variables at the Time of Termination Study

At the time of termination the patient was asymptomatic with a few exceptions. He had returned to a fairly
active social life in his community and resumed working at
the family company again. Drinking, which had been a problem at the time of initial study but was not then recognized,

had subsided considerably. His potency had improved. He
was less demanding of his wife and of other people, particularly those in his business, and was considerably more
understanding of them. He still had some symptoms, however.
There was some anxiety and occasional phobia. He was much
happier than he had been and was very grateful for having
been helped. There was one brief note in the therapy records
which pointed to a much larger problem with the patient's
father than had been recognized or than was worked with in
the treatment. The major finding at the time of termination
was that the patient had passed the five-year mark for
recurrence of carcinoma, therefore the main conflict trigger
had been removed and with its removal the patient's symptoms
had largely abated. Furthermore, the nonrecurrence of the
carcinoma removed a stress.

The supportive elements in his life continued to be
excellent. The relationship with the parental family was
good, although the relationship with the father in the context of the family business was a mixed blessing. The marital situation continued to be good, and the financial support was considerable. An obvious support, and one which
unquestionably helped this man regain his equilibrium, was
the silent supportive and continuing relationship with the
therapist and with the Menninger Foundation. There is much
evidence to indicate that the wife, the therapist, and the
Foundation were, in the aggregate, the symbolic security-
giving mother figure for him.

Opportunities for growth were abundant; he could make
his business grow, he could go into other kinds of business
of his choosing, he had adequate operating capital and personal skill. His marital relationship was excellent, but
the relationship with his son was somewhat strained. The
patient apparently was intent upon forcing his son into the
occupational mold that had been forced upon him by his
father, and the son was rebelling. By and large, the overall environment was quite need-congruent. This was a man
who had made his mark in business and in the community, and
the community and the business welcomed him. The relationship with the wife was probably the most need-congruent
aspect of all. Although the therapy was a very supportive
element, the absence of recurrence of the carcinoma was the
one single factor which coincided most obviously with his
recovery.

4. Summary of Situational Variables at the Time of Follow-up
   Study

At the time of follow-up, a number of changes had taken place in this patient's life. He had partially withdrawn from the family business, devoting more effort to a project of his own, and also to managing the investment of funds of his own and of some relatives. The patient had noted considerable change in himself and in his functioning in the company. He was more fair to the employees and they were more fair to him. His business ventures continued to be very successful; this included the family business but also the new project. The father still upset him almost as much as ever; he never complimented the patient nor any other employee on anything they had ever done. The patient was quite active in his business, he was a director in eight other companies, but he wished to withdraw from business. His dream was to spend three months of the year in the North and three months of the year in the South. It was noted that he did not plan to retire, but on the other hand he was beginning to think of retirement at an early age. One can wonder whether this fantasied shedding of responsibility in some way reflected a regression and simultaneously a shedding of conflict triggers. The fear of closed-in places and people persisted and were about the only signs, in his opinion, of the old illness. His social life had been resumed.

Obviously the core conflicts had not been resolved. Although this man had continued to maintain his adjustment, it was evident that certain situations continued to trigger his core conflicts of separation and castration anxiety. It may be that he was not completely convinced, even though he consciously denied this, that his carcinoma had really disappeared. It seems likely that the relationship to the Menninger Foundation, a good relationship with his wife, and the fact that his carcinoma had not reappeared in the five years offset these core anxieties, but something kept him from functioning optimally, and something also caused him to flirt with the idea of reducing his responsibilities. Supports continued to be abundant. Need-congruence was plentiful - this refers to the good relationship with his wife and opportunities for being a responsible man in the various business adventures.

5. Summary

This case illustrates rather nicely the stressful impact, but also conflict-triggering impact, of a threat to life. This man had established a good equilibrium in his life adjustment. However, permitting himself to continue to be dominated by his father suggests that he had never really resolved his oedipal difficulties. This is reflected also in his jealousy toward his son, both while the son was growing up and in later years. There was a clear problem with the son in later years.

With the development of the carcinoma the patient became anxiety-ridden and phobic, fearing he would die alone, unattended. He regressed and found comfort from his wife, who became a mother figure whom he had to have with him every moment. Fortunately the wife could respond to this need. He also found additional security at the Menninger Foundation. With the continued support of the Foundation and his wife, and the gradual loss of the conflict trigger (in the form of a threat to life by the carcinoma), the patient slowly but progressively began to reintegrate. His adjustment attained an adult level again but his symptoms continued to persist with diminished intensity. Some, such as anxiety in the barber's chair or dental chair, were still there. The castration threat was obvious. His inability to regain his original level of adjustment can be explained by the fact that once having regressed, the conflict trigger (the cancer) had not been completely removed, although the patient consciously stated he was completely reassured on this score.

This is an especially clear example of an external event being both stressful and conflict-triggering. It was, of course, the unconscious conflicts which were activated by the conflict trigger that produced the illness and not the purely stressful impact of the carcinoma.

SYNTHESIS OF SITUATIONAL VARIABLES - CASE #5

1. Brief History

The patient, married and childless, came for an evaluation when she was in her late twenties. She complained of her infertility, nervousness, and depression. Her past history revealed that her parents had split up several times, always reconciling only to split up again. The father was a very strict man, an alcoholic, and a person whom the patient eventually came to hate. The patient and her mother were never close. There was much tension in the home, and amidst the family squabbles the patient found herself siding with her mother despite her inability to be close to her. The patient felt painfully self-conscious all of her life, and felt like an outcast most of the time.

Disgust towards sexuality developed early and seemed, in part, to be related to the fact that she witnessed parental coitus several times and frequently saw her father walking around nude. Her introduction to menstruation was traumatic, reinforcement coming from the fact that she had to wash out old cloths in order to provide herself with fresh sanitary napkins. A prudish attitude towards sexuality developed very early in life and she used to slap boys who tried to kiss her. Symptom formation occurred shortly after her first experience at heavy petting, during which her boyfriend somehow managed to ejaculate on her slacks. Soon thereafter her mother died. These symptoms eventually became more quiescent.

The patient was married in the mid-forties to a quiet, gentle, passive man. She soon wanted a baby but at the same time recognized that she was extremely fearful of becoming pregnant. She continued to work as a nurse (she had become a nurse in defiance of her father), but stopped working after two years of marriage in order to increase her chances of becoming pregnant. Chronic pelvic disease was finally diagnosed. She underwent surgery but her sterility persisted. A period of extreme anxiety developed when her menstrual

121

period was overdue twenty days.

The first major decompensation occurred shortly after
she and her husband adopted an infant boy. The patient went
through the motions of taking care of the child but she made
curious remarks such as she "did not like the baby being
so cute and happy"; she had the impulse to grab the baby
and shake him "as if you are mad at somebody and you want
to hold him and shake him." She became increasingly upset
and doubt-ridden about her ability to take care of the baby,
recognizing her inability to feel towards the child as a
mother should. She became obsessed with urges to hurt the
child. Once or twice she took hold of the baby and shook
him to the point that both he and she cried. After having
had the child for six months, both she and her husband agreed
that it would be best if they gave up the child. This decision followed her hospitalization in a psychiatric hospital
elsewhere. The patient began her analysis at the Menninger
Foundation, where she was never hospitalized.

2. Summary of Situational Variables at the Time of Initial
    Study

The core neurotic problem at the time of initial study
was centered around her identity. Hers was a mixed mascu-
line-feminine identity. The roots of this problem were
oedipal and a strong dependency. The patient was very
envious of men, felt competitive towards them; she felt she
needed to be in control; she was obstinate. On the other
hand, there were marked childlike dependent qualities in
her. The primary conflict triggers at the time of initial
study were her wishes to be a mother and a better wife; in
short, to fully live out the feminine role. Although she
tended to deny it, the fact of the matter was that she ab-
horred sexuality, and to be intimate with a man aroused her
phallic rebellious tendencies as well as her oedipal guilt.
The patient was extremely determined to overcome her problems.

Very little stress was noted at the time of initial
study although living in a house trailer could have been
considered a minor stress. Her father was still alive but
vegetating in a nursing home. This may be considered somewhat stressful, and also conflict-triggering to a degree.
The supports in her life revolved primarily around the fact
that she obtained gratification from her work as a nurse
and from her husband. He consistently stood by her, provided well for her, and at the outset seemed to support her
wish for treatment. Opportunities for growth seemed quite
good. The husband had a professional identity which

permitted having a good social position. Both she and her
husband wanted to make a home and have a family.

Need-congruence was fairly good at the time of initial
study; that is to say, this patient had a home and a husband
which acted as stimulating factors towards greater growth
and maturity. However, the husband was somewhat need-
incongruent in a sense. He was a very compliant and passive
man and in this respect was somewhat lacking in ability to
bring out the woman in his wife. Had he been more forceful
he would have become more conflict-triggering. Nothing was
immutable at the time of initial study except that they
were Catholics and divorce was more or less out of the question. That she probably could not conceive seemed likely;
however, adoption was always a possibility for her.

3. Summary of Situational Variables at the Time of Termi-
    nation Study

By the time of termination the husband had already
moved in order to establish his practice. He issued an
ultimation to the patient that she follow him. This caused
her to terminate the treatment sooner than she and her
analyst wished. It seems to be the general consensus that
the patient was moderately improved by the time of termination. Her anxiety was considerably less, her insight was
greater; but at the same time it was clear that her problems
were by no means resolved. For instance, she wondered how
she could leave the analysis without having made peace with
her mother. Such a statement reflects the unsettled state
of her unconscious oedipal problem. Rebelliousness and
obstinacy still remained, and the patient felt considerable
trepidation about adopting a child. She still had not been
able to have one of her own, although no physical reasons
could be found other than the old diagnosis of the chronic
pelvic inflamatory disease.

The conflict triggers at the time of termination were
essentially the same. These were the demands from the environment (they were her own demands of herself) that she
live out the woman's role. She still avoided an intimate
relationship with her husband, the thought of having a child
was still anxiety-provoking. She felt more comfortable with
herself and among people, and felt that she would attain
her goal of adopting a child even though she doubted, to
some extent, that she would be able to follow through if
she did adopt one.

There were no stresses in her life other than

childlessness. The father had died, and special note should
be made of this fact; not only had a stress been removed by
his demise but also a conflict trigger. The husband continued to be quite supporting; he had a good job, their
finances had improved, and they were becoming part of the
community.

Her opportunities were still good. The husband was
rated as a plus and minus factor insofar as need-congruence
was concerned. He was need-congruent insofar as he was a
man, gave her a home, and provided the opportunities for
her to become a woman; however, he was not as much of a
man as he might have been and thus blended to some degree
with the nonfeminine aspects of his wife. The situation was
still relatively mutable except for the fact that they were
Catholic and could not divorce.

4.   Summary of Situational Variables at the Time of Follow-up
     Study

     The most notable fact at the time of follow-up was that
the patient had adopted a baby girl. She left treatment
with the resolve that she would do this. She began working
in a nursery, thereby finding satisfaction on the one hand
but becoming anxious on the other. She went into long
religious retreats and "stormed heaven," and finally got a
tongue-lashing from her priest who told her to knuckle down
and fulfill her duties to her husband. This tongue-lashing
coincided approximately with the time that she adopted her
child. She had a great deal of support from the Catholic
organization in her community in connection with the adoption. They let her pick out the child she wanted; they let
her get to know the baby before she actually adopted it;
the church provided tension outlets (in the form of prayer),
and she received counseling from one of the priests.

     The quality of the adoption experience, the relation-
ship of the patient to the adopted child, and the eruption
of symptoms in the patient following the adoption, all
showed very clearly that this adopted baby was a pronounced
conflict trigger. The patient became worse symptomatically
immediately after the adoption; she became irritable, she
began resorting to drugs of various sorts, she slapped the
child a few times and seemed unusually harsh with it. The
patient reflected an unusual amount of will; she said that
she would never return to Topeka without a child, and she
made good her promise. There were no real stresses in her
life; the supports were plentiful; the husband continued
to stand by her and he was very fond of the child. Their

place in the community was growing; they had a home of their
own.

5. Summary

This case illustrates the intimate connection between
conflict triggers and core conflict very clearly. It also
illustrates the blending of neurotic personalities in
marriage. This patient developed along somewhat unfeminine
lines so that by the time she reached young adulthood she
had not found her femininity. There was a masculine controlling streak in her which seemed to be an expression of
an unresolved oedipal conflict. Despite these masculine
elements in her nature she married but, as might be predicted,
she picked a man who was passive and not fully masculine.
However, the healthy aspects in both of them led to the wish
for a family.

The patient became markedly decompensated when she
brought a child into her life. It should be noted that her
first brush with sexuality before marriage aroused much
anxiety in her. She had always been standoffish as far as
boys were concerned. The underlying basis for her rejection
of femininity, her hostility toward males, and her difficulties in adopting the baby became quite clear in the analysis.
When the patient stated that she defied God by becoming a
nurse, she was probably saying that she was defying her own
oedipal wishes to consummate a marriage with God (the father)
and have a child by him. Work for her was an escape from
marriage. It is clear that oedipal guilt, rejection of the
feminine role, and envy of the man's position in life, as
well as her own wish to be given to in the dependent position rather than be giving to someone else who is dependent,
were the main factors that stood in her way of a happy and
successful heterosexual adjustment.

All of the assessments at termination of the analysis
showed that this treatment was incomplete. However, it must
be noted that although she left treatment still somewhat
rebellious, still anxious about having children, and still
childless, she nonetheless "blessed" the analyst and thanked
him. She herself even wondered if there might not be more
change in her than she recognized at the time of termination.
The fact of the matter is that the patient did bring the
major conflict trigger (the baby) into her life, something
she had not been able to do prior to treatment. It should
not be overlooked, however, that she received massive support
from her environment during this development. (This refers
to her husband and to the Catholic organization in her city.)

It is questionable whether she could have accomplished the adoption without the support from both the husband and the church.

It seems correct to say that enough of her core conflict had been resolved that she could now do what she had not been able to do before. To what extent the intrapsychic reorganization can account for the adoption and to what extent her willpower and the massive environmental support can account for the adoption is not clear. All factors obviously played a part. It must be noted, also, that this patient had, from the very beginning, contributed a very powerful inner push to achieve her goal. Where the energy came from for such motivation can only be speculated about.

Despite what one has to say about the treatment, the facts are that she was able to do after treatment what she had not been able to do before, regardless of how much support she may have gotten from her environment. There is one fact that must not be overlooked and this has to do with the father's death. It is quite possible that the father's death permitted the oedipal problem to recede just enough to make the adoption possible and with the help of treatment achieve that which had not been possible before.

SYNTHESIS OF SITUATIONAL VARIABLES - CASE #6

1. Brief History

This woman came to treatment in her late twenties because of severe rage attacks during which she beat up her
children, dissociative states, marked marital discord, dissatisfaction with life in general, and a history of a severe
snake phobia since early puberty. Because of a long waiting
list for treatment at the Menninger Foundation she began
psychotherapy in another city but had an unsatisfactory
experience there. Interestingly enough, however, her snake
phobia disappeared during that time but her overall adjustment continued to be highly unsatisfactory.

She was treated by psychoanalysis at the Menninger
Foundation for a period of 2½ years and for more than 500
hours. She was seen periodically by her analyst during the
follow-up period. During the analysis itself the patient
lived in Topeka and on weekends visited her home where her
family continued to live. Her husband's business commitments precluded the entire family moving to Topeka.

At the time of initial study there were three living,
prepubertal, children. A fourth child, a baby, had died
just prior to the patient finally seeking psychiatric help.
Her parents and both in-laws were living in the city where
the patient had lived with her husband.

2. Summary of Situational Variables at the Time of Initial
Study

The patient's core conflicts at initial study were defined as primarily phallic-oedipal. The snake phobia was
believed to conceal her strong wish for and intense fear of
the phallus. She was bitterly disappointed with her life
as a child, and was continually sustained by the fantasy
that some older man would do something nice for her, rescue
her. This seemed to mean that he would give her a penis,
or that he would give her marriage, romance and a child.

127

That heterosexuality was the primary conflict trigger can be inferred from the circumstances surrounding the onset of the snake phobia. The patient's mother told the patient a story of someone finding a snake in their bed. From then on (the patient was then approaching puberty) she became phobic of snakes. This fear progressed in intensity and finally became nearly incapacitated by the time she sought psychiatric help. We have no detailed account of the effect of the birth of each child; however, we do know that she frequently flew into rages at them and eventually was nearly unable to function in her home. The final straw was the death of the fourth child, which she believed she hastened by the way she managed him.

It would appear, then, that the demands of womanhood, heterosexuality, motherhood, were the primary conflict triggers. These external factors were reinforced by the close proximity of her own parents as well as the in-laws. There had been many thoughts of divorce and many criticisms of her husband.

The only stress at the time of the initial study was the recent death of her last child. There were considerable supports in her life and, despite the negative feelings toward the parents and in-laws they were, nevertheless, present and helpful. The husband provided her a home and had an adequate income. He was interested in her sexually, but at the same time maintained a certain emotional distance from her. Her appearance was supportive in that she was an attractive woman. The opportunities for improving her life adjustment were ample. She had a home, she had potentially a good place in the community, and she had three young children. These same factors that provided an opportunity may also be considered as need-congruent. All provided the means by which she could live out the woman in her. The husband may be considered somewhat need-incongruent in that he was a shy, retiring person socially and managed to use up much of his spare time with hobbies of his own away from the home. Her own neurotic conflicts were the barrier to her adequately using these need-congruent aspects of her life.

3.   Summary of Situational Variables at Time of Termination Study

It is very significant to note that during treatment this patient seemed to have improved considerably. While living in Topeka she attended a university and graduated with honors. Her symptoms disappeared in large part, and the termination team suggested that a considerable amount

of conflict resolution had taken place. The analyst described her as being markedly improved and stated that she
was asymptomatic and had considerable insight. The area of
greatest symptomatic improvement was in the patient's management of her children. She had formerly been extremely
harsh with them, beating them, and so forth. At termination
they no longer appeared to be a threat to her; she was able
to experience a good deal of positive feelings towards them
without having to act out the opposite. She no longer needed
to treat her little girl as a deprived person. The oldest
son, who had taken a considerable amount of mistreatment,
was no longer treated by the patient as her disliked male
twin. She had, in addition, developed some other channels
for hostility and did not appear to use hostility as a
weapon against her husband.

The treatment team suggested that the core conflicts
were not resolved completely but were reduced in intensity.
The core neurotic conflicts revolved around the unresolved
phallic problems which complicated her own identification
as a mature woman. Relationships with the husband were not
particularly improved, however. Arguments did go on between
them and there was a hint that the sexual adjustment was
not satisfactory. It seems, then, that at termination the
children were less conflict-triggering than before; the
best evidence for this, of course, was that the patient's
relationship with them had improved. The husband, however,
was still somewhat conflict-triggering for the relationship
with him was more or less unchanged. Symptoms were much
less at the time of termination. There were no stress
factors in her life; the opportunities for a good life were
plentiful; she still had her home, her family, her position
in the community.

Need-congruent factors were the same ones that provided
her the opportunity for the future. She had a husband,
children, family, and the position in the community. We
should note, however, that the husband was somewhat need-
incongruent in that he stayed away from home a good deal of
the time and wasn't as heterosexual a being as he might be.

4.   Summary of Situational Variables at the Time of Follow-
     up Study

At the time of follow-up there were a number of interesting developments. Apparently as soon as this woman returned to her home town she became quite symptomatic again.
At one point she even said that the symptoms were a thousand
times more intense during the follow-up period than they

had been prior to treatment. There is a hint that the snake phobia had returned to some degree, she was depressed much of the time and suffered from intense head pressures, the only escape from which was to be found in sleep. There was, however, a freedom from fear, and this was one of the big changes that took place. The rages were still present, however, according to an interview with the husband. The patient had, however, accepted her femininity to a greater extent and appeared to be less competitive with men. Fatigue was a prominent symptom and probably was a manifestation of her depression. The patient now had fog states about every day, along with the "terrific" pressures in her head. Somehow, though, she was more accepting of her symptoms and less frightened by them.

She eventually had another child and was able to write a fairly cheerful letter to her former doctor about her life which made it appear that she was considerably more content. It was evident that the role of woman, homemaker, mother, was still conflict-triggering for her; however, it appeared to be somewhat less so. At the same time, it must be noted that her children were considerably older than they used to be and hence had less of a direct impact on her. She was managing herself in her home better and particularly in the role as a mother and woman. She was involved in some social activities. There were no stresses. Opportunities for a better life were abundant and, of course, her environment was as need-congruent as it was before; in fact, it was probably more so. The husband himself went into treatment and appeared to have changed some. It was now possible for the patient and her husband to talk together; in fact, she said they never ran out of something to talk about. The family enjoyed group projects in which all of them participated. That she can do all of these things implies some resolution of conflict.

5. Summary

This patient was made vulnerable to a severe neurosis by virtue of marked unresolved phallic-oedipal conflicts. The first trigger for this repressed conflictual constellation appeared to be the snake story her mother told her. This occurred about the time of puberty when heterosexual object-finding first makes its appearance. The patient had sufficient strength, however, to marry and bear four children. Marital life was stormy for her, however, and it is clear that her own underestimation of herself as a woman (she never felt perfect), and the demands of heterosexuality (motherhood, wifehood, homemaker) eventually produced a

decompensation. That is to say, these external demands
triggered her unconscious conflicts sufficiently that the
end result was a severe decompensation. She was phobic,
unable to function adequately as a mother, and at times was
assaultive to her children.

Psychoanalysis took place while the patient was away
from home much of the time. It seems reasonable to suppose
this arrangement for the treatment imposed a certain limitation on the extent to which her unconscious problems were
resolved. However, some resolution obviously did take place.
It is noteworthy that she improved markedly while she was
away from her home. This fact can be explained by the
absence of conflict triggers, the supportive effect of her
treatment, and some slow but progressive resolution of the
unconscious problems. Soon after returning home, however,
this patient became quite symptomatic again. This fact can
be related directly to the heavy impact her environment had
on her, an environment which for her was still conflict-
triggering.

However, after reeling under this heavy and stagger-
ing onslaught from the combined effect of the external triggers and the unconscious triggered conflicts, the patient
managed to rally and eventually seemed to establish an adjustment that was reasonably satisfactory to her. She was
symptomatic, however, still having depression, some anxiety,
some arguments with her husband, some sexual difficulties
and so on, but she was not nearly as incapacitated as before.
This improvement can be explained in the following way: (a)
there had been some resolution of core conflict; (b) the
conflict triggers were somewhat removed by virtue of the
fact that the children were older and she had full-time help
in her home; and (c) the husband was more need-congruent
than before. His having changed through treatment offered
an opportunity for an outlet of the woman in her. This
happy interaction between them certainly must have fostered
the maturational process in both of them.

Of course success as a woman breeds further success,
and no doubt the patient continued to apply the insight she
gained in her analysis to her postanalytic life. One can
speculate that the insight into the nature of the snake
phobia led to the disappearance of the phobia, and that the
depression now came from her sense of inadequacy as a fully
evolved and developed woman, something she would have to
develop in the course of time. It would appear that she was
slowly coming to peace with herself, but this occurred only
after a phase of intense discomfort where she even considered

committing suicide as a means of escaping her life dilemma. It would appear that this patient had slowly but finally tentatively accepted her femininity and, as such, was able to cope with the demands on her as a woman. But this was a reluctant acceptance and the role still created a great deal of tension and dissatisfaction in her, a fact which indicates that the core problems were by no means gone and that she still clashed with the demands from the environment that she be a woman.

SYNTHESIS OF SITUATIONAL VARIABLES - CASE #7

1. Brief History

The patient was in her late thirties when she came for
treatment. She was the wife of a physician and the mother
of two prepubertal boys. Her symptoms were primarily alcoholism, two suicidal attempts, a long-standing inability
to fill the role of mother and homemaker adequately, and
moderately severe arthritis. She apparently managed to care
for the first child but she resented the second child, who
was unplanned and a male. She experienced much difficulty
towards this child and always had a strongly negative attitude towards him. Her illness became acute several years
prior to her coming to treatment when the second son developed a serious crippling illness. She became depressed,
felt guilty, began drinking excessively in order to carry
out her duties as a homemaker and mother. She found it increasingly difficult to care for the sick child. At one
point she was so regressed in her adjustment that she totally neglected the crippled child's broken extremity.

Eventually it was considered dangerous to leave the
patient in her home alone for on one occasion she flooded
the house by letting the bathtub overflow with her in it.
The husband feared that she might set fire to the house.
The patient was hospitalized, and began psychoanalysis five
times a week and accrued over 100 hours. The husband and
children remained at home while she was in Topeka for
treatment.

2. Summary of Situational Variables at the Time of Initial
   Study

The woman was a patient in the hospital when she began
her analysis. The core conflicts were defined as a profound
oral dependence, a hostile feminine identification with her
own phallic-aggressive mother, a pronounced envy of and
competitiveness with men, and a rejection of her own femininity. It seems clear that being married and forced into

133

the feminine position aroused the aforementioned conflicts
with her own need to be given to. This became most clear
with her inability to be mothering and helpful to her
crippled child. It was at this time that her alcoholism
increased sharply. The patient had been unable to take care
of her home, she neglected her children in general and, at
the height of her rejection, made a shambles of her home
and her own functioning in it. She had been unable to be
loving towards her husband for a long time. The patient's
mother was a profound conflict trigger, as were these other
factors in her immediate environment, despite the fact that
the mother was not in her immediate vicinity. The mother
was a very harsh, domineering woman who had very little good
to say towards the patient. The patient's inability to be
feminine stems in part from the identification with her
mother, who had similar difficulties, but was also derived
from her envy of and competitiveness with men. Her environment was, at the same time, considered to be moderately
stressful. The sick child was unquestionably a burden on
her, the mother's open ·coldness was a stress.

Despite the many conflict-triggering and stressful
factors in this woman's life, there were many supports.
Her husband provided very well for her financially, he
offered her a good social position, and, in his own way,
he seemed to have loved her, curiously enough. The husband
had done everything possible to make treatment available
for her to the extent that he dipped dangerously into his
financial resources. There was not, however, much intimacy
or true mutuality in the marriage and in this sense the
marital sexual situation was conspicuously lacking in support. She was rather deeply involved in civic activities
and unquestionably found support in these pursuits. She
had been quite successful as an amateur ornithologist, and
in the past had made several successful speaking engage-
ments on radio. A great deal in this woman's life was need-
congruent insofar as offering her the possibilities to develop the woman in her. She had a good home, children, and
a place in the community.

The husband, however, was somewhat need-incongruent
insofar as bringing out the woman in her was concerned. He
was very much a little boy, quite Casper Milquetoastish
and he eventually became impotent some time during the
marriage. The two of them did, however, carry on a rather
active social life, there being many cocktail parties and
functions of various sorts. It seems safe to say that the
husband resonated in large part with those elements of her
personality which were derived from conflict. That is to

say, he blended with the neurotic elements in her to a
greater extent than he was need-congruent with the latent
woman in her. The opportunities for a better life were
certainly plentiful in her circumstances in her home town.
Unless the husband changed, it seemed unlikely that a truly
heterosexual relationship in the broad sense of the word
could ever develop with this particular man. There was really
nothing immutable in her life except the boy's physical
disability. She was not bound to her marriage by religious
scruples.

3. Summary of Situational Variables at the Time of Termin-
    ation Study

    The patient had been in the hospital for about six or
seven months, she had over 100 hours of analysis, but she
terminated treatment on her own volition. She made many
excuses for terminating, the most prominent of which was
that her husband could not finance treatment any longer.
She had been carrying on an affair with a homosexual man
(he was married but still overtly homosexual) whose wife
was not in Topeka. Although her drinking subsidied considerably, early in the treatment she smuggled alcohol into
the hospital and it seems reasonable to believe that she
drank periodically during the post-hospital phase of treatment. The patient's decision to leave Topeka seems to have
revolved around the impending arrival of the wife of the
man with whom she had been having an affair. Upon the
arrival of this woman the patient became severely depressed
and then decided to leave Topeka.

    It is clear from the record that the post-hospital
phase of treatment was by no means an easy one for her,
requiring, in addition to her analysis, full-time day hospital care. The patient returned home to a situation that
was about the same as it was when she left it. A full-time
housekeeper had been hired during her absence, both children were living at home, the husband was very busy at his
work. The in-laws were still there; the old circle of
friends, as far as we could tell, was relatively unaltered;
and the husband, as far as we could see, was no different.
The research assessments at the time of termination indicated that the core conflicts were unchanged. Her dependence,
her mixed identification, narcissism, hostility towards
women and towards men - all were unaltered. In view of
that fact, the home situation in all of its ramifications
was considered to be conflict-instigating.

    The husband, the children, the responsibilities of

being a wife and homemaker, the intimate sexual situation, can be viewed as conflict triggers still. The children were a little older and perhaps, therefore, less demanding on her. There is little information about the patient's own mother, but presumably the in-laws were as cool towards her as they were before. There was some difference with regard to the children. Plans had been made for the older son to go away to college and the younger had had some corrective surgery which had led to a private nurse being hired for him.

The responsibilities which fell to her were somewhat less at termination than at the time of the initial study. The supports were quite adequate; the husband, in his own way, was trying to keep things together and the patient was planning to seek psychiatric help in her home town. Again, the home situation family life was all considered to be quite need-congruent. It has never been too clear how much this woman and her husband had in common insofar as interests were concerned, except for an interest in bird watching. It seems unlikely that there was really much between them. His passivity persisted, as did her aggressivity. Again, nothing immutable could be seen in her life.

4. Summary of Situational Variables at the Time of Follow-up Study

It was interesting to note that the psychological tests indicated a better level of integration at the time of termination than at the time of the initial study or at the time of follow-up. Much had happened to this patient during the follow-up period of two years. She had divorced. We don't know who initiated it; the record merely states that the patient and her husband had an amicable divorce. It was agreed that the patient would have the two boys with her during the summer vacations and that they would be with their father during the remainder of the time. She was given adequate alimony.

During the follow-up period the patient returned to Topeka, sought further treatment at the Menninger Foundation but was refused because she refused to accept conditions of treatment. She obtained private psychiatric help from a practicing psychiatrist in Topeka and remained with him for several months. During this period she struck up a romance with a very sick patient of the Foundation who was many years younger than she. He was transferred in his work and she went with him.

At the follow-up interview it seemed to us that the patient looked a little neater than she had been when she lived in Topeka. The Treatment Variables team, however, thought otherwise, feeling somewhat shocked by how much older she looked and how sloppy she was. The patient said that she felt a considerable relief of pressure following the divorce. She said this was because she got away from association with her husband's family, and that she was away from the abnormal home life which resulted from her husband's preoccupation with his work. She also complained of the unsatisfactory sexual relations in her marriage, the long periods of absence of her husband - which were her rationalizations for gravitating into a more Bohemian kind of life. She said she had never experienced closeness in her marriage and she experienced considerable relief getting away from him. She did not feel comfortable in the high-brow social circles of his family. She described her relationship with her young suitor as very satisfying.

Of course it is questionable how much of her story can be believed, particularly her remark that there had been a diminution in her drinking. She stated that she still continued to drink but that she didn't get completely drunk anymore. The relationship with the mother was still tense; the patient referred to her as "Madame Hitler." She said that her fear of thunderstorms had diminished considerably, as had her drinking, yet we have other evidence that her phobia about thunderstorms was not very reduced at all. The patient remarked that her arthritis had gotten much better and she attributed this to her move to a different climate. She was doing very little that was constructive; she and her suitor beachcombed, and presumably she was seeing a psychiatrist on an on call basis.

The most obvious change at the time of follow-up was the absence of conflict triggers. This was due to the marked shift in her external environment and not due to resolution of the core problems. She had, in fact, shed most of her conflict triggers. She was now away from her husband, children, the in-laws and, by and large, she was away from her mother although the mother remained somewhat in the background.

The patient complained considerably about the difficulty in making social contacts, and it is believed that this degree of isolation was conflict-arousing for her dependence and deep sense of loneliness. This fact could explain to some extent her continued need for alcohol. The dependent conflict may now have been more activated by

virtue of the lonely life she was leading despite the fact
that she had her suitor with her. A woman who looks as
absolutely disheveled as she did will be slow in making
friends and will have a difficult time finding work. She
already was complaining of that fact. The patient's alimoney arrangements were an obstacle to remarriage. Should
she remarry, she would lose her monthly support.

There were no actual stresses in her life other than
the residual pain of a divorce and a feedback stress of
alcohol. Despite the divorce, there were a number of supports in her life. She had the alimony, she could see the
children again, she was in supportive therapy, and she was
living in a common-law relationship.

Opportunities for this woman had become considerably
more limited. At one time her opportunities were quite
plentiful; she was blocked only by her illness. Her illness
forced her out of her need-appropriate environment in which
there were plentiful opportunities and now there was very
little open to her insofar as bringing out the woman in her
was concerned. The relationship with Mr. ___ was need-
incongruent; he was much younger, a passive, weak fellow
whom she no doubt dominated.

5. Summary

This was a woman who was severely burdened by a variety
of nuclear conflicts. She was profoundly dependent, she
rejected femininity, she was envious of men and reinforced
her penis envy by having identified with an aggressive
phallic mother. Because of her need for intimacy in the
mothering sense this woman married a man who could provide
her much security. Unfortunately, he expected her to be a
wife and homemaker as well. She failed miserably at this
task. It is very clear how the increasing number of conflict triggers activated the core conflicts which then produced a progressive disintegration. She fled from treatment and then eventually shed her conflict triggers. She
divorced and left the life that provided an opportunity for
her to become a mature woman. There is one exception in
this statement and this revolves around the characterologic
passivity of the husband, who in that sense was need-incongruent for her. Her main purpose for leaving the marriage
was that she could not accept the responsibilities of
woman, wife and homemaker. She divorced, took up with a
much younger man whom she could dominate and with whom she
felt comfortable. She continued her drinking, perhaps on
a somewhat diminished level of intensity and, if she told

the truth, she was able to experience some less tension in her life. This is probably true. Although she may have escaped the major conflict triggers in her life, in doing so she cast herself into a world which probably caused her more loneliness than she had before.

SYNTHESIS OF SITUATIONAL VARIABLES - CASE #8

1. Brief History

This patient came for treatment at age 30. At that
time she was the mother of two sons, ages six and four.
She had many somatic complaints, nervousness, irritability
and weakness for the 18 months preceding the beginning of
treatment. The history of somatic illnesses dated back to
childhood. Her anxiety was so great that the evaluating
physician recommended that she be placed in the hospital
for the completion of her evaluation.

The patient stated that she had never felt loved and
had always been a lonely child. She had been an active
youngster, however, having taken part in extracurricular
activities and having had many friends. She met her future
husband while in high school and dated him during the latter
high school years and, after a prolonged courtship, married
him at age 22. He was 23. They had been married eight
years at the time of the evaluation. The patient stated
that during the marriage she frequently had somatic complaints - weakness, excessive fatigue, occasional irritability and nervousness. She had hoped the marriage would
be a solution for some of her feelings. At the time of her
evaluation the marital adjustment was so bad that the hospital doctor privately predicted that a divorce was in the
offing for her.

It is clear from the history that the illness may have
been of long-standing but took a definite turn for the worse
not too long after the marriage so that by the time she came
for treatment she was spending a good part of the day in
bed, getting up around 10:00 or 11:00 in the morning and
then going to a cocktail party or bridge tournament in the
evening. With the birth of the first child the patient had
been unable to take care of it adequately, requiring the
husband to get up in the night and take the role of the
mother for the baby. In addition to this, they had a
full-time maid who took care of the baby in the daytime.

140

Shortly after the birth of the first child the patient
periodically got so upset that her husband would have to
take her on trips, leaving the baby behind with the husband's mother. The husband stated that he had to meet
many of the children's needs because of his wife's inability
to do so. She could hardly manage the first child but seems
to have been able to do a little better by the second one.
By the time she finally came to the hospital she was subject
to the symptoms mentioned above, as well as crying spells
and "hysterical" attacks. The patient had, in effect,
totally abdicated the responsibilities of the wife, mother
and homemaker. The husband actually feared that she might
kill one of the children in her frequent fits of uncontrollable rage.

2. Summary of Situational Variables at the Time of Initial
    Study

    There were two major core conflicts identified at the
time of initial study. On the one hand there was a profound oral disturbance which presumably accounted for her
demandingness, narcissism and her inability to be giving.
The second conflict was the phallic-oedipal one which she
managed by having made a hostile identification with a
phallic-aggressive mother. Aside from the clinical evidence
for inferring such a conflict, it should be noted that at
age 20 she had a very intense love affair with a man over
twice her age. When marriage with this man was clearly impossible, she married her husband with whom she had a
stormy honeymoon. She was an extremely narcissistic and
demanding, hostile woman, not content with her role as a
woman, threatened by men, still tied to her father, and
hostile towards her mother. The mother remained a profoundly conflict-instigating factor. The husband was a
conflict trigger in that he represented the forbidden father
figure. The children demanded that she be a mother and
that she be giving to them. She could fulfill none of these
responsibilities. All of the factors around her, husband,
children, home - all of which demanded that she be a giving
women - were intensely conflict-triggering for her. The
marital sexual situation was especially conflict-triggering.
She was frigid, could only have intercourse when she was
intoxicated. Sex was experienced by her as an attack.

    There were no actual stresses in her life, as such,
other than the feedback variety which her own behavior precipitated. There may have been some stress in having come
from a lower socioeconomical level than her husband's.
The drug intake was a stress of a feedback variety.

The husband was very supportive. Not only did he
provide her with a home and financial security but he also
assumed many of the household duties that she should have
taken care of. In this sense he was need-incongruent. In
addition to this, she had full-time hired help. Her husband seemed to have been quite devoted to her and tried
for years to get her treatment but she refused. Hospitalization obviously was a support at the time of initial study.
Opportunities were plentiful for this person. She had a
home, family and a place in the community. They were prominent pillars in their city and there were numerous opportunities for her to grow, mature and find her place, not
only in the home but in the community from which they came.

Clearly the patient's relationship with her mother was
need-incongruent. The mother had experienced this patient
as a difficult child from birth on, and one about whom she
"never knew what was going on." The rest of her life may
be considered to have been need-congruent with the exception of those areas of responsibility which her husband had
to assume for her. She had a husband who was a good provider and apparently a good father, she had children at
home, and social status. Her own conflicts and character
aberrations clashed with these external factors. There was
nothing immutable in her life.

3. Summary of Situational Variables at the Time of Termi-
    nation Study

This patient had less than fifty hours of psychotherapy.
The therapist stated that she developed an immediate transference resistance, seeing the therapist as one of the real
objects of her former life. There were long silences;
there was a continual flood of feeling which made speech
impossible. Her feelings ranged from violent hatred to
positive feelings. The therapist seemed to resemble the
patient's mother in these transference developments. In
short, nothing whatsoever happened in the psychotherapy
insofar as resolution of core conflicts was concerned. She
began missing her hours, she eventually left the hospital
to return home with her husband approximately eight months
after she entered the hospital. The patient, oddly enough,
said she felt so well that she was willing to undertake
the home responsibilities. She went home but was readmitted to the hospital within three months because of her
inability to function in the home.

She resumed psychotherapy. The second round of psychotherapy lasted three months. She was seen only once a

week. Again, nothing was accomplished in the psychotherapy.
Upon leaving the Menninger Foundation hospital and her
psychotherapist, she was transferred to a state hospital.
The patient was essentially the same at termination as she
was at the time of the initial study. She may have been
more suicidal and potentially homicidal at the time of
termination. She threatened the doctor's life, the husband's life, as well as her own. Although somewhat removed
at the time of termination from all of the conflict triggers
listed at the time of initial study, the responsibilities
were all still there. Thus nothing had changed at the time
of termination over the time of initial study. The core
conflicts had not been touched in the slightest and the
husband, home responsibilities, children, as well as the
mother, were all as conflict-triggering as ever.

Stresses were about the same. Supports continued to
be the same, although there was probably by now some talk
of divorce on the part of the husband. In this sense one
must note that the supportive elements in her life were
diminished by virtue of her husband's withdrawal from her.
On the other hand, however, there were greater supports in
the form of the Menninger Hospital and finally the state
hospital. Although talk of divorce might be viewed as a
loss of support, a divorce also would bring with it a sharp
reduction in a number of conflict triggers in her life.
The opportunities for the future were still there, although
not as available to her by any means because of her progressive decompensation. Similarly, the need-congruence
was all potentially there, but she was in no way able to
make use of it. Nothing was immutable in her life.

4. Summary of Situational Variables at the Time of Follow-
    up Study

Unfortunately, we know very little about what happened
to this patient by the time of follow-up. We know that she
was divorced and that the husband had the children. We
don't know whether or not she was living with her mother,
although this is a possibility. We infer, however, that
the mother may have been physically closer to her than prior
to the divorce. Despite the fact the mother was a hateful
person, therefore somewhat stressful as well as conflict-
triggering, she did, on the other hand, manage to stand by
her daughter to a considerable extent. The very fact of
the divorce and the fact that she had lost her home and
her children means that there had been a sharp reduction in
conflict triggers. Whether or not this was coincided by a
diminution of symptoms would be very important for us to

know, but unfortunately we do not know. We do know that
at the time of follow-up the patient was quite paranoid
in her attitude towards her former therapist but she was
not in the hospital and this certainly speaks for something.
Presumably, therefore, she was less symptomatic at the time
of follow-up than she was at the time of termination or at
the time of initial study. We know that the need-congruent
aspects of her existence were diminished. We don't know
what the stresses were in her life. We know that her opportunities were somewhat diminished. Again, there was nothing
immutable in her life.

5. Summary

Although the data in this case is somewhat sparse,
this patient is an example of a woman's inability to master
her responsibilities. Evidence of emotional instability
was clearly present prior to the marriage, but she was not
so symptomatic that she could not get along. It was after
marriage that she began to decompensate. Her symptoms
gained in intensity, not only after marriage but, in particular, after the birth of the first child. This fact
indicates clearly how the demand of the environment that
she be giving and fill the mother's role triggered the
unconscious orality, dependence and narcissism as well as
the oedipal problem of taking mother's place within a family constellation. In short, she finally abdicated all of
her responsibilities as a mother, wife and homemaker and
then eventually shed those responsibilities by provoking a
divorce. She first escaped into the Menninger Hospital on
two different occasions and there, interestingly enough,
apparently became quite improved symptomatically. This
can be explained on the basis of the removal of her conflict triggers. After her second hospitalization she was
transferred to a state hospital. Apparently soon thereafter her husband left her. We don't know what the exact
timing was, but when she was contacted for the follow-up
studies she had already been discharged from the hospital.
One could well imagine that this patient would be more or
less asymptomatic by now. This is a clear example of how
the patient solved her life adjustment by shedding conflict
triggers.

SYNTHESIS OF SITUATIONAL VARIABLES - CASE #9

1. Brief History

    At the time the patient came for treatment she was in
her early forties. She had been referred by psychiatrists
who had attempted to treat her for a brief time. She complained of being unable to sleep, having "hysterics," and
in general was unable to get along in her home with her
husband and child. She was hospitalized at the Menninger
Foundation, given electroshock, and eventually entered expressive psychotherapy for over 300 hours on a three-times-
a-week basis.

    The patient was an only child. Her father died when
she was about two years old; she was then left in the care
of her mother, who entered a professional career and achieved
a high position. The patient saw little of her mother and
was essentially raised by the maternal grandmother whose
influence she strongly felt. This person was a stern, strict,
demanding woman. Violent quarrels ensued between the grandmother and mother because of divergent opinions regarding
the patient's upbringing. She was a precocious child musi-
cally and scholastically, and was scheduled to go to a
school of one of the arts when in her midteens but this did
not materialize because the mother developed cancer. After
the mother's death the patient proceeded to go on to a large
city where she fell in with a Bohemian crowd. These people
fascinated her, but despite this she apparently made a good
social adjustment. In her late teens she met a brilliant
young professional man (whose profession was the same as
her mother's), and upon the insistence of an aunt who was
looking after her she married. This marriage was a failure.
A pregnancy led to abortion, and divorce soon followed.
She returned to her home town to live with her grandmother
and there met her second husband who was allegedly a solid
citizen, son of a wealthy businessman, but a person who
shared none of her Bohemian interests. Soon after their
marriage she experienced abdominal pain and underwent a
bilateral salpingectomy and unilateral oophorectomy. The

145

marriage proceeded on a rather casual plane. She felt tired much of the time and frequently was unable to carry on her wifely duties. They adopted a baby and it was around this event that the patient became noticeably worse and found herself unable to give much, if any, care to the child.

Shortly after adopting the child she and her husband moved to a large city. Her physical symptoms returned in full force after they moved into a small apartment where she would have to do all of her own housework and care for the child. Although she felt weak and helpless she did some volunteer work.

After several years the patient became interested in an employee of her husband. Although the husband was aware of the mutual attraction between his wife and this man, he was not aware of the sexual relationship between them. The husband returned to their former home, leaving his wife in the large city with the adopted child. Details are not too clear, but it seems that the patient was in therapy in the city where she was living sometime during this period. After the husband threatened to divorce the patient, she finally returned home but quickly became severely symptomatic, was seen by a psychiatrist who, in turn, referred her to the Menninger Foundation.

2. Summary of Situational Variables at the Time of Initial Study

The core neurotic problems in this patient seemed to be two in number. On the one hand, there was a profound oral problem; on the other hand, the oedipal theme which manifested itself largely as identity difficulties (rejection of femininity) seemed quite evident. Without question the most significant conflict trigger was the adopted son.

This woman had managed to adjust to marriage, although not very well, but it was not until she adopted the child that she became seriously symptomatic. Note that the earlier pregnancy had led to abortion and eventual removal of her reproductive organs. Following the adoption of the child she not only became more symptomatic but she was unable to care for the child, pick it up, mother it, etc. This interplay of conflict trigger and core conflict caused her to flee from her role as a wife and mother. She was openly promiscuous in the large city, engaged in "Bohemian" pursuits, and badly neglected her child. She was able, however, to remain out of the hospital under these conditions. On the husband's ultimatum, she had to return to

her home city, and it was when she was forced to be a mother
and homemaker that she became symptomatic to the point of
requiring hospitalization. It is clear that the role of
wife and mother activated the unconscious factors which
generated thse symptoms in her.

There were few stresses in her life, although the
husband was a bit dull. He tended to sleep when he came
home in the evening; however, this form of escape undoubtedly related to the kind of woman she was. The supports
were fairly abundant in her life. She had her own circle
of friends; her husband had always been supportive. Opportunities for the future were good. She had the home, potential position in the community, and the child.

With regard to need-congruence, it again appears that
there was much that was need-congruent in her life insofar
as promoting growth and maturation in her was concerned.
She had the child, a husband, and a home. Her husband was
a simple, homeloving man, not given at all to the Bohemian
way of life, and had few artistic interests. The patient,
on the other hand, was more artistically inclined, had
lived around a big-city crowd for a long time, and thus she
had very little in common with him.

3. Summary of Situational Variables at the Time of Termi-
    nation Study

The patient had been hospitalized for about five months
and had had a long series of ECT when she started psychotherapy. Soon thereafter she went into the Day Hospital
and within two years of her termination had begun working
as a volunteer music therapist.

The life situation of this patient was markedly changed
at the time of termination in contrast to the time of the
initial study. Now she was living alone in Topeka, again
having an affair now and then. She was working in the field
for which she had been trained, and she did not have her
husband or child with her. The relationship with the husband rapidly became estranged, divorce was in the air for
about a year, and they finally divorced a few months before
treatment was terminated.

By and large, the conflict triggers were removed at
the time of termination. The assessment of the treatment
by the Treatment Variables team, and our own impressions
gained from the research data, indicates that the core conflicts in this woman were relatively unchanged despite the

psychotherapy. The patient was somewhat symptomatic at
termination. We note that she still had difficulty getting
up in the morning, moped around considerably, let the house
get into a state of disarray, and tended not to take action
unless someone else would initiate it. No stresses were
noted in her life.

The main areas of support were her friends and her work.
She socialized freely, had a number of friends, had a boyfriend or two who were quite interested in her. One particular lover, a blind man, seemed to be especially supportive to her. She eventually came to see that this individual
was not the love of her life, however. Insofar as bringing
out the woman in her, her life was somewhat less need-congruent at the time of termination than it had been at the
time of initial study. She no longer had a husband or child
or home. In another sense, however, her life was considerably more need-congruent for she could live out those interests that had been developed in her for a long time. These
interests refer to her socializing tendencies, her interests
in music, and her interest in a more Bohemian kind of people.
Opportunities for the future were rather good. She had her
profession, and talent which would permit her to develop
in that direction. She had a small inheritance and she was
young enough and attractive enough to marry again provided
her own neurosis did not stand in the way.

4.   Summary of Situational Variables at the Time of Follow-
up Study

The patient lived in Topeka for a long time after terminating her psychotherapy, but began to feel lonely here
and eventually returned to her home town where she obtained
work. She taught music for beginning piano students and
rented a home near her place of work. It should be noted
that she maintained some contact with her former husband
and adopted child. She stated that although she had no
direct responsibility for the youngster, she nevertheless
taxied him around some. By now he had become a teenager
and she felt considerably more comfortable with him. The
patient was considerably freer of symptoms by the time of
follow-up than she had been at the time of initial study.
It should be mentioned, however, that it was still believed
that the core conflicts had not been worked out in any essential way but here, again, there were very few conflict
triggers in her life at follow-up. It should be noted that
the patient was able to marry again and so it could be
supposed that the new husband might be somewhat conflict-
triggering. There is no evidence to make such a statement,

however, because as far as we could tell her marital adjustment was quite good, although there was no child in this,
by now, third marriage of hers. We picked up the thought
somewhere that the man was a latent homosexual although
this is not confirmed. He was somewhat of a Don Juan, however, who had been a bachelor for years and had a girl in
every port.

Supports were quite plentiful. The patient had an
alimony settlement and her new husband was quite well-fixed
financially. Of special note is the fact that this man was
considerably more need-congruent than the former husband
had been as far as interests were concerned. They enjoyed
concerts and a whole range of activities that the patient
never shared with her former husband. Opportunities for
the future were reasonably good. Parenthood was obviously
out of the question.

5. Summary

This case illustrates very nicely the impact of marriage
and, in particular, the impact of parenthood as conflict
triggers. She got along reasonably well in her life adjustments insofar as not being particularly symptomatic was concerned until she married. Her first marriage was a failure
and ended in an abortion and gynecological surgery which
left her sterile. She became symptomatic fairly soon after
she remarried, experiencing fatigue, inability to carry out
her duties and so on but managed, nonetheless, to make a
marginal adjustment. With the adoption of the child she
became markedly worse, had to have psychiatric treatment
in the large city where she lived, began an affair, had to
leave home by going to work, and more or less deserted her
child and husband. The husband eventually left her in the
city, and although the child remained with the patient he
was left pretty much on his own. When her husband forced
her to return to live with him, she was forced into a
highly conflict-triggering situation. Again, under these
external conditions which had such a profound neurotic
meaning for her, she became so sick that she had to be
hospitalized and given electroshock.

Although the therapy certainly helped her in a variety
of ways, it is clear that her psychological improvement also
coincided with the removal of the conflict triggers. She
was markedly improved by the end of therapy and during the
follow-up period was able to marry again. It should be
noted, however, that by the time of the third marriage
there were no longer any expectations of her to be a mother.

In addition, she was able to live out her professional interest, and the man she married was more compatible, shared more interests, and so on. Apparently the challenge of satisfying the needs of a small child, as well as the oedipal conflicts that had remained alive in her, made it impossible for her to succeed with either her first or second marriage. By the time the demands on her to be a mother had disappeared she was able to lead a relatively asymptomatic adjustment and was even able to marry for the third time and presumably make a success of it.

SYNTHESIS OF SITUATIONAL VARIABLES - CASE #10

1. Brief History

At the time of the patient's evaluation she was 30
years of age and single. She was referred by a psychiatrist
who had attempted to treat her by psychotherapy as an outpatient. This failed, and hospitalization was deemed necessary, and it is of note that the patient was brought here
against her will. For two years prior to her seeking psychiatric help the patient had felt that her life was becoming progressively less satisfying to her. She began resorting to barbiturates to help her sleep and forget her
troubles. Her intake of this medication increased progressively so that eventually she was taking huge doses
and on a few occasions had been found to be semicomatose.
Prior to coming to Topeka she had been found wandering
around the halls of her apartment building, confused and
clad only in her undergarments.

Her father was a general practitioner who highly valued
sons and devalued women. So sure that his second child
would be a son, he had already called his relatives notify-
ing of this happy event before he actually knew that he had
a daughter. The parents never got along well and divorced
when the patient was about 17.

The patient apparently identified more with her father
and with men than with women. She, herself, wanted to become a physician but was talked out of it by her father who
insisted that the woman's place was in the home. As a
compromise she took up laboratory work. She took up this
work harboring the fantasy that she would some day find the
cause of cancer. Her emotional difficulties apparently
dated back to the time of the parents' separation. She
became depressed at this time, apparently because of that
event; she found herself unable to carry on with her school
work and made attempts to get her parents to reconcile but
failed. She managed to rally, however, returned to
school, was successful in her classwork, and to some extent

151

in her social adjustment, but eventually was dismissed from
school for reasons that are not clear. There is some suggestion in the history that this might have been due to
homosexual activity. Trained as a medical lab technician,
she secured work in cancer research and also enrolled in
night school at the university. She would have graduated
with an A.B. degree had she not had to enter the hospital.
Working as a lab technician and going to school sharply
limited her social life. However, she felt she was not
ready for marriage for she felt unsure of herself as a
woman and prospective mother. She worried a great deal
about feelings of immaturity and indecision, and was beset
with fear that she would marry the wrong man. Her mannish-
ness had been noted by various psychiatrists who had treated
her.

2. Summary of Situational Variables at the Time of Initial
    Study

    This patient lived with her mother on and off follow-
ing the parental divorce. It is evident from the history
that the patient's mother had a depreciated opinion of
women, and it is clear that the patient's father felt this
way.

    The core conflicts that were delineated were, on the
one hand, a fierce competitiveness with men and, on the
other, her character makeup seems to have been derived in
part from an identification with the mother. The end result was that she experienced herself as a second-rate
person, as a woman who compensated for these feelings with
strong masculine strivings. The oedipal basis for her unsuccessful efforts to establish femininity is obvious. The
patient did not fully identify herself with women nor did
she have a good object (the mother) with whom she could do
so. She tended to try to make herself into a boy in order
to gain her father's love. In order to have the loving
father she identified herself with him. Dependency strivings appeared to play some role in her neurosis and character disturbance. She continued to live with her mother,
and one can speculate that this fulfilled the dependency
but also permitted her to live out a kind of masculinity
(take the father's place) in relation to the mother. The
most obvious conflict triggers were the parents. A very
powerful potential conflict trigger was the demand to be a
woman, something she wanted but feared she could not do.
The father's derogatory attitude towards women was stressful. The mother attempted to be helpful but was too per-
missive actually. This might be viewed as stressful. She

had taken up with a Bohemian group of people. This way of
life might also be considered somewhat stressful. Her
physical appearance was stressful; she was described as un-
attractive, having a large head, short extremities and a
masculine appearance.

The supports in her environment were few in number.
Her parental family, of course, had tried to help her through
her illness, and the mother had given her a place to live.
Her work had been supportive. Little in this patient's
life could be considered need-congruent from the point of
view of helping her develop her own femininity. To live
with the mother certainly was not. The absence of a man
in her life was a large lacuna in the environment. Her
work was need-congruent for those elements of her personality which demanded that she do something very important
in life. This aspect of her nature seemed to be derived
largely from her conflicts, however. On balance, her life
situation was not very need-congruent. Opportunities for
the future existed. It was always possible for her to
marry but her unattractiveness limited her possibilities.
She could always go on with her work if she chose and were
able. Her opportunities for the future were limited some
by her illness.

3. Summary of Situational Variables at the Time of Termi-
    nation Study

This patient began psychotherapy and was treated for
over 200 hours. She made good progress during the treatment. She left the hospital, went into Day Hospital, and
then took up private residence after she had worked for
about a month. She had finished her college work and married approximately three months prior to the termination
of her treatment. The therapist was opposed to this marriage because of his belief that the patient was acting out.
It should also be noted that prior to the marriage the
patient had made some changes towards femininity. She began to dress differently, she developed strong erotic feelings for the therapist, and it was probably at the height
of this development in the treatment that she displaced
her affects and wishes and made an object choice. The man
she picked was a passive man who had been homosexual. Her
therapist described him as a "passive castrated man" whom
the patient dominated just as she attempted to dominate
(and outwit) the therapist. In fact, the therapist referred
to this whole episode as having been outmaneuvered by the
patient. Therefore, although the marriage had some of the
earmarks of heterosexuality, the role reversal and the

acting out aspects of the event would indicate that in
fantasy the patient was living out her domineering, masculine tendencies, and to a lesser degree some feminine tendencies.

The core conflicts presumably remained about the same;
however, the events just described suggest that there may
have been some slight resolution of the nuclear problem.
Two conflict triggers were somewhat removed. These are the
two parents. Not only was the patient more physically removed from her parents by virtue of the active efforts of
the personnel of the Foundation, but the attitude of the
parents had changed towards her somewhat, particularly the
father's attitude. She complained, however, that the mother
was still attempting to interfere and control her and the
patient seemed to do little about it. This indicates that
the mother was still conflict-triggering. Although there
was little direct evidence, it seems that there may have
been some difficulty in the marriage. Therefore it might
be reasonable to rate the husband as a mild conflict trigger
although at the time of termination there was very little
actual evidence for this.

The parents were still somewhat stressful although
their attitudes had softened considerably. The husband had
periodic bouts of alcoholism which may be considered to
have been stressful. Supports were rather plentiful. The
father's attitude toward the marriage was very supportive
and the mother had maintained her steadfast, although somewhat interfering, interest in the patient. The marriage
and her work were supporting. There were a number of
friends and co-workers who were also very supportive to the
patient. Opportunities for the future seemed rather good.
She could always continue working. She could have children if she were able. Need-congruence is perhaps the most
interesting element in this patient's environmental interaction. In one sense the husband was hardly need-congruent
at all. He was a very passive, meek, castrated, homosexual
man, who could hardly bring out the woman in the patient.
There was a blend of femininity and masculinity in each
person.

4. Summary of Situational Variables at the Time of Follow-
    up Study

During the follow-up period the patient terminated
her work and became pregnant two months later. However,
she miscarried in another two months. She did eventually
bear a full-term child. The husband had remained sober up

to the time of his graduation but then went on a spree to
celebrate. The husband's treatment terminated, at which
point both the patient and her husband moved to another city
where the husband planned to attend graduate school. Some
post-follow-up indicates that the husband left the patient.
It is interesting to note that after the christening of
the child he disappeared for a time, presumably for several
months. Subsequent information, however, indicates that
he returned to the patient.

During the follow-up interviews the patient complained
that her husband was too demanding sexually. They quarreled
some but the marriage was apparently holding together, but
her lack of interest in housekeeping led to some arguing
between them. The relationship of the parental family had
improved during the follow-up period. The patient, interestingly enough, now got along better with her father than
with her mother.

Although the marriage, despite the subsequent separation that we know about, seemed stable, there were quarrels
which always ended by the husband's apologizing and crawl-
ing back to the wife like a bad little boy. Evidently
part of the reason the marriage had managed to survive was
the husband's acquiescence to his wife and he frequently
said, "She knows best." When his hostility towards her
built up, he turned to alcohol. It is noteworthy, however,
that most of the symptoms that brought her to treatment
(this refers to the addiction, depression, and so on) were
gone by follow-up. The aggressivity in her personality was
still present; however, she had been able to marry and make
a home and become pregnant. This would indicate that some
change in the core problem was accomplished during the
psychotherapy. On the other hand, it should be noted that
the parents, who were major conflict triggers, were much
more remote in the patient's life at follow-up. The marital
sexual relationship, however, was a conflict trigger for
it is quite evident that this patient could not fully step
into the woman's role. She avoided sex, minimized its importance, was probably frigid. She dominated her husband,
and so on. There were no stresses to speak of except the
husband's drinking which occurred episodically.

Supports were many. The parental family, particularly
the father, was simply overjoyed by the patient's marriage.
She was involved in church work, had a number of friends,
had a home, and was accepted on many fronts. Opportunities
were plentiful. Need-congruence was moderate only. She
did have a husband and a home, but he wasn't much of a man

and in this sense was not need-congruent for the feminine potential in her. There was a remarkable neurotic blend between the patient and her husband.

5. Summary

At the beginning of treatment this patient was, in a manner of speaking, more man than woman. She depreciated femininity and although identified to some extent with her mother, the mother also had depreciated femininity. She clearly had identified with her father, was very competitive with her brother and, indeed, had sought to develop her personality and her life along masculine lines. Although there is nothing masculine about being a medical laboratory technician, the meaning she attached to the job, namely becoming an expert and doing something great such as finding the cause of cancer, is evidence of her depreciation of femininity and her appreciation of masculinity. She had strong homosexual leanings and had probably been involved in a few overt affairs. She was living with her mother and undoubtedly derived a lot of dependent gratification there and, at the same time, was also taking over the father's role with the mother. However, there was enough woman in her that she was dissatisfied with the kind of life she was living. She eventually became depressed and took barbiturates in order to help her maintain her equilibrium.

Two major events would appear to account for the happy changes that took place in this patient. For one thing, the Foundation helped her extricate herself from her entanglement with her mother and father. In one letter from the hospital doctor the parents were told in no uncertain terms to get out of the patient's life. Thus we see that these two major conflict triggers were progressively pushed away from her. At the same time the therapist undoubtedly made some kind of a dent in the nuclear problem. Certainly a strong positive erotic transference developed towards the therapist. The underlying meanings were, on the one hand, the blossoming femininity and, on the other hand the patient was probably attempting to demonstrate her superiority under the guise of a developing femininity. What she did in essence, according to the therapist, was outmaneuver him and get married too soon. The man she picked was himself a homosexual, passive and essentially castrated. It appears, then, that she left treatment before she became fully a woman. Even so, this was a rather remarkable shift because the patient did marry, did get pregnant, and did ultimately have a child. The husband, curiously enough,

did complete his education, and although he deserted the
family for a time after the birth of their child, he apparently returned to the patient and the child.

The outcome, then, would seem to have three major
elements in it. Some major conflict triggers were removed;
the patient resolved enough of her core problems that she
could marry; and the man she married blended with her own
incompletely developed feminine personality. In short, the
point this patient reached in her treatment was an equilibrium which may prove to be successful. How successful
it will be in terms of furthering the maturation and healthy
development of the child remains for the next generation
to see.

SYNTHESIS OF SITUATIONAL VARIABLES - CASE #11

1. Brief History

This patient was a 30-year-old married housewife and former nurse when she came for treatment. She was the only child of parents who apparently had never established a good marital relationship. The patient believed that during her early years her mother was never happy; she complained constantly, was picky, and nothing was right for her, no one could please her. In the patient's eyes, the father was mostly conspicuous by his absence but was considered to be consistent, loving and kindly and, of the two parents, the more understanding. The patient's father, according to the patient's husband, was a passive, weak individual who left home when the pressures from his wife became excessive. His absences were supposedly fishing or hunting trips and on one occasion, when the patient was nine years old, he was gone for two years "for business reasons." He invariably returned, but his pattern of leaving for extended periods of time persisted through the years. The patient remembered wishing that her parents were closer together but she always felt that the mother chose her for close interpersonal relations over the father.

Having lived on a farm most of her life the patient, after much pleading on her part, persuaded her parents to move into town. It was while she was in junior high school that she became aware of her nervousness for the first time. This took the form of stuttering, anxiety, withdrawal from social contacts, and severe picking of her nails and fingers. She completed nurses training feeling that she had "for once in her life done something on her own." She enjoyed this training, studied hard and did quite well, and she was successful as a nurse after graduating.

After a courtship of approximately a year she married her husband, who was then a medical student, and again she felt she had done something worthwhile when she married. She claimed that the initial phase of their marital

158

adjustment was satisfying to them both. However, approximately a year and a half after marriage, in the course of
discussing sex one evening, she asked her husband whether
or not he had ever had premarital sexual relations. In
response to his affirmative reply she felt hurt, shaken,
lonely and let down. It was as though "a beautiful dream"
had been shattered. She became hostile and antagonistic
towards her husband, repeatedly bringing up the question
of his premarital sexual relations, pressing him for details,
and always harping. Her distress apparently subsided some,
and during the time she was carrying her first child she
felt unusually well and untroubled. Almost immediately
following the delivery she suffered a return of her old
doubts about her husband and her self-doubts; her anxiety
reappeared, and her hostility towards her husband returned
with renewed force. Much strife developed in the family.

After attempting several jobs which satisfied neither
her husband nor her, he opened a general practice where he
remained for a number of years. Following the birth of a
second son the symptomatic patters that had emerged after
the birth of the first reappeared. Not only did she have
her own emotional disturbance to contend with, but she
noted that her husband was withdrawing from her. She felt
that neither of them was doing right by their children.
Friction within the family increased; she grew further and
further from her husband, and upon his insistence she
sought psychiatric care. After hospitalization for eight
weeks she returned home symptomatically improved, but when
she learned that her husband had confided in his office
nurse about his personal problems she suffered a return of
all of her previous symptoms in exaggerated form. She
questioned her husband's fidelity constantly, now believing
that he was unfaithful to her. She had difficulty managing
the children. Finally, in desperation, she accepted the
recommendation that she come to the Menninger Foundation
for an evaluation. By "accident" she became pregnant for
the third time during this period just prior to coming for
treatment.

2.   Summary of Situational Variables at the Time of Initial
     Study

The patient was never hospitalized, and shortly after
her evaluation she began psychotherapy. She was in the
Day Hospital half-time, however, and worked the other half-
time. Her psychotherapy ended when her therapist left the
employ of the Foundation. She was evaluated at that time
for psychoanalysis and this was begun. She was in analysis

for a total of 891 hours.

The core conflicts were primarily at two levels. There was the oral dependent, demanding, narcissistic core (apparently her infantilizing relationship with her mother never allowed her to have adequately given up this libidinal position). The second conflictual level was the phallic-oedipal one.

The conflict triggers in this patient's life are quite clear. Although we don't know what was going on in her life during the seventh grade when symptoms appeared, it appears that the upsurge of sexuality during puberty resulted in social anxiety. It is evident that living intimately with a man in marriage served as a conflict trigger and caused her to ask the question, the answer to which shattered her "dream." This refers to her discovery that the husband had been with another woman prior to his marriage to her. Interestingly, the patient felt quite well when she was pregnant. Immediately after the birth of her child the family constellation became even more conflict-triggering; the patient became much worse symptomatically. The birth of the second child again added to the conflict-triggering environment and, finally, the conflict trigger which broke the camel's back was the realization that the husband had confided his troubles to his office nurse. At this point the patient was unable to stay in her environmental situation any longer and took flight, first to a hospital and then to Topeka.

By the time the patient began treatment she had already placed some physical distance between these conflict triggers and herself. Conflict triggers were the husband (and his nurse confidant), the children, the demand on her to be a mother, homemaker, wife. In addition to these factors triggering her oedipal conflicts, all of these same factors placed demands on her that she be a giving person rather than one who is given to. The mother was considered conflict-triggering in that she kept alive the infantile tie (the oral dependent problem), as well as the oedipal guilt. The major stress, and the only one at the time of initial study, had to do with being separated from her husband and at the same time pregnant.

Supports were plentiful; she, of course, had the support of treatment; her husband supported her financially; and she had always known that, despite the gulf between her and her mother, the mother would help her materially if she needed it. Her occupation as a part-time nurse was

quite supportive since she had always enjoyed this work.
Opportunities for the patient seemed plentiful; she could
either develop professionally or she could develop as a
mother and wife, provided her illness could be worked out.
The patient's mother, despite her supportive aspects, was
considered to be highly need-incongruent in that she tended
to inhibit the patient's maturation; that is, she tended to
infantalize her. We don't know too much about the husband
as a person, but it does not seem that their interests or
character traits were of such a nature as to make them in-
compatible. They had once found quite a lot of happiness
together and so we must assume that he was need-congruent
in a personal sense, and offered her a need-congruent environment in that she was provided the opportunity for
developing as a mother, woman, wife, homemaker, and member
of the community. There were no immutable factors noted
at the time of initial study.

3. Summary of Situational Variables at the Time of Termi-
    nation Study

    During the patient's treatment her husband announced
that he wanted to divorce her. About the time that her
husband stated his wish for a divorce, she returned home
with a statement from her therapist attesting to her ability to care for her children. She did not want a divorce,
but, rather, desired a reconciliation. After her return to
Topeka, psychoanalysis was considered more seriously and
she began this form of treatment. It should be noted that
undertaking psychoanalysis in Topeka separated her from her
husband and children.

    By the time she completed her psychoanalysis she was
considerably less symptomatic; her analyst believed that
she gained good insight into many of her mental mechanisms
as well as the genetic roots of her personality and her
emotional disturbance. It should be noted, however, that
her manner during the court hearings was believed to have
contributed to the loss of all but one of her children.
Also worthy of note is the fact that she seemed to show very
little response to having actually lost her children. The
patient reacted to the former husband's second wife in the
same way that she had reacted all of her life to her mother.
About this other woman, she had the thought, "She has me
under her thumb."

    Despite the psychoanalyst's assertion that the patient
was a changed person, it is very difficult to accurately
assess the state of her core conflicts after treatment. She

certainly gained insight into her neurosis and into the
mechanisms she used for managing it. There can be no doubt
that her opinion of herself changed some, some of her symptoms abated, and psychological tests indicated that her
anxiety tolerance had increased considerably. At termination, however, the patient was an unhappy person; a state
which is easy to understand in view of the loss of her
family. Most notable of all with regard to situational
variables, however, is the fact that she was much freer of
conflict triggers at the time of termination than she had
been at the time of initial study.

All of those factors which were designated as conflict-
triggering were now removed, with the sole exception of her
one small child; but even here she was not around this child
all the time, having gone back to work. The patient's
father had died and this removed another conflict trigger.
Although the mother was still alive, she lived quite some
distance from the patient. We are unable to attribute her
symptomatic improvement to the resolution of core conflict
despite what the analyst said about her having gained a
great deal of insight. Other than having to live alone
and provide for herself to some extent, the fact of having
lost her family was a stress in its own right.

Supports were moderate. The husband had kept her in
treatment and was paying her a reasonable alimony settlement; the mother had continued to contribute to her financial support and offered personal support as well, although
this had been hard for the patient to accept. Opportunities
for this woman were somewhat limited by now. She, of course,
could develop professionally and work full-time as a nurse.
Opportunities along these lines were fairly abundant. On
the other hand, to remarry and have an established family
life was considerably less possible for her at this point.
She was older, had three children, the smallest of whom
was with her. She was not attractive.

Need-congruence from the point of view of helping her
find herself as a woman was considerably diminished. She
had given up all of those factors (husband, home, family
life) which could have helped her consolidate the gains
she may have found through analysis. Her smallest son was
need-congruent in that he gave her an opportunity to be a
mother; but not having a husband or not living in the constellation of a family restricted the need-congruence of
the environment. It may be that the patient's mother
softened some and was in some respects more need-congruent
than at the time of initial study. Again, at the time of

termination there were no immutable factors.

4. Summary of Situational Variables at the Time of Follow-
   up Study

During the follow-up period the patient had moved back
to the city where her mother and other relatives lived. She
worked as a nurse and the mother took care of her smallest
child, but was not enthusiastic about it. The patient
described a very confused period during her stay at home,
a state which improved after she got someone to look after
her child. The patient's low self-esteem continued; she
was, by and large, unhappy and moderately depressed. There
were some hopes of getting her other two children, but
these hopes were eventually shattered by the courts.

Because of her small child's own disturbance and his
need for treatment, she returned to Topeka. Communications
with the therapist and the evaluation of the research team
indicates that this woman was extremely unhappy and lonely.
She was by no means over her illness, although in some ways
she was less sick than at the time of initial study. She
experienced a great deal of social anxiety. She gave
many rationalizations about not being able to find a man.
She doubted her ability to care for her small child properly.
In addition to these more personal problems, she was bitter
about her life situation.

It was our impression, and also that of the Treatment
Variables team, that the patient was still pretty much
caught in her neurotic conflicts. Although there was some
improvement in her relationship with her mother, this relationship was by no means what it should be. Her expectations of her mother still betrayed her dependence and her
submissive attitude towards her. The patient recognized
that she was not willing to assume the role that mother
had wanted her to take. This apparently meant to become a
mature woman herself. At times she had been able to relate
to her mother as woman and not as child. It should be
noted that the mother was not living in Topeka so that, in
fact, most of the conflict triggers were again absent.
She still experienced exquisite loneliness. Having to
function in a responsible capacity before people always
created anxiety in her; presumably her low self-esteem was
triggered by these challenges.

There was some stress in her daily living. She not
only had to be a mother to a child, but also a breadwinner.
Her working arrangements were not the easiest in that she

had to get up rather early in the morning and get her child
ready for the day, and then leave him with the baby-sitter.
Having been a married woman and then having her family life
disintegrate was stressful. Supports were in evidence.
Her ex-husband continued to support her financially and her
work was supporting. She had a few friends who were supportive, one of whom was a quite elderly person who was
obviously a mother substitute. Very little in this woman's
life was need-congruent at the time of follow-up. Her work
was congruent with those aspects of her that were expressed
in her wish to work, but there were no outlets for a full
expression of mothering and wifely intentions.

5. Summary

     This case illustrates a number of things; however, the
most significant from the point of view of situational variables is how some improvement in this patient's psychic
state seemed, in part, to be related to the removal of conflict triggers. The importance of not breaking up a family
in order to treat one'member is clearly illustrated by the
treatment course and outcome. The overall impression from
all of the data is that although the patient gained considerable insight into her personality patterns and attitudes and, to some extent, the genetic roots of her illness,
she by no means resolved her illness. Marked dependence
remained which was reflected, in part, by her having moved
back to Topeka in order to be close to the treating institution and her former therapist. The problem with the
mother was by no means settled, although improved. The
father was dead so it's not possible to ascertain how the
relationship to him might have changed.

     She consciously wished to save her marriage and her
family, and after losing her family she expressed the wish
to remarry. She did not do this, nor did she try very hard,
and we take this as evidence that the oedipal problems were
not fully solved. She could, however, look back into the
strife of her marriage and see that a great deal of it was
her doing, but knowing this and being able to behave differently are not equivalent. Her analyst even observed that
although she gained a lot of knowledge about herself, all
of this insight had yet to be put into action. Therefore,
by one process or another, this patient managed to shed
all of her conflict triggers. In the beginning her illness
convinced the doctors that she was too sick to be treated
elsewhere. She presumably was offered this possibility
but said that she could not leave Topeka. Later in the
analysis she was not transferred to where her husband was,

nor was this even given serious consideration when it became clear that a divorce was pending. We must conclude,
therefore, that the diminished severity of some of her
symptoms is to be accounted for by the removal of some
major conflict triggers. She gave up her family life,
something she could not accept because of its triggering
effect upon her own oedipal and dependent problems.

SYNTHESIS OF SITUATIONAL VARIABLES - CASE #12

1. Brief History

At the time of her evaluation this patient was a 24-
year-old white widow. She was a self-referral whose complaints were depression, irritability, insomnia, occasional
attacks of acute anxiety, worry over raising her children,
constant quarreling with and a distressing hatred of her
mother - all of which appeared subsequent to her husband's
death about a year prior to her coming for treatment. She
also stated that she did not want her second child, and
then listed secondary complaints of low self-confidence
and excessive anxiety in relation to almost everything.

The patient's parents had been married ten years before
their only child, the patient, was born. Her earliest
memories had to do with the fear of being left or punished.
She claimed to have had asthma since the age of two, and
it was the patient's mother, a former nurse, who induced
the patient's father to move the entire family from the
Northeast to the Southwest because of this asthma. Because
of the asthma and some spells that were considered to have
been epileptic, the patient was an overly protected child
from the very beginning, but one who was extremely strong-
willed. She was a shy but popular child in school, having
started at age eight. She knew all the answers and was
considered to be a teacher's pet. The mother never allowed
her to do any of the household duties; and a vivid memory
has to do with the mother telling her at age five that men
were nasty, would abduct, rape and kill her. She was given
to temper tantrums throughout most of her life.

Her main interests were being married and being a
designer. After a year and a half of correspondence with
a pen pal whom she knew from a fraternity-sorority magazine, they married in the late forties when she was 19
and he was 20. She had been living in the Eastern United
States at the time, but due to the mother's insistence she
and her husband moved back to the Southwest where her

166

parents lived.

The patient's husband was a kind, handsome man but one who, presumably, was rather passive. The patient was frigid in the sexual relationship. Her main grievance then was that his work took him away for so many hours, and she was often uneasy when he was away from home. In order to supplement their income the patient worked. A daughter was born. The patient was pregnant a second time when her husband was killed in an accident. Soon thereafter she began to feel in an exaggerated way what she had experienced most of her life. She became more and more unsure of herself, craved help from others for her sorrow, especially from her mother who continuously fell short of the patient's expectations. Although she looked forward to the birth of her second child, her unhappiness and mutual agitation with her mother increased. Apparently her father slapped her, and the parents threatened her with commitment and putting the children up for adoption if she didn't snap out of it. She was called lazy, self-pitying, and a poor Christian by her physician and minister; no one seemed to understand her. She came alone with her two children to Topeka and sought outpatient treatment. This took the form of a psychoanalysis.

2. Summary of Situational Variables at the Time of Initial Study

The Patient Variables team defined the core conflicts in this case as being three in number. The first and most important were those surrounding the oral-aggressive drives. These conflicts were manifested by her demandingness, rages, and tantrums when her gratifications were not forthcoming. A second core area related to her stubbornness, which implies anal difficulties; and a third core area had to do with her phallic sexuality which related to her having identified with her dominant, aggressive, phallic mother. Although the husband's death antedated treatment, the continuing impact of this event was viewed as a conflict trigger. His demise apparently activated the unconscious death wish towards men and separation anxiety.

The death caused another very important and drastic shift in her life. She was thrown back into close proximity with her mother, and it was this relationship which was probably the most conflict-triggering of all. The mother dominated, infantilized, exercised absolute control, all of which activated the patient's conflict centering around submission. The loss of the husband may have had the meaning of the loss of a nurturing object, and thus

some of the deep oral and very early infantile needs may
have been activated. Her dependence made her particularly
vulnerable to the challenge of being the only parent of two
very young children, both of whom were, in fact, dependent
upon her. The mother's dominance activated all of the
oedipal and preoedipal conflicts in relation to the mother
and, although it wasn't so stated at the time of initial
study, the fact that she was thrown back into her parental
home with two children, and being this close to her father,
may have contributed some to the difficulty.

She took the first step towards improving her life by
physically leaving all of these conflict triggers (with the
exception of the loss of her husband) and coming to Topeka
for help. The most obvious stress of all was the recent
death of her husband, and having to be the only parent of
a very small child and one soon to be born. The constant
disharmony between the patient and her mother, although in
part a function of her own unconscious conflicts, certainly
was stressful. The mother, in her own right, was quite a
handful. In fact, she impressed one of us as looking like
Winston Churchill or an English bulldog.

The supports were relatively minimal. She had adequate
finances because of her husband's insurance. There was one
aunt who was stabilizing and helpful, but other than that
she was on her own. She found very little solace from her
parents. The opportunities for her seemed rather plentiful
for she was a young, bright woman, who could either marry
or pursue a career. The most obvious need-congruent aspect
of her life was the fact that she was already launched in
the direction of motherhood but, of course, the fact that
she didn't have a husband made her life rather need-incongruent. Having had to live in her mother's home was need-
incongruence in the extreme.

3.   Summary of Situational Variables at the Time of Termi-
     nation Study

This patient was seen in psychoanalytic treatment for
over 800 hours. It is interesting to note that the analyst
indicated the bulk of the analytic work centered on her
oedipal struggles, on the idiosyncratic manifestations of
her penis envy, and dependency striving and their relation
to her object choices. The patient was quite committed to
her treatment and apparently was satisfied with the outcome.
During the course of treatment she had had her second child,
had obtained an undergraduate and a graduate degree. She
was planning to find work after treatment terminated. It

should be noted that the patient had desired to be in the
same kind of profession as her analyst. The analyst noted
that what wasn't analyzed away in this patient was penis
envy.

The patient, at termination, still felt cheated and
shortchanged; however, she controlled these feelings better
by termination. The analyst also noted that he did not
know how good her sex life was, that she wasn't married
and he considered it quite possible that she was sexually
inhibited, but probably not as much as before. She had no
sexual affairs during the analysis. The analyst wasn't
sure she would remarry. In short, this patient was considerably healthier at the time of termination. She was
able to be with her children some of the time, she found
some sublimated outlets for her envy of men. She was also
physically removed from her mother and father, and had
worked through the loss of her husband - all had been conflict triggers.

A conflict trigger that remained was living alone,
which undoubtedly triggered her loneliness and dependence,
but she was by no means as isolated from life as she had
been for now she had professional associates and friends,
not to mention the mothering significance of the Menninger
Foundation. Notably absent was a husband and the demand
that she be a woman in the full sense of the word. In
fact, she was relegating a good bit of the care of her
youngsters to hired help. On the other hand, the patient
did describe an improved relationship with her mother, but
in the same breath she noted that she and mother were many
hundreds of miles apart. The mother's behavior had softened
some.

It is evident that the core conflicts had been resolved
to some extent, and it is equally evident that the conflict triggers were fewer at the time of termination than
at the time of initial study. Her symptoms were, accordingly, considerably less.

Other than having to be responsible for two small
children, there were no stresses in her life. Supports
were fairly plentiful; she now had a profession, she was
living close to the Menninger Foundation, the mother's
attitude had softened some, and there were adequate finances. The opportunities were still plentiful for her.
She could grow either professionally or in the direction
of mother and wife if she were able or chose to. The
parents were somewhat more need-congruent now than they

were at the time of beginning treatment. The mother did
not now try to impose herself upon the patient as much as
she used to. The children were need-congruent in that they
could bring out the woman and mother in her. The fact that
there was an absence of an ongoing heterosexual relationship made her environment not as need-congruent as it
might have been.

4. Summary of Situational Variables at the Time of Follow-
   up Study

During the two-year follow-up period the patient worked
and was self-supporting. Although she had some trouble with
her boss, a person who, in fact, was somewhat like her own
mother, she managed to survive at work and did a creditable
job. She was courted by a widower with several preadoles-
cent children. After a courtship of a few months they were
married. As soon as she met this man she began having
anxiety attacks, and by the time of the follow-up study
she was having the worst attacks of her life. She was
frigid sexually and she felt very inferior to his first
wife. Her parents felt that she was taking on too much,
and his parents thought that he was marrying beneath him.

The notes of the patient's analyst, who took her back
into analysis, made it clear that our estimation of the
degree of resolution of the core conflicts at the time of
termination was inaccurate. This woman had by no means
overcome her oedipal problems, and certainly she had not
overcome her problems revolving around submission, overdetermined as this conflict was. She began having much
difficulty in the marriage, and by the time of follow-up
there were real factors in her life which became conflict
triggers by virtue of the fact that there was much core
conflict remaining in her. The core conflicts were clearly
oedipal, on the one hand, and the penis envy conflict on
the other. We note, for instance, that she had an anxiety
attack right after she had been alone with a young boy.
The associations in connection with this attack were clearly
oedipal in nature, and in part revolved around the feeling
that she, the patient, could never adequately replace the
husband's first wife. It is our hunch that she had, therefore, displaced her sexuality on her stepson and experienced
the anxiety in relation to him. In any event, it is clear
that the core conflicts had not been resolved and that the
surest test of her state of health had been making a home,
being a wife and mother, and that she was unprepared to do
this because of her unresolved conflicts. The patient was
extremely troubled by taking the feminine responsibility in

the marriage, and there was a parallel loss of the sense
of autonomy in that relationship - she was not as free as
she used to be.

There were a number of supports in the patient's life;
she still had some income of her own and now, of course,
she had a husband and her own family life. In addition to
this, she had the profession which she could use if she
needed to. The stressful elements were the several children for whom she had responsibility. It should be noted
that she did not have any hired help.

Although her environment was now much more conflict-
triggering than it was at the time of initial study or at
the time of termination, it was also, at the same time,
more need-congruent. The fact that the patient went back
into analysis after the follow-up evaluations were done
makes it evident that she wanted to resolve the conflicts
which prevented her from adapting to her new need-congruent
environment.

5. Summary

Although this patient was not particularly symptomatic
at the time she was married to her first husband, it is
interesting to speculate whether she might not have become
so in time. We can say this now in view of her reaction
to her second marriage. The fact that she became symptomatic after her husband's tragic death can be explained by
the conflict-triggering and also stressful effect that
his death had upon her. The death was an actual loss; it
doubled her responsibilities and it also activated the
marked dependence in her. It seems reasonable, in light
of the subsequent marked penis envy that emerged in the
analysis, that the husband's death provided a fulfillment
for the unconscious death wishes she harbored towards men.
His death then threw her back into her mother's influence,
thus contributing further to her neurosis by activating
the submission conflict centering around the aggressive,
dominant, phallic mother.

Subsequent data make it clear that another reason for
her symptomatic worsening originally had to do with being
placed so close to her father with two children of her own.
This undoubtedly activated her oedipal fantasies. She escaped from a good number of her conflict triggers by coming
to Topeka, and in this relatively conflict-triggering free
environment she launched into a lengthy analysis. Instead
of making tentative heterosexual involvements during the

analysis, she seemed to develop in an opposite direction; that is to say, she developed sublimated outlets for her penis envy and, although she worked on her relationship with her mother and gained awareness of her conflicts, she by no means resolved them, her Oedipus complex in particular. This became glaringly evident by the time of the follow-up study. She had married during the follow-up period and was beginning to experience more intense anxiety than she ever had before. Marked interpersonal difficulties soon appeared in the marriage; she found herself frigid.

SYNTHESIS OF SITUATIONAL VARIABLES - CASE #13

1. Brief History

The patient was a teenager when he came for his outpatient evaluation. The precipitating reason for the re-
ferral was the patient's bizarre behavior at school.

The patient was the older of two children. He first
saw a psychiatrist at the age of six because of severe
headaches. Little information exists about his preschool
relationships except that the mother always felt close to
him and in many ways bent over backwards to meet his needs.
Because he was so much faster intellectually than his
classmates there was little for him to do but daydream and
challenge his teachers. He entered a private school at
the age of thirteen.

He always felt different because he never felt that
he was either a Christian (his mother's religion) or a
Jew (his father's religion). His school difficulties continued, and on one occasion he had to drop a subject because he had the belief that his teacher was stabbing him
in the back following his classroom discussion.

A year prior to his coming to the Menninger Foundation
he was seen by a psychiatrist because of complaints of
inner emptiness and feelings of unreality. He was isolating himself in his room, and was frequently angry and depressed. Because his doctor felt he was on the verge of
a schizophrenic break, the boy was placed on small doses
of Miltown and encouraged to visit Europe that summer.
This he did, but after returning to school in the fall he
began feeling that the left side of his body was falling
asleep; he felt small in a big world, and that people were
looking down at him. Instead of attending to his studies
he secluded himself with other boys and discussed philosophy. He was finally withdrawn from the school and brought
for treatment. His evaluation noted the struggle for eman-
cipation from his parents and his search for a personal

173

identity. It also became clear that he suffered from a
severe illness.

2. Summary of Situational Variables at the Time of Initial
Study

     The patient came from an extremely unconventional home.
There was little discipline or order in his home and, in
addition, there were the mixed cultural influences of the
parents. Although the central conflict in the patient was
defined as an identity problem, it also seemed likely that
there were oral, anal and, especially, phallic aspects to
the identity disturbance. The fact that he had fears about
homosexuality, had a dominating, castrating mother and a
passive, somewhat effeminate father, certainly suggested
that he had not resolved his oedipal difficulties and that
his maturation and, in particular, his identity formation
suffered as a result.

     The conflict trigger at the time of initial study was
the demand from life that he become something - not only a
man, but a man with an occupation or a professional identity.
It is clear that both of his parents were still conflict-
triggering. The tie between the boy and his parents was
strong. It was noted, for instance, that they visited him
every weekend at school until his boredom with their visits
led to a reduction in their frequency. The mother was infantilizing, overcontrolling and subtly castrating, and the
father did not offer him the kind of direction he needed.
His behavior at school was an effort on the one hand to
emulate his highly unconventional parents (he had a bar in
his room, he dressed in a sloppy and outlandish manner and
carried on discussions about philosophy) and, at the same
time, represented a rebellion against the demands from the
environment that he become a mature man.

     The overall environmental milieu in which this boy
grew up was considered to be stressful. His mother constantly expected a high intellectual performance from him.
Even though the parents were stressful, and certainly
conflict-triggering, they also provided a great deal of
support. This support was probably more of a material
nature than personal, but nonetheless supports were fairly
abundant. Clearly, the hospital was the most supportive
element of all for him at the time of the initial study.

     Not only were the parents conflict-triggering, they
were highly need-incongruent. The quality of their life
went beyond uniqueness. He was poorly equipped to fit in

anywhere, but in a more specific sense his father's passivity, frailty, and tempermental, sensitive nature hardly was
need-congruent. Similarly, the mother's infantilizing tendencies and her own bizarre behavior impeded the maturational processes in him. Small wonder, then, that he not
only felt that he did not fit in, a feeling derived in part
from his oedipal struggles no doubt, but in fact he did not
fit in anywhere with his environment because of the personal
environment with which he had become identified.

3.   Summary of Situational Variables at the Time of Termi-
     nation Study

This patient was admitted to the hospital and later
became a full-time Day Hospital patient. From there he
went to a foster home. During the latter part of his stay
in Topeka he was living in a home with two other boys. He
was seen in psychotherapy for less than 100 hours, three
times a week. His treatment was terminated because the
father was no longer willing to support it financially. He
wanted the boy to return to the East to be with the family
and go to Europe with them later.

Psychological tests made at termination indicated considerable tightening up of ego controls. Anxiety tolerance
was somewhat greater. The treatment team noted that there
was still considerable anxiety. Apparently there were both
phobic and obsessional symptoms; withdrawal to daydreaming
and sleepiness seemed to have diminished some. The patient
was less bizarre, somewhat less grandiose, but in many respects he was very much the way he was when he came for
treatment. In general, however, it could be said that he
had improved and that his symptoms had quieted down some.
He was in better control of himself. He tried less to make
a display of his bizarreness.

The core conflicts at termination seemed to be essentially unchanged. In the course of his treatment his very
close attachment to his mother became more apparent. His
high ideals became exposed but also his rebelliousness about
reaching those ideals and his inability to really try to
attain them. This problem seemed to reflect his fear of
accomplishment. Any kind of challenge to be successful was
conflict-triggering; his parents continued to be conflict-
triggering. His environment in Topeka was probably the most
need-congruent that he had ever been in and it seemed that
having lived here and having been exposed to normal, or at
least seminormal, people may have had some beneficial effect
on him in that a more favorable environment was available

for him to straighten out his identity struggles. There were
no real stresses. Supports were fairly good. He had the
Day Hospital, foster parents, and he had a therapist and a
house doctor, both of whom liked him. The parents continued
to support him financially up to a point and then insisted
that he leave Topeka. Opportunities were quite good for
this boy. His parents had enough money to educate him
along any line that he might choose. There were many contacts that the family could provide.

4. Summary of Situational Variables at the Time of Follow-
up Study

During the period from termination to follow-up the
patient progressively extricated himself from his parents.
For a time he stayed with his parents, traveled with them
in Europe and did very little, if anything. They didn't
get along well together and he became progressively aware
of the entanglements between all of them and he resolved,
upon returning to the United States, that he would leave
home. He did this eventually and claims not to have received even financial support from his parents for a time.
Later it came out that he received some financial help
from his parents to supplement his own earnings. He apparently had various odd jobs. He became allied with a teacher
and saw in this person someone with whom he could identify.
Not only did he identify with this man but he also seemed
to make a father figure out of the father of his girl friend.
These people had apparently been friends of his parents for
a long time. During the first phase of his breakaway from
his family he sank quite low in his own adjustment. He
stayed with "beatniks," took marijuana and ate peyote.

By follow-up this patient was living an independent
existence, apparently feeling much better as a result of it.
During the course of the follow-up interviews the intensity
of his attachment to his mother became apparent. This was
a relationship, however, which he changed considerably by
breaking away. In fact, he claimed to see his parents very
seldom. Symptomwise the patient seemed to have changed considerably. No mention was made of any recent migraine,
fainting, temper tantrums, somatic complaints, difficulties
in eating or sleeping. Phobic symptoms, obsessional symptoms
and suicidal ruminations were not in evidence or were absent. Daydreaming continued to some extent. Feelings of
estrangement probably occurred under severe stress. Loneliness was considerably less. The identity problem was
identified as still being present and severe, as were the
sexual difficulties.

The work inhibition was considerably less. Psychological tests revealed the patient's thinking was no longer
flagrantly peculiar nor as expansive. There was no evidence
of psychosis. These changes, according to the psychologist,
could be accounted for by constriction, denial and avoidance and, although more firmly integrated, there was evidence
of vulnerability to disorganization.

Core conflicts were by no means resolved. This was
manifested by his more obvious concern about homosexuality
and his inability to feel love feelings for his girl friend.
He frankly stated he dreaded the responsibility of marriage,
although he wanted to marry, fearing that he would be unfaithful to his wife. What seems to have developed by the
time of follow-up is that the bizarre adolescent psychotic
type of ego disorganization that was apparent at initial
study had undergone transformation so that the patient showed
a more classical kind of character disturbance in which
concerns about masculinity appeared more clearly. More
typical neurotic symptoms were appearing, such as anxiety
about responsibility, marriage, sexuality.

The following factors in his environment were conflict-
triggering. First and foremost, it should be noted that
the parents were not as conflict-triggering as before, not
because they were different or because the core conflicts
were resolved but because of the patient's having extricated himself from the entanglements with the parents. They
no longer lived together and there was an unspoken agreement that they would have little to do with each other. He
had shifted his libidinal attachment from his parents to a
girl friend and it was quite clear that the girl had, in
turn, become a conflict trigger for him. This relationship coincided with the development of fears about homosexuality, masculine inadequacy, dread of responsibility,
and so on.

His life wasn't too stressful by the time of follow-up.
Supports were there. He knew his parents were standing
behind him silently and they were, in fact, giving money
towards his living expenses. He had a number of friends
from whom he mooched, and the parents of his girl friend
obviously served as parent surrogates.

Opportunities continued to be good although they were,
perhaps, somewhat limited by the boy's unconventional makeup.
It would be hard for him to find a place in a business,
for instance, and it seemed most likely that he would carve
out a life for himself along some unconventional lines.

His work with his teacher was perhpas the most need-congruent aspect of his life. Also need-congruent were the
parents of his girl friend and, of course, his girl friend
was need-congruent. All of these factors had a stabilizing,
maturation-producing effect upon him. That he had gotten
away from his parents and saw so little of them contributed
to the need-congruence of his life. That he had a tendency
to run with beatniks, of course, suggests that a portion of
his environment was quite need-incongruent, but the picture
we get is that he was progressively extricating himself from
these kinds of involvements.

5. Summary

     This patient developed classic dependent and oedipal
conflicts. In addition to this, however, this patient's
parents were highly unusual and unconventional people and
both quite ill. Therefore, not only did the patient develop
the above-mentioned core conflicts, but he developed an ego
disturbance as well. At the time of adolescence he became
quite ill. He was unable to work and succeed, and there
was marked social anxiety. Probably to some extent as a
result of his stay in Topeka, and possibly because of his
own awareness of where the difficulties lay, this boy
gradually began to disentangle himself from the highly
conflict-triggering, need-incongruent environment that his
parents provided him.

     Having made the break from them, he floundered for
awhile, sank quite low in his social adjustment, but gradually seemed to latch onto some serious work and at the
same time affiliated himself with some people who had a
stabilizing identity-producing effect on him. His turbulent
intrapsychic condition began to crystallize out so that the
more classical masculinity-femininity, aggressivity-passiv-
ity struggles began to appear in him. He developed classic
neurotic fears about homosexuality; the love-sex split
appeared and he found himself sexually attracted to a girl
but unable to feel love for her. In making the break from
his parents he found a more need-congruent environment for
himself. The girl, his teacher, and the way of life surrounding these individuals was more need-congruent. Because of
his own unconscious conflicts these environmental factors
were new conflict triggers. The general trend in his life
seemed to be a positive one.

SYNTHESIS OF SITUATIONAL VARIABLES - CASE #14

1. Brief History

When this patient came for treatment she was a 20-
year-old, unmarried college student. She had seen a physician because of attacks of uncontrollable crying, depression, and difficulty in getting along with her fellow
students and teachers. She admitted that she was depressed
and said that she felt the way she had felt at the time of
her mother's death.

The patient was the third child born of a blue collar
worker. The mother was in her late thirties at the time of
the patient's birth. The patient believed, and there is
evidence in the clinical data, that the parents had wanted
a boy and because of this she felt that she was a disap-
pointment to them. She described herself as having always
been a very rebellious person who was never afraid of parental discipline. She frequently would not mind her mother
and seemed not to be swayed by frequent spankings. Apparently there was considerable chronic tension between the
parents. The father was a rebellious man who had great
difficulty getting along with fellow workers and superiors.
As a result of this problem the family moved quite often.

In her early teens she was shocked by the vile language,
the uncouthness of people and the open display of sex. She
stated that it horrified her and that she was constantly
embarrassed, particularly with regard to being razzed about
being such a prude and a "goodie-goodie." She always felt
as though she was an outsider. Despite these feelings, she
was president of the senior class in high school, she had
leading parts in school plays, she was the organist in
church, and generally excelled in music. She belonged to
many clubs and was a recreation leader for some other organization. It was during this time that the mother became
ill and a good deal of the housework fell to her. She
accepted this domestic responsibility but did not like it.
The patient noted something of a personality change during

179

this time; she became more resentful, more aloof, and had a chip-on-the-shoulder attitude. She grew disinterested in the activities of boys and girls her own age and, by and large avoided dating. She had one boyfriend, however, with whom she was extremely provocative and who, because of this behavior on her part, finally jilted her and took up with her worst enemy. In retrospect, she felt that she might have done well to stick with him and marry him. Menstruation had been a great shock to her. Mother had never helped her to understand any aspect of sexuality.

After graduation from high school the patient went to a university for approximately two years. It was during this period that she had her only heterosexual experience. This was with a young man who was about to be married and she, therefore, felt there was no possibility of anything coming of it. This incident occurred about one month before her mother's death.

During the second year in college she became involved in an overt homosexual relationship and for the first time felt that she was really loved by someone. It was because of her unhappiness at school and discontent with herself that she took a summer job. It was during this time that she had her one attempt at heterosexuality. Her mother's impending death caused her to return to her home. The father sent her back to school after the mother's death and homosexual entanglements soon reappeared. She withdrew from her friends, cut classes, became depressed and was having hysterical episodes. Because of the intervention of some school officials, she was placed on probation and psychiatric help was recommended.

2. Summary of Situational Variables at the Time of Initial Study

The core conflicts at the time of initial study were at two levels. On the one hand, there was the oral-dependent attachment to the mother, and on the other hand the oedipal conflicts. Although anal stubbornness and rebelliousness are referred to, it is probable that these behaviors were related to the wish to be a boy and the reluctance to submit to males or to the phallic mother. It is evident that she struggled with a mixed identity problem.

There were a number of conflict triggers at the time she came for treatment. The most pervasive conflict trigger was her wish that she could establish a heterosexual relationship. It should be noted that she had been very

provocative towards the boy who was fond of her and whom
she wished she had married. She became frankly dissociated
for about four days when some boys told her she was in no
position to tell them what to do. It was the mother's
death in particular, however, which probably had the unconscious meaning of opening up the possibility of taking
mother's place with the father, which then sent her head-
long into a defensive homosexual position. She made a
feeble effort to establish a heterosexual relationship, but
was completely unable to sustain this effort.

The stresses at this time in her life were rather
severe. The main stress was the loss of her mother. The
patient, in essence, was an only child because her sibs
were many years older. She had been very dependent upon
the mother. Although the father was somewhat of a distant
man, this very distance itself might be considered somewhat stressful. Certainly very stressful were the homosexual entanglements that the patient got herself into.
Not only did these entanglements violate the social mores,
they violated her own sense of self-esteem, despite the
emotional satisfactions gained and the defensive functions
they may have served.

Supports were minimal. In his own way, the father did
support her; he provided money for school, he paid for treatment and he bought her a car. The teachers and administrators at school were supporting. Her schoolwork and her
fortunate relationship to some of the school administrators
may be considered the only need-congruent forces in her life
at the time she came for treatment.

It was highly need-incongruent for her to be embroiled
in homosexual relationships; there were no boys in her life.
As removed as she was from her father, he hardly had a
positive effect on her. The relationship with him was over-
ridingly conflict-triggering rather than need-congruent.
Opportunities for a young girl such as this were plentiful.
She was bright, attractive, somewhat talented, and certainly
socially competent. Nothing in her life was immutable except for the death of the mother.

3.   Summary of Situational Variables at the Time of Termi-
      nation Study

The patient was treated by supportive-expressive psychotherapy for less than fifty hours. The father had remarried; the patient had graduated from college and she
had begun teaching. She lived with one of her old

homosexual partners.

It is clear from the interviews with the therapist and his supervisor, and from the description of the changes the patient made during treatment, that treatment was nothing but a supportive relationship and that those changes which occurred can be attributed to transference cure and support. Genetic roots were not searched out, and by the therapist's own account he was very passive with her and dealt with her only along supportive lines. It is, therefore, evident that the core conflicts were not altered at all; however, her environmental arrangements were somewhat improved. She now was independent, and by virtue of her job she increased her contacts with her sister who appeared to be taking on a mother role for the patient. Because of her phallic-oedipal conflicts, the heterosexual demand remained a conflict trigger; however, there really was very little of a conflict trigger of this sort in her life for she simply avoided men. Nor were there many opportunities to come into contact with men because of the nature of her life situation - those men who were around were married teachers at her school; she made no efforts to meet eligible bachelors.

Parents were presumably as conflict-triggering as ever; however, the father was less so because he now had a wife, which would tend to exclude the patient from the opportunities with him that she unconsciously believed to exist. There were no stresses in her life, as such, except the continued homosexual entanglements. The religious, ethical, and cultural background of her family was supporting; she had a good education, the father had helped her financially, and gave her a car so she could get to her treatment and school. The stepmother showed evidence of being accepting of the patient. The patient's sister was supportive.

Again, opportunities appeared unlimited; she continued to be attractive, although somewhat mannish in her appearance, and she was bright. Many need-incongruent factors existed in her life, the most notable of which were the homosexual entanglements. These relationships played right into her neurotic needs and did not offer her an exit from her illness. There was nothing in these experiences that promoted growth and maturity; rather, these relationships fed her neurosis at all levels. The therapist noted that her pattern was to be the aggressor, and once having conquered the other woman she slipped into a very dependent role with the partner, obviously fulfilling pregenital neurotic wishes in the relationship. It might be that teaching

was somewhat need-congruent in that the subject she taught
offered her the opportunity to exercise certain feminine
potentialities and interests.

At the time of termination the patient was obviously
feeling better but, as has been noted, she was still mannish
in her appearance and she admitted that she still had difficulty getting anywhere on time. The patient's relationship with her father had improved after he remarried.

4. Summary of Situational Variables at the Time of Follow-
    up Study

Nothing much changed in the patient's life during the
period other than the father having died prior to the follow-
up study. It is of particular interest to note that during
the follow-up evaluation the patient expressed the opinion
that this was her last chance to really come to grips with
her problems. The upshot of the follow-up was that the
patient had a formal consultation at the Foundation and
eventually reentered psychotherapy in the city where she
was living.

One can speculate about the fact that now that her
father was dead this patient could at long last consider the
possibility of becoming a woman. She again grew dissatisfied with herself as a homosexual and with her life in general and wished to resolve her problems. For the most part,
however, her life was relatively unchanged. She had continued to teach, she was very busy in school activities
but had no social life outside of these functions. She
carried on with two or three different women in overt homosexual relationships and could not enter into heterosexual
relationships. It is noteworthy, however, that during the
follow-up interviews she stated that she did wish to marry,
that she realized without help she would never be able to
accomplish this objective.

During the follow-up evaluation no stresses, as such,
could be seen other than the legal action involving the
settlement of her father's estate. There were relatively
few supports in the patient's life; she was totally self-
sustained. The job and her contacts there were quite supportive; she had friends at the school and, of course,
there were the homosexual partners who offered a support of
sorts. The core conflicts were clearly unresolved and the
conflict triggers the same.

This woman, at the time of follow-up, seemed to have

crystallized a homosexual identity; however, this may not
be completely so because of her wish to marry and her eventual reentry into treatment during the post-follow-up period.
There are some interesting things to note in this connection. A careful review of the outbreak of the symptomatology
(the overt homosexuality) seems to support the rather central presence of the phallic-oedipal conflict. It should
be noted that the patient first got involved in a homosexual relationship when she was an adolescent girl. The
overt homosexuality reached its peak at the time after the
mother's death (when the father was more "available") and
then began to subside gradually after the father's death.
She claimed to have broken off the overt homosexual experiences with one of her partners about nine months prior to
follow-up, and with another partner a couple of weeks prior
to coming to the follow-up. Thus, by the time of follow-
up she seemed to have renounced her active homosexual way
of life.

Having to teach young students about normal sex phys-
iology and function was conflict-triggering for her. Women
were conflict-triggering and so were men. Opportunities
still seemed to be plentiful; her life unfortunately was
quite need-incongruent. Homosexual involvement, although
presumably curtailed shortly before coming to the follow-
up period, by no means furthered the maturation process.
Her work offered some congruent aspects in that she was
offered the opportunities to socialize and exercise her
skills and talents. In a somewhat remote way, she could be
mothering to younger children. It is significant that
shortly before follow-up the patient had stopped living with
a homosexual and had, instead, taken on a woman counsellor
as a roommate. This relationship broke up when the woman
counsellor learned of the patient's previous homosexual
involvements.

5. Summary

This patient nicely illustrates defensive flight into
homosexuality in the face of heterosexual demands. The
parents had always been conflict-triggering in the sense
that the tension between them did not permit the patient to
resolve her own oedipal problems adequately. As the patient
became an adolescent she grew away from her father and became somewhat anaclitically attached to her mother - a
relationship which developed highly need-incongruent aspects.
With the coming of puberty and the demand to form heterosexual object relationships, she began to develop symptoms.
The earlist symptom erupted when some boys challenged her

bossiness and pointed out that she was in no position to
give orders to anyone. This so upset her that she developed
a dissociative reaction which lasted several days.

The patient was progressively drawn into sticky involvements with women, and this quality to her sexuality
became overt before the mother's death. Actually, the
mother had been quite ill for a number of years before she
died. The first overt homosexual affair occurred about six
months prior to the mother's death. The patient made one
desperate effort to establish a heterosexual relationship
by leaving the conflict-triggering situation and going to
another city. Upon the mother's death she was thrown into
a closer relationship with her father. Under these conditions her behavior deteriorated, her homosexuality blos-
somed and she finally had to come for treatment. A transference cure of sorts was accomplished, the patient managed
to finish school, she became self-sustained, but settled
into a homosexual existence even though she was by no means
satisfied with this way of life.

During the two-year follow-up period she lost her
father. He was injured and became bedridden for about a
year prior to the time we saw her, and died a few months
before this time. It is significant that the father's in-
capacitation and death coincided with her efforts to re-
nounce homosexuality. One can be a bit skeptical about
how sincere these efforts were; however, she did kick one
partner out, took up with another, but eventually got her
out of the house and then lived with a nonhomosexual woman,
or a woman who had at least sublimated her homosexuality.
Especially important to note is the fact that her wish to
reenter treatment and presumably reach the objective of
being able to marry and have children (something she said
she wanted during one of the interviews) developed more
fully after the father's death.

A bit of information that comes from the post-follow-up
period from the doctor who took her into treatment after
her follow-up evaluation is that she made a suicide attempt
after some sexual transactions with a male. It seems quite
clear that this occurrence confirms the conflict-triggering
aspect of heterosexuality. She provoked the man into making
advances, and then when she rebuffed him he became forceful
and tried to choke her. She then made a suicide gesture.

SYNTHESIS OF SITUATIONAL VARIABLES - CASE #15

1. Brief History

The patient was in his early thirties when he came to
Topeka for psychiatric help. He was admitted to a hospital
because of fear reactions which gripped him in almost every
social situation. His anxiety was so acute that by the
time he was admitted he was unable to walk down the street.

The patient's father apparently was an alcoholic whose
relationship with his wife was chronically strained. According to the patient, the mother usually succeeded in driving
the father out of the house or forced him to be quiet when
he was drinking. The patient very much wanted attention
from his father but their relationship was always distant.
Mother was a dominating woman. He had always resented his
mother because of her dominance, but at the same time appreciated her willingness to do anything for him. He never
disobeyed her.

Developmental history was not available when he came
for treatment, but he recalled no difficulty with feeding,
sleeping, and urinary or bowel control. His earliest
recollection went back to age three at which time he thought
he heard a woman call him; he ran up to her only to be told,
"I don't want you." A feeling of not being wanted persisted
throughout his life.

Although he was a successful youngster and collected
more merit badges in Scouts than anyone else, he never felt
he deserved them. He was always busy in school with extracurricular activities, was either a president or a leader
of almost every club. He learned about masturbation at age
12 but experienced profound guilt about this activity. His
father died, and he soon experienced the first attack of
anxiety (he was a senior in college at the time). Occasionally he would feel trapped in a barber chair or at gatherings and would have to leave. He graduated with a professional degree near the top of his class and then was accepted

in the ROTC, staying there for 18 months. He was at the
top of his class at Officer's Candidate School, and it was
around the time of his graduation that he had his first
heterosexual experience. During an overseas duty assignment he again became quite nervous in the performance of
his duties and was seized by the impulse to flee. There
were a few heterosexual experiences.

Upon release from the service he taught for a while
and did well. He noticed the onset of difficulty while
lecturing to large classes. He would be seized with the impulse to flee the lecture room but felt trapped and unable
to leave. These reactions spread to include discussion
groups. He became engaged and was to have been married but
he became so much worse symptomatically that he finally resigned his job, gave up his marriage plans, and began
psychotherapy.

He derived some benefit from this treatment but was finally hospitalized. He remained in the hospital for over a
year and then obtained some outpatient treatment from several
therapists. When his last therapy ended he was much improved, and was incapacitated in only two areas of his life -
he was extremely anxious if he had to speak before groups,
and he was always extremely anxious if there were any prospects of his getting too close to a woman. It is of interest to note that he once had blamed his mother for all of
his trouble. He was offered a teaching position but instead he moved back home to live with his mother and take
up private work. Prior to returning home to live with his
mother he had been courting a girl. Because his anxiety
began increasing again, he began his psychoanalysis.

2. Summary of Situational Variables at the Time of Initial
   Study

At the time of initial study the patient was teaching
on a part-time basis and living by himself in a room with
bath in a private home. Social contacts were quite limited.

The core conflicts that were defined at initial study
were the oral-dependency problem and an oedipal attachment
to the frightening, castrating, yet nurturing, mother. It
was presumed that this wish for his mother as an oral and
phallic object was the main obstacle blocking him from a
successful heterosexual adjustment, and that these unconscious intentions were the primary basis for his symptomatology. The most significant conflict trigger in his life
was the mother, with whom he maintained close geographical

as well as emotional proximity.

Intensely hostile towards his mother, he was, never-
the less, unable to give vent to his anger lest the dependence
be threatened. One of the most pronounced conscious fears
that he had at the beginning of his treatment was that he
would fall into the control of a woman. He recognized that
he was unable to endure intimacy with a woman or with friends
in general. It was quite clear that a heterosexual relationship and responsibility in the form of work were conflict-triggering to him. In both of these situations he
became incapacitated by anxiety.

3. Summary of Situational Variables at the Time of Termi-
    nation Study

This patient was in psychoanalysis five times per week
for six years. During this time he filled a prestigious
teaching appointment and had been considered for an administrative post. He acquired a group of friends through the
years, becoming quite popular. He maintained a relationship with his girl friend, spent a great deal of time with
her, but avoided making love to her. He supported her,
however, and even bought her furniture once when she was
forced to move. Landladies and other individuals assumed
there was a sexual relationship with this woman, but according to the information from the analysis there was not.
His symptoms had improved considerably so that he was now
able to lecture in front of large groups, but even so he
would find himself becoming uncomfortable. We know from
sources outside of the treatment that he had ejaculatio
praecox even after the termination of his analysis.

The symptoms were not essentially different at termination although some were less severe. He was considerably more integrated by the time of termination so that he
could face situations much better than at the time of the
initial study.

The core conflicts did not seem to be completely resolved at the time of termination. Not only were oedipal
castration fears still in evidence, the prephallic fears
of losing control, being annihilated, disintegrated and so
on, were perhaps more evident. This data came from the
analysis. He was considerably more settled in his life
and he was better able to tolerate his anxiety. He was
somewhat less distant in his interpersonal relationships,
in particular with the girl whom he had dated for a number
of years. At one point near the end of his analysis this

woman made the observation that when he kissed her it was
like he meant it, like she existed.

There seems to have been some improvement in the
patient's childlike oral demandingness. He had achieved
some independence from his mother so that he could stay
away from her without excessive anxiety or guilt, but he
still became impatient or irritated by her and was always
glad to leave. Although largely impotent, he still engaged
in sex play. It was evident that the mother continued to
be a conflict trigger; and that women, particularly his
fiancee, were conflict triggers. In a broader sense, all
of the demands of heterosexuality were potential conflict
triggers. Work seemed to be less conflict-triggering than
before.

At termination, as at the time of initial study, there
were no significant stresses in his life. Supports at
termination were considerably more than at the time of
initial study; he had his job, he had a steady girl friend,
and he had begun to build up a circle of friends and professional associates who respected him. He was appointed
to a number of committees. These appointments greatly enhanced his self-esteem. His job, the woman who seemed devoted to him, his friends and his place in the community
were all need-congruent.

4. Summary of Situational Variables at the Time of Follow-
    up Study.

By follow-up this patient had continued to be very
successful; his community involvements had increased some
and he was held in high esteem by his associates and
students. He had purchased a home and was planning to marry
his longtime girl friend. It is of particular interest to
note that his mother had died midway during the follow-up
period. It was at this point that he made the remark, "It's
all over now," and in a few months he decided he was ready
to get married. He still taught his large classes, experiencing some difficulty with these but was able to do it.
He got along well with his colleagues but he felt that his
life was somewhat empty. He felt himself to be a teacher
and not one of the boys anymore. The old feeling of being
unwanted, the feeling of being a tolerated intruder, persisted, but he said this didn't bother him so much anymore.
Other symptoms were still in evidence; he occasionally experienced fatigue; he still had difficulty with sexual relations and urinary frequency, a symptom he had for years
and which still persisted to some degree.

At follow-up it would seem that there had been some
resolution of his core conflicts. The pervasive anxiety
and severe panic attacks were not as great nor were the
rest of his symptoms, and his social adjustment had improved a great deal. His self-concept had changed some so
that he no longer thought of himself as a "three-year-old"
and had come to see himself more as a man. The fact that
he was planning marriage is probably the most significant
development during the follow-up period, and indicated that
something had changed within him. It would seem that the
improvement in his life was directly related to his treatment, but his intensified heterosexual relationship with
his girl friend and his plans to marry may also be related
to the fact that a major conflict trigger, the mother, was
no longer present. It is as though he had more completely
shifted his libidinal cathexis from mother to girl friend.

There were no stresses in his life other than the
responsibilities of being a teacher. Supports were in
abundance, the primary ones being his devoted girl friend
and a circle of friends. Opportunities for growth existed,
and very significant was the fact that his life was need-
congruent. He was a respected member of the community,
enjoyed his work very much and had the opportunity to grow
as a teacher. His private life was rapidly becoming increasingly need-congruent.

5. Summary

This patient's illness was largely autoplastic and
tenaciously resistant to change. He, nevertheless, did
improve through the years. It is evident that the patient
gained a great deal of insight and that his life adjustment
as well as his symptoms improved slowly but progressively
during the six-year treatment period. He by no means resolved all of his conflicts because all of his symptoms
persisted to some degree, the most notable of which was the
marked sexual difficulty. Whether or not he would have
married had his mother not died is difficult to say, but
it does seem probable that her death removed the major conflict trigger in his life and thus permitted him to take a
major step forward. The crystallization of marriage plans
came after her death.

This case is a rather good example of a person staying
in the same environment during his entire treatment period
and being able to do after treatment what he could not do
before. It should be noted, in retrospect, that he became
symptomatic for the first time three months after his

father's death. This may have had the meaning that now,
at last, he could take the father's place. It is also of
interest to note that he finally was able to crystallize
the wish to marry a few months after his mother's death.
That is to say, the absence of the father was a decided
conflict trigger which may have precipitated the illness
(along with all of the other demands that he become a responsible man). Before the father died he extracted the
promise from the patient that he would always take care of
his mother. It should be noted that the patient always
sent flowers on the same days that his father had done for
so for many years. With the mother's death the conflict-
triggering environment was largely gone. The girl friend
was still conflict-triggering and certainly the demand to
be a responsible man was also conflict-triggering but not
to the degree that he could not manage these demands. The
improvement in this patient, then, can be attributed to
resolution of core conflict and the disappearance of a major
conflict trigger.

SYNTHESIS OF SITUATIONAL VARIABLES - CASE #16

1. Brief History

The patient was a fortyish, unemployed married man, the father of five children. His primary complaints upon arriving for treatment were chronic alcoholism and an inability to work. He was the son and heir-apparent of a very active and successful man who owned and ran one of the major companies in this country. There was an older brother and a younger sister. The patient's brother, a few years his senior, was a poor scholar but very popular. He worked as a salesman for the family firm but became alcoholic in his twenties and died in his late twenties as a result of an accident he caused while drunk. There is little relevance in the sister's history insofar as this patient is concerned except for the fact that she, too, was a severe alcoholic.

The patient was brought up in high social circles, enjoying all the advantages of extreme wealth. He was cared for by a nurse until he was five, and apparently his early years were not clouded by psychological difficulties. He went to public school and in the course of his trips from home to school he became very close to the family chauffeur who taught him to fight and to drive and also became a father figure for him. From age nine to fourteen he attended a private school, then went to prep school where he surpassed his brother scholastically and in sports but was not popular. He graduated at age 16. He had wanted to study architecture but could not turn down an offer from his parents to send him abroad to school. At 18 he entered the same university his father and grandfather had attended, and at his father's suggestion picked subjects which, in the long run, would help him when he presumably would enter the firm. He spent vacation time working in various departments of the firm.

He had a highly successful four years at college and he met an additional qualification that his father asked of

192

him, namely, to refrain from drinking until he was 21 and
thereby win a prize of a thousand dollars. The brother had
been a heavy drinker and it regularly fell to the patient
to put him to bed at night. On one occasion the patient
disgustedly let the brother manage for himself and the
brother apparently started the fire which took his life.

The patient was commissioned as an officer and remained
in the service until the mid-forties. He never saw combat.
He met and married his wife while still in the service. He
was presumably symptom-free during his military service.

Upon his separation from the service he went to work
for his father's company. By then he and his wife had two
children. By the late forties he was receiving rapid promotions within the company, and it was during this same
year that his father retired from the business. At this
point the patient became sharply worse. His drinking increased in earnest, he became more withdrawn and irritable
towards his wife and children. The wife stated that at
times he was unable to go to work. Sexual relations with
his wife diminished. She stated that the patient always
had a warm and close relationship with his children until
the late forties when his obvious decompensation began.
Around this time the president of the company informed the
patient's father that the patient was drinking too heavily
and that this was interfering with his work on Mondays. It
was shortly after this that the patient burned down his own
house when he was drinking. Fortunately the family was
away and the patient escaped without injury. By the mid-
fifties he took a leave of absence from work and was treated
in a sanitarium, and within a few months he resigned from
his father's company. He soon came to the Menninger Foundation.

2. Summary of Situational Variables at the Time of Initial
    Study

At the time of initial study the patient was still
hospitalized and had begun his psychoanalysis. The Patient
Variables team defined this paitent's core conflicts as
being primarily at the oedipal level, pointing to a very
obvious struggle with the father which emerged when it came
time to take the father's place in the business. Apparently
getting married, having children, being an officer, were
not conflict triggers in themselves, or at least if they
were not sufficiently intense to activate symptoms. However, it was clear that stepping into the family business,
with the objective of ultimately taking over the father's

place in the company, proved to be the conflict trigger
which launched this patient into a slow but progressive regression. Everyone in this patient's family, on both sides,
in contrast to the patient, had been highly successful
people. A secondary core conflict had to do with the oral
one, and it is believed that the alcohol satisfied some of
this need. Quite clearly, though, the primary function of
the alcohol was to help this man escape from an intolerable
life situation; it also served his self-destruction. There
is little direct evidence that the wife or the children were
conflict-instigating. It would seem that the combination
of being a husband, father of several children, and breadwinner in the position previously held by his father, were
the conflict-triggering factors.

There were no stresses, as such, except of a feedback
variety brought on by the patient's drinking. It is quite
possible that the heavy responsibilities in his father's
company would eventually have become stressful, and it is
conceivable that the patient's father was a bit meddling
and interfering but, by and large, the patient had a very
comfortable life. They had a summer home, adequate finances
for vacations, luxuries, and so on.

There were many supports in this man's life; he had a
good background, family tradition, and more than adequate
wealth. He had a large number of contacts, including a
wife and children and fairly close family ties, all of which
can be considered supportive. Opportunities for fulfilling
himself were abundant. Need-congruence was good. This man
had already made a home for himself, had established a
marriage, and the outlets for work within the company were
good. However, the psychological tests pointed out that
this patient was a somewhat shy, passive, introversive man,
and it should be noted that this is hardly the kind of personality that is suitable for stepping into the presidency
of one of the major houses of this country. Perhaps, then,
the job may have been somewhat need-incongruent as well as
conflict-triggering. The patient, in some ways, was a
victim of his birth, never having had the opportunity to
live out his own interests but, rather, always having had
to comply with the wishes of others, most notably his
father.

3. Summary of Situational Variables at the Time of Follow-
    up Study

This patient's psychoanalysis was terminated after
something over 200 hours of treatment. He had refused to

remain in the hospital, choosing instead to leave against
medical advice. He had been warned that all treatment would
stop if he made this move. He frequently became severely
intoxicated and on occasion would become assaultive when
drunk.

His family moved to Topeka a few months after he began
his psychoanalysis. His treatment proved to be stormy, and
it was when he insisted on being discharged from the hospital after several previous admissions that it was decided
to discontinue his psychoanalysis. The marriage had deteriorated badly during this brief period in treatment, the
relationship with his wife being complicated by heavy drink-
on both their parts. The wife ostensibly had gone home and
refused to return. Her leaving the patient coincided approximately with the time the analysis was terminated.

Obviously none of the core problems were solved. The
conflict triggers would, at first glance, seem to have been
somewhat removed in Topeka. There was little hope that the
patient would again join the family company, although it
may be that the patient felt inwardly that he should return,
and, indeed, a place would be made for him if he ever re-
constituted adequately. The intense discord with the wife
suggests that the children and the wife were conflict-
triggering. That his wife was a mother figure was manifested by his persistent efforts to set up an essentially
mothering relationship with her in which she would baby him,
cater to his needs, and tolerate his behavior, whatever it
might be. In the course of treatment he managed to rid
himself of his wife and children just as he had managed
earlier to rid himself of the demands of the job in his
father's firm.

The kind of life the patient was leading was stressful
in a sense; both he and his wife were drinking, there was
much turmoil between them, he was at odds with his doctors
about whether he would stay in the hospital or not. Supports continued to be rather good; there was always adequate
financing, the wife and children did stick by him for a
time, and there is little question that the parents were
solidly behind him in his treatment efforts. Opportunities
still continued to be good; need-congruence had been good
prior to the wife's departure from Topeka; the patient did
have a family, he had found a job in Topeka for a brief
time. The patient found much support from the head of the
company for which he worked.

4. Summary of Situational Variables at the Time of Follow-
up Study

Approximately six months after the termination of his
psychoanalysis the patient was dead. During the post-
treatment period he had continued to drink heavily. He was
in training at work and was slated to become an estate
planner eventually. For a time he lived alone in a house
he had purchased here, but then he moved to a hotel. He
apparently contracted pneumonia and meningitis and died.
From all appearances it would seem that his alcohol played
a central role in his death. That he committed suicide has
not been conclusively shown, although his death is clearly
the end product of a long self-destructive life course.

5. Summary

This patient came from a very prominent, successful
family. There is some question as to how much maternal
warmth greeted him when he entered the world, for it should
be noted that much of his care fell to a nursemaid. Subsequent attitudes of the patient reflect a very strong
attachment to his mother. In his married life he frequently
criticized his wife for falling short of what his mother
used to do.

He completed his college work, was commissioned in the
service, and served as an officer for approximately five
years. He married and had five children, and throughout he
remained asymptomatic. Alcoholism always lurked in the
background, however, but was rationalized away as being
merely social drinking. Trouble began for him when he tried
to enter the father's company with the goal of eventually
taking the father's place in that organization. At this
point he began to falter in his adjustment and he slowly
went downhill. His regression ended in death. Before he
died he had managed to shed his primary conflict trigger,
the challenge of taking the father's place in the family
business, but he also shed other environmental factors which,
in his regressed state, had apparently also become conflict
triggers. These were his wife and children. At the time
of his death he ended up essentially alone and, by and
large, unable to be self-sustained. The loss of his wife
and children was undoubtedly a heavy blow to him, even
though their absence lightened the conflict-triggering load
on him.

SYNTHESIS OF SITUATIONAL VARIABLES - CASE #17

1. Brief History

    At the time of the psychiatric evaluation this patient
was in his late thirties, married and the father of one
child. He had been feeling resentful, was depressed, and
at times had suicidal thoughts. There was difficulty in
concentration for about six months, and some difficulty
with his sexual potency.

    He was the youngest of three sons born to a lower
middle income group. The mother, in particular, had very
much wanted the third pregnancy to bring a girl. She let
him wear curls until he was two, and then cried bitterly
when they were cut off. One of his early memories had to
do with running his fingers through a girl's long curls.
He was always a rather quiet, reticent, passive boy.

    He married in the late thirties, and describes a care-
free and happy marriage during the first year. After a
year, however, the patient's wife underwent pelvic surgery
and then in the next year was again subjected to similar
major surgery. This surgery altered the relationship between the patient and his wife somewhat; the wife became
less active and more dependent on the patient, and their
sexual relations were interrupted for long periods of time.

    The patient was overseas during the mid-forties, being
assigned to duties which were primarily office work. Upon
his return from overseas his wife had already moved back to
live with her parents, and had developed a very dependent
relationship to them. The wife had become physically and
emotionally ill during his overseas duty. She suffered from
periods of apathy, had numerous somatic complaints, and
was occasionally depressed. Because of her illness a psychiatrist advised the patient to give in to her demands.
The wife assumed no responsibility for his care or the care
of the home so that housekeeping, nursing the wife, attending to the meals and so on devolved upon him. He continued

197

this pattern of being nurse, mother, housemaid and husband
for a number of years.

In the late forties his father died leaving a nearly
bankrupt business to the patient and his two brothers. The
estate was divided; the patient never really took charge of
the business which he finally got control of through the
financial help of his father-in-law. He eventually gave up
this business. For a few years, perhaps three or four,
prior to coming for the evaluation the patient had begun
feeling tired and angry and insecure. He felt that he had
too much to bear, taking care of the child, his wife, the
home, and the business (before he sold it). He had begun
to feel useless and he entertained ideas of suicide.

An increasing independence in his wife became manifest
to him during his visits to Topeka, whereas he had previously
had to take care of her. He accordingly no longer had the
opportunity to do this and apparently he felt his wife was
drawing away from him. Interestingly, he believed his symptoms worsened as his wife's independence increased. The
patient had used alcohol for a number of years to escape
the very real tension that existed between him and his wife,
and he wasn't sure that he could live without it by the time
he began treatment. When the patient started his psychotherapy the wife was still in the Menninger Foundation hospital and the patient moved to Topeka.

2. Summary of Situational Variables at the Time of Initial
Study

The core problems were defined as a marked dependence
and as phallic-oedipal. Presumably he found gratification
for his dependence in the intimate relationship with his
wife. It is evident that he must have believed he made this
relationship secure by waiting on her and catering to her
every need. It might be supposed that having to be giving
in so many respects conflicted with his own dependency needs.
It is curious to note that evidence of improvement in his
life (when the wife improved during her hospitalization),
flimsy as that improvement was, seemed to be a provoking
external factor insofar as his own subjective discomfort
was concerned. It would, then, appear that as his wife
gained in independence, his dependence upon her was threatened. It is probably correct to speculate that as she became less dependent herself and more independent (grown up)
the demand that he become more of a man and less "of a
woman" in the house increased. It would almost seem that
as long as he could "be a woman" in this household he was

relatively asymptomatic, although obviously somewhat dissatisfied with himself in that role. Thus, the possibility of losing the intimate relationship with his wife was
conflict-triggering, and so was the hidden demand that he
be more of a man with his wife (as she emerged from her
illness).

Having to take care of such a sick woman was certainly
stressful to some degree. The role of the woman that he
assumed with his sick wife was highly need-incongruent
insofar as bringing out the man in him. It seems quite
probable that living under these need-incongruent surroundings contributed to his depression, for he was aware that
he was not fulfilling himself as a man. Unfortunately,
however, the challenge of assuming a different kind of role
in the relationship (he believed that he became definitely
worse as his wife showed promise of improvement) was conflict-triggering, while at the same time more need-congruent.
It is evident that his conscious recognition of the role
reversal contributed to his depression and alcoholism and,
of course, these symptoms received a big boost when he was
faced with the challenge of becoming a man, for then his
inadequacies became more apparent.

Opportunities were only meager. There was some wealth
in the wife's family but this was not available to the
patient. He had had a business that he might have made grow
had he been more aggressive, but by the time he was in
treatment he had given up the business and was a man without
a job and without much training for anything in particular.
Opportunities were, therefore, somewhat limited. Supports
were moderate only. The wife could hardly be considered
supportive, but having a child was a support of sorts.
There was no job to reinforce his self-esteem or offer any
actual support. The father-in-law gave some financial support of course, but the conditions were always attached that
the money be spent just as the father-in-law dictated.

3. Summary of Situational Variables at the Time of Termi-
    nation Study

This patient was treated twice a week for something
over 100 hours. During the time he was in psychotherapy he
disposed of his business which, for a time, he had tried
to keep running by making trips back and forth from Topeka.
The patient and his wife set up housekeeping as soon as he
came to Topeka, moving into a house with their child. The
father-in-law for a time seemed to have stifled the patient's
efforts to get a job by offering to support the family if

the patient could not get a job. The patient did, however,
obtain work with a comapny doing office work and handling
other matters for a construction company. It should be
noted that the wife ridiculed his job, saying that their
maid earned more money than he did.

The wife continued in psychotherapy and their child
entered treatment. A second child was born during the period
the patient was in treatment. Quite a change took place
in their home life. With the patient off to work every day,
the wife had to learn to get along with the maid. Obtaining work made it possible for him to step out of the mother-
housemaid role that he had been in for so many years. The
patient paid for his own psychotherapy out of the money he
earned. The father-in-law continued to support the family
modestly. Drinking at nightime ended, by and large. The
patient and his wife joined a supper club and began to
make friends in the community. The patient was very proud
of his job and stated that he was finally beginning to feel
his importance, feeling that he had something tangible to
give his employer. Home life was happier and more satisfying, particularly because the patient could stand up to
his wife and not give in to her every whim; "I feel more
like a man standing up for my rights, people are interested
in what I have to say, and I don't have to have a drink in
order to be in a conversation."

Because this was primarily supportive psychotherapy,
we must assume that the core neurotic problems in this man
were not touched. However, the patient's behavior was
markedly different. His subjective feeling about himself
was different, and his level of adjustment had changed
equally markedly. His symptoms had diminished to a great
extent. He could do many things that he formerly could not
or would not do. He was working, he was drinking less, he
was spending more time with his children, he did not kowtow
to his wife to the extent that he used to, and he felt much
better about himself. His depression was gone.

We would have expected that these new pressures on
him, all of which may be subsumed under the title of adult
male responsibilities, would be conflict-triggering if it
were true that the core problems had not been resolved.
This, however, does not appear to be the case for the man
was living a much more involved life in the adult masculine
sense, and he remained relatively symptom free and was a
great deal happier. We must assume, therefore, that (1)
either the original assessments regarding the unconscious
conflicts were incorrect, or (2) he gained ego strength in

treatment and, relatively speaking, the unconscious conflicts were outweighed and, therefore, exerted less impact
on him, or (3) unconscious conflicts were resolved through
new life experiences during treatment without the benefit
of insight.

This man was taken in hand by a very positive and
directive psychotherapist who pointed out his deficiencies
and his highly need-incongruent way of life. He responded
to this relationship and discovered that he could do the
things that other men can do. It would seem, then that
intrapsychic change occurred. Whether or not this included
resolution of unconscious conflict is hard to say, but it
is evident that what was potentially conflict-triggering
once, was conflict-triggering at termination to a minimal
degree. We refer here to adult male responsibilities. His
life, at the same time, was a great deal more need-congruent.
He had a home with two children; the wife was making more
effort to be the wife and mother although she was by no
means fulfilling these roles adequately. He did have a
job, and he subjectively felt that he had found his worth
and self-esteem. Supports were more plentiful in some
respects. The most obvious support of all was his work.
There he had established good relationships with co-workers
and his employer. His relationship with his children was
supportive, as were his involvements in the community.

4. Summary of Situational Variables at the Time of Follow-
    up Study

During the follow-up period the patient's mother died.
One of his brothers had become friendly and visited him
occasionally. The patient had established a farily close
relationship to his oldest son and he was quite proud of
this young boy The patient had continued the same kind of
work but was with a larger company where he supervised
three men and had considerably more responsibility than in
his former job. The second company bought out the older
company. There had been several salary increases; his fear
of authority and, in particular, his boss, had diminished
a great deal. He claimed to be able to say more of what
he felt rather than stifle it as he previously had done.

As stated in the summary at termination, we have only
indirect evidence that the oedipal and dependent conflicts
were still present. If all of the changes in his life which
can be lumped under the heading of adult male responsibilities were conflict-triggering, we should see more symptoms
in him. But this was not so. Other than some anxiety and

perhaps moderate drinking, the old symptoms were, on the
whole, gone. Remarkably different was the man's passivity.
Unconscious conflicts appear to have been resolved somehow
on an experiential level by virtue of the treatment and the
changes that took place in his life pattern. We must conclude that there was very little that was conflict-triggering
in his life. Stresses were still there, the wife being the
primary stress. She continued to be a difficult person to
live with. Supports remained about the same; the father-
in-law helped with the living expenses. Opportunities for
growth had improved somewhat, although there were definite
limitations on how far he could go in his company. Need-
congruence continued to be good. He had a job, children
and a wife.

5. Summary

      This man started adult life not too badly. He was
able to marry and, for about a year, established a happy
relationship with his new bride. His wife obviously, however, was not able to accept the role of a woman and, this
being so, we assume that he was not able to accept the role
of the man. Subsequent events in his life bear out this
assumption. The patient eventually assumed the woman's
role rather completely in relation to his wife. He became
nurse, housekeeper, mother, cook and, in the process,
relinquished his male responsibilities. Although for a
time he tried to run the business he inheritied from his
father, he eventually gave up all of this. Because he was
not totally satisfied with this role reversal, he grew increasingly dissatisfied with himself and eventually became
depressed, alcoholic and moderately suicidal.

      In part because of his wife's treatment, and in large
part because of his own, he was able to reverse the role
reversal. He found a place in a man's world, he became a
father in the truer sense of the word, a breadwinner and,
under these happier conditions, he gave up most of his symptoms. Some anxiety and tendency to alcohol remained. Since
he did not have insight-giving therapy, one must wonder just
how these changes came about. One might suppose the changes
were the result of a transference cure. This change (conflict resolution) took place as a result of experiencing
the mastering of life's challenges in a way that he had
never been able to do before on his own. Such a view, of
course, is at variance with the belief that intrapsychic
change must be associated with insight. This case would
seem, in part, not to support that assumption.

SYNTHESIS OF SITUATIONAL VARIABLES - CASE #18

1. Brief History

   This patient was a 34-year-old white, single educator who held an administrative position when he came for treatment. He was a self-referral, hoping to be treated by psychoanalysis because of uneasiness with women, jealousy of his superiors, and a feeling of insecurity with people.

   At the time of the evaluation the patient's father and mother were in their mid- and late fifties. The father owned an automotive garage where they specialized in ignition repairs. He was described as poorly educated but an excellent tradesman who was honest and conscientious. The patient and his father were always distant and, by contrast, the patient was close to his mother. She was always available to the patient and his younger brother, talked to them a great deal, went on outings, picnics and hikes, and for years it was their custom to take long hikes. The mother taught him to dance. The patient saw his parents as having always lived in conflict and being chronically antagonistic towards each other. He apparently was the confidante of both parents in later years, and the relationship to the mother remained close throughout.

   As a child he was popular and successful in school; he was valedictorian of his class, active in student council, played basketball and football and was captain of the basketball team. Later he got out of these sports on the pretense of physical illness. Dancing was important to him and he stated that up to the present he had a great love for dancing, that nothing released him like dancing did. His recreational interests were all active ones such as cycling, camping, climbing and walking. The father was crushed when the son did not go into the family business and elected to go to college instead. He had won a scholarship to college, his mother secretly helping him. He graduated in the forties.

Because of defective vision he memorized the eye chart and was accepted in the armed forces. After completing OCS he was commissioned a second lieutenant and transferred to another camp where he was placed in charge of a component of troops. Eventually he was stationed in the Pacific. He contrasted his safety in his service assignment with the assignments of his classmates by noting that 80 to 90 percent of his officer class were casualties.

After discharge from the service he returned to his old university where he accepted an administrative position. While there he obtained a master's degree and a doctorate and then taught in a college. He didn't like his first year of teaching because he felt threatened by the students.

He first went into psychotherapy in the mid-fifties; his symptoms then were essentially those he complained of when he started his analysis in Topeka. His complaints revolved around his sex life which may be briefly summarized as follows. He first began to go steady with a girl who was slightly older. He liked the role of being the eligible bachelor, and he was treated like a prince. He broke off with his first love in college, using the impending service obligation as an excuse. He did very little dating in the service. After returning from the service he met a divorced woman twenty years his senior. Although attracted to this person he was also revolted by her, and developed psychosomatic pains when she urged him to kiss her on one occasion. While working on his doctorate he married for the first time. This marriage proved to be unsuccessful largely on the grounds of sexual incompatibility. He complained that she was overly sexed and she complained of sexual inadequacy on his part, although he claimed to have been capable of two or three ejaculations a night. It was during this marriage that he first sought psychiatric treatment. It is significant to note, therefore, that committing himself to a woman coincided with an increase in symptomatology sufficient to lead him to seek treatment. This marriage was soon terminated.

2. Summary of Situational Variables at the Time of Initial Study

At the time of initial study the patient was a bachelor living in an apartment by himself and held an administrative position in an educational institution. The Patient Variables team defined the patient's core neurotic conflict as being primarily oedipal. The patient believed his father to be impotent and ineffectual, while he considered his

mother to be warm, protective and seductive. The Situational
Variables team agreed completely and could find no evidence
of further core problems of significance. The narcissistic
qualities in his personality were a feature of his character.

Actually, there were very few conflict triggers in
his life at the time of initial study. Potential conflict
triggers were for him to be in a position of responsibility,
marriage and parenthood. There was no woman in his life at
the time so that actually there were no conflict triggers
other than the relationship to authority figures at work.
He had previously lived out his oedipal problems with older
and unsuitable women. It should be noted that his marriage
coincided with his seeking psychiatric treatment for the
first time. There were no stresses in his life. Supports
were rather abundant; he had a good position, he was a
friendly man who made friends easily; his life was need-
congruent in that he had good outlets for his abilities at
work. Because he had not yet established a home, outlets
for fatherly and husbandly tendencies were not available.
Opportunities were quite abundant.

3. Summary of Situational Variables at the Time of Termi-
    nation Study

The patient was treated for nearly 1000 hours, five
times a week. During this period he so provoked his superiors that he lost his job. After his resignation he
obtained other work and did very well at this job.

In the earlier part of his analysis he was very promiscuous. He always managed to find women older than he
whom he would seduce. He had also met a young woman of
whom he was growing fond. This relationship finally became
intense. They were married during the fourth year of the
analysis. Their first child was born just prior to the
termination of the treatment.

By termination he had been married several months,
he had a new child, and he had contracted to buy a home.
His life was not as idyllic as it seemed. He occasionally
still felt his old competitiveness towards his boss at work,
noting that a certain distance sometimes developed between
them. Hostility with his wife flared up occasionally when
she did not mother him to the extent that he had wished it.
For instance, he admitted during the termination interview
that he liked to have his wife do things for him, plan for
him, and prevent all possible pitfalls.

His wife claimed that he was not as sexually active
as she wished. His promiscuity had disappeared. The relationship with his parents seemed considerably changed.
It was noted during one of the interviews that he stated
that he managed to avoid arguments with his father now,
whereas he used to bring things up knowing that these were
touchy spots and that wrangles were sure to follow.

Comparing his life before treatment with how it was
after treatment, one is struck by the number of significant
changes. He was considerably more successful at work, provoking authority less. He had married, was the father of
a child, and was preparing to buy a home. He had been unable to do any of these prior to treatment. It is of special
importance to note that these major shifts in his life
occurred during treatment itself. One can wonder whether
or not he would have been able to bring about these changes
by himself after treatment had terminated. This patient
paid for his own treatment.

We believe that some resolution of core conflict took
place, although the psychologists and the Treatment Variables
team seemed to believe that he was only slightly changed
intrapsychically. We question this. The fact of the matter
is, he had been able to do after treatment what he could
not do before. He was genuinely fond of his wife, and was
very fond of his son. He was less provocative with authority figures at work. He had stopped his Don Juan activities
and, indeed, it would seem that he settled into a more mature heterosexual adjustment.

All of this does not overlook the fact that the patient
still had a marked narcissistic streak in his personality,
that he tended to exploit people, that he was exhibitionistic. It seems safe to say that this new position that he
found himself in was itself, to some extent, conflict-triggering, which of course means that the core conflicts were not
completely resolved. There were arguments with his wife
that were brought about by his unrealistic expectations of
her and his need to provoke her, which created distance between them. He had some tendency to estrange his relationship to his boss.

There were no stresses in his life; his life circumstances were highly supportive. The wife was quite devoted
.to him, his co-workers admired and respected him, as did
his bosses, and he had a number of close friends who liked
him. He was a handsome, vigorous man who fitted in well
with others. Opportunities for the future were quite good.

One of the great shifts in his life was that the life situation at termination was highly need-congruent. He had a good job, he acquired a lovely wife and child, and had made a home for himself. All of these factors would tent to stimulate the maturational process in him. They were also somewhat conflict-triggering, as was noted earlier.

4. Summary of Situational Variables at the Time of Follow-up Study

During the follow-up period the patient had been promoted at work on more than one occasion; there was another child; but at the same time he recognized some difficulties within himself. He began feeling more uncomfortable on the job with his colleagues, particularly with his boss, and he recognized they were both uncomfortable in each other's presence. Recognition of some of the possible dynamics involved made him wonder if he didn't need more treatment. His relationship with his wife, although good in many respects, was not as idyllic as it had been portrayed to be at the time of termination. There was no question about going ahead with the marriage, although early in the relationship there had been some doubt in their minds as to whether they could stick it out. Through a non-research source it is known that the patient's wife felt that she should get some help somewhere because of some of the difficulties that were cropping up between the two of them. Their sexual adjustment was by no means even. Periods of intense "togetherness" alternated with periods of distance and aloofness. The patient attributed these latter phases to stored up resentment, which he recognized were not reality-based.

By the follow-up period the patient was, however, getting along better with his father than his mother. At the same time he noticed quite an estrangement toward his mother which bothered him rather deeply. He stated at the time that he suspected his problems were with his mother more than with his father as he had thought most of his life. It was, therefore, evident that the core conflicts were not completely resolved. In some respects this patient was not as well adjusted at follow-up as he was at termination. There was greater discontent at work and in some ways there was more trouble in the marriage, although at the same time there were periods of greater tranquility and solidity in the marriage also. The sexual relationship was probably not as conflict-triggering as it had been in the past, but the mother was more decidedly a conflict trigger and the father less so. This is interesting in that this development occurred when the patient actually married, a fact which

apparently triggered the mother aspect of the repressed conflicts. The patient's job appeared to be somewhat conflict-
triggering as did all of his responsibilities. These included the wife, the children, and making a home for all of
them. There were no stresses in his life.

There were many supports; all that were enumerated at
termination continued to exist at follow-up. Opportunities
continued to be good; need-congruence was plentiful. That
is to say, the marriage offered him good opportunity for
growth, as did his job. There is some question about his
suitability for this particular job, although it should be
noted that when he was a fund raiser for his alma mater he
was extremely happy. He was doing essentially the same kind
of work currently. It would seem, therefore, that his dissatisfaction at work related to the conflict-triggering
aspects of the work rather than to its being need-incongruent.

5. Summary

This patient was a strongly femininely identified man
at the time he came for treatment. These characterologic
aspects would seem to be rather clearly erected for defensive purposes against the core oedipal problem. The patient
was close to his mother and distant from his father. He
was a Don Juan, who liked to play the role of the little
prince who was seduced by the more aggressive and/or older
woman. Heterosexuality was difficult for him, and the sexual
situation was highly anxiety-arousing. The patient was discontented with himself and sought treatment. It should be
noted that he actually began treatment the first time in his
life when he had his first attempt at marriage. It would
appear that the conflict-triggering aspect of marriage so
mobilized the unconscious oedipal problems that he became
symptomatic and required help. As a result of his treatment it would seem that he resolved his core problems to a
considerable degree. He was able to marry and, in fact,
chose a very lovely young woman for his wife. All of this
occurred during the analysis. One can wonder to what extent
these developments were acting out as well as a newly found
level of maturity. In any event, he made good the choices
and found considerable happiness with them.

His adjustment took a slight dip in some respects during the follow-up period, and in other respects became
healthier. By the time of follow-up he was the father of
two, and had received several promotions at work. A bit of
post-follow-up information, however, revealed the fact that
he went back into once-a-week therapy. The patient reported

this as having been very valuable to him. We know that he was transferred to another branch of the company and was promoted at the same time. His marital adjustment appeared to be satisfactory although it should be noted that he was traveling much of the time and was not at home as much as some husbands are.

SYNTHESIS OF SITUATIONAL VARIABLES - CASE #19

1. Brief History

When this patient came for an evaluation she was a
21-year-old single, unemployed, drama and ballet student.
She had done very poorly at the university. The parents
felt they could not handle her at home any longer and because of their increasing concern over their daughter's
deteriorating life adjustment she was brought for treatment.
The patient had been very rebellious which, in part, was
manifested by having associated with undesirable companions.
She was the youngest of three sibs.

The patient described her father as a weak man, without principle, who was very inconsistent in his values;
she claimed to have no respect for him. The mother was
described as equally inconsistent who, the patient believed,
suffered all her life from a kind of ugly duckling concept
of herself. The mother evidently wished to live vicariously
through her daughter, for on one occasion when she was
probing the patient about her sexual activities she said,
"You shouldn't object to my questioning. Any mother has
a right to live a little bit vicariously through her
daughter."

The patient was described as having been a beautiful
baby but one who early revealed marked exhibitionistic
tendencies. Her parents encouraged her to express these
tendencies through dancing and singing. Her attractiveness
and high intelligence placed her at the top of every social
and school situation. At age eleven her older brother
seduced her into some sex play which continued intermittently from ages eleven to sixteen. Presumably their
activities included nearly everything short of actual
intercourse.

Her father began pushing her to perform well at about
the same time she was finishing high school and ready to
enter college. The patient passed the entrance exam for

university work and then began her college career. During
her first year she did marginal work only, became increasingly disorganized and involved with a clique of girls.
She returned to college for the second year but was dismissed from school at the end of the first semester because
of complete failure in all of her courses. During the
summer between these two years at school she had been in
drama school where she had become enamoured with a much
older man. She later told her mother that she had slept
with this man but that nothing had happened. After leaving
the university following her expulsion she refused to go
home but instead took up various odd jobs. Her mother
visited her and found her living in deplorable circumstances.
She was making her living posing in the nude for a photographer.

During the following summer, as a result of her parents' efforts, she obtained work in a girls' camp. It was
there that she became involved in some homosexual activities. One partner was an older woman towards whom the
patient felt enamoured, and there was also a younger girl
who came from a lower socioeconomic class. At this point
the mother wanted a doctor's opinion regarding the advis-
ability of carrying out the father's orders that the
daughter return to college.

She began psychotherapy in the mid-fifties, and at
the same time enrolled in a university. Instead of stick-
ing with this plan, the patient decided that she wanted to
study ballet and acting. The parents endorsed this plan.
While in a large city she very quickly gravitated to a
most Bohemian group and began to identify herself with the
underdog. She befriended homosexuals and associated with
obviously ill people. She did not work, became involved
with an older Negro who was married and had children.
There was considerable sex play with this man but she denied
ever having had intercourse with him. At this juncture
in her life her parents brought her to the Menninger
Foundation.

2. Summary of Situational Variables at the Time of Initial
    Study

Although the Patient Variables team did not emphasize
the phallic aspects of this girl's difficulty, the Situational Variables team believed that the major conflictual
fixation level was phallic-oedipal. It was noted that she
was quite preoccupied with men's penises and to some extent
her own nudity. There was a nearly absolute avoidance of

intercourse. The patient quite clearly made a travesty of
normal mature living. She sought out the Bohemian atmo-
spheres and environments and unsavory characters of all
sorts. When she was at home with her parents she revealed
a marked rebelliousness towards them. Obviously the parents were conflict-triggering, and in a general sense the
demand to live a normal mature existence was highly conflict-triggering. Although one might say that the prolonged
sexual activity with her brother was already symptomatic
behavior, the actual disturbance or the first clear symptomatic eruptions occurred when she was about fourteen.
At this time she developed an intense love for a much older
man.

After she left for college she began to regress in
earnest. It is about this time that heterosexual object
choices are made and, of course, her behavior at that time
was nearly completely symptomatic and expressive of not
only her phallic-oedipal conflicts but dependence as well.
The latter seems to be more lived out in relation to the
homosexual women. The stresses were primarily of a feedback nature brought on by her own illness. The stress at
the time of initial study refers primarily to the chaos in
her life. Supports were limited. Her parents in their
own way had tried to be supporting but they were far too
lenient with her to have really figured as significant
supports in her life. It is true, however, that they always stuck by her and finally fished her out when she got
in over her head. Opportunities for this girl were quite
good. She was an attractive, engaging person, young,
bright, and given the proper home climate she could have
developed well. Need-congruence at the time of initial
study was nil. All of her contacts and the whole way of
life in general fed her neurosis. Even the parents were
not need-congruent. The mother had a subtle way of stimulating the illness in this girl for it seemed that she
wished to live vicariously through the daughter's misconduct.
The research team believed that neither parent genuinely
loved the child just for what she was but rather loved her
for what she could do for them. The daughter realized this.

3. Summary of Situational Variables at the Time of Termination Study

This patient was treated by psychotherapy for a total
of over four hundred hours. The treatment may be described
as having been quite chaotic. The patient eloped and
married and then returned to Topeka to resume psychotherapy.
There was much talk of having this marriage annulled.

There was some question of whether both parties should be
kept in treatment or not in view of their rebellious acting
out behavior, but it was finally decided to keep them in
treatment and not insist on an annullment. The parents
did not want the marriage annulled (probably because of
the extreme wealth of the family of the boy the patient
married). The patient and her husband set up housekeeping
but immediately began fighting, which included physical
assaults. The husband was frequently gone overnight, running around with a crowd of delinquents. The first child
was soon born. The patient terminated her treatment abruptly
and instead began seeing a Christian Science worker. Although this is a bit of follow-up data, it should be mentioned here that there is some evidence that the patient
felt that she had to terminate the therapy before she could
get a divorce. She presumably believed that her therapist
was against a divorce. She was pregnant with a second
child by the time she terminated treatment.

It would seem that very little had changed in this
patient. Certainly the core neurotic problems were untouched. Although she had married, this was by no means
a rational act but a clear acting out and, as might have
been expected, the marriage was characterized by continual
dissention between the two partners. Thus it appears that
being married and all that this implies (wife, mother,
homemaker) were the new conflict triggers in her life.
She had, through a counterphobic maneuver, plunged into
"maturity" and failed miserably.

The husband was clearly conflict-triggering as well
as stressful. He was a very difficult, disagreeable and
immature young man. The parents remained conflict-triggering although geographically removed. The patient was a
very poor housekeeper and seemingly took delight in shock-
ing her parents in this way. The responsibility of caring
for the house, conflict-triggering as it was, fell to a
maid. She was out of her house much of the time and relied
heavily on babysitters. Although there was a shift in the
life pattern it was essentially as symptomatic as before.
The core conflicts were the same and now, instead of the
parents and the broad, ill-defined challenge of a heterosexual existence being the conflict triggers, she had crystallized out the conflict triggers by acquiring a husband,
baby and home. Her life was certainly stressful. There
were supports of sorts, the most stable of which, of course,
was the therapy. The husband provided for her adequately.

4. Summary of Situational Variables at the Time of Follow-up Study

During the follow-up period the patient gave birth to a second child and also obtained a divorce. She was granted her home and a very liberal alimoney support until she remarried. Trust funds were set up for her children. She continued to live in her home for about a year and had a couple live with her. She then moved to a run-down, mixed neighborhood where she lived in an apartment. She was promiscuous, had friends among Negroes, stayed away from her children much of the time, found it difficult to care for her home and, in short, lived a very chaotic life. On the positive side, she did volunteer work for a number of charitable organizations. Her pattern with men was to pick socially inferior men, get them enamoured, and then reject them scornfully, demanding to know why they thought they had any hold on her. This life pattern confirmed the belief that her core conflicts were by no means resolved. She now felt completely free from her parents and because of this had a more kindly feeling towards them. She refused to move back near her family.

Conflict triggers, by the time of follow-up, had diminished. She had continued to extricate herself from the emotional ties that she had had with her parents. She was divorced and her relationships with men were transient and superficial. The primary conflict triggers remaining were the two children and the need to make a home for them. In some ways she seemed somewhat more tranquil and less disturbed at follow-up than at termination. Much of the care of the children fell to paid help. She spent most of her $1000 a month. She hoped that when her ex-husband completed his treatment he and she might remarry.

This patient's life may be viewed as moderately stressful by virtue of the chaos in it. Supports were minimal although financial support was adequate. Need-congruence was only moderate. The patient had two children, which tended to stimulate the maturational process in her. Unfortunately these need-congruent factors were also conflict-triggering. Opportunities were good provided the patient could overcome her illness.

5. Summary

This patient was a highly disturbed individual whose illness erupted during puberty. There had been some somnambulism early in life but the gross disturbance became

manifest during adolescence. She exhibited a polymorphous
perversity, participating in all sorts of perverse activities, including homosexuality and romances with much older
men. It is clear that the unconscious conflicts erupted
at a time when nonincestuous object choices are first made.
Practically every facet of the challenge to live a normal
life was conflict-triggering. The most significant conflict triggers were the parents. The patient became
noticeably worse after she had been around her father.
While in treatment she acted out her unconscious conflicts
by impulsively marrying a patient who was also a patient
of her therapist. As might be expected, the demands of
marriage, heterosexuality, parenthood, etc., proved to be
highly conflict-triggering. The behavior in both parties
of this match remained grossly symptomatic if not actually
becoming worse than it had been. The patient then divorced,
and although her life by no means became tranquil she seems
to have been somewhat calmer than either before treatment
or during treatment when she was married.

This case illustrates how the external form of a
psychiatric disturbance may be altered some over time but
the unconscious meaning is essentially the same. Very
little happened in this treatment in the way of bringing
about intrapsychic change; instead, the patient merely
sought to reorganize the external aspects of her life.
She substituted her chaotic Bohemian existence prior to
coming to treatment for a strife-filled impossible marriage
which brought two children into existence. Taking a very
long view, one might suppose that some intrapsychic change
had taken place, for the patient had been able to marry.
She had been able to define one of her goals in life as
wanting to live the life of average middle-class people,
but this sort of opinion might well have crystallized in
time without any professional intervention. The core conflicts remained unchanged; the conflict triggers merely
shifted in form. The patient substituted the moderately
supporting parents for a poorly supporting husband and,
finally, more supporting friends and paid help. She
apparently found a good deal of support from the church
and by the time of follow-up her life was more need-
congruent than it had been in the beginning. She had two
children to bring out the woman and mother in her.

SYNTHESIS OF SITUATIONAL VARIABLES - CASE #20

1. Brief History

At the time of the evaluation the patient was a 29-year-old white, single, medical student. He had been be-having unethically with patients, doing pelvic examinations in the night under nonprofessional conditions. He was sus-pended from school and referred for the evaluation.

The patient's mother, age 52, was described as poised, friendly, intelligent, and rather attractive. The father, a farmer, was a somewhat shy, inhibited, schizoid individ-ual who, nonetheless, was very hardworking, but also a hard-drinking man. The patient's birth was normal but it is noted that he had jaundice at about the age of five months.

The patient felt that he was somewhat withdrawn from other children until about the fourth grade when he became much more obviously outgoing and sociable. He retained this style of social interaction all during his high school years, being active in all of the extracurricular activities. He won track honors, as well as being elected to the National Honor Society for high school students. He worked a great deal on the farm and prided himself on being able to do "a man's job." During the summer between the patient's junior and senior years in high school he developed some dizziness which was eventually diagnosed as neurocircula-tory asthenia. It should be noted that he was suffering from compulsive masturbation at the time and finally he was advised to get away from home for awhile. He lived with an aunt and uncle and his symptoms did improve but did not disappear completely until he entered the military service in the mid-forties.

His entry into active combat was delayed somewhat by surgery but following this surgery he went into the combat zone for seven months. He was under heavy mortar fire for a period and he functioned well under these stressful

216

conditions. The onset of heavy drinking coincides in time
with his first efforts at heterosexual experiences. Upon
discharge from the service he returned to his home where
he worked on the farm. His drinking continued there and
he continued to drink heavily until he started college.

After he matriculated he stopped the heavy drinking,
settled down, worked very hard and made extremely high
marks. He completed a premedical education, and the pattern
of tension and drinking reappeared in medical school. It
had been his plan to marry during these years in school and
it should be noted that his worst period with regard to
drinking and tension coincided with the time when his marriage seemed most imminent. Because his girl friend was
unfaithful to him he broke off with her. The patient had
trouble all through his medical education and even some on
the farm at home during the summers. He complained of
tension, he drank excessively, and there were periods of
depression. He became most distrubed when he was on the
psychiatric service in medical school. He apparently had
an amnestic episode and examined some female patients in
the early morning hours. There had been a similar incident
earlier but an intern was blamed.

2. Summary of Situational Variables at the Time of Initial
    Study

At the time of initial study the core conflict was defined as being primarily phallic-oedipal. Conflict triggers
were the increasing demand that he be a responsible person
and ultimately become a physician; more specific conflict
triggers were the intimate exposures to women patients.

The parents were considered to be conflict-triggering,
particularly the mother. It is obvious that the most important conflict trigger was the possibility of succeeding
and becoming a physician. During his fugues he demonstrated
his curiosity and fear about genitalia. The dependency
problem must have been a central issue in this man, although
at the time of initial study not too much was made of this
nuclear conflict. The stresses were not remarkable other
than those of being a medical student. The supports were
moderate. The parents had certainly supported him all the
way and he had managed to get financial support from an
uncle. His good grades in school and his affiliation with
the student body of medical students were supportive to
some degree. Opportunities, of course, were abundant.
Need-congruence was good. Being in medical school was the
fulfillment of a lifelong dream.

3. Summary of Situational Variables at the Time of Termi-
    nation Study

The patient was treated by psychoanalysis for nearly
700 hours, five times a week. He overcame his symptoms;
there were no more dissociative states. During treatment
he worked as a psychiatric aide. He was married in the
middle of his analysis. He returned to medical school and
then reduced his hours from five to one per week. He eventually increased this to three times a week, and then graduated after treatment terminated.

The assessment made by the Treatment Variables team
at termination was that his conflicts had been significantly
worked through. This assumption, based on information from
the analyst, coincided with his markedly improved behavior.
He had married, returned to school, was no longer drinking
or having any of the other major symptoms which were present
at the time of the initial study. It therefore seemed that
very little was conflict-triggering in his life with the
possible exception of the sexual situation. He was able
to go back to school and be an outstanding student and was
particularly well thought of by his professor of medicine.
The stresses were those of a medical student. Supports
were still abundant. Opportunities were good and his life
on the whole seemed very need-congruent.

4. Summary of Situational Variables at the Time of Follow-
    up Study

During the follow-up period the patient was still
married, graduated from medical school and completed an
internship and then joined a group practice in a fairly
small community. He couldn't get along with any of the
doctors. He began taking drugs. He remained there less
than a year, then took the place of a retiring physician
in another small community. This was a private practice
arrangement where the community provided him with an office
and other needs for him to carry on his practice. He
managed to hold up for about two months but was hospitalized for extreme behavior which included wild driving,
other forms of alloplastic behavior, gross exaggerations
about what he accomplished in his practice, ingestion of
drugs, and so on.

It is evident that at follow-up the core conflicts
were not resolved at all. His wife (with whom he fought
continually) and the demands which were placed upon him
as a physician all proved to be highly conflict-triggering.

He eventually fled from all of these conflict triggers and
returned to the family farm. Post-follow-up information
revealed that he remained on the farm for a couple of years.
He then tried to set up private practice again but this
was complicated by a series of physical illnesses as well
as depression. He died, presumably from heart disease
although the scene where he was found dead had all the earmarks of a suicide.

It is evident that the demands of maturity were conflict-triggering. The stresses were not unusual, although
the stress on a young physician starting a practice or
attempting to enter practice is above average. Supports
were moderate; he had a wife, and the communities welcomed
him with open arms. His life was highly need-congruent.

5. Summary

This is an excellent example of the importance of
follow-up studies. The information taken from the analyst
at the time of the patient's termination of his analysis
indicated that his core problem had been worked through
and that significant intrapsychic change had occurred.
Indeed, his behavior in life supported these inferences.
It is probable that the extent of his illness was underestimated in the beginning. History has it that he had a
megalomanic streak in him from early life on. When he was
in practice he made gross exaggerations about the number of
patients he treated in a day, the number of deliveries,
and so on. This case illustrates the effect of the conflict-triggering impact of the environment and how this
patient attempted, as so many others have, to solve his
dilemma by shedding the conflict triggers.

SYNTHESIS OF SITUATIONAL VARIABLES - CASE #21

1. Brief History

    This patient came for a psychiatric consultation in
his mid-twenties. At time he was a graduate student in
psychology. He had previously been in psychotherapy and
was now again feeling the need for it as a result of having
been unable to hold a girl friend. In addition to his inability to sustain a heterosexual relationship, he complained of severe anxiety with which was associated frequent
urination. He found that tears rolled down his cheeks
without apparent reason on several occasions. He was an
extremely shy man with low self-esteem who felt that he
could never succeed at much in life. There was a tendency
to withdraw; there was a hint of some sleep disturbance as
well as gastrointestinal disturbance.

    His parents apparently never got along together. He
was an only child. The father had been married previously
and had a grown son who was out of the home. The father
was a printer by trade and an alcoholic. The mother also
worked and presumably was the dominant figure in this match.
The patient had slept in the parental bed until he was four
years old and then was moved to an adjoining room. He insisted, however, that the door between their rooms be kept
open. He developed enuresis at this time and continued to
be enuretic until age 13. The father did the housework
because the mother didn't like to do it. The father was
out of work for long periods of time. The patient grew
up as a shy, sensitive fellow whose main interests were in
academic and intellectual areas and he did well at this
kind of pursuit. Social contacts were always difficult.

    After he finished high school he went to a large uni-
versity forty miles away. The patient first saw a psychiatrist there to get some advice about getting help for his
father and mother. There apparently was a great deal of
friction between his parents at this time. It appeared
that he seemed to be on a mission which was to bring harmony

220

to his parents. He began seeing this psychiatrist regularly, however, and this continued for a period of about a
year. As he continued in therapy he began to see his own
anxiety more clearly, as well as his sense of inferiority
and shyness about girls. He always had the feeling that
girls did not like him, that they would reject him because
he was unacceptable to them. He was able to have a relationship with a girl for a time but she broke off with him.
While in college the patient would impulsively hitchhike
home to see his parents because of feelings of loneliness.
The goodbyes were particularly painful because the father
generally cried when they parted. It should be noted that
his girl friend at the university decided to leave him after
his return from one of his visits with his parents.

Recognizing his need to get away from his parents, he
transferred to a more distant university. Because he wanted
to be financially independent of his parents, he applied
for and gained a scholarship. He worked as an overseer at
a dormitory. This parting from his parents was perhaps the
most difficult of any, but after he left he felt better
than at any time before in his life. The first few months
were very happy ones. At one of the early fall dances he
met a girl he liked very much and began dating her. They
seemed to have had much in common and enjoyed each other;
however, he could not hold this girl, and it was at this
point that he began to consider getting further treatment
and applied to the Menninger Foundation. He didn't want
his parents to pay the bill.

2. Summary of Situational Variables at the Time of Initial
    Study

The core conflicts of this patient were at two levels.
At the deepest level was a profound oral-dependent attachment not only to his own mother but to a motherly father.
This was manifested by the sticky relationship between
him and his parents from which he so desperately was trying
to emancipate himself. The second level of psychosexual
conflict revolved around the phallic-oedipal difficulties
with associated guilt and anxiety. These being the core
conflicts defined at initial study, it was quite clear
from the life pattern of this patient that his parents were
the most significant conflict triggers. It should be noted
that his first serious girl friend left him right after he
returned from a visit home. It might be speculated that
he behaved in a way that was more noxious to her right after
this visit because of the parents' conflict-triggering
impact.

The effort to establish a heterosexual relationship was clearly conflict-triggering. In such a relationship he felt inferior, inadequate, subject to rejection and unable to make the grade, and it was this fact that sent him to treatment the first time and again into treatment the second time. It would appear that he courageously tried to establish a heterosexual relationship but became anxious and forced the girl into a more maternal role, with the patient himself taking on the identity of a little boy. He wanted to be mothered and yet he rebelled against it, and at the same time he was afraid to be manly.

The stresses in his life were considerable. The alcoholic, infantilizing, passive father was a stress. The constant quarreling and bickering between his parents was certainly a stress; and there was some economic insecurity; however, this was really not of much note. The supports were there in that the parents, despite all of their psychopathology, seemed quite fond of their son; they gave him money and other material things, as well as their own obvious affection. Opportunities were certainly good; he was an intelligent fellow given to academic pursuits; he had won a scholarship and he wasn't completely repugnant to the opposite sex by any means, despite his shyness and indecisiveness. Need-congruence was not high; parents such as his hardly fostered maturation in him; however, being at school, having a job, was all quite need-congruent.

3.   Summary of Situational Variables at the Time of Termination Study

The patient was seen once a week for over 200 hours in expressive-supportive psychotherapy. During treatment he got a master's degree in psychology. In his first job he got along rather well with women supervisors. He met a girl at a church function and began a courtship. He avoided marriage because his psychotherapist had recommended psychoanalysis. He drove a cab after hours in order to earn extra money. The sexual relationship with this girl was not good; he necked with her, partly disrobed her but ejaculated in his trousers. Masturbation was his main sexual outlet. It appears that the primary gain from his treatment in his own eyes was that he was able to gain some weight (something he had wanted to do for a long time) and he was able to sustain a relationship with a girl. This girl wanted to get married but he avoided it.

At termination he had become even more independent of his parents and was able to reject some of the gifts they sent him, including clothing. Urinary frequency diminished and probably even disappeared before termination. His shyness subsided to some extent; depression and feelings of anxiety lessened to some extent; he was still quite a shy man. Anxiety, in fact, was still considerable; homesickness had diminished. The Treatment Variables team was of the opinion that the core conflicts had changed some. They believed that the oral problem was partly worked out and that the more predominant core conflict at termination was the phallic-oedipal one.

The therapist told us that he did not think the core neurotic problems had been resolved, or at least he didn't think much change had taken place at this level. The therapist saw some symptomatic change but he didn't think this was due to a resolution of core conflict; he felt that the patient had some greater awareness of his core problems, particularly his hostility toward women. Something changed, however, between the patient and his parents. He was able to refuse the mother's money and was able to send back some of the clothing they sent him. If his core problems were not resolved by treatment, then these changes were probably due to some maturational trends in him as well as to the treatment, all of which led to a strengthening of his ego.

It should be noted that by the time of termination the patient's father was not drinking, and there was not only a geographical distance between the patient and his parents but a greater psychological distance too. Thus it would seem correct to say that the parents were less conflict-triggering at termination than they were at the time of initial study, not because the core conflicts were changed so that there was nothing to trigger, but because of the distance he had been able to put between himself and his parents.

Work apparently had never been too much of a conflict trigger for him. However, his efforts to establish a heterosexual relationship were still clearly conflict-triggering, and although he could now sustain a heterosexual relationship, he could by no means carry it off well and without symptoms. He still felt somewhat inferior in a heterosexual relationship and suffered from a severe potency disturbance. Stresses were of no significance at termination. Supports came primarily from his work, some from his girl friend, and some still from his parents whom he recognized were benind nim. His life was considerably more need-congruent at the time of termination than at the time of initial study. He had extricated himself from a pathological entanglement with his parents, he now had a girl friend, he was making his own way in life.

4. Summary of Situational Variables at the Time of Follow-up Study

The patient took his therapist's advice that he obtain a psychoanalysis. His analyst asked how he could work on his sexual problems if he had never had any sexual adventures. The patient apparently took this as advice to get married, which he then did. The girl he had been going with had wanted to get married and despite his severe potency disturbance they married. He then obtained work in the field of special education. The information we have suggests that the marriage did not go well, that the potency disturbance continued, and that the wife had become subject to periodic depressive episodes. In the two years of marriage he never succeeded in having intercourse. The patient's wife was aware of his sexual troubles before their marriage but thought that they might go away after marriage. The wife noted that he was uncomfortable around children and did not know whether he wanted to have them or not. She would have liked to have children. He was more affectionate with his wife than early in the marriage, something which encouraged the wife about the future.

The symptoms at follow-up were as follows. There was no evidence of depression; there was severe premature ejaculation and inability to have intercourse; anxiety was still moderately present but less than at initial study; feelings of inferiority persisted but may have been somewhat less intense; there was still some evidence of homesickness although by no means as severe; there was no evidence of sleep disturbance, eating disturbance, or obsessions. The patient was now a breadwinner and family man, although an inadequate one in the sexual sense. He continued to find independence from his parents. The urinary frequency had disappeared.

Core conflicts seemed relatively unchanged at the time of follow-up. Because he had emancipated himself from his parents to a considerable degree, the parents were much less conflict-triggering than they were at the time of initial study, or even at the time of termination. This man, unfortunately, had hopped out of the frying pan and into the fire for he had taken a woman into his life, which then introduced a new conflict trigger. Although he had certainly increased his involvement in life and increased his commitments and responsibilities, he nonetheless had been

unable to consummate the marriage. He could, however,
express some tenderness toward his wife. When he first
took his job he had some difficulty with his supervisor,
but apparently this had been resolved and so it would appear
that the work situation was hardly conflict-triggering at
all at this point. There were no stresses. Supports were
rather abundant from his wife, and from his work and work
associates. The wife, in particular, was patient, helpful,
and gregarious enough to keep pushing him into social
activities.

Opportunities were fairly good and the marriage provided continued gratification and room for growth. Need-
congruence was much better at the time of follow-up than
it ever had been before. Now he had a wife and a job and
if he could overcome his internal difficulties he was in a
climate which would foster maturation in him. One can
wonder, however, about the wife's own personality; we suspect that her more aggressive gregarious nature blended to
a certain extent with his passivity. That she would marry
an impotent man makes us wonder how really need-congruent
she was, and whether in subtle ways she might not stifle
further change in him.

5. Summary

This patient was the product of very disturbed parents.
The father was a weak, passive man and the mother a more
aggressive, dominant personality. Since the patient was
an only child, both parents apparently fulfilled many of
their own neurotic needs through him. The best evidence
for this is that they kept him in their own bed for four
years, probably between them as a kind of guardrail. A
profound dependence developed in the patient, as well as
an unresolved oedipal conflict.

Despite these marked conflictual handicaps, something
propelled this man forward and he recognized his need to
get away from his parents and he also recognized his inability to establish a heterosexual relationship. He twice
sought and received psychiatric treatment and, although his
treatment was never extensive or intensive, he made considerable progress. He was able to emancipate himself
from his parents, the primary conflict-triggering and need-
incongruent but also supportive factors in his life, and
he established a fairly independent existence. He began
earning his own way, pushed these two conflict triggers
and need-incongruent factors out of his life and was able
to make it on his own. However, he met with considerable

trouble, as one might have expected, when he attempted to
establish a heterosexual relationship. He could not hold
his women, recognized his failure and sought treatment for
this. He married, but picked a fairly assertive, gregarious
woman who was satisfied to have an impotent husband. He
found himself completely unable to penetrate and troubled
by severe chronic premature ejaculation. Despite these
difficulties, he continued to grow in his professional
developments. Not only did he originally receive a master's
degree, but he progressed through three successive jobs and
established an independent existence. Obviously his core
conflict and derivative characterologic problems of passivity and inferiority remained; there were still symptoms.

It should be noted that when he got away from his
parents the first time he had never felt so happy in his
life, and this sense of happiness persisted for quite awhile.
When he again attempted to intensify his object relations
with young women his sense of distress increased. He did
not flee from this, however, but progressively increased
his commitments and took on more responsibilities.

SYNTHESIS OF SITUATIONAL VARIABLES - CASE #22

1. Brief History

When this patient came for his evaluation he was a
30-year-old, white, married attorney. He previously had
been hospitalized and was then transferred to the V.A.
Hospital in Topeka. He complained of having an unbalanced
personality and that he fluctuated to extremes of behavior,
that he was a chronic liar and an embezzler, and that he
had recently escaped criminal action because his father had
made financial restitution. Because his father had not
been able to make complete financial restitution, the
patient was unable to return to his home state.

The father was a very successful and hardworking attorney. The mother met him when she was working in his organization. It was reported that while the father was an
aggressive lawyer, he was ruled by his wife and daughters
at home. He was, however, a man of warmth, while the
mother appeared colder and more critical towards the patient.
The father always provided well for the family and had been
quite indulgent with the patient. The patient said about
his mother, "I love her when I'm away from her but I can't
get along with her when we're together." Because of feeling discriminated against by playmates as a child, mostly
by children of a higher social class, he developed a profound hatred for this social strata.

Following graduation from high school he entered the
law school but left after one semester to enlist in the
Army. He saw overseas duty and was in a combat zone for
approximately six months where he was wounded. He allegedly
was awarded several combat awards. He claimed at one point
to have captured a large number of prisoners. He enjoyed
Army life, began a wild way of life drinking, dating,
smoking and doing things that were forbidden at home.

He eventually returned to his university and completed
law school and then entered the practice of law in his

227

father's office. He claimed to have always loved the practice of law, particularly jury trials involving civil wrongs.
He especially enjoyed opposing an attorney if he was from
a higher social class, and he described himself as being
openly vicious in his strategy.

Sexual activity in the form of masturbation began at
the age of 16 and he had continued this, although he had
had intercourse frequently. Early in his life he was afraid
to approach a girl, but once he began experiencing success
in his law practice he set out to make the acquaintance of
the most beautiful models and women in cafe society. He
never gave up until he had seduced the girl he set out to
conquer. He would then discard her as callously as
possible.

Early in his law career he began to feel uneasy in
relation to people. He became even more concerned about
himself because he lost several cases which he should have
won easily, and some of his financial investments began
going badly. Because of his declining practice and his
spendthrift activities he began to get into financial difficulties. In order to bail himself out he falsified
records, forged documents and embezzled money. His activities were finally discovered by his father who made an
attempt to pay all of the outstanding debts which totalled
many thousands of dollars. The patient was spared disbarment through the influence of his father. Later information indicates, however, that he was disbarred. All of
this occurred in the same year he met and married the
daughter of a well-to-do family. Within a few months he
entered a hospital for the first time. Because it was
advised that he should begin psychoanalysis (advice given
by a psychoanalyst) he was discharged from the hospital
and taken as a patient in the outpatient facilities at the
Menninger Foundation where this kind of treatment was
available.

2. Summary of Situational Variables at the Time of Initial
    Study

By the time the patient began treatment at the Menninger Foundation he had already found a job and his wife and
child had moved to Topeka. He began psychotherapy once a
week. Core conflicts at the time of initial study seemed
primarily to be an oral-aggressive sadistic problem. He
had an insatiable wish to take in, to devour, and to destroy. Not stressed adequately, we think now in retrospect,
were the phallic-oedipal problems. His Don Juanism, the

conquering of upper-class women (a symbol for the mother),
and the way he turned his wife into a mother by his expectations of her, all point to the significance of this core
conflict, as well as the oral sadistic one.

The conflict triggers at the time of initial study,
and during that phase of his life when he became acutely
ill, were clearly the work situation with the father and,
later, marriage. Rather than succeed in his work and thus
join with his father, he tried to destroy the father and
himself. We think this failure reflects an externalization
of his infantile oedipal struggles. The fact that he loved
his mother and idealized her but could not get along with
her when he was in her presence shows that she, too, was
an active conflict trigger in his life. The fighting and
the bickering undoubtedly served to help him control his
erotic feelings toward her. During this decompensation
the patient saw fit to (alloplastically) add another conflict trigger to his life. He married, and it was after
that marriage that he finally withdrew from professional
life altogether and entered the hospital.

At the time of initial study the opportunities for
this patient had been good and chances are he could have
continued to grow professionally once the charges against
him had been lifted. His life was quite need-congruent;
he had a wife, good social standing, and a profession.
Supports were adequate. Interestingly, after his evaluation at the Menninger Foundation he was told to go out and
make a life in Topeka for one year and return and then he
would be considered for treatment. The patient did this.
He bought a home, got a job, and returned to apply for
treatment on the anniversary of his evaluation. Psychoanalysis was not recommended.

3. Summary of Situational Variables at the Time of Termi-
    nation Study

The patient was seen in psychotherapy approximately
one hour a week, sometimes more often, for over 100 hours.
During this period he and his wife had a second child.
For a time he did so well in his work that they were going
to give him a significant promotion, but because they discovered the history of embezzlement in the past he was
fired. He then obtained work with another company, but
then he discovered that the old problem in his home town
had been cleared up and that no charges were pending
against him. He got very cocky and hostile towards his
family and his in-laws and told them off in various ways.

He decided that what he really wanted to do was live back in his home town and return to the practice of law. He began writing bad checks about that time.

In addition to some bad checks, his attorney informed his wife about a sizeable fee he owed the attorney. These difficulties, heaped on her chronic discontent with her husband, led her to sue for a divorce. She returned to her home with the two children. Because of his debts he went into bankruptcy, losing house, furniture and automobile. The bad check writing continued and at one point he was jailed overnight.

After his wife left he seemed to have turned over a new leaf for awhile; he stopped drinking, started going to church, and began working ten hours a day. He was constantly preoccupied with the question of whether or not his wife would return if he straightened up. He began to make money in his work, again became cocky, and occasionally missed his therapy hours at the point when he was beginning to succeed again. At one point he returned home, displaying himself as a success. He bragged about his income, and so on. Immediately after this he developed a physical illness and eventually was unable to work at all, and he then again fell into the hands of his creditors. He finally disappeared and failed to show up for his treatment.

It is of interest to note that he managed to succeed for awhile, but at the point in his treatment when he became successful and was about to be promoted he began to regress again, and at this point he rid himself of major conflict triggers - the wife and two children. Interestingly, after they left he improved for a time, despite the fact that he was somewhat depressed and shaken by his wife's departure. Apparently his having succeeded served as a conflict trigger for he began to go steadily downhill and finally left treatment altogether.

It is obvious that his parents and the possibility of returning to his practice was a silent but ever present conflict trigger. The opportunities for this man had always been good. He had a need-congruent life, the wife, children, work of any kind. He was an affable man who seemed to get along in almost any kind of job, and supports were rather abundant.

4. Summary of Situational Variables at the Time of Follow-
    up Study

    During the two-year period we lost track of this pa-
tient for a time. He was eventually found in his home
town living with his parents. He had, in the meantime,
been divorced. He had obtained work approximately three
months prior to the follow-up interview. He claimed to see
his wife occasionally and to contribute financially to the
support of his children. In a telephone conversation with
the mother we received information that the patient actually
spent all his money on himself and even had to ask his father
for money on occasion. The mother also said that he was
no longer writing bad checks but now openly asked his father
for money when he had exhausted his own funds. As far as
the mother knew, he never did get back his license to practice law. Because he got in arrears with his payments to
his wife for the care of the children she refused to let
him see them.

    It was evident at follow-up that none of his core
problems were solved. For a period of time during the
treatment he seemed to improve, but by follow-up it was
evident that his successes led to further regression and
his ultimate shedding of all the conflict triggers. He
returned home, however, and thus was still in the presence
of some major conflict triggers, that is, the father and
the mother. Work must be considered to be conflict-triggering to some degree. The psychological tests, however,
showed considerable improvement. He was more contained;
less preoccupied with sex; in general, less disturbed.
This fact may be directly correlated to the fact that he
had shed his conflict triggers, at least this empirical
relationship did exist. Opportunities were still good for
him, although not as good at follow-up as at the time of
initial study because of his disbarment. Need-congruence
was not as great as it had been, for he had now lost his
family and was not practicing the profession for which he
had been trained.

5. Summary

    This case illustrates rather nicely how the parents
and the effort on the patient's part to identify with the
father can be conflict triggers. He was somewhat disturbed in the university but nonetheless he managed to
complete school and graduate and pass the bar examination.
It was when he went to work in the father's firm and began
doing well that he began to fail. He sought bad

companionship, he embezzled funds and, in essence, destroyed himself, and in the process nearly destroyed his
father, something he unconsciously probably wished to do.
His efforts at succeeding and becoming a man included
marrying. This only added fuel to the fire and he soon
had to be hospitalized. The prospect of treatment seemed
to have done more for him than the treatment itself. During
the year's waiting period he did rather well, but again
it should be noted that this success, coupled with even
greater success during the treatment period, led him again
to his own defeat. The upshot of all this was that he
eventually shed all of his conflict triggers in the course
of his regression. Not only did he lose his status in
life, but he lost his family as well. These losses significantly lowered the demands on him.

Interestingly enough, by follow-up, after he had shed
all of these triggers, the psychologist reported that he
was a much less disturbed man in many respects. Much is
made of his need for revenge toward the parents. By the
time of follow-up the man was working and had again begun
to succeed to some extent. At the same time, his infantile
needs were being met through alcohol, by living at home
close to his parents, and getting funds from the father.
It would seem that he struck a balance of sorts between his
mature and neurotic sides. He found a place where he could
sufficiently gratify his infantile wishes and at the same
time moderately succeed at what he was capable of doing.
Under these conditions he seemed to be relatively stable,
at least more stable than when he was on his own and succeeding in life with a wife and children to support.

SYNTHESIS OF SITUATIONAL VARIABLES - CASE #23

1. Brief History

    At the time this patient came for treatment she was
an unmarried college student in her late teens. Her chief
complaint was anorexia alternating with bulimia since early
adolescence. She was transferred to our hospital from
another hospital where she had been hospitalized upon the
advice of her doctor. Her doctor had hospitalized her
primarily because of the patient's tendency to involve her
parents in her illness and in her treatment to the point
that it was interfering with therapy.

    The patient's parents were a middle-aged Jewish couple;
the patient was a wanted child, born five years after the
marriage. She had one sibling, a brother two years younger.
The patient had always been a good eater who loved her
bottle and apparently made no objection to the transfer to
the cup. She was toilet trained very early and established
both bowel and bladder control by the age of two. There
were many relapses in bowel control later. The mother
described the first eight years of the patient's life as
being quite happy, and it should be noted that the father
traveled a good bit of the time and was not home very much.
The mother felt that the family was fairly closely knit
and harmonious during this period.

    Early in the patient's school years she became very
competitive and would often write much longer themes than
were required, and everything she did caused an expenditure
of an exhausting amount of energy. As a child she was
closer to her father than to her mother. She became money
conscious early in life, and this pleased her father a
great deal. The patient's menarche occurred when she was
12. During the same year the patient's mother had a mastectomy and was ill for some time thereafter. About this
operation, the mother told the patient, "Don't ever let
them do this to you." Her menstrual periods were irregular
early in her life, and she seemed to be acutely uncomfortable

about any physical contacts with her parents. It was around this time that she began to have a problem about eating. She recalls that right around the beginning of puberty a doctor told her that she could have a nicely rounded female figure if she would eat more. When the patient was 13 the mother had a thyroidectomy, and two years later a second mastectomy.

After the second mastectomy the patient would barely go to the mother's room to speak to her. She knew that she should be growing closer to her mother but had the feeling that she could not because "Mother somehow seemed so incomplete." She began to get hostile and openly defiant towards both parents, and overtly rebellious and stubborn. The serious eating problem appeared about this time. She would sit at the table with her family but often would not eat, then later at night she would raid the refrigerator. The patient became very jealous of her brother's relationship with their father and she began to compete scholastically with the brother. There was a brief period of psychiatric help during her mid-teens. Because of her intense desire, the parents allowed her to go to the university of her choice, but there she skipped her meals and then stole food from the kitchen. During her freshman and sophomore years the patient's desire to steal food reappeared but she was able to refrain. Finally, early in the sophomore year the school asked for her to be removed. From here on out she eventually found her way into a psychiatric hospital and then was transferred here.

2. Summary of Situational Variables at the Time of Initial Study

At the time of the initial study the parents were living in a large city and the patient was an inpatient at the hospital. She had just begun her psychoanalysis. The primary conflict in this patient was defined by the Patient Variables team as being at the oral level, but evidence of the anal and phallic conflicts were seen as well. The oedipal conflict was manifested largely as her struggle against femininity. On the one hand she tried to make herself slim and trim like Peter Pan, and on the other hand she tended to overeat and, in her opinion, become too fat. The fact of the matter is that when she was heavier her figure was quite feminine in appearance. Her weight seemed quite appropriate for her age.

The most obvious conflict triggers were the parents, who were somewhat removed, and her own expectation that

she would blossom into a young woman. It may be somewhat
more difficult to see this as an external variable; however,
it was a social norm toward which she felt drawn. Thus
heterosexuality in its broadest sense was a triggering
challenge for her. At the same time, of course, her own
instinctual strivings were pushing from within. That the
father was conflict-triggering can be observed in the
patient's extreme discomfort when close to him physically.
The oedipal rivalry in relation to the mother, and the
patient's image of the mother as an unsuitable identification object, can be seen in her extreme discomfort around
the mother.

There were no stresses in this patient's life; supports were quite abundant; her parents were solidly behind
her; she had the hospital for a time but eventually she was
living on her own. Opportunities for this young person
were nearly unlimited. Need-congruence was rather poor.
Her parents had always been too indulgent and had played
into her conflicts. The father, with his seductiveness,
was hardly congruent, and the mother with her too giving
attitude, and the lack of controls imposed upon the patient
by them was need-incongruent. In short, not only were the
parents conflict-triggering, but they were hardly need-
congruent variables in her environment even though at the
time they were supportive.

3.   Summary of Situational Variables at the Time of Termi-
     nation Study

The patient began her analysis and was seen for over
500 hours, terminated, and then reentered treatment in
another city after leaving Topeka.

Some of the important events during this period are
as follows. Early in treatment she continued her stealing,
she began a relationship with a boyfriend (whom she eventually married); there were two attempts at suicide, one
by wandering into the river and the other by taking an
overdose of sedatives. She began to dress more appropriately and appeared more as a woman than a sexless girl.
The relationship with the boy thickened and she found her
parents were, at least on the surface, accepting of him.
She attended university courses towards the latter part of
the analysis. She got along much better with her family,
and they were so impressed by her improvement that they
were willing to agree to her marriage. Because her boyfriend wanted to go to school elsewhere she terminated
her analysis and lived with him several months before they

married. The stealing stopped early in her analysis; however the overeating and fasting never did disappear completely. The patient was in treatment briefly elsewhere and then finally married the young man she had met in Topeka.

At the time of termination both she and her future husband were students at the university. It is evident that the patient gained considerable insight into her core problems, and it is noteworthy that she was able to marry, something one would hardly have expected to be possible. The basic conflicts were touched at least to some degree. She also had been able to extricate herself from her family, something her earlier hostility towards them no doubt was designed to accomplish, thus making it possible for her to marry. Her stealing was under control but her overeating and fasting were not.

That she was still quite a troubled girl was evidenced by the fact that she had some difficulty in the intimate aspects of her marriage, she still had difficulty accentuating her beauty and appearing as feminine as possible. She was frigid a good part of the time and noted that she reached orgasm less after marriage than she had before. The analytic evidence for a pronounced phallic-oedipal core conflict is abundant. A good part of her analysis had to do with trying to avoid the feminine role on the one hand and, on the other, she made herself have a pot belly and look pregnant. Competitiveness with men was quite clear, and underlying this no doubt was the early relationship to the brother as well as the wish for the penis. She experienced considerable difficulty in bringing her husband to the parental home, but she was able to do it. She said jokingly at one point that evidently her father was not able to imagine her sleeping with a man. We can, therefore, say that the challenge of becoming a woman was still conflict-triggering. The husband was certainly conflict-triggering in two ways. On the one hand he kept alive the oedipal problems, and on the other hand she lived out some of her competitiveness in relation to him. The parents were still conflict-triggering but clearly less so, but of course it should be noted that there was a much greater geographic distance between them.

Despite the fact that there has been criticism leveled at the first analysis, it would seem that these views are not wholly correct. It appears that more of the neurosis was resolved during that experience than might first meet the eye. Of course when the patient was in the analysis she was going through a maturational period in her life,

and some of the changes can be accounted for by these maturational processes.

4. Summary of Situational Variables at the Time of Follow-
    up Study

       By the time of follow-up the patient and her husband
had moved to another large city. Both had graduated with
a college degree and she had gotten a scholarship for postgraduate study in the same general area as her husband's
primary area of interest. They were living on the money
they had and refused help from her parents. By the time
of follow-up it would seem that her level of adjustment
was just about the same as it had been at the time of termination. There were still gross difficulties in the sexual
area. She now stated that she never had orgasm since she
left treatment in Topeka. She could cook for her husband
but was unable to sit and eat with him. Her compulsive
overeating interfered with social engagement for the simple
reason that any time food was to be served she didn't want
to go. On the other hand, she could partly fulfill the
role of wife and homemaker but she still needed her husband's help with these tasks. She found that she could
dress more femininely on some occasions but not on all,
and she was unable to use nail polish.

       That the parents were still somewhat conflict-trigger-
ing is evidenced by the fact that the patient and her husband got along much better with the father when he came
alone than when both parents came together. Clearly, the
husband and the need to be a homemaker were still conflict-
triggering. The patient was pregnant once, but aborted
spontaneously.

       Supports were rather good; the patient had the full
support of her husband's parents; the husband was extremely
supportive in that he helped her with many of the home
responsibilities. Need-congruence was fairly good, she
had a home of her own, but her husband was really not too
much of a man; in fact, a great deal in the husband resonated with the neurotic elements in her. More of a man
would never have put up with the unfeminine qualities in
her. The parents were need-congruent in that they objected
to the somewhat Bohemian style in which the patient and
her husband lived and they tried to foster a more conven-
tional outlook towards life in both of them. It seems that
the patient's father was more accepting of the marriage
than the patient's mother. Having outlets to pursue her
intellectual interests was need-congruent. This was an

intelligent girl with obvious capabilities as a linguist
and it was useful and need-congruent for her to be able
to exercise these talents.

5. Summary

As overdetermined as this young person's neurosis was,
it would seem that the challenges of heterosexuality precipitated the illness. The pregenital determinants led to
the compulsive eating, stealing, the stubbornness, but as
the analysis unfolded it became clearer that the phallic-
oedipal problems occupied a central position in her neurosis and in her character makeup.

The mother's surgery seemed to have a triggering effect
on this patient and may have contributed to the outbreak
of her illness. The mother was stripped of some of her
femininity. This may have complicated the girl's identification with her mother and may have contributed to her
reluctance to have a feminine body lest she surpass her
mother whose femininity had been marred. Oral roots to her
overeating, as well as the phallic ones, were uncovered.
There was the wish to devour "breast-penis." By far the
overriding problem was for her to somehow avoid becoming
a woman. She was fiercely competitive and envious of the
penis, and guilt-ridden about taking the mother's place,
and threatened by the thought of female sexuality. The
parents' attitude towards the patient tended to keep these
conflicts alive. She, however, managed to extricate herself from her parents and eventually placed much geographic
distance between herself and them.

That she was able to take a man in her life and eventually become somewhat more feminine points to some resolution of the intrapsychic problem as well as to some spontaneous maturation that she may have achieved during the
time she was in treatment. While in treatment she was of
an age when maturation normally takes place. But even
though she married, she was by no means able to fully live
out the feminine role. Evidence for this is abundant and
it is clear that she picked a man who was rather weak.
His passivity blended with the nonfeminine elements in her.
He was need-incongruent from the point of view of bringing out the best of the female in her.

This case illustrates how, through treatment, the
patient resolved some of her conflicts and was able to do
after treatment what she could not do before. On the other
hand, some of her ability to move forward may be accounted

for by the removal of the conflict triggers. Finally, it
is evident that the man in her life was a conflict trigger
for she could not eat with him, had found it difficult to
become pregnant or to remain so, and she remained frigid.

SYNTHESIS OF SITUATIONAL VARIABLES - CASE #24

1. Brief History

    This patient was in his early thirties and single when
he came for his evaluation. He complained of being quite
upset; he felt that he was not getting enough out of life,
nor had he been able to realize his potentialities in his
professional work.

    The patient's father was a taciturn, moralistic, hard-
working man, and a financially unsuccessful salesman. The
patient had always been ashamed of his father's occupation,
and claimed never to have witnessed his father doing the
nice, gentle or sweet things for the mother which the patient
felt should be done. His relationship with his father had
always been distant and he disapproved of his father's ways.
Mother was described as a kindly but secretive, possessive,
and jealous woman who would sit endlessly in her chair
dozing. She never seemed to cook a meal but rather warmed
up leftovers. He was ashamed of both of his parents as far
back as he could remember, and angry with them for being
so poor.

    The patient was the youngest of three male sibs spaced
five and ten years apart. He was an unwanted child, born
when his mother had started the menopause. He was always
a solitary, sensitive youngster who experienced his childhood as bleak and he felt that he lived in a half-lighted
world in view of the fact that his family was always turning off lights in order to save money. He was afraid of
other children and clung to his mother, usually playing
close to her or alone. He grew up to be indecisive, inhibited, but managed to establish a series of relationships, all of which had been marked by dependence on his
part, accompanied by feelings of helplessness. He was a
slow, perfectionistic person who exasperated others by this
behavior. He consciously felt himself to be a mama's boy
and recognized that he was stubborn and tended to pout and
to be possessive of the people he was dependent on. He

won a scholarship and attended a university. Because of
the excellence of his work he attained a second scholarship and took two more years in his chosen field. He liked
to associate with homosexuals but never got overtly involved.

After completing this work he went into the service
where he was urged to enter officers' training but he felt
unqualified. He hated his service experience, and after
completing it he returned to the university and completed
a five-year program. Because of some seductive overtones
in a male friend's behavior he decided to leave. Another
reason for his leaving was his increasing concern about
his parents for whom he felt responsible. He obtained em-
ployment but left after three months because he could not
accept their philosophy. He easily obtained another job
where he was able to work more independently. He spent
nearly five years in that city and during this time established a pattern of working five days at his job and then
going home for the weekend to be with his parents. He made
a number of attempts to change this pattern but was unable
to do so. He wanted a relationship with a woman but felt
no woman would want him, and was unable to reach this goal.

Although his character illness had existed for many
years, he dated the recognition of his need for treatment
to a weekend with his parents where there had been a great
deal of discussion about his building a home for himself
and his parents. He had returned to work on Monday and as
he tried to work he became increasingly uncomfortable,
with a vague sense of apprehensiveness which eventually
became an acute anxiety attack. He took two weeks leave
and stayed home with his parents during this time. During
this period he decided he would come to Topeka and he began his treatment in the mid-fifties.

2. Summary of Situational Variables at the Time of Initial
   Study

The massive inhibition and compulsive character traits,
as well as the passivity, implicated the core neurotic
problem as revolving around the anal and phallic-oedipal
phases. The evidence for the oedipal problems are the
gifts to the mother and the indirect disparagement of the
father, and the lack of heterosexual life. The conflict
triggers were quite clearly the parents, to whom he was
inextricably tied, and the challenge of establishing a
heterosexual relationship. Success at work appeared not
to be conflict-triggering although even there it was clear
that he had not completely fulfilled himself, despite his

successes at the university. The possibility of building a home and moving into it with his family seems to have been the trigger which precipitated the acute anxiety attack which, in turn, finally sent him running to the psychiatrist. The parents, because of their clinging attitude toward the patient, may be considered moderately stressful.

The supports for this patient were fairly abundant. He had a lot of supports from his work, of course, and in their own way the parents were supportive in their attitude towards him. Need-congruence was limited solely to his work situation. It was highly need-incongruent for him to remain so closely tied to his parents, to live in a single room in a rooming house, and to have no friends to speak of. Opportunities actually were rather good for him but the horizons receded because of his neurotic limitations.

3. Summary of Situational Variables at the Time of Termination Study

This patient's analysis, at the rate of five times a week, totalled over 1000 hours. The most obvious effect of treatment was that he gained 30 pounds. The psychologist reported more anxiety but a greater ability to tolerate it; he was freer of depressive feelings; sexual conflicts still seemed to be a live issue but stimulated acute anxiety less; he seemed to be more capable of putting up with his relationship to his parents.

In the behavioral realm, however, not much change took place; he continued to live in a room in a rooming house; he had no serious female attachments; his work continued at about the same level of creativeness. And it was quite evident that despite his lengthy analysis no significant alteration took place in his core conflicts; this being so, all of those environmental factors that were conflict-triggering at the time of initial study still had this effect. He did, however, become a little more comfortable with other men and with his father. He was somewhat less preoccupied with thoughts of providing for his parents. At termination he insisted that he was not interested in girls. Stresses were about the same at termination; supports about the same; and need-congruence about the same.

4. Summary of Situational Variables at the Time of Follow-
up Study

By the time of follow-up the patient was still working for the same firm that he was at the time he began his
analysis. He was still terrified of women, frankly admit-
ting this to one of the research members; he still lived
in the same quarters and, although shocked at himself for
living in such circumstances, he seemed rather content with
his surroundings. He carried the belief that something
would happen to improve his life without his having to
raise a finger. As mentioned, women still terrified him;
he was more or less friendless. In short, other than his
involvement at work he was extremely uninvolved in life.
He still visited his parents in much the same way he did
at termination. He still had the urge to build a home for
his parents, but he recognized that it would be a mistake
to do that because they would find the care of a home of
their own a real burden. He continued to spend nearly
every Sunday in their home.

5. Summary

This is an example of nothing much being accomplished
by treatment. The patient had developed an acute anxiety
state when he, presumably, was being pushed into a closer
relationship with his parents. It may be that his counter-
urges to totally extricate himself activated intense separation anxiety. We are not clear just what this initial
attack of anxiety was about. It is evident, however, that
this was a man who was more or less uninvolved in life
except for the work area. He remained closely tied to his
family and other than these two areas in his life had no
meaningful interaction with the world around him.

He went into analysis, which presumably proved to be
a highly intellectualized experience, and although he may
have gained a good deal of intellectual insight he never
reached new ways of adjusting to life. He may have come
to know himself somewhat better, but the old life patterns
persisted. In short, nothing much really happened in this
treatment; he may have arrived at some sense of having
been accepted by the analyst, he may have overcome some
of his guilt. The dependent gratification of the analysis
may have offset his anxiety some; he became somewhat less
symptomatic but again, in essence, remained an unchanged
man.

This case illustrates beautifully the importance of

having a patient become involved in life while he is in treatment; otherwise the insights are never worked through in the context of life experiences. Furthermore, the un-involvement in life precludes a full attainment of insight because unconscious conflicts unquestionably remain dormant.

SYNTHESIS OF SITUATIONAL VARIABLES - CASE #25

1. Brief History

      This patient was in his mid-teens when he came for his
evaluation. He had been caught running naked near some
houses on two occasions, riding horseback naked, and there
was a history of poor school adjustment and complaints of
anxiety.

      The patient was the grandson of the founder of a
well-known manufacturing concern. He recalled little of
his natural mother. She left home when he was a very small
child, and is said to have been alcoholic and promiscuous.
The patient saw her intermittently for a few years until
his father remarried. He feels (correctly) that his mother
was never very interested in him. He referred to her with
a good deal of anger and contempt. The father, an invalid,
did not get along well with his own father and left home
to live elsewhere and work for one of the father's busi-
nesses. The patient was fond of his father, happy with
him, but does remember a number of occasions on which he
was chastised. He recalled wishing his father was dead.

      The father did die when the patient was not yet a
teenager, the day after having punished the boy. The
father had asked for his heart pills right before his death
and the family has intimated that the patient was a little
slow in bringing them. The stepmother was in her mid-forties
at the time of the patient's evaluation. The patient was
bitter towards his stepmother because she talked so much
of the unhappiness in her past. He felt obligated to her
and felt quite torn between her and his paternal grandfather who was his legal guardian and who was openly antagonistic toward the stepmother.

      As a boy the patient was friendly and made superficial
friendships with boys his own age, but he did not have any
close friends. Relationships with girls were usually platonic. He was quite naive sexually, regarding masturbation

245

as disgusting. The patient began to feel responsible for his father's death and to fail in school.

In his early teens he accidentally injured his stepmother and he felt that she believed he intended to hurt her. He could never be successful socially or in sports, although he had wanted to play basketball. Shortly prior to his evaluation he had been seized with an impulse to run naked through his grandfather's property, "to give me a sense of freedom." He did this on two separate occasions and also recalled having ridden a horse while naked when he was not yet a teenager. He denied having masturbated while nude in the grandfather's garden (this was an accusation), or that he was deliberately exhibiting himself. At the time of these events the patient was living alone with his stepmother across the street from his grandfather's home. One brother had been killed in Korea and the other was living elsewhere.

2. Summary of Situational Variables at the Time of Initial Study

The core conflicts that were defined at the time of initial study were at several levels. There was the object loss and the sense of oral deprivation revolving around the early loss of his mother. The major conflict that appeared on the psychological tests had to do with the conflict between conforming and rebelling. Just what the basis for this conflict was is not clear; whether this is conflict at the anal level or whether this is a passive homosexual conflict is uncertain. We know that the tests do show that he was deeply conflicted about sexuality. The phallic-oedipal conflict is implicated, as well as the oral dependency and object loss conflicts.

Conflict triggers were several, the worst of which was the absence of stable loving objects around him. Conditions of life such as these could only aggravate his sense of loneliness and loss. One can speculate that living alone with his stepmother must have been extremely conflict-triggering to him. Also conflict-triggering was the cultural background from which he came. The eminence of his family was a standard that he probably felt he could not live up to with any degree of success. It is quite likely that his need for freedom reflects an unwillingness or inability to accept responsibility. Therefore, any kind of demand from the environment that he persist and succeed is rebelled against for to succeed would be conflict-triggering. The grandfather's open rejection was conflict-triggering.

Stresses were plentiful, the primary one being the
cold, rejecting, unsympathetic grandfather. The emotional
vacuum in which he lived was a stress. Supports were only
moderate and these were primarily financial. It should be
noted that the stepmother, who seemed to have some genuine
interest in him, was prevented from maintaining a relationship with the patient by the grandfather, and it should
also be noted that the Menninger Foundation went along with
the wishes of the grandfather. There was nothing need-
congruent in this person's environment other than the
foster homes in which he was placed. The grandfather with
his harshness was not; the stepmother may have been moderately need-congruent; private schools may have had something to offer him, but a lonely, insecure, lost boy such
as this needed the warmth, acceptance, guidance, and stability of a home. This he did not have. Opportunities were
quite good. The grandfather unquestionably could have put
the world at this boy's feet had the boy been able to
succeed at anything.

3. Summary of Situational Variables at the Time of Termi-
    nation Study

The patient was in expressive-supportive psychotherapy
for over 200 hours on a twice-a-week basis. He was in
several foster homes. He didn't care too much for the first
one, he liked the second one, and he especially liked the
third. He completed high school and then prepared to enter
the university. It should be noted that he became disturbed shortly thereafter and had to enter the hospital.
He attempted to do volunteer work; he also completed one
semester at the university, and wanted to marry a girl
friend he had known for some time.

The grandfather complained about the cost of treatment, and it is interesting to note that a month later the
patient began to show disinterest in his therapy and his
day hospital activities. The therapy was soon terminated.
He hadn't been going to therapy regularly for some time.
The grandfather tried to have the patient work for one of
his enterprises but this was an abortive experience. The
patient became somewhat disturbed after having had a
couple of sexual affairs and reentered the hospital for
approximately one month. About this time the termination
study was done. Between hospitalizations he was living
in a foster home.

At termination his core conflicts were defined at two
levels. The phallic exhibitionistic voyeuristic oedipal
conflict and the dependent object loss conflict were still
evident. Anxiety indicative of castration anxiety seemed
to be more in evidence. Basically he was unchanged. There
may have been some redistribution of his anxiety and ability
to control it; there was some evidence of insight but in
the main he was an unaltered patient. The core problems
were clear by the time of termination but they were unaltered.
Much aggression toward the stepmother appeared; these were
fantasies of tearing, clawing, murdering and raping. He
was fearful that he might shoot his grandfather as he had
accidentally shot his stepmother. The most obvious conflict-
trigger was the grandfather.

Similar again was the absence of stable parental figures.
This situation had improved somewhat in that the foster
parents took a genuine interest in him. It was also obvious
that any effort to succeed, either at work or school or with
a girl, was conflict-triggering. Stresses were about the
same; the grandfather continued to be domineering and rejecting, but other than that there were no particular
stresses. Supports were more plentiful at the time of termination. There were the genuinely interested foster parents, and the grandfather continued to supply the money.
Opportunities as usual were unlimited; his life was a bit
more need -congruent than at the time of initial study.
What had changed was that he had some foster parents who
saw some growth and maturational needs in him.

He married and had a child, and the grandfather died.
The patient attempted various business ventures, including
some real estate deals which flopped. Through an intervention by a senior member of the Menninger Foundation the
patient was able to get back into college, but this collapsed.
He complained of being unable to hold himself to a regular
schedule. The marriage, interestingly enough, went rather
well in some respects. He found a lovely young girl for a
wife, who herself had been a patient. She seemed quite
content with homemaking, wished to be a mother and eventually became one, and seemingly a good one. She tolerated
his sudden absences quite well. What most characterized
the patient, however, was his inability to really come to
roost either within his own family or with any kind of work.

4. Summary of Situational Variables at the Time of Follow-
   up Study

The core conflicts were obviously not changed; however,

he had gained some strength from somewhere for he was able
to marry and by the time of follow-up had two children. It
is conceivable that his strength came from the relationship
with the foster parents. It is unlikely that he carried
with him any fond feelsings toward the Menninger Foundation.
It should also be noted that one of the major conflict
triggers (the grandfather) had been removed by the time of
follow-up. Similarly, by having a wife and child much of
the loneliness and sense of deprivation was no longer triggered; but on the other hand, having a wife and children was
somewhat conflict-triggering. More conflict-triggering
than anything had been his inability to assume work responsibility. There were no stresses in his life; supports were
fairly good. He had the foster parents and the wife and
children. Need-congruence was improved. To have his own
family was certainly need-congruent, despite the fact that
the family was also conflict-triggering. The foster parents continued to be need-congruent. Opportunities were
abundant.

5. Summary

     This patient's illness erupted while he was living in
a highly conflict-triggering situation. Ever present was
the absence of close meaningful interpersonal relationships
which could offset the early object loss and later object
losses in his life. Significant is the fact that he was
living alone with his stepmother at the time he exhibited
himself nude. Although eventual hospitalization provided
him some security and protection, and despite the fact that
he entered a psychotherapeutic relationship, all the evidence
indicates that none of his intrapsychic difficulties were
essentially changed. He did, however, have a very meaningful relationship with his foster parents and probably to
some extent with his psychotherapist. He gained strength
somewhere, probably through the inherent maturational
process going on in him (in view of his age) and from these
meaningful, trusting, dependable relationships. He was able
to marry and have two children, and obviously these new
objects in his life permitted the sense of deprivation and
loss to recede deeper into his unconscious. At the same
time, the wife and two children had noticeably increased
his anxiety; he had gotten considerably fatter, and he was
still unable to hold a job or really stick to anything for
any length of time, and this includes just staying around
his home with his family. It is evident that any kind of
permanent or enduring commitment to life remained conflict-
triggering for him.

Post-follow-up information reveals the marriage to have failed at a time when the children were in their own oedipal years.

SYNTHESIS OF SITUATIONAL VARIABLES - CASE #26

1. Brief History

This patient came for treatment when he was in his
early forties. He was a physician who had been in private
practice, was married and had two adopted children. His
father was a well-known physician who was retired at the
time of the patient's evaluation, and who was described as
a shy, retiring man but one who was interested in his career,
had worked hard at it, and who wished that his money be
spent for his family and not hoarded and passed down after
his death. The mother was a more flamboyant person,
emotionally expressive and, in light of subsequent data
that has emerged about her, she was quite a castrating,
domineering type of woman. Nonetheless, the patient always
felt closer to his mother than to his father. The patient
had a brother two years younger, not as brilliant but who,
nevertheless, specialized and became successful.

The patient's early life was punctuated by some physical illnesses but none prevented him from growing up in the
style of a fairly active, energetic boy. He was popular
and had the advantage of an excellent education. In the
course of his education he followed his father's footsteps,
obtaining two professional degrees. The basis for his not
being appointed to a certain institution was that he was
too much of a loner and could not work closely with other
people.

As was customary in this family, the two sons were
allowed a year in Europe, during which time they could study
and travel. Prior to leaving for Europe the patient met a
young woman of whom he was quite fond. It should be noted
that he was drinking quite a lot during this period in his
life, presumably living out an identity that his mother
admired very much. This refers to hard drinking. There
was an understanding between the patient and his girl that
they were committed to each other and during the year in
Europe his drinking reached extreme proportions.

251

Upon his return, and because of the belief that his
girl friend was pregnant, they married secretly. It was
at this time that the drinking became even worse, and it
was then too that he had his first severe accident in which
he badly damaged his hand. About this marriage, the material
from the analysis reveals that at one point he said to his
mother with regard to having married, "Please forgive me,
I'll never do this to you again." He also began medical
school when he married, and both of these events coincide
with the onset of his drug addiction. He stated that he
felt trapped in the marriage; the wife was a frigid, bitchy,
sarcastic type of woman who was, in many respects, similar
to his mother. Nonetheless he went through medical school,
completed an internship, completed residency and studies
for a second degree, obtained a commission in the service
and served for two years. There is some evidence that he
was freer of some of his symptoms while in the service.

After military service he began private practice and
adopted some children. His behavior began to progressively
deteriorate and in two years he was quite decompensated.
He was taking large doses of drugs intravenously. He had
an auto accident in which he sustained a severe injury. He
had become destructive in his home, once assaulted his wife,
and finally moved out. His father retrieved him and had
him evaluated, after which there was a brief effort to return to work, but he then decompensated again and was
brought to Topeka. He stayed in the hospital one year,
funds coming from his parents' retirement savings. He began his psychoanalysis approximately two months after entering the hospital and was seen five times a week.

2. Summary of Situational Variables at the Time of Initial
    Study

Although the Patient Variables team found evidence of
conflicts at all levels of psychosexual development, the
phallic-oedipal level seemed to be the primary area of difficulty. It should be noted that the conflict triggers are
those of adult male responsibility. The first evidence of
the conflict-triggering impact of the environment was when
he became interested in a girl whom he felt he would marry,
thus suggesting that an impending heterosexual relationship was conflict-triggering. Even though physically removed from her for a year he began drinking then and upon
his return the conflict triggers became more intense. He
not only married this girl but started medical school and
thus was launched towards a professional development that
paralleled that of his father, a man whom he greatly admired.

When he did marry and start medical school his symptoms
became worse. It was at this point that his addiction
first appeared. The accident was obviously a self-destructive act; he did receive a severe injury and it occurred
during a drunken binge. We don't know just how conflict-
triggering the added responsibilities of the two adopted
children were.

There may have been a period of partial relief during
the time he was in the service. The patient stated that
that the two years in the service were his very best for
he was free of symptoms and for the most part he was free
of drugs. It should be noted that under those circumstances
he was not following his father's footsteps directly and he
was physically removed from his parents, although he probably
had his wife with him. We don't know, but she may have
been working. When he returned from the service he began
private practice and his symptoms reappeared. This private
practice was in a community neighboring that of his parents.
The practice of medicine and being a family man were obviously conflict-triggering for at this point his symptoms
became much worse.

The stresses were considerable during these years;
most of these were of a feedback variety associated with
the intake of drugs and alcohol. On the other hand, private practice is a stressful occupation; however, this
alone certainly could not account for his symptoms. The
supports were seemingly abundant. He knew that his parents
admired him; in fact, somewhere in the story the father
referred to him as the apple of his eye, but interestingly
enough the mother was probably not as supportive as castra-
tive. When he confessed his drug taking to her she pledged
not to tell anyone about it. This can hardly be truly
supportive but, rather, played into his sickness. It
should be mentioned that the mother's ambition for the
patient was that he be an English teacher in a girls'
boarding school.

Opportunities were abundant for this man. Need-congruence was limited. On the one hand, his profession was
quite need-congruent (it is evident that he was deeply
identified with his father and if he had not been intrapsychically conflicted he would have been able to live out
that identity). On the other hand, however, the mother
was not need-congruent, and to some extent the father's
personality was not either. The father was too passive,
the mother too aggressive. Their personalities were not
need-congruent insofar as helping him find himself as a man.

The most need-incongruent person of all insofar as helping him mature was the wife. She was a hostile, castrating type of woman who would tend to inhibit the development of his masculinity. However, he did have a marriage, a home and children, which would tend to bring out the best in him.

3. Summary of Situational Variables at the Time of Termination Study

The patient was treated by psychoanalysis five times a week for over 1000 hours. He moved out of the hospital after one year and began to see his present wife, who was a patient of his analyst. He applied for and received his Kansas Medical License and began a practice shortly thereafter. He later took a job at a hospital. The patient decided to divorce his wife while in treatment. He made a major step forward when he was able to read a paper at a medical meeting.

Four years after the onset of his treatment his mother, father and brother had serious illnesses. He withstood these crises fairly well. He married the woman who was in analysis with his analyst; both were still in treatment at the time although he was about to terminate. He was elected to membership in a prestigious organization. His wife became pregnant prior to this termination. The patient's adopted son came to live with them. When the patient terminated treatment he was working as a physician, he had established a home, had his wife's own three children and his adopted son, and they had a baby of their own. His adjustment was good.

The patient's analyst defined the core problems as being largely oedipal and explained his symptoms, including the severe alcoholism, on this basis. The passive homosexual conflict emerged, as did the fear of success. In short, all of his symptoms, including his failures, were classically oedipal in nature.

The patient had established a good relationship with his father before the latter died, and he saw his mother in much clearer perspective. His success in marriage and at work, and the absence of symptoms, would, therefore, suggest significant resolution of the intrapsychic problems.

There were some environmental changes that might be viewed as changes in the conflict triggers. He was no longer living in the old environment in private practice

and with the same wife as before. The patient made the
remark that he doubted his improvement would have held up
had he returned to the old environment. He noted that his
medical work was at a considerably lower key than when he
was in private practice. Although he was able to work,
which reflects some resolution of core conflict, it is also
possible that his ability to work to some extent reflects
a lessening in intensity of the conflict-triggering environment. He certainly could be a father now, whereas he
could not do this before. He also could stand family life
better than he could before, evidence that the conflicts
had been somewhat resolved. A major change had occurred in
his choice of wives, however. The first wife was a hostile,
castrating woman; the second wife was quite different insofar
as personality makeup was concerned. Thus it seems reasonable to say that he had found a woman who was more need-
congruent. She seemed to resonate with the more adult and
mature elements in his personality in contrast to the first
wife who resonated more with unconscious neurotic elements.
The father was no longer living, and this removed a major
conflict-trigger. It should be mentioned that plans for
marriage antidated the father's death by approximately a
year and half and that the marriage occurred over a year
before the father died. There is some evidence, however,
that all of the core problems were not resolved and that
he used work as a means for avoiding family life.

There were no stresses at the time of termination with
the exception of all of the children he had to take care
of, but he could get away from them through his work. There
were some supports; he had his wife, the Topeka community
with which he had become a part, and his former analyst
still lived in that community. Opportunities were quite
rich for him and his life was very need-congruent.

4. Summary of Situational Variables at the Time of Follow-
    up Study

At the time of follow-up the patient had moved closer
to town, he had his wife's three children, both of his
previously adopted children, and two children from the
present marriage. He was working at a hospital. There
was no evidence of a recurrence of his symptoms, with the
possible exception of some drivenness. He admitted that
sometimes he was tempted to jump into action, but that he
managed to curb himself. The marital adjustments seemed
to be satisfactory although he noted that one has to work
at a marriage to make it succeed. Psychological tests
indicated quite a lot of change in his makeup, yet there

were many hints of conflict in the sexual area. He denied any disturbance in his sexual functioning, however. All in all, his adjustment seemed at least to have sustained itself if not improved somewhat during follow-up. Core conflicts were about the same as at the time of termination; that is to say, considerably worked through, with much insight and evidently considerable resolution. There were very few obvious conflict triggers in his life. In this case this was so because there were fewer conflicts to be triggered. Need-congruence was good; the man had a family.

5. Summary

This case illustrates especially clearly the conflict-triggering impact of the environment. The patient first became obviously symptomatic when he entered into a close heterosexual involvement. As he took active steps to become a physician and ultimately follow his father's footsteps, unconscious conflicts were increasingly mobilized. He finally decompensated when he had assumed a number of adult responsibilities. There were the practice of medicine, home life, the role of a husband, father, and breadwinner. It would seem that the favorable outcome in this case relates to changes in two areas. There was a significant reduction in core conflict, and there were some environmental changes too. He had changed his practice of medicine from a highly competitive, more taxing kind to a less stressful institutional type of work; he got rid of a need-incongruent wife and found one who was considerably more need-congruent. In addition to this, his father had died, but it should be noted that his relationship to him had improved markedly before the father's death.

SYNTHESIS OF SITUATIONAL VARIABLES - CASE #27

1. Brief History

This patient came for an evaluation when he was in his late twenties. He was unmarried, had been seen at a clinic, and because of the severity of his illness was admitted to our hospital. He was a severe alcoholic, his interpersonal relationships had deteriorated, and he was unable to work.

The patient came from a family with a strongly religious tradition. He was the second child and only son of a businessman who, like his father before him, had been very successful in the business. The father, however, was viewed by the patient as somewhat weak in relation to his mother who was the more dominant one of the pair. In addition to this, she had independent wealth which seemed to reinforce her position of strength. Shortly after his birth the mother had to leave for health reasons and, therefore, he missed out on the close mother relationship in the beginning days of his life. The mother was subject to depressive episodes and alcoholism, requiring hospitalization for these illnesses. It is noted that from the time the patient was a young child the parents slept in separate bedrooms.

The patient ground his teeth as a child, he was enuretic until he was six, and he recalls many nightmares during his youth. With the coming of puberty the patient got into a running open conflict with his father, frequently threatened to kill him, assaulted him, and on one occasion the father moved out of the house. At the time of puberty the patient developed marked feelings of inadequacy, compulsive masturbation, and started drinking heavily in his midteens. His alcoholism was punctuated by periods of blackouts and amnesia. He had one good period in his life for about three years when he worked in a business similar to his father's. The father had gotten his son this job. The patient worked up from errand boy to a higher position.

Upon entering the Army he began drinking again and apparently this was a continuous problem throughout his two years in the service, one year of which was spent overseas. Just prior to his coming for treatment he had had a somewhat extended affair with a woman five years older than he. He had left home, ostensibly to get a new start in life, but then picked up with this older woman and continued his downhill course and finally sought treatment on his own initiative.

2. Summary of Situational Variables at the Time of Initial Study

The core conflicts in this case are quite clearly oral and phallic-oedipal. The open running battle with his father is perhaps the best evidence of the latter conflict. At one point he stated that dating girls was a nightmarish experience for him; he was beset with feelings of inadequacy and compulsive masturbation. He evidently did not have a strong father with whom he could identify and who would prevent him from developing too strong an attachment and eventual identification with his mother. It is quite clear that the parents themselves were conflict-triggering and tended to keep alive the repressed infantile conflicts. To succeed at work was conflict-triggering, and certainly the demand to establish heterosexual object relations was the most conflict-triggering of all.

Supports had been somewhat plentiful in his life; his parents had given him a good cultural background, education was available to him, and he might have stepped into his father's footsteps in the business had he been able to accept this. This implies also that the opportunities for becoming something were good. The business and cultural environments were need-congruent for this patient; however, the patient's own family was not very need-congruent. This was so because the mother was a dominant, aggressive person and the father more of a weak man who failed to offer the patient a good identification object. The patient did not have much of a private life of his own and therefore this area is grossly lacking in need-congruence.

3. Summary of Situational Variables at the Time of Termination Study

The patient entered the hospital and approximately eight months later began psychoanalysis five times a week, for a bit over 500 hours. This had not been a classical analysis. At one point, because it was believed he was

not analyzable, he was sat up and treated by psychotherapy.
It should be noted from the progress notes of the therapist
that after he sat the patient up the patient's adjustment
improved remarkably, and that when the analysis was resumed
the patient did poorly again. The treatment was permanently
changed from psychoanalysis to psychotherapy, whereupon he
began to do better again.

After his discharge from the hospital he began a full-
time job in a store but because of sexual acting out,
drinking and missing hours he had to be hospitalized for a
few days. He then worked as a salesman and did rather well
at that. Both of his parents died within a week of each
other about midway in his treatment. Because he was doing
poorly in his treatment there was a reevaluation conference
and it was recommended again that the patient be transferred
to psychotherapy. Since the patient was dissatisfied with
this he decided to go elsewhere. The consultant agreed to
let that happen, thus the treatment was not completed.

It is obvious that this treatment was a complete failure,
that psychoanalysis was not the treatment choice, and that
somehow the therapist was not up to handling this patient
adequately. Therefore the core conflicts were unresolved
and the conflict triggers remained essentially the same.
These, in brief, were the responsibilities of maturity,
and more specifically the conflict-triggering impact of
establishing a heterosexual relationship. None of his relationships with women succeeded, nor did his efforts to
work.

Loneliness unquestionably was a conflict trigger, and
the fact that both of his parents died removed two significant conflict triggers but their very death may have activated the loneliness and early object loss problem in him.
Stresses were the parental deaths and the feedback stress
of drinking. Supports were sharply diminished at the time
of termination, and his money was beginning to run out.
Opportunities were somewhat less now because the father
could no longer offer him entry into the business world.
Very little was need-congruent in his life.

4. Situational Variables at the Time of Follow-up Study

This man continued to drink and live a vagabond's
existence for nearly two years after termination. At the
time he reached rock bottom he was finally disowned by his
sister. He then met a woman whom he started to look after,
but it turned out that she began looking after him. He

described her as a very powerful, broad-shouldered, strong person who seemed to bring stability to his life. After he met her he started going to AA and then eventually he began working. He got simple work at first and finally, by the time of follow-up, he was working for a company and living in a kind of common-law relationship with this woman.

Since the core conflicts in this patient were not resolved, it must be presumed that responsibility and a heterosexual relationship were still conflict-triggering. There seems to be a paradox here, however, because he was now able to work and maintain a relationship of sorts with a woman and still not drink and, in fact, if we can take his own account seriously he was better off in his adjustment than he had been for years - perhaps ever in his life with the possible exception of a brief period in the early fifties.

When one considers the personality characteristics of the woman it becomes a little clearer why his adjustment may have improved. Not only did he reach rock bottom and discover that something had to change, but the woman he chose for a heterosexual object relationship was a dominant one. She combined two characteristics - there was a tendency in her to mother him, which must have suited his oral dependent needs, and she was strong and aggressive sexually, a quality which apparently resonated with his own sexual passivity. Another interesting development just prior to the follow-up study was his renewed interest in religion. His faith in God was restored, and this may reflect some ongoing intrapsychic identification process. It is noted in his termination interview that he had been angry at God, that he had had difficulty in accepting the concept of God because earlier in his life he had identified his father with God. Subsequent information indicates that the patient did marry this woman, she was pregnant, and the patient had continued to remain sober.

5. Summary

By our usual criteria, a conflict-resolving therapy did not take place. Since heterosexuality and responsibility had been the conflict triggers at the time of initial study, and in view of the fact that at follow-up the man was working, sober and essentially married, one wonders what had happened to him intrapsychically to make these changes possible. Post-follow-up data indicated that he did marry, that his wife was pregnant, and that he had continued to work and receive raises and promotions. It is

noteworthy that his interest in religion reappeared and that
he somehow found peace with God.

Several possibilities present themselves. It could
be that he gained much more insight from treatment than he
was willing to admit or give the therapist credit for, and
that he could only put these insights to use after he had
left the treatment situation, thus claiming the credit for
himself. It could be that his treatment initiated some
intrapsychic changes which then progressed by some spontaneous means so that intrapsychic conflict continued to
be resolved after he terminated. His changed attitude toward women, the fact that he could marry and get his wife
pregnant, and could remain on the job, are certainly indicative of some kind of intrapsychic change. Not to be overlooked is the fact that both of his parents, with whom he
had so alloplastically lived out his unconscious oral and
oedipal conflicts, were dead. This fact may have permitted his unconscious conflicts to sink into the deep
recesses of his unconscious, thus making it possible for
him to establish a heterosexual relationship and be more
responsible. Of course it could be that some of the intrapsychic change was a function of the natural maturational
process. The fact that he had clearly emerged to a higher
level after his illness than he ever had before his illness makes one think of the integrating effect that an illness process may have.

SYNTHESIS OF SITUATIONAL VARIABLES - CASE #28

1. Brief History

The patient was a married housewife in her mid-twenties
and the mother of an infant boy. Her husband was a student.
Her complaints were obesity, compulsive overeating, tension,
nervousness and guilt feelings; there was rather marked
marital discord; she stole money from her mother. There
was a more or less running battle with her mother. She had
a brother, four years older, with whom she never got along.
She had shoplifted as a child.

The parents were socially prominent in a small town,
and her father was a civic leader. The mother was described
as an irritable woman who carried a grudge, she was extremely
unpleasant if crossed, and very obese. She was a spotless
housekeeper but personally slovenly.

The patient stated that she had been nervous all of
her life; graceless, clumsy and prone to drop things. She
was a cute, chubby child but began to gain weight when she
started to school. She had few dates in high school, not
because she didn't have an interest in boys but because
she felt awkward and socially unpoised. The patient stated
that she was a sweet child until her teens and then had to
learn to rebel, fight and fight back at her mother or else
be swallowed up by the mother. Since that time there had
been nothing but bickering and arguing between the mother
and the patient.

During her freshman year in college she dated a great
deal and her grades were poor. She slowed her social activities during her sophomore year and improved her schoolwork. Because she wanted to get away from home, and in
particular from her mother, believing that this was the
only way she could develop any independence, she went out
of state for her third year, and there her study habits
improved markedly. She transferred to still another college
and there met her husband who was a serviceman. When he

262

returned from military service she quit school to marry him
and he enrolled in premedical work. He was two years younger
than the patient but in her estimation clearly superior to
her mentally and emotionally. She became pregnant immediately after marriage, had an easy pregnancy and delivery.
With only one serious affair to her name before she married,
her initial sexual adjustment with her husband was difficult partly, she thinks, because they honeymooned with his
parents. The patient subsequently developed a sadomasochistic relationship with her husband. Apparently she would
provoke, a fight would ensue, she would feel guilty and
attempt to atone and then, under these conditions, be able
to feel sexual arousal.

The final precipitant that led her to come for treatment seemed to have been the marriage. Whereas on the surface her reality situation appeared to be much better,
that is, she was away from her mother, was married to a man
she admired, and had a child, she actually became more
acutely aware of her psychologic disturbance. It would
seem, then, that she managed to maintain a sick equilibrium
up to the point of marriage, but soon after marriage found
herself needing help.

2. Summary of Situational Variables at the Time of Initial
   Study

The core conflict at the time of initial study was
thought to be sadomasochistic in nature and also an unresolved oedipal problem which she endeavored to resolve
through a hostile identification with her mother. The
treatment team did not stress the oral dependence but we
think that this was also a large component of her central
conflicts. She had been a nail-biter, garrulous, a heavy
smoker, spoke of her need to "fill an inner emptiness."
It is hard to say whether her outbursts of excessive eating were compulsive in nature or whether they reflected a
feverish effort to fill this inner emptiness. The oedipal
meaning is rather clear, for to overeat made her unattrac-
tive as a woman.

It is evident that the patient's parents were conflict-
triggering - the father because of the patient's intense
erotic attachment to him, and the mother because she triggered the oedipal submission and hostile aspects of her
oedipal problem, as well as the sense of oral deprivation.
The most significant conflict trigger, and the one which
apparently sent her off for treatment, was marriage and
motherhood. Presumably her efforts to commit herself to

a man and have a better marriage than mother was too much for her. The husband had begun to lose interest in her because of her obesity. Furthermore, her own efforts to become slim and attractive in order to secure her position with him became conflict-triggering. This would have made her more beautiful than her mother. The patient also equated slimness with weakness, and to be slim meant to her to be weaker than her mother. To be more attractive than her mother made her mother's rival. The husband clearly triggered the oedipal problems in the patient.

There were not many actual stresses in her life although the kind of mother this patient had could be considered stressful to some degree. Her own obesity was stressful for she was embarrassed about this and felt socially uncomfortable. There were some supporting elements in her life, most notable of which was the father, who consistently supported her treatment. There was a fair amount in her life that was need-congruent. She did have a husband, she had a home and a baby. The picture we got of her husband, however, was that he was weak, and in this sense he could not be considered to have been fully need-congruent. There was good opportunity for growth and maturation. If she wanted to develop some aspects of her personality outside the home she had a university atmosphere in which to do this. Her development as a woman may have been hampered somewhat by her husband because of his immaturity and passivity. Nothing was immutable in her life.

3. Summary of Situational Variables at the Time of Termination Study

This patient was treated by psychoanalysis five times a week for five years. A few weeks after she began analysis her husband admitted that he had been having an affair and he left home. There was a brief reconciliation but they gradually grew more distant and were finally divorced a little less than two years after treatment was begun. Upon the husband's insistence, the patient agreed to get a divorce. It should be noted that at the time this developed the patient had become increasingly hostile towards her mother. The patient's father died about midway in her treatment, and from then on the patient really had no men in her life save a few dates here and there. Her relationship with her mother steadily improved after the analyst pointed out how unjustified some of her criticisms were. It should be noted also that the patient's relationship to the mother improved after the divorce and after the father's death when there were no men in her life.

The patient terminated her analysis considerably less symptomatic in many respects; she was more content with herself and she was managing her child fairly well although she still had some help with it. She had started going to school and her relationship with her mother had improved considerably. She left analysis as obese as ever, however. She could not finish work on her Master's degree. She continued to live on her inheritance. She was described as less rebellious, less controlling, and less castrating. She was not yet working at the time of termination.

The treatment team stated that the biggest change had been a move in the direction of a firmer feminine identification with less protest against this. Signs of masculine protest were reduced in intensity. They noted that the patient's disturbance in the relationship with her mother had been reduced and that there was psychological test evidence to suggest there were less intense hostile feelings towards her. On the other hand, there was evidence that this shift toward more feminine identity produced some anxiety and insecurity in her. Strong oral-passive yearnings were believed to have remained, but the struggle over rebelliousness and autonomy seemed reduced.

The patient described herself as being more thoughtful of other people, and she managed to care for her small son adequately. It should be noted, however, that some definite changes had taken place in her external situation. First and foremost is the fact that there was no husband. Clearly, then, one of the main conflict triggers had been removed. A second major conflict trigger was removed through the death of the father. In view of the removal of these two major triggers, one has to wonder whether the improved psychological test picture and her improved behavior was so much due to resolution of conflict rather than the fact that conflict sank more deeply into the unconscious. Apparently the mother had changed somewhat, too, and seemed to have softened her attitude some. The mother was probably not essentially changed but it seems that the softened behavior in the patient may have caused the mother to react less fiercely to her. The mother continued to be very good about taking care of the patient's child.

The patient had two supportive relationships; one was the mother and the other was another motherly lady who lived in the same apartment building. The relationship with the brother had grown worse. The patient recognized that she provoked fewer arguments with her mother and at the same time had gained a much better understanding of

her. The patient felt she could separate herself better
from her mother and prior to treatment the mother had represented all of her own faults. At termination she felt that
she saw her mother as a separate individual and even recognized that she loved her mother. She found a second mother
in the person of the landlady of the apartment building,
who was extremely supportive, took care of the child, and
was really the only close contact with another person that
the patient had. There continued to be some financial
support from the father's estate.

Need-congruence was worse in some respects and slightly
better in others. The environment was less need-congruent
because she had lost her marriage. On the other hand, the
relationship with her mother had improved and, therefore,
this segment of her life was more need-congruent. Opportunities for development were fairly good, with the main
obstacle, of course, the continued personal difficulties
as reflected in the obesity.

4. Summary of Situational Variables at the Time of Follow-
up Study

During the follow-up period the patient got a job in
a public school. She met her boyfriend, who was a teacher
and who wanted to be an entertainer. She lost weight but
was still obese. She visited her former analyst a few
months prior to having reached the lowest level in her
weight. After she was down to her lowest weight she managed to maintain a fairly good level of weight but when
the relationship to the boyfriend became serious and they
began talk of marriage she noticed that she promptly began
to gain weight again.

By follow-up the psychological tests indicated that
there had been a marked increase in the sexual identity
conflict amounting to a full reappearance of the homosexual
conflict. The test picture at follow-up appeared to be
essentially the same as it was at the time of initial study.
At follow-up the treatment team indicated the patient
showed moderate anxiety and they indicated that the relationship to the mother had become somewhat more hostile
than it was at termination. The relationship with the
possible husband reflected serious conflicts; for instance,
they had done nothing but very platonic petting during a
courtship of several months. The patient was able to work
for only one year and was not asked to return. She no
longer shoplifted, there was no sex life with her boyfriend,
who appeared to be inhibited if not impotent. Both the

oral and oedipal conflicts were implicated in the follow-up
assessments, and it seemed to the treatment team that little
resolution had taken place. She still spent money excessively. Although the treatment team and the tests indicated very little resolution of conflict, the Situational
Variables team suggested that there probably was some resolution. She was by no means the sloppy, narcissistic,
self-centered person she had been at the time of initial
study. It remains to be understood, however, what accounted
for this change. Two major conflict triggers in her life
were removed. It is notable that when a man entered her
life (the new boyfriend) she began to gain weight and her
relationship with her mother again became strained.

Opportunities for the future were fairly good, the
patient could work if she wanted to or was able to. If
she could lose weight she certainly could find a man because her real beauty began to show through when she was
thinner. Need-congruence at follow-up was about the way
it was at termination.

5. Summary

This was by no means a skillfully done psychoanalysis;
however, the patient was seen for an extraordinarily long
period of time and for a large number of hours, and it
cannot be assumed that her analyst functioned inadequately
during the entire period of her treatment. It seems quite
evident from our interviews with her that she gained some
insight into herself on many levels, and she certainly saw
into her relationship with her mother rather extensively.
Another improvement was that she did so much better with
her child. It seems correct, then, to say that the patient
at least saw into her conflicts and probably reduced them
to some extent. However, at the same time some major
changes took place in her life, changes which existed at
the time of the termination evaluation. She had lost her
father and she had lost her husband. In short, there were
no men in her life at all. Under these conditions it appears to be possible that the conflicts in her were not
only less triggered at termination but were less triggered
during a major portion of the treatment itself. That is
to say, the person of the analyst could not alone adequately
trigger her unconscious conflicts thus making them available for working through and resolution.

Something, however, happened to her unconscious problems because her test picture at termination seemed considerably better than at the time of initial study. It

should be noted also that she did not lose weight until
there were absolutely no men in her life, including her
analyst, and as soon as a man came into her life and with
the talk of marriage her weight began to reappear. This
suggests that conflicts in her still existed and that they
were subject to activation by this more intensified involvement with the opposite sex. Interestingly, the test picture
at follow-up again showed signs of greater illness; in fact,
it was considered to be very similar to that done at initial
study. One of the basic questions which has to be answered
in this case is whether this relatively poor outcome was
directly the responsibility of the analyst, that is to say
that this was not a thorough analysis, or whether the life
circumstances around this patient during the analysis precluded the possibility of a thorough analysis. The assumption underlying this latter statement is that had her father
been alive, had she continued her marriage, she might have
been able to do more extensive analytic work and resolve
her unconscious conflicts.

SYNTHESIS OF SITUATIONAL VARIABLES - CASE #29

1. Brief History

This patient came for an evaluation when she was in
her late teens. She failed in her first year of college,
drank episodically, and had become overtly homosexual.
While the patient was successful academically she told
fantastic stories about herself, such as being pregnant,
but it was largely the inability to get along with people
and her overt homosexuality which had been discovered that
led to her expulsion. Prior to these symptoms the patient
had been episodically belligerent and "hysterical" with
her parents, seemed to have become withdrawn and quite
self-centered and preoccupied.

The patient was the older of two children born into
a middle class family. The father was described by both
the patient and her mother as passive and a problem drinker.
The patient's mother was an aggressive woman who was active
in community affairs. The patient originally felt quite
close to her but in recent years had felt distant from her.
The patient thought that her mother was to blame for her
dislike of her father on the grounds that she would have
liked him better if the mother hadn't always been running
him down. She enjoyed a great deal of attention from her
parents during the first years of her life, particularly
from her father. Her brother was born when she was five
and because of his chronic illness the parents focused the
bulk of their attention on him believing that other relatives looked after her adequately.

The patient first began to show difficulty around age
11 or 12 when she became very difficult, if not impossible,
to discipline. She was "unconquered" by punishment such
as spanking and seemed to withdraw into an attitude of "You
can't hurt me." These difficulties grew worse as she went
through high school. She became uncontrollable, was heterosexually promiscuous and showed a strong need to express
contempt for the man by being cold and unresponsive. Her

269

difficulties seemed to come to a head while she was away
at a fashionable girls' school. She had become interested
in dramatics and thought that she could best develop her
talents at this school. As a result of an intense homosexual relationship which was discovered, the patient moved
into the Dean's home for the remainder of this semester
and then left school. She refused to see a psychiatrist
in her home town. It was when her parents discovered a
letter she had written to her homosexual friend that they
arranged for her to be seen at the Menninger Foundation.

2. Summary of Situational Variables at the Time of Initial
    Study

    The core conflicts in this patient were at several
levels. She was, first of all, a narcissistic person who
was very demanding and dependent in her aims. She was also
confused in her identification, having established a mixed
identity. This confusion seemed to stem from identification with a phallic-aggressive mother, and her own rejection
of her femininity which is associated with a male identification. The Rorschach supports the view of the centrality
of her penis envy and mixed identity. It was quite clear
that the theme of "not having gotten enough" stemmed from
the oral level, but probably also from the phallic level.
Her brother was born when she was five years old and this
sick boy took away practically all of the attention that
she used to get. A very close relationship developed between the patient and her mother. Submitting to external
control had been a conflict-triggering situation for her
most of her life. It seems probable that for her submitting or even cooperating with the environment was tanta-
mount to an admission of weakness and subjugation, something which in her mind characterized women. Her rebelliousness became most intense at puberty and coincided with
the promiscuity with males. The combination of the instinctual pressure from within and her involvement with
boys which, in turn, served as conflict triggers, leads us
to believe that she defensively then took flight into overt
homosexuality. To what extent her school work was conflict-triggering is not known. We do know that girls were
probably conflict-triggering in that they awakened her
latent homosexuality. Having more or less renounced boys
and substituted wild fantasies about her relationships
with them (such as getting pregnant) she intensified her
relationship with girls. We take note that one girl in
particular aroused acute anxiety in her. It's evident,
then, that both males and females were conflict-triggering.
Her identity disturbance was best illustrated by her typical

dress which consisted of blue jeans, a man's shirt with
shirttail out, and a mannish hair style.

The parents were conflict-triggering but in view of
their geographic distance from her it seems unlikely that
they exercised much of a conflict-triggering effect while
she was here in Topeka. There were no actual stresses as
such other than those of the feedback variety. There was
dissension in her parental home but this was at a distance.
The overt homosexual relationships were somewhat stressful
in that it was a socially unacceptable way of life.

Supports were fairly good. Despite the dissension
in her parental family, both parents wanted the very best
for her and supported her both emotionally and materially.
Opportunities were quite good. She was an attractive young
woman who could easily find a man and could develop a marital life if she could overcome her conflicts. She was
sufficiently appealing that she could pursue a career if
she desired. Her life was not particularly need-congruent
at the time of initial study. The father was too wishy-
washy, the mother was sticky. Living alone in an apartment was not good for her in the beginning. Hospitalization was need-congruent at the time of initial study but
she lost this as soon as she moved out.

3. Summary of Situational Variables at the Time of Termi-
    nation Study

The patient was in the hospital for about a year. Her
first effort at psychotherapy, which consisted of only a
few hours, was during the period she was in the hospital.
This never seemed to go very well. Her second psychotherapy
period began after she left the hospital, and was twice a
week for over three hundred hours. The patient lived in
an apartment, worked at various jobs and, initially after
leaving the hospital, was promiscuous in both heterosexual
and homosexual relationships. She also did a lot of drinking. Suddenly during treatment she bought some feminine
clothes and had her hair cut in a feminine way and dyed it,
but it is interesting to note that not long after that she
became intensely involved in a homosexual relationship,
thus illustrating the conflict-triggering effect of trying
to be feminine. She lost her job and continued her homosexual relationships rather freely. The girl with whom
she had the overt homosexual relationship was a few years
older.

The psychotherapist told us that he, in essence, helped

her adjust to a homosexual way of life and that he in no
way touched the core neurotic problem. This is a very re-
pressive girl who found great difficulty utilizing the psychotherapeutic process in an introspective exploratory
manner but on the other hand took very well to suggestions
and directions by the therapist.

The patient left psychotherapy a confirmed homosexual.
The symptoms were changed in the following ways. Heterosexual promiscuity had ceased; homosexuality had become
more severe and had become an ego syntonic pattern; hysterical outbursts had changed from severe to mild; she was still
narcissistically aloof; drinking ceased being a problem;
frigidity was still severe in her contacts with men. Depression was minimal; belligerence was minimal; impulsivity
was somewhat less; she was still compulsively neat. The
psychologist felt that the identity crisis was less in that
the phallic problems relating to this disturbance were not
as active at termination, a fact which we relate to her
having give up heterosexual goals.

Upon completing her psychotherapy the patient moved
to another city where she went to work in some large department store. There were no stresses in her life as
such other than the continuing homosexual existence, but
in view of the fact that she had more or less accepted this
way of life and was living in a large city it would appear
that this was a minimal stress.

There were not as many supports in this girl's life;
material support was nil. The relationship with the mother
was good, however. The core conflicts in this patient were
essentially unchanged. The main fixation seemed to be oral
dependence to a hostile phallic mother in relation to whom
she felt completely overwhelmed. The oedipal problem was
also a central issue with her. The therapist reported that
her dreams were always of a phallic nature, that she was
riding a bicycle, or that there was some machinery between
her legs. The most obvious conflict triggers for this
woman were men and the kind of life that a woman would live.
She avoided all of these conflict triggers by living a
homosexual existence, reporting that she still felt distant
and tense and uncomfortable around men, and in particular
around her father. She didn't even like male homosexuals.
Women still continued to be somewhat conflict-triggering,
and living alone triggered her loneliness.

Opportunities were still somewhat plentiful. The
opportunity for marriage was quite limited because of her

illness. Need-congruence was low. A heterosexual way of
life would be the most need-congruent of all for her and
this was completely lacking. Her interpersonal relationships resonated with the sick elements in her and in this
way helped perpetuate the illness. Her work was need-congruent, and with regard to work her mother was a helpful
factor. There was nothing immutable in her life.

4. Summary of Situational Variables at the Time of Follow-
    up Study

During the follow-up period the patient continued to
work in a department store. She had friends among the
homosexual crowd, shifting from one homosexual partner to
another. Interest in outside activities was completely
lacking. There were some depressive signs showing during
the follow-up interviews. The patient was living an aloof
type of existence. The examiner felt that should she experience a sudden rejection by a homosexual lover she might
even become suicidal. The patient, however, felt that she
was getting along somewhat better than she had at the time
of termination study. It was evident that she was completely committed to a homosexual way of life.

The symptom picture at the time of follow-up was about
the same as at termination. There was no heterosexual
promiscuity; homosexuality was severe; she was still moderately aloof; she was not drinking; anxiety, depression,
belligerence, impulsivity were all mild to moderate. She
was still a neat person.

In general the patient was less symptomatic in all
areas with the exception of the crystallized homosexuality.
This symptom picture is completely understandable in view
of the fact that she avoided all conflict triggers which
would resonate and activate those latent conflicts that
were never worked through in her therapy and which prevented
her from becoming a woman. This refers to her inverse
resolution of her Oedipus complex and the reinforcement
this area of conflict had received from pregenital factors,
most notably the dependent attachment to the angry submissive mother which had become her superego at this point.
By avoiding men, by carving out a little homosexual world
of her own, she had been able to divorce herself from all
of those demands of society which would activate these
unconscious conflicts. Instead, she fed her illness through
her homosexual behavior and by so doing lived in a most
need-incongruent environment. All that was need-congruent
was her work which must have given her some satisfaction

and self-respect and, of course, provided for her materially.

5. Summary

This girl developed the way she did because of her aggressive, masculine mother and passive, alcoholic, weak father. Parents of this sort and the trauma that occurred with the birth of her brother seemed to have sent her off into nonfeminine direction of development. Conforming to the standards of society was impossible for her because this meant establishing a feminine identity and developing male object relationships. She could not do this, and it is of special interest to note that her overt homosexuality broke out after a flurry of promiscuous heterosexuality. This flurry of promiscuity was her desperate effort to establish herself as a female. She retreated and finally settled on overt homosexual relationships. Dependence was manifested by overeating and drinking.

This patient was completely unable to utilize expressive psychotherapy except possibly for achieving insight at the most superficial level. Instead, she soaked up her therapist's guidance like a sponge. This kind of fatherly acceptance of her sexual inversion on the part of the therapist precluded resolution of core conflict, a fact the therapist freely admitted but defended because of her inability to work expressively in psychotherapy. The patient finally found relative quiescence in her life by avoiding all of those external demands which would arouse the unconscious conflicts that stood in her way of becoming a woman. Instead, the therapy helped her change the environment in a way that her neurotic needs (which outweighed the health in her) were best satisfied. In so doing she became relatively asymptomatic.

Although this patient probably had changed a great deal symptom-wise, she was essentially a very sick person when one thinks of the inverse identity that she had finally established. It is entirely possible that a different therapy might have helped her establish a feminine identity, especially if the therapist had more actively directed her toward that goal.

SYNTHESIS OF SITUATIONAL VARIABLES - CASE #30

1. Brief History

    This patient came for his evaluation during his late
twenties. He was a married physician who had been unable
to continue his residency. The crowning blow seems to have
been finding his wife in bed with another man. He gave the
man a terrible beating and, presumably because of this
episode, his own periods of depression, anxiety, and apathy,
and difficulty in working, he came for treatment.

    The patient was the oldest of four children born of
a successful physician. They were upper-class and strongly
identified with convention and proper living. Soon after
his birth the mother told the father that they should not
let this child divide them. His father was a cold, aloof
man with whom the patient presumably never developed a
close relationship, and the mother apparently had some
difficulty in rearing him. A good portion of his care was
relegated to maids.

    Always a shy, timid child, he first experienced diffi-
culty when he moved from his first home. The next period
of difficulty appeared when he started school. He had
trouble separating from his mother and experienced intense
anxiety. The mother apparently was uncertain about how to
handle her child for he remembers her frequently going out
to study groups to learn how to rear her child correctly.
As he approached his teens he remembers that he began
worrying about himself excessively. He became possessed
with feelings of inferiority, guilt and separateness from
his fellows and family. Although a large boy, he was afraid
to fight and often was bullied by peers. Masturbation began at age 13, something about which he developed extreme
guilt. He was depressed during his early to midteens and
at one point wrote a long confessional letter to his father
about his masturbation.

    Because of his interest in a promiscuous girl he became

so disturbed that his father referred him to a psychiatrist.
This man was kindly and supportive and reassuring, but surprisingly enough advised the patient to practice courtship
with his mother! After this first appointment the patient
never returned for the second. He continued to complain
of being a coward and a fraud or a phony. He did poorly
in college, flunked out once because of inattention to his
work and depression. He managed to get through college;
however, he had periodic psychiatric interviews. He began
medical school and married a year later. The marriage was
a stormy one from the beginning; he was never affectionate
with his wife; he used her for sexual gratification; and
later became sexually assaultive. The wife contributed in
a large measure to their financial support.

In the mid-fifties, after attending a wedding, he became elated and had to be admitted to a hospital for about
a month. He received electroshock and immediately improved.
In connection with this illness he felt that he had powers
over people, could stare at them and make them leave. He
returned to school and graduated and began his internship
soon thereafter. He did not do well during his internship
and had a particularly bad time on the OB service, but had
a rather good time on the eye service. The day before his
internship ended he felt he could no longer take it and
told his immediate supervisor that he was emotionally ill
and could no longer work. He was hospitalized for about
a month with depression and suicidal preoccupation. He
received several electroshocks and responded promptly.

He began medical residency, wished to switch to psychiatry but was refused. He took a residency in neurology
instead but again began to neglect his work. At about this
time he caught his wife in bed with another man, severely
beat the man and was then brought to the Menninger Foundation for an evaluation. He entered the hospital in an
elevated mood. He had just been granted a divorce. He
obtained work as a physician at a hospital even though he
was still an inpatient. He then entered a family care
home and began his psychotherapy.

2. Summary of Situational Variables at the Time of Initial
Study

At the beginning of his psychotherapy the patient, as
noted, was living in a foster care home and practicing
medicine at a hospital. The core conflicts were defined
at this time as a profound oral aggressive fixation to the
mother and an equally profound oedipal conflict.

In looking back over the history, it is clear that he had been very sick from early life on, however a more pronounced and manifest illness seems to have erupted during his early teens when he became stimulated from within by the coming of puberty. This activation of conflicts which occur during puberty unquestionably was reinforced by his efforts to establish object relationships, most notable of which, as recorded in the history, was the promiscuous girl. Presumably as a result of the periodic psychiatric attention he received, and also from the ever present support of his parents, he managed to get through school and finally enter medical school and marry. His behavior began to deteriorate some in college but it did not seriously begin to deteriorate until after he got married.

His increased symptomatology appeared in the form of depression, some suicidal thoughts, and fierce feelings of inferiority. It is obvious that as he advanced in life and came ever closer to the position of a married, practicing physician, his symptoms grew progressively worse. The crowning blow came when he found his wife in bed with another man. Thus it can be seen that all along the primary conflict triggers had to do with heterosexual object relations and work. When he was a small boy his parents were obviously severely conflict-triggering, and the advice of the psychiatrist didn't help this any when he suggested that the patient practice romancing with his mother.

At the time of the initial study he had, to a considerable extent, shed many of the conflict triggers. He was no longer actively involved in any kind of work; he had physically removed himself from his parents, thus lessening their current conflict-triggering significance, and he was divorced. That the wife had been severely conflict-triggering is clear from the nature of his attitude towards her and also from the referring physician's statement that she resembled the patient's mother to a great extent. It would seem likely that any woman would be conflict-triggering for him and so would any kind of work; however at the time of initial study, as we indicated, such triggers were absent.

There was hardly any stress in his life other than the disorganized existence which his own illness had created. It was somewhat stressful to find one's wife in bed with another man, however, the conflict-triggering aspect of this experience was the last straw. Supports were plentiful. Despite the fact that his father was a cold, aloof man, he loved his son and in his own way tried to stabilize

and support the patient. This support included liberal
financial assistance. Opportunities were good; he was a
big, handsome man, he was keen intellectually and a physician. Need-congruence at the time was not particularly
great. He had lost his wife and was not working. It seems
unlikely that the wife had been a very need-congruent person
in the first place. Nothing was immutable.

3. Summary of Situational Variables at the Time of Termination Study

   This patient entered supportive-expressive psychotherapy and was seen two to three times a week for over 300
hours. Approximately six months after starting psychotherapy he opened an office for the private practice of medicine.
He had been drinking some but stopped and his practice went
well.

   While on vacation he met his second wife-to-be and
after a relatively brief courtship married her while in
treatment. It's very interesting to note that he began
feeling depressed and again had mood swings not too long
after his marriage. He required some medication. Within
a few months, however, his mood swings subsided and the
marriage became considerably more satisfying. It is particularly interesting to note that the therapist volunteered
the information that by the time this man began psychotherapy things had settled down in his life considerably
and that there never were any very serious crises in the
course of the treatment. There were serious problems at
times, but no crises.

   The therapist noted that right after the patient
married the second time he struggled some with ideas that
his second wife might also be unfaithful to him as the
first had been. The therapist was very supportive throughout and clearly helped the patient establish himself in
life. The therapist noted that the patient had some trouble
feeling for his wife despite the fact that he could do all
kinds of things for other people. The therapist said he
never saw any mood swings in this patient, and that he
deliberately left the unconscious conflicts alone, that he
felt there were many problems that existed and that some
day the patient might go into a psychoanalysis. He also
noted that the second wife was quite different from the
first. The therapist felt a little bit uncertain about
what might come of the patient in the future.

   It is quite evident that the patient was markedly

improved, that he was able to work successfully, and that
he had a reasonably successful marriage. The patient himself said that he felt much different and that he didn't
feel like a boy any more, and that he felt like another man
alongside his father. He felt like he belonged in Topeka.

The two psychosexual levels implicated in this illness
were oral-aggressive and phallic-oedipal. There is considerable evidence that the patient had a pronounced castration fear towards his father and excessive closeness to
his mother and sister. Based on what the patient told us,
and also what the therapist told us, it seems correct to
say that these core problems and their derivatives were not
dealt with interpretively. Transference phenomena were not
interpreted nor did the therapy ever take much of a retrospective view of things. The therapist pointed out that
the patient had a reflective potential but that he had
designed the treatment along different lines because of the
presumed ego weakness in the patient. The therapy, then,
had been designed largely to further the patient's maturation and strengthen his ego.

From looking at the patient's behavior, it would seem
that work and marriage were significantly less conflict-
triggering at termination than they had been at the time of
initial study. The marriage had been decidedly conflict-
triggering in the beginning for they got off to a very
stormy start, and it was evident that despite his ability
to succeed in his marriage he still reacted to his wife
somewhat symptomatically and during periods of sexual
intimacy could not permit himself to really be there with
his wife. He experienced impotence periodically with the
second wife and continued his masturbation.

It would seem, then, that the fact that he could now
take on two major involvements which were potentially conflict-triggering (the wife and work), something he had not
not been able to do successfully before, is in part related
to the ego-strengthening effect of the treatment and the
many corrective emotional experiences he had been able to
have while under the stabilizing impact of the treatment
relationship. That his self-concept seems to have changed
so much he could marry and work, and since his view of his
father was apparently so altered, indicates that there may
have been some silent resolution of intrapsychic conflict
that went on without the benefit of interpretation. On
the other hand, the fact that his second wife was so much
like his sister and, in fact, in many ways has had a
career almost identical to his mother's would indicate that

some of the core problem had not been resolved. This certainly coincides with the therapist's view of the fate of the patient's core neurotic difficulties. There were some stresses in his life; starting a private practice is not the easiest venture. Supports continued to be plentiful. The therapist had been openly supportive throughout the treatment, his wife was, and the many feedback gratifications that came from his involvement in the community were all supportive. Work was highly need-congruent and supported growth and maturation in him. The wife was a much nicer person that the first wife had been, and similarly functioned as a need-congruent factor.

4. Summary of Situational Variables at the Time of Follow-up Study

The patient left treatment, entered the service, and was stationed overseas. While there, we gather, he didn't practice too much medicine but his duties were administrative. He apparently got along pretty well with his superiors, something he had had difficulty with in the past, but the wife noted that his immediate boss was a man who was interested in retiring and really wasn't much of a supervisor.

This couple enjoyed their time overseas and while there had a baby. The patient was possessed by some thoughts that this was not his child, but these fantasies never influenced him to any extent. He did have a few suspicious thoughts about a friend who visited their apartment. His anger became evident when he once shook the baby too hard for crying and apparently his wife interceded. By and large, however, he was quite happy with the baby and in no way hesitated to show this to the research teams. The marriage continued to run smoothly; in fact both the patient and his wife said that they had grown closer and that they talked things out more than they had been able to do before.

Upon returning to the United States the patient felt close to his father and recognized a genuine fondness for him. His attitude towards his mother was not much changed, however. He anticipated entering a group practice, and he had some thoughts of working as some kind of traveling physician. The general direction, however, in his life seemed to be towards greater maturity, greater stability, more commitment to wife, child and work. There were no symptoms in evidence.

The psychological tests, both at termination and follow-
up, showed considerable settling down and there was less
evidence of disorganization; however, the follow-up tests
indicated that the patient was still somewhat unsure of his
identification, that he held no particular pattern of object
ties and that he appeared to be somewhat incapable of lasting relationships or allegiances. They noted a certain un-
committed quality in him. There was still a hyperalert
paranoid quality. They noted that much of this man's appeal
was that of the innocuous, charming, castrated little boy.
Anxiety was diminished, however, and there was an increasingly effective use of denial and projection and avoidance.
They suspected that his adjustment rested rather heavily
upon external supports and that one might expect a cutoff
from this kind of unilateral gratification that he sets up
with the woman would quickly cause him to revert to the
angry borderline psychotic-like state that was seen at the
time of initial study. This evidence is cited to support
the view that core conflicts were not extensively resolved,
but interestingly enough marriage and fatherhood had not
produced pathology.

When seen at the time of follow-up a major conflict
trigger had not yet been taken on; we refer to work responsibilities. It would seem that his parents were considerably less conflict-triggering, but one has to note that he
was quite distant from his parents. It is possible that
work might be conflict-triggering although post-follow-up
data would be required as evidence. His life was quite
need-congruent, he was planning good work outlets, had a
nice wife and a new baby. His parents were behaving appropriately with him.

5. Summary

This man's illness was derived from oral and phallic
conflicts and finally erupted in gross symptomatic form
at the time of puberty when the pressure from within was
great but when there was also a simultaneous demand that he
invest himself in the opposite sex. As his effort to take
on external responsibilities increased, his illness increased until finally his marriage and work reached such a
high degree of deterioration that he had to be hospitalized. In the course of leading up to his final hospitalization he shed all of his conflict triggers. With the
kind and skillful help of his therapist he gradually got
back into life and was able to carry on effectively. How
much of this was due to conflict resolution is difficult
to say. It seems most likely that a good part of his

improvement can be accounted for by the introjection of the stabilizing, loving, father-figure therapist. Unquestionably the growth-stimulating effect, that is need-congruent impact of work and remarriage, contributed through their corrective emotional experience impact to his improvement. It seems this improvement endured for he eventually became a father, and it seems most likely that his behavior will continue to stabilize when he finally enters private practice.

This case illustrates, among other things, the impact that a therapy of a non-core conflict-resolving kind can have. It remains to be seen whether or not the patient will remain asymptomatic when he is fully committed to the practice of medicine and has a growing family.

SYNTHESIS OF SITUATIONAL VARIABLES - CASE #31

1. Brief History

This patient, a housewife and mother of four, came for treatment when she was in her early thirties. She had become tense, anxious and subject to periods of intense inner turmoil for a number of years, and finally became so incapacitated that she had to be hospitalized.

The patient was the third of six children born to a wealthy family. The girls were considered second-rate in this family, while the boys were valued more highly. The patient idolized her father; she loved to get attention from him and was jealous of any attention he gave to the other children. She considered her mother to be lacking warmth and understanding in spite of putting on a front of affection. She never felt comfortable in her mother's presence and never felt the mother was interested in her.

Instead of going to public or private school, she obtained her education from tutors. The patient lived in the country a good part of her life and pursued vigorous, solitary, outdoor activities of a tomboyish nature. She described herself as having been a mediocre student, erratic, doing well only in subjects she liked. She was never a socializer and scorned boys. Her aim was to enter the family business after a period of training.

She worked for a while in various parts of the country. While working she met a newspaper correspondent who was considered to be brilliant but unpredictable and a troublemaker. After a whirlwind courtship they married. The patient believed she had finally found the husband she was looking for. She saw in him an aggressive, dynamic and brilliant man who would set the world on fire. However, it didn't turn out this way. Almost immediately after the marriage he stopped working, picked up with some of his old mistresses, told his wife she did not appeal to him sexually, and so on. Despite this unhappy marital

relationship four children were born to this couple. Almost immediately after the marriage her adjustment began
to deteriorate. There was constant bickering, she was dissatisfied, and as her family grew she became progressively
decompensated. She finally sought individual psychotherapy
but quit, according to her therapist, when her denial of
her own weakness and helplessness began to fail. The patient began having periods of turmoil during which she was
extremely anxious and unable to organize her thoughts. She
became immobilized, withdrawn, relied on alcohol, and eventually had to be hospitalized. She came to the hospital
on her own volition.

2. Summary of Situational Variables at the Time of Initial
   Study

     The core conflicts at the time of initial study re-
volved around extreme competitiveness with males and, of
course, associated with this was a depreciation of femininity. Obvious oedipal conflicts were apparent in her deep
attachment to her grandfather and father. There also
seemed to be a certain dependence in her.

     The primary conflict triggers in her life were the
demand that she be a wife, mother and homemaker. All the
children were conflict-triggering, the husband was, and
domestic life appears to have been too.

     She came to Topeka, leaving all of her children with
her husband and maids. The patient lived in fairly close
proximity to her mother, a person who appeared to be regal
and distant. It would seem that the mother also triggered
unconscious conflicts. The stresses in this woman's life
were considerable. It was most stressful to have a husband
who was openly hostile, promiscuous, unpredictable and un-
reliable. Having four children is somewhat of a stress
but probably not in this household because of the abundance
of hired help. There were two full-time maids. The supports from a material point of view were quite plentiful.
The mother, although cold and aloof, steadfastly stood by
the patient throughout all of her difficulties and regularly stepped in to help when she was desperately needed.
The husband was absolutely not supportive, and conspicuously lacking were the warm dependable supports that come
from friends.

     Opportunities for this woman were quite abundant in
a professional direction, but not so insofar as her marriage
was concerned. She had a very bad marriage, and in addition

to her own neurotic difficulties, which blocked her from
developing as a homemaker, mother and so on, the personality difficulties of her husband were clear external blocks.
Need-congruence was only partial for her; she did have children for whom she could be a mother; she had a home; she
belonged to the upper-class social set, all of which afforded
her outlets for her personality. She could have worked
had she desired. The husband was strikingly need-incongruent. He may have had talent but he had no strength of
character and in no way provided a psychological stimulus
for furthering maturation along feminine lines in this
patient.

3.   Summary of Situational Variables at the Time of Termi-
     nation Study

This patient entered the hospital and was discharged
to Day Hospital a year later. The husband filed for divorce
a year after she began psychotherapy. She brought her four
children and an older woman to help to Topeka. The older
woman left shortly because they didn't get along. The
patient changed therapists and followed the new therapist to
another city upon his termination at the Menninger Foundation.

During the course of her treatment the patient moved
even further away from her parental family. She set up a
household for herself and her children in a large city and
began socializing some there. There were old friends, she
became active in an association and met a bachelor, quite
a number of years older than she, and eventually married
him. She became pregnant by this man after the marriage
and terminated her psychoanalysis.

At the time of termination there was no evidence of
her turbulent episodes; her emotional inhibition and aloofness was mild to moderate; there was no obsessional rumina-
tion; drinking was probably moderate; her competitiveness
towards men and rejection of the feminine role was mild to
moderate; masochistic interactions with her husband were
considered mild with the second husband; there was no
evidence of heterosexual promiscuity by the time of termination; she was considered to still have moderate difficulty handling her children; manifest anxiety was moderate;
depression was considered mild. This amelioration of her
symptomatology was correlated with the fate of her core
conflicts.

The treatment team indicated that the core conflict
was somewhat ameliorated. It was noted, however, that with

the first therapist she would not cooperate and with the second therapist she triumphed in a sense by breaking analytic structure although she cooperated better in many other ways. She felt appreciated as a woman by her second analyst, but had triumphed by taking liberties with the rules of analysis, and felt superior over men by having picked the kind of man that she did. On the other hand, it was noted that she did feel more feminine, was better with the children, and that some of her symptoms had abated. That the core conflicts were not thoroughly worked through would lead us to believe that marriage, homemaking, motherhood, being a wife, were all somewhat conflict-triggering still. However, she was not as competitive with men as she had been at one time. She also saw her mother more realistically than she used to. Thus it would seem there were fewer conflict triggers in her life for two reasons: there were fewer triggers in the sense of the mother being away, and the core conflicts had been reduced quantitatively to some extent.

It should be noted that the second husband was like the first in some respects. The second husband had avoided heterosexual commitment for a long time, in fact he never married until he was in his fifties. The oedipal overtones in this choice seem rather obvious, but on the other hand this man was a kinder person in many ways and somewhat more successful than the first husband. In the second marriage, as in the first, they lived on the patient's money. This husband was a good deal more interested in the children, however, and he was certainly kinder to the patient and in this respect was more need-congruent than the first man had been.

There were no stresses in her life other than the five children, but here again she had help with them. Some of her children were problem children. Monetary supports were plentiful, and she had some friends and social outlets. Opportunities seemed rather good. She had reestablished home life and had outlets for professional or semiprofessional interests if she chose. Need-congruence at the time of termination was considerably better than at the time of follow-up. This husband, although obviously neurotic himself, was, at least in the beginning, more willing to be a husband and a father. His being more of a man may have been more of a conflict trigger than the first husband.

Psychological test data at termination indicates that she had gained considerable insight into her oedipal conflicts, that there had been some resolution of these

conflicts with consequent development of greater initiative,
autonomy, self-esteem and a much clearer idea that one can
be a woman and still find gratification through femininity.
There was a diminution of denial and avoidance but some
greater increase in anxiety, but this was less disabling.
The deeper pregenital needs, particularly the oral ones,
seemed to have become fixed in her character structure.

4. Summary of Situational Variables at the Time of Follow-
    up Study

During the follow-up period the patient was euphoric
for a time after she married, but the relationship between
husband and the children soon began to deteriorate. After
her baby was born her relationship with her husband deteriorated and she became frigid. She lost respect for him,
she tended to lose friends because of him, she considered
him to be very dogmatic and arrogant. At social gatherings
he talked of subjects that were of no interest to others
and she felt ashamed of him. She complained also that the
husband was not particularly involved in his own career,
and some assessments of his work indicated that his pro-
ductions were quite mediocre. This assessment was confirmed by some of the researchers who had seen his work.

At the time of follow-up the patient no longer had the
extreme turbulent episodes but it was noticed that she still
had emotional outbursts towards her children. The patient
had begun using alcohol again; depression had progressed
from mild to moderate; and anxiety had increased. Her
difficulties with the children were moderate. There was
no apparent promiscuity but the patient had become frigid
with her husband, and masochistic interactions with her
husband had become moderate to severe. Her rejection of
femininity was still considered to be mild to moderate.

Psychological tests suggest that there had been significant resolution of her core conflicts as well as a reorganization and strengthening of her defenses. Apparently
there had been major changes in the reorganization of and
expression of affect; reality testing seemed to have improved; there was a greater acceptance of femininity. The
treatment team indicated that the core problem was essentially the same as it was at termination. These problems
revolved around her penis envy, rejection of herself as a
woman, and hostile competitiveness with men. They noted
that these ongoing unconscious problems appeared to have
been greater than thought at termination. It is evident
that the recommitment to a man and again attempting to live

family life in which she is the mother, homemaker and wife proved to be conflict-triggering to her. Many of her old difficulties had returned although probably not to the intense degree that she formerly experienced them. While the husband was somewhat more of a man than the first husband was, there were many qualaties in his personality which make us consider him to be need-incongruent. He seemed to be the long-awaited-for father figure, but he also was a weaker, depreciated, hired-for-help kind of male in the house whom she could dominate and feel superior to.

5. Summary

This patient was an aggressive phallic woman who appears to have been fixated primarily at the phallic-oedipal level with some pregenital components, mostly of an oral-dependent nature. She saw little value or worth in femininity and believed that the only way she could be a worthwhile person was to pursue the objectives that her father and his father before him had. Because of her wish to be a woman and mother she eventually married, picking a man she thought would set the world on fire in a way that she had wished she could. As it turned out this man was weak, irresponsible and decidedly need-incongruent insofar as bringing out the woman in her was concerned. They managed, however, to have four children despite his extreme degree of irresponsibility, and this increased involvement with the husband and children proved to be sufficiently conflict-triggering that she slowly decompensated and finally required hospitalization. This man was the worst kind of husband and thus contributed to her unhappiness, but she needed this kind of man to blend with the neurotic elements in her. She escaped her conflict triggers by coming to Topeka and into the hospital. She began to pull herself together, improved in her adjustment, eventually left the hospital and had her children rejoin her.

Her first analysis did not work, no doubt in part because of her unwillingness to commit herself to it but also due to some definite limitations in the first analyst. Her second analyst worked with her intensively but introduced certain modifications in technique which may have limited the outcome although this is by no mean certain. She "triumphed" over her analyst by provoking a breakdown of the analytic structure to some degree. It would seem that her second marriage, in part at least, was an acting out in which she chose a man very similar to her former husband in a number of respects. Upon committing herself to this man and upon having another child, many of the old

difficulties reappeared. She began drinking, she became
frigid, there was marked marital discord between her and
her husband, she felt ashamed of him and, in short, began
recognizing her poor choice. The worsening of her symptom
picture and her interpersonal relationships occurred despite
the fact that both the treatment team and the psychological
tests indicated some resolution of core conflicts. In all
probability there was some resolution but not enough to
make it possible for her to again attempt to commit herself
to a man and to family life without symptoms reappearing.

This case illustrates beautifully the development of
an illness with the onset of commitment to the opposite
sex, the worsening of that illness as the conflict triggers
increased in number, the amelioration of the illness with
treatment but also with the removal of conflict triggers,
and finally the return of the illness to a significant degree with the reappearance of conflict triggers. Not only
was the environment conflict-triggering, but it was need-
incongruent to a significant extent. The children certainly
were need-congruent.

This patient illustrates, among other things, the
tenaciousness of intrapsychic problems and the great difficulty one encounters in attempting to bring about funda-
mental, that is, essential intrapsychic reorganization.
The therapy no doubt bolstered her ego; she had certain
corrective emotional experiences during the treatment by
finding that she was appreciated, but she did not resolve
her core conflicts to any significant degree.

SYNTHESIS OF SITUATIONAL VARIABLES - CASE #32

1. Brief History

At the time of her evaluation the patient was in her early twenties, married, and severely incapacitated by phobic anxiety.

She was an only child. Her mother had had a previous pregnancy and was considered responsible, because of her vigorous physical activities, for the stillbirth of this pregnancy. The father was a successful self-made professional man. The history indicates that the mother infantilized the patient during her childhood. The patient revealed marked separation anxiety when she started nursery school despite the fact that she was an active extroverted child. She overcame her childhood phobia.

The patient dated the onset of her illness to her mid-teens. She was attending an experimental school and was trying very hard to break through some clique lines. She was also struggling with her own sexual feelings at the time. She dated quite a bit at this point, was kissed by several boys at a party and then severely censored by the clique leader. She was excluded from this group and at that point became very anxious and was so terrified about going to school that she had to remain at home. She was seen by a psychiatrist for a time and then was seen on a once-a-week basis for the next several years. Her anxiety returned when she was 16 and apparently she had to have someone with her all of the time. She was able to do some work in her father's office.

Between the ages of 16 and 18 she was excited and preoccupied with her present husband whom she had known since childhood; he had been a babysitter for her. They were married when the patient was not yet 20 and the husband was slightly over 20. The patient commented that she had no trouble at all with any of her symptoms immediately prior to her marriage or during the time he was in the

service. After about eight months of marriage her symptoms
reappeared in full strength. Even though she claims to
have been symptom free during these eight months, it is
evident that she was still anxious for she had to have someone with her at night. Upon returning to her home town
after her husband's discharge from the service, the patient
matriculated at a university but had to quit again because
of her phobia. She attended class with her husband, however,
even though she was not formally enrolled. She was continuing to see her psychiatrist who advised the patient and
her husband to move away from her home town.

She was referred to a psychiatrist in another state
and she and her husband moved there when the patient was
just past 20 years of age. Her pattern of shackling her
husband and virtually making a mother out of him progressed
to the point that he could not carry on his work. He issued
the ultimatum that she either get treatment or he was going to divorce her. The patient's psychiatrist backed the
husband, and she came to the Menninger Foundation.

She was admitted to the hospital and remained an inpatient for less than one year, and started her analysis
after she had been discharged from the hospital.

2. Summary of Situational Variables at the Time of Initial
    Study

The core conflicts at the time of initial study were
viewed as being primarily at the oral level. We agreed
with that, but we saw striking evidence of the phallic-
oedipal conflict. The patient seems to have had a masculine aggressive streak in her, associated with which was
a definite rejection of femininity. There were no real
stresses but, on the other hand, her life was not need-
congruent. Her husband was about as meek and passive as
a man can be. He considered himself to be a noncomformist
and dressed the part. He wore curious clothing, and assumed most of the household duties, at least while the
patient was in the hospital and after she began coming home
for extended trips. In some respects this patient's parents were need-congruent. They tried to bring some order
into the chaotic lives of their daughter and her husband.
The home that this young couple had established was a mess
and the parents tried to help them straighten it out and
bring some order into their lives.

The parents were not only need-congruent in certain
respects but they were also very supportive. They

steadfastly stood behind their daughter, giving emotional
support and ample financial assistance. The financial
support may have been excessive, and may be considered
somewhat need-incongruent for it tended to foster the in-
fantilism in both the patient and her husband. Opportunities for this young woman were abundant, provided she
could overcome her illness.

3. Summary of Situational Variables at the Time of Termination Study

    The patient was treated by psychoanalysis for over
one thousand hours. During this time she had one child
and became pregnant for a second time. Her husband was
working locally and had also gotten a college degree. By
the end of her treatment the patient was considerably less
phobic, had become a mother, she had managed to take care
of part of her home although she had hired help, and she
socialized a good deal more than she had been able to during the height of her illness. Her husband had begun work
on a postgraduate degree. She had been offered a good job.
The husband, married life and motherhood were all conflict-
triggering at the time of initial study and were somewhat
so at termination. It was quite clear, on the one hand,
that the patient welcomed the obvious changes in herself
and similarly the changes in her husband, but that these
very changes seemed to still activate unconscious conflicts.

    The patient was threatened by her husband's growing
masculinity and assertiveness and success in school;
therefore it seems correct to say that the husband was becoming considerably more need-congruent but also somewhat
more conflict-triggering at the same time. The parents
were still somewhat conflict-triggering. It should be
noted that the analyst observed that most of the patient's
old symptoms returned almost in full force every time her
parents visited. At termination the phobic reactions
occurred only in special situations, but were especially
severe when around her parents. The nned for the presence
of a protecting figure had practically disappeared. She
continued to have some psychosomatic symptoms which are
generally associated with a need for mothering.

    At termination the oedipal conflicts in this patient
had become much more apparent. She not only had rejected
her femininity, but she was envious of men and was deeply
attached to her father.

4. Summary of Situational Variables at the Time of Follow-
up Study

During the follow-up period the patient moved away
from Topeka and her husband continued his studies at a univ-
sity. A second child was born, and finally she had a third
child. All of these gains indicate resolution of core conflict; however, it should be noted that she could not manage
her children and her house alone but had some hired help.
Of particular interest is the way in which her husband's
success provoked her. At one point she admitted that had
she known that her husband would turn out so well she probably never would have married him in the first place. She
easily recognized and openly talked about her competitiveness with him. She had had a real showdown with her mother
and apparently both found their place in relation to each
other.

These developments indicate a growing maturity and an
increasing acceptance of femininity. At the same time, not
all of the conflicts were resolved because she reacted
negatively to the growth in her husband, and in particular
it should be noted that all of her old symptoms reappeared
whenever she was around her father.

It would appear that she was more generally phobic
at follow-up than she had been at termination. This is of
particular interest because her involvement in various
elements of life was considerably greater than at termination. By now she was the mother of three, her husband was
quite clearly going to be successful, and in some ways she
was more distant from her parents, a fact which must have
triggered her dependency. She wanted more children but at
the same time she wanted to invest more of her energies
into the academic sphere and compete with her husband. She
still hadn't given up the idea of professional life. She
was torn between the possibility of having another child
or being content with the three she had and soon returning
to school to get a Master's degree. At follow-up the
father no longer contributed money to them directly but
he had arranged investments for them which nicely supple-
mented their income.

5. Summary

All of the assessments indicate that this was a very
dependent girl who was closely attached to her mother and
who never got through the phallic-oedipal phase of psychosexual development, and was fixated phallically and

masculinely identified. This identity no doubt derived
from a strong attachment to her father and no doubt also,
at a deeper level, some identification with her own phallic-
aggressive mother. Separation anxiety seems to have been
triggered when she was separated from her mother when she
started to nursery school. Later, at the onset of puberty,
when sexuality made its appearance, she again developed
phobic anxiety and dreaded to be left alone. She responded
to a mothering kind of psychotherapy for a number of years
and, interestingly enough, chose a man to marry who had
once been her babysitter, and this is what she made of him
after she married him. Extremely passive, and quite clearly
a mother for this patient, he nonetheless was a male and
because of this was somewhat of a conflict trigger. Through
her involvement with this man her phallic-oedipal and all
of her unconscious conflicts were again mobilized and a
phobia developed. This severe illness demanded that her
husband relinquish his claim to masculinity and become a
mother for her. In so doing she fulfilled her dependency
and she emasculated her husband, something her phallic competitive conflicts forced her to do. Fortunately her husband refused to be completely emasculated and because of
his ultimatum, and also no doubt because of her suffering,
she was hospitalized and treated by psychoanalysis.

Through this psychoanalysis she gained a considerable
range of insight and made some definite changes towards
greater maturity. She eventually had three children, was
able to take reasonably good care of them, she could break
the infantile attachment to her parents to some extent,
and could be a better wife to her husband.

Although there were these gains, her gains were by no
means complete. She resented her husband's successes, she
still felt competitive with him, she could not function
completely adequately as a mother, and most of her symptoms
returned even at the time of follow-up if she were in the
presence of her father. The conflict-triggering aspects
of her husband, of the role of wife, mother and homemaker,
and of her father, are unmistakably clear. Of particular
interest is the dynamic interplay between the patient and
her husband. At the time of initial study the husband was
somewhat conflict-triggering and hardly need-congruent at
all; in fact, his own personality characteristics, primarily
his passivity and ineffectualness, played right into her
neurotic needs. As she changed he changed, but those very
changes seemed to have provoked the unconscious conflicts
which she resolved in her analysis to a great extent but
never completely.

SYNTHESIS OF SITUATIONAL VARIABLES - CASE #33

1. Brief History

This patient was a physician in his late forties when
he came for his evaluation. He was admitted directly into
the hospital.

He came from conscientious, God-fearing, hard-working
people. His father had been a rather successful physician,
having built up a clinic when this patient was a small child.
The patient was separated from his mother for several
months when he was less than two years of age. During this
time he was cared for by an aunt who neglected him, and was
then sent to the grandparents' home. It is said that he
had a gastrointestinal disturbance during this entire five-
month period.

Little else is known about his early history until he
was six years of age. During this time several relatives
came to live in the home. He was brought up to be a hard-
working boy who earned extra money by having his own garden,
by selling his products, and so on. He was described as
easygoing, agreeable, and fat, and was frequently called a
sissy. It is known from the analysis that he first began
homosexual practices when he was 11 or 12 years old. He
compensated for his reputation of being a sissy by going
out for football and playing a very good game even though
he did not like it. He was always popular and stood at
the head of his class. In medical school he was in the
upper ten percent. From there he went to a residency
where, after a number of love affairs with nurses, he met
and married his wife. He had been going with a nurse whom
he presumably had impregnated and it is believed that his
marriage to his wife, who was older and also a medical student, may have been related to his having gotten the nurse
pregnant.

He entered the service in the early forties and following a tour of duty in this country he was appointed to an

administrative position overseas. He returned to become
a professor of a medical speciality.

It is noted somewhere in the record that he told his
father once that he went through quite a depressive episode
after leaving the service. While in the service in this
country he was with his wife but was subsequently separated
from her when he went overseas. It would appear that his
depressive episode after separation from the service coincides with his being reunited with his wife.

He gave up the professorship and in a short time entered a private practice with two other doctors. Soon after
starting his practice, which from the beginning appeared
to be very successful, his marital difficulties began, or
at least grew more intense. He began to drink more and
more. His wife, although very brilliant, was unable to
manage the home. As a consequence the patient had to get
breakfast if the children were to get to school on time.
Despite this discord in the marriage four children were
born. It was at the time of the birth of his last child
that he became impotent. The wife began treating him med-
ically by giving him male hormones. She then got some books
on homosexuality and finally encouraged him to take a male
lover, who for a period of time lived in the home.

During this period of chaos and increasing difficulty
he had less and less to do with his parents, particularly
his father. If the father visited in the home the patient
would go outside to avoid him. The patient's drinking became so bad that he finally had to give up his practice.
He was first taken to a sanitarium where they recommended
that he stay away from his wife for a whole year. She took
all of their money and went East to get further medical
training, leaving the children with his parents.

The patient came to the Menninger Foundation, and began his analysis after having been hospitalized for several
months. After about a year or so he entered the Day
Hospital and lived in a family care home for a time. He
obtained work as a company physician.

2. Summary of Situational Variables at the Time of Initial
   Study

At the time of the initial study the two primary conflicts were oral-dependence and the phallic-oedipal conflict. His passivity, his abhorrance of aggression, his
inability to be successful, all pointed to a homosexual

solution of the Oedipus complex.

The conflict triggers were the usual ones. He managed
to maintain his equilibrium until he had to settle down into
a heterosexual adjustment right after his discharge from
the service. It is possible that separation from the service activated his early separation difficulties, but at
the same time a woman was permanently introduced into his
life.

There followed a depressive episode from which he
recovered, but when he then tried to take on a high level
professional position he experienced difficulty and left
that for private practice. It was in the face of success
and with a growing family that he decompensated severely.
Therefore it seems correct to say that success at work,
the responsibilities of being a father and a husband were
the conflict triggers for oral and oedipal conflicts. It
should be noted, however, that he had a terrible woman for
a wife. She was a castrating, diminishing, competitive
female who sought to destroy her husband. Instead of being
supportive and empathic and understanding, she began to
suggest that he was lacking in male hormones, that he, in
fact, was probably troubled with homosexuality and the way
to find out was for him to embark on overt affairs. Therefore the wife was highly need-incongruent, and she was not
supportive.

The parents were also conflict-triggering but at the
same time were supportive. At the height of his illness
his father tried very hard to straighten out his son and
on one occasion took him to a resort motel for two weeks
to see if he couldn't get order back into his life and get
him stabilized. It should be noted that when the father
visited, the son would avoid him. This seems an especially
clear expression of the patient's tendency to avoid the
conflict triggers, that is to say, the presence of the adult
father activated the infantile relationship to the father.

Stresses in his life were quite considerable. A very
busy private practice is stressful, and the kind of wife he
had was stressful. The need-incongruent elements in her
makeup were also stressful. The drinking and the homosexual
experiences and the fights were all the stresses of a feedback variety, but he had the opportunity to be head of the
household, he had the opportunity to be a successful physician and father. Opportunities were quite plentiful,
although the opportunities within his marriage were considerably limited by the personality of his wife.

3. Summary of Situational Variables at the Time of Termination Study

This patient was seen five times a week for well over one thousand hours. This was a very stormy treatment and ended when the patient died.

After working as an employed physician, he worked for a time in private practice, and then obtained work at a hospital in Topeka. It is very interesting to note that as his wife rejoined him and as each of the children successively rejoined the family, his symptoms became progressively worse.

In the course of his analysis each of his parents had serious illnesses but neither died. When the mother became seriously ill the patient remarked that he would die too when his mother died. There were homosexual episodes during the analysis and he had to be readmitted to the hospital twice for alcoholism. After he began his job at the hospital he started taking drugs. Towards the end of his treatment, when he was reunited with his entire family and working full-time at the hospital, there were many signs of suicidal preoccupation and there were numerous accidents which injured him slightly to moderately.

At the time of his termination his anxiety was more severe than at initial study; alcoholism and drug addiction continued throughout; homosexuality never disappeared and there was no permanent improvement in his potency or his passivity. The analyst noted that when the patient became potent for a period during his treatment he got quite frightened and began taking some drugs for this. His passivity remained unchanged and the somatizations, such as colitis, nausea and vomiting, never disappeared. Depression became a predominant symptom in the later phases of treatment, with frank suicidal preoccupation. On one occasion he talked of putting a bullet through his head because his days were numbered and there was nothing to do but kill himself.

The Treatment Variables team saw little evidence of the phallic-oedipal problem. We disagree with this completely. The oral problems were certainly there, but evidence of the phallic-oedipal conflicts were in great abundance. The therapist told of the problems that stood in the way of the patient getting well. That is to say, to get well meant that he had to be an adult, to be grown up, to have a penis, and to release his anger appropriately.

For him, to be a man meant taking over from father, and it
meant possessing mother, but this meant losing his penis.
The therapist reminded the research team that as a boy he
had always manifested a lot of curiosity. When he was age
five the father decided he needed a circumcision, so the
father gave him the anesthesia and the uncle cut off the
foreskin. Too much of the foreskin was removed and all
the kids accused him of having part of his penis cut off.
This occurred at the height of the oedipal period. It is
also evident that the patient was deeply attached to his
mother at an oral level. Prior to treatment he had clawed
at his stomach and said that he wanted to get his mother
out of there. He made comments to the effect that when
mother died he would have to die so as not to be separated
from her, that in fact they were one. This latter remark
emerged during treatment.

It appears, then, that none of these core conflicts
were resolved at all despite their clarity.

As the patient assumed his responsibilities of physician, father, husband, he took on many conflict triggers.
These triggers activated the unconscious conflicts and he
went progressively downhill with the introduction of each
new conflict trigger. His life was further complicated by
his very need-incongruent wife. Every time he did make
temporary gains in his treatment, his wife seemed to get
very upset and tended to undercut him.

5. Summary

It is probable that the parents, by their own personalities, molded or caused the inverse resolution of the
oedipal situation or the pregenital conflicts. Two traumatic experiences occurred in his life also. One was the
separation from the mother for a period of about five
months when he was 17 months of age. We also know that
the mother probably was quite a doting woman and may have
wished that he be a girl. It is hard to say how true it
is, but the patient's wife claimed that his mother had
treated him more as a girl when he was a little boy; she
gave him dolls to play with and that sort of thing. In
any event, it seems that a very close attachment between
the patient and his mother and, conversely, a distant relationship between the patient and his father, developed.

The second traumatic event was the circumcision when
the patient was at the height of his oedipal period. These
two traumatic events, with the daily closeness to the mother

and the distance from the father, seemed to have caused
this patient to be unable to get over his deep dependent
attachment to his mother or to resolve his oedipal problems.
He grew up to be a sissy but he overcompensated for these
tendencies, became successful in sports and academically
and, indeed, he continued to succeed well up to the point
where he took a woman into his life. At the juncture in
his life (upon his release from the service) when he tried
to live with a woman continually he began to develop symptoms. These were the drinking and drug taking and the constant marital discord. As his family increased in size and
as he began to become increasingly successful in the practice of medicine, in short as his heterosexual and mature
commitments intensified, his symptoms also intensified.

He was hardly able to hold his own against this onslaught from his unconscious, and his efforts were further
inundated by the overt attitudes and characterologic makeup
of his wife. This woman was a harsh, masculine, castrating,
unsympathetic, unfeminine person who materially contributed
to his defeat.

He eventually shed all of his conflict triggers, managed to pull himself together well enough to leave the
hospital and resume the practice of medicine. As his family
rejoined him a step at a time he became progressively worse
each step of the way so that by the time he had all of his
family back together and was practicing medicine he was
declining sharply in his adjustment. This decline was
complicated by the illnesses of his parents, particularly
the illness of his mother with whom he seemed inextricably
entwined. But the main difficulty seemed to be the estab-
lishment of an independent, heterosexual, responsible,
life. He grew more and more despondent, thought increasingly of suicide, and finally ended his life.

It should be noted that the patient's father had been
a physician (as was his uncle) and at one time had been
rather outstanding and successful. Not only could the patient not be a husband and father, he could not be a succesful physician. A side note on this is of interest in
that the patient's mother allegedly once said that she
doubted that the patient should ever have gone into medicine,
that he seemed better suited for a different career, an
area in which he had excelled earlier.

SYNTHESIS OF SITUATIONAL VARIABLES - CASE #34

1. Brief History

This patient came for a consultation when she was a 30-year-old professional woman. Earlier she had been dismissed from a job because of some difficulty with male patients and inability to get along with her supervisors. From this consultation it was revealed that she had had chronic difficulty in getting along with people, particularly men. She was unable to marry, was promiscuous, and always broke off the relationship when it threatened to become serious. She had had one year of psychotherapy. She was subject to depressive episodes and felt unloved and unwanted.

The patient was the middle child of five children. All of her living sibs were boys. She was particularly rivalrous with a brother a year and a half older than she, but was old enough to have contributed to the care of her youngest sibling. Twins were born to the family but died shortly after birth. Her father, who came from an old stock rigid family, was 13 years older than the patient's mother. The mother seemed chronically unhappy, discontented, argumentative around the home, but away from home was gay and lively.

As a child the patient loved flowers, animals, birds, etc., took to dolls and sewing, but later in life tended never to be aware of her talents for feminine pursuits. Early in puberty she tried very hard to be a tomboy, her favorite game being Tarzan. She found herself to be quite anxious in school and especially so if she had to get up and speak before a group. Her grades suffered in high school. She had a few high school crushes but only dated a few young men. In that respect she seems to have been attracted to the "psychopathic" type of personality. Late in high school she discovered that by being seductive she could have any boy she wanted, but by and large she kept a safe distance from the boys.

Around age 17 many of her girl friends were preparing hope chests but she did not. She felt that she had seen enough of married life for the past 17 years or so and apparently wanted nothing of it. The patient admitted that although she was never aware of it she must have wanted to be a boy and she did feel at the time of her evaluation that she could do anything a man could do and some things even better. However, as a youngster she discovered that this actually was not so, that she wasn't physically strong enough to do some of the things the men could do.

Despite her father's strictness the patient actually saw him as a mild, well-meaning, ineffectual man, which is in contrast to her image of her mother which was that of a managing, controlling, punitive, unloving mother. Her chronic dissatisfaction, depressive feelings and her disturbed interpersonal relations led her to seek psychiatric treatment.

2. Summary of Situational Variables at the Time of Initial Study

The core conflicts were defined primarily at two levels, the first being the phallic-oedipal and the second the oral. Most obvious was her hostility toward men, her envy of them, and her wish to have had a penis and to have been a man. That there are also oedipal attachments seem rather clearly revealed by the psychological tests, in particular the TAT story in which she reveals the deep love for the father. Underneath these phallic-oedipal difficulties there was a streak of oral dependency in her; she wanted very much to be loved, to be taken care of, and to receive narcissistic supplies of one sort or another. The conflict trigger in her life, therefore, would seem to be the challenge of a heterosexual relationship. She was attracted to men but involvement with a man inevitably led to symptomatic behavior. She also could not get along with female supervisors. It seems correct to say, then, that women supervisors activated the maternal elements in her unconscious conflicts. Her work seems to have thrown her into somewhat more intense conflict-triggering situations in that she had to be intimate with patients, both male and female. That she got into difficulty with a male patient is not surprising in view of her phallic-oedipal problems.

There were really no stresses in her life as such. Support came from her work. Little support seemed to be coming from her family inasmuch as she seems to have broken off her relationship with the sibs and parents alike. Her

life was moderately need-congruent. Her profession provided
mothering outlets for her and undoubtedly gave her the
opportunity to express some of her learned skills. Insofar
as her heterosexual adjustment was concerned, however, her
choice of men was not need-congruent. She gravitated to
unsuitable males. Opportunity was quite good for her; she
certainly could go on with her work, and she certainly had
the native talent and ability to attract men. Unfortunately
her unconscious problems prevented anything enduring coming
out of these transient relationships.

3. Summary of Situational Variables at the Time of Termination Study

This patient was treated by expressive psychotherapy.
She never overcame her inability to marry. She worked at
various jobs, including some private work. She caused her
psychotherapist some embarrassment in the way she recommended him so strongly to other patients. She got into all
kinds of difficulty while in treatment; she became pregnant
and had to be aborted. She was promiscuous, and eventually
she got into such a difficult and unresolvable transference
jam that she began going steadily downhill, finally losing
her job.

The psychological tests indicate that not only did the
patient become more alloplastically inclined but also more
paranoid. The tests also indicate depressive periods that
now, in contrast to initial study, had a suicidal quality
to them. The patient failed to pay her income tax and got
into financial difficulties by overspending with charge
accounts. None of her symptoms were improved; in fact,
anxiety and depression and interpersonal difficulties were
rated worse at termination than at initial study.

It is clear that the unconscious problems in this patient were untouched, and despite the therapist's claim
that there were periods in her treatment where she gained
good insight into herself, it seems highly unlikely that
this insight produced any basic change. Instead, treatment
seems to have mobilized her conflicts; she acted them out,
projected them, and got into a terribly entangled transference jam which finally led to a breakdown of treatment.
She began missing appointments, she accused the therapist
of robbing her of the best years of her life, doing nothing
for her, and so on. Her behavior indicates that in addition to there being no resolution of core conflict, there
also was no change in those environmental factors that were
conflict-triggering. Quite obviously the therapist became

the most significant conflict trigger of all. Men continued to be conflict-triggering; work was; women supervisors
continued to trouble her. Even having to conform to ordinary rules of life was conflict-triggering. She worked her
full work day but she established her own schedule and would
not adhere to the work day that was prescribed for her.

The only stresses in her life were of a feedback nature
that she brought on herself. This refers primarily to the
pregnancy, the interpersonal difficulties and so on, and
the loneliness. There were practically no supports other
than her job and the treatment itself. Her life was highly
need-incongruent. There were no outlets for the feminine
side of her personality. Her work, however, was need-
congruent but she even managed to ruin this. Opportunities
continued to be somewhat plentiful. Her abilities had led
to good job offers. She was still an attractive woman at
termination but she managed to avoid men or would choose
unattainable men, including married ones.

4. Summary of Situational Variables at the Time of Follow-
    up Study

Considerable difficulty was encountered in trying to
locate this patient for the follow-up study. After her
usual initial reluctance, she eventually cooperated with
the follow-up teams. She stated the condition, however,
that she see only one person and not be seen by a group.

The story of her life during the follow-up period is
a pathetic one. Her level of work had dropped considerably;
even her few friends chided her for sinking to a low level.
Her father died during the follow-up period. She returned
home and promptly got into a running fight with her mother.
However, she did not hesitate to accept funds from her
mother and brother periodically when she found herself des-
titute. Information suggests that she continued to rely
somewhat heavily upon drugs and alcohol. This was new information. She indicated that she thought she would have
been better off dead.

Most of her symptoms were about the same. She had
lost her sexual interests, however, and perhaps was somewhat less promiscuous during the follow-up period than
previously. To some she appeared more depressed. In
general she had lost interest in life. She had a hyster-
ectomy. Her increased detachment from life, although in
itself reflecting her sickness, nonetheless coincided with
the psychological test report which describes some improvement.

She seemed a little less volatile, perhaps a little less
projective, and in the course of the follow-up evaluation
settled down so that, by the time it was concluded, she
seemed to be less of a suicidal risk than she had originally
appeared to be.

Core conflict certainly was unchanged but there were
some changes in the conflict triggers. The father was now
dead; she had pushed men further out of her life; there
were no women supervisors with whom she fought. She was
perhaps a bit more tranquil than she had been. The treatment team described all of the old symptoms as still being
present but, as noted, the tests suggested that she was a
little less volatile and turbulent.

All of the conflict triggers listed earlier were still
potentially there and some of them were actually there,
most notably the challenge of a heterosexual adjustment.
A major conflict trigger had been removed from her life,
however, and this was the person of the therapist. Stresses
were of her own making. Opportunities continued to be
present although perhaps not as plentiful as before, and
her life, by and large, was need-incongruent. She was
living alone, not fully expressing her professional capabilities, and she was by no means interacting with an environment that would bring out the woman in her, something
she had always wanted.

5. Summary

This patient was an orally and phallically-oedipally
fixated woman with an ego structure that precluded much
coming out of an expressive psychotherapeutic effort. She
was externalizing, projective, alloplastic and, despite
some evidence that she had a reflective capacity, it
appears that she really was lacking in true psychological-
mindedness and reflectiveness. During the eight years of
psychotherapy practically nothing was accomplished, and if
we take into consideration the normal gains that should
come during an eight year period at the prime of life, it
is evident that this patient deteriorated severely. Her
treatment finally broke down as a result of an insoluble
transference and possibly countertransference jam. We
feel charitable toward the therapist, however, and we think
that almost any therapist would have gotten into these
difficulties as a result of a really sincere effort to
work with this patient expressively.

All of the elements of a heterosexual, mature adjustment

were conflict-triggering for this woman. This refers primarily to the challenge of being a woman, a mother, a wife; in short, committing herself to a man. In addition to these conflict triggers, the patient also was unable to get along with women. She got into repeated arguments with women supervisors, and she had great difficulty conforming to rules and regulations. There was no resolution of core conflict. This patient, like so many others, seems to have found a partial solution to her dilemma by more or less isolating herself from conflict triggers. She quit treatment, she began withdrawing from men, she found work that precluded much contact with women supervisors and, in short, settled for a rather lonely and isolated life.

SYNTHESIS OF SITUATIONAL VARIABLES - CASE #35

1. Brief History

This patient first noticed symptoms when she was in
her second year of professional training. She had stooped
to pick up a dropped pencil and experienced a feeling of
dizziness and fright and feared she would collapse. After
that she had the same symptom periodically without much
relief. These symptoms became worse after the birth of
each of her children, three in number, and most severe after
the birth of her last child. For this she sought psychiatric treatment for one year and felt a little better. She
and her family moved to another city, at which point her
symptoms promptly became worse again. She had to force
herself to go shopping and could not stand to be alone in
a car away from home.

This patient was the second of three girls. The
father was an ineffectual man; he never made a very good
living, and he died when she was six years old. An uncle
helped them move into a better neighborhood but because
the mother went to work promptly the patient experienced
another kind of loss at about the same age. The youngest
sister had been born shortly before the father's death.
When the patient was 13 her older sister, then 19, suddenly died.

The mother stressed the importance of education and
particularly the importance of a person being able to take
care of himself. It was probably under the impact of the
mother's pressure that the patient went into nurses training after two years of college even though she hated it.
After her training course was completed she took more
college work which qualified her to be a public health
nurse. She met her husband while they were both in college.
They were approximately the same age, he being a few months
younger.

He entered military service before their relationship

had progressed very far but upon his return they renewed their acquaintance and were married. There were three children. As noted earlier, the patient's phobic symptoms became worse after the birth of each child. During each of her pregnancies she had a rash that covered most of her body and which itched terribly.

Therapy notes indicate that the patient's marital life had been quite hectic. She evidently screamed at her husband, who had to get his own breakfast. She felt that she was wasting her time being a housewife; she recognized that she tried to control her husband by feeling bad; she felt very bad when he left the home; at the same time her husband was a crutch for her.

2. Summary of Situational Variables at the Time of Initial Study

The Patient Variables team defined the most central core conflict in this patient at the oral level. The problem of loss was also obviously a significant factor in the formation of her illness. The father had died when she was only six and the mother had to leave the home every day in order to work.

The second core conflict had to do with the feeling of dissatisfaction with her sex. It is noted that the parents had wished for a boy, and although the Patient Variables team noted penis envy in this patient they did not think this was a central problem, but one that existed nonetheless. Hostility towards men certainly existed and her efforts at diminishing her husband and forcing him to do things around the home certainly betray her phallic-oedipal problems. She depreciated and belittled men and tried actively to compete with them. It is not clear what conflict triggers or conflicts related to the dizziness when she was in the second year of professional training. It could be that having to do for others when she wanted to be dependent and be taken care of was the basis for her disturbance then. We do know that each pregnancy produced a somatic reaction in her and then she became markedly more anxious if not frankly phobic after the birth of each child. It can be speculated that the appearance of each child frustrated her dependency wishes all the more and also activated phallic-oedipal problems. Each child forced her to be more of a woman, something she unconsciously rebelled against and may have felt guilty about. We believe that having to move away from her mother was conflict-triggering. The appearance of anxiety was much worse after the move.

There was nothing really stressful in her life as such. Supports were rather good; the husband stood by her quite faithfully, he earned a good living, was understanding and helpful. Opportunities were practically unlimited; she had all the advantages of marriage, home and a good income, and had she not been ill she could have made a good family life for herself. She was trained professionally also and could have worked. The marriage, the family and the home were all need-congruent. It is possible that the husband was somewhat need-incongruent by virtue of his passivity and willingness to be manipulated by her illness, something that she quite coldly did and recognized she was doing.

3. Summary of Situational Variables at the Time of Termination Study

This patient was treated by psychoanalysis. Without attempting to review this treatment, it is our general impression that not too much came of it insofar as the patient making essential intrapsychic changes are concerned. We note, for instance, that the analyst did not keep the patient on the couch, but when her struggle against change became intense permitted her to sit up. He rationalized this to himself on the grounds that he believed she would have become psychotic had he insisted that she proceed within the original psychoanalytic structure. We note that on one occasion he cried in front of his patient and that he shared private information with her. All of these data suggest quite clearly that this treatment broke down, and because it did it seems unlikely that basic change took place in her.

These assumptions are supported by other assessments. The psychological tests, for instance, indicate that the patient was perhaps more vulnerable to disorganizing anxiety. They note continued presence of phobic symptoms, the increase of dysphoric affects; the psychologist was struck by her harshness, her suspiciousness, and sarcastic manner. Tests indicate a strong sense of sexual inadequacy and a depreciation of her role as a woman. Her estimation of the therapist was quite low. Her opinion that the therapist was dead except for his leg, and that he tries to work magic but knows that he can't do it, beautifully reflects her unwillingness to be changed into a woman by a man.

The treatment team noted that anxiety and phobias were still present, and they noted her projective capacities but did not believe that she was psychotic. They make

special note of the conflict of the masculinity and femininity, which confirms our impressions at the time of initial
study that this patient had much phallic-oedipal conflict.
The other sources of information indicate, however, that in
some ways the patient was better. She was sometimes willing to go places with her husband, she seemed to function
somewhat better in the home, and occasionally could even
go places by herself, including to and from her hours. She
was able to do some volunteer work in the community. All
of the old conflict triggers, though, were still there.
These refer to the mature responsibilities of a woman. That
she was less symptomatic obviously suggests that something
happened and it may be that having found the therapist to
be a kind gentle man somehow strengthened her ego and thus
made it possible for her to contain the pressures from her
unconscious more adequately. It seems unlikely, from any
of the data we have studied, that any conflict resolution
occurred.

There were no stresses, as such, in her life and,
again, supports were quite plentiful. The husband stood
by her throughout, the therapist was most supportive.
Need-congruence was quite good with one exception. By the
time of termination it appeared clearer than ever that the
husband seems to have been quite a meek man. We think that
had he been able to be more assertive and forceful with
his wife he would have facilitated her treatment and in
that way aided in the resolution of conflict. Unfortunately he continued to play into the neurotic character elements and in this way worked against constructive changes
in her.

4. Summary of Situational Variables at the Time of Follow-
    up Study

During the follow-up period the patient moved and was
again living near her mother. She picked up with her old
friends and reestablished her relationship with her mother.
She took a part-time job. She was very proud of her children; the oldest boy was now 16, the second boy was an A
student, and the girl was nine years old and apparently
quite bright. She was very happy that she moved back to
her home town. The mother was only 30 minutes away. With
regard to her symptoms, the patient still had some difficulty driving by herself and in particular through tunnels.
She still became anxious and perspired freely when driving
15 to 20 miles to the city where she worked. Interestingly,
she noted that her driving difficulties were worse in the
evening when the sun was setting.

She was still irritable and nasty at times. She
apparently had thought very little about her former analyst
and even remarked that she had felt sorry for him. She
was dissatisfied with her husband's obsessiveness and indecisiveness; she would have liked for him to make decisions
but apparently he could not. Their sex life had deteriorated to a considerable extent. The patient remarked that
she didn't really know whether treatment had helped, and
wondered if she had had her mother around she might not
have needed it. The treatment made her feel that somebody
cared, she liked her analyst but felt that he was weak.
She didn't like to lie on a couch because she was a patient.
Sitting up made her feel like she had more of a friend and
that she was less of a patient.

The husband noted that she attacked him less and there
were fewer rage attacks since they had moved. He reported
that his wife was frigid much of the time and that he had
little interest in her. She handled the finances. The
anxiety symptoms were rated as mild, the phobia was considered to be moderate, rages were mild, depression mild
to absent, somatization such as obesity, headache and so
on were mild to absent, competitiveness towards men was
still moderate, sexual difficulties were still moderate.

The treatment team suggested that the conflictual constellations still continued to be present at follow-up
although somewhat reduced in their external manifestations.
At the time of follow-up the resentment against the mother
and the younger sister was still quite strong, for instance,
but, as noted earlier, the patient was less symptomatic
in some respects.

The fact that she was still hostile and derogatory
and competitive toward her husband is further evidence of
the unresolved conflicts. Psychological tests note that
this patient was happier than when last tested. The overall impression we gained from the test report, however, was
that all the old problems were there but that her defenses
were functioning better. The environmental changes may
have affected her improved symptom picture as well.

We think one of the most significant factors in her
improved state is that she was close to her mother again.
The support from the mother seems to have had quite a beneficial effect on this patient much like the phobic patient
who can be symptom free in the presence of the security-
giving figure. There were other changes that had taken
place through the years which may have entered into the

picture. For one thing, her children were much older and no longer demanding so much from her. Recall that her symptoms became pronounced after the birth of each child. Now that her children were well into latency and adolescence, the dependency conflict, and probably the phallic-oedipal conflict, was less triggered. The patient had also taken herself out of the conflict-triggering situation by returning to work. This made it possible for her to have to face the challenges of being a woman less persistently. The husband had finally withdrawn from her. In short, there were fewer conflict triggers and those that were there were less intense. As mentioned, being in the supportive presence of her mother had undoubtedly contributed to the amelioration of her symptoms. None of this should minimize the supportive ego-building effect of the therapy.

Opportunities were still there; need-congruence was only moderate. The patient herself recognized that her husband's meekness, passivity, and ineffectualness had somehow held her back.

5. Summary

This patient first became ill when she had to take care of others and was, in fact, embarking upon a way of life that she secretly resented having to do. Not only did she want to be dependent rather than independent, it seems likely that she would have preferred to have pursued marriage rather than a profession. This last remark is an inference only. In any event, she began to develop phobic symptoms, could not be alone, and it is interesting to note that even after treatment some of her phobias while driving were most severe at sunset. It is at this time that loneliness is most intensely felt. Loss was a basic conflict in her due to the loss of her father and then later separation from her mother because of the mother's having to return to work. Because of the character makeup of the parents and the sudden interruption of the family constellation at the height of the patient's oedipal period, this patient did not work out her phallic-oedipal conflicts. These conflicts, as indicated earlier, may have been triggered when she embarked in the direction of a career.

She married a man who was meek and passive and who blended with the aggressive dominant aspects of her own personality. After the birth of each child she became acutely worse symptomatically because, we think, the child was a conflict trigger by forcing her to be a mother, a

woman and a wife. She finally decompensated to the point
that she had to have extensive treatment. Her phallic-
oedipal difficulties, which she experienced as a masculinity
versus femininity struggle, caused her to make a shambles
of the treatment. That she could do so was contributed to
by the analyst's weakness and inability to stand up to her.
Be that as it may, she seems to have managed somehow to
strengthen her ego to some extent by virtue of this interpersonal experience and was eventually able to leave treatment, but she found her way back to within 20 miles of her
mother. It was noted earlier that with the passage of time
the conflict triggers became less intense. As a result her
symptoms were less intense but the research data indicate
that all of the old conflicts were there. The patient returned to work half-time as another effort to find some
kind of suitable life adjustment for herself.

SYNTHESIS OF SITUATIONAL VARIABLES - CASE #36

1. Brief History

This man first came for an evaluation because his wife
threatened to divorce him because of his perverse sexual
practices and heavy drinking.

The patient was the third of four children born into
a very wealthy family. Two older children died before the
patient's birth. A sister, two years younger than the
patient, was in her late twenties at the time of the evaluation, married and she had two children. The father had
died of a coronary. The mother was 68 at the time of the
evaluation. The patient stated that when his mother was
sober she was sweet and kindly but many times she behaved
in a highly seductive way towards him when intoxicated,
often requiring his assistance to get to the bathroom where
he would watch her urinate.

When he was three or four years old his parents took
an extended trip, leaving him with nurses. He recalled
that at that time he urinated while looking at a picture
of a woman. A few years later he and his sister used to
watch each other urinate. The patient derived satisfaction from placing bugs in the toilet bowl and having his
sister urinate or move her bowels on them. As noted earlier,
it was during his adolescence that the patient used to enjoy taking his intoxicated mother to the bathroom and
watching her urinate on pieces of toilet paper that he had
placed in the bowl.

During his earlier school years he was a tall, gangly,
awkward, shy boy. Following graduation he attended a univ-
sity for two years and then spent two years at another
university from which he graduated with an A.B. degree. It
was while at the university that he began to drink. He
and his fraternity brothers often visited houses of prostitution and it was then that he began to ask prostitutes
to urinate on live objects in the toilet bowl. During

314

these years he gained his greatest sexual satisfaction out
of frequent masturbation which was preceded by fantasies
of a woman urinating on various kinds of small animals or
on a slave tied in the toilet or himself in the toilet.

He was inducted into military service and during his
six months of training married a girl whom he had known at
the university. A few months after his marriage he was
taken out of special training because of lack of leadership.
He was unhappy in the service and drank heavily. Upon discharge from the service he entered a school and remained
two years. He lazily surveyed the job situations and finally settled on one he obtained through connections. His
work was unsatisfactory; he drank and frequented houses of
prostitution. Two children were born into this marriage
despite his alcoholism and inability to work steadily or
effectively. It appears that his drinking worsened after
the children arrived.

The patient did not accept the conditions for his
treatment the first time and he and his wife and children
left Topeka. The patient's wife divorced him as she had
threatened she would and he returned to his home town where
apparently about all he did was drink. Prior to the divorce
he had attempted psychotherapy once a week away from Topeka
for eight months but got nowhere. Before his wife actually
divorced him he quit drinking for three months and tried
to win her back but failed. Because of severe financial
difficulties his attorney agreed to help him if he would
accept treatment. On his return to Topeka he entered the
hospital despite his reluctance to do so.

2. Summary of Situational Variables at the Time of Initial
   Study

The core conflicts at the time of initial study were
rather difficult to define. It would seem that oral and
anal conflicts were associated with his perversions. Phallic-
oedipal conflicts were implicated by his extreme difficulty having heterosexual intercourse. The perversions may
have had a defensive significance in relation to the phallic-
oedipal conflict. It is a bit difficult to know just what
the conflict-triggering environment was in this patient.
We note that he began drinking (which probably marks the
beginning of his regression) when he was a college student.
This was a time when he had to begin preparing for a life's
work and a time when he began to attempt to establish
heterosexual relationships. It seems likely that his frequent trips to the houses of prostitution were associated

with the beginning of his alcoholism.

Despite his illness he managed to get through school and fulfill his military obligations. He didn't do well and his drinking increased. He got married and his drinking increased even more, and after his children were born his drinking increased even more than that. It is quite likely that he had perverse fantasies most of his life but it was when he began going to prostitutes that the perversions really began to erupt. This suggests that it was heterosexuality which led unconscious conflicts to take the form of manifest perversions.

As the regression deepened he began to have panic attacks which seemed to have been precipitated by being alone. In view of the eventual loss of all meaningful object ties, the separation problems, dependence and so on must have been constantly triggered by his lonely existence. To sum it up, it would seem that being alone triggered separation anxiety and dependence, and that responsibility and heterosexual closeness triggered pregenital as well as phallic-oedipal conflicts.

Most stressful in this man's life, of course, was the drinking and the recent divorce. The degree of aloneness that followed may be considered somewhat stressful as well as conflict-triggering. Hospitalization was most supportive to him. Prior to coming here there was very little support for him other than an attorney who finally bailed him out of his troubles and got him into treatment. Opportunities were abundant because of his wealth and connections. Nothing was very need-congruent by the time he came back and actually started treatment. He had no job, he had lost his family, and most of all other meaningful contacts. He was at odds with his sister to the point that they were not speaking to each other. Nothing was immutable in his life.

3. Summary of Situational Variables at the Time of Termination Study

This patient started treatment in earnest after his return to Topeka and remained in therapy for over 500 hours. He was seen three times a week for about three years, twice a week for about six months, and then once a week for several months. There were intermittent contacts for about a year until the treatment terminated.

During treatment his ex-wife and two children were killed while they were on their way to visit him. For a

time the patient had worked and also made efforts to affect
reconciliation with his wife. The wife, however, had made
it quite clear that she was not interested in remarrying
him.

During the course of the treatment, and even prior to
the death of his ex-wife, the patient entered into a long
series of involvement with other women, the pattern of which
was almost identical. He would find a woman who looked
attractive to him sexually, would rush her, and the moment
she showed interest in him or he succeeded in winning her
he became frightened and anxious and provoked a rupture of
the relationship. He attended courses at a university in
preparation for a speculation which he later went into
quite heavily. It was about this time that he first began
taking drugs. Following the death of his attorney the
patient became addicted to tranquilizers that had been prescribed for him following this man's death.

He met his future wife and, unlike the other girls,
he could not provoke her to leave him. He interrupted
treatment and married this woman but soon thereafter he
came to his former therapist in panic, saying that he
wanted to resume treatment because he felt like he was in
a trap. He resumed treatment and began work. The patient
was married and working, but then injured a pedestrian with
his automobile and resumed his drinking and drug taking.
The therapist gave him a choice between drugs and therapy,
and the patient chose drugs and broke off his treatment.

It is clear that the core neurotic conflicts in this
patient had been untouched. It is also clear, however,
that something had changed because he had been able to get
married again. Furthermore, he had been able to work. He
remained impotent and, in fact, never had intercourse with
his wife. Thus it appears clear that the ordinary demands
of life, such as making a living, heterosexuality, etc.,
were still conflict-triggering. He felt trapped after he
had married and this suggests that the closeness to his
wife activated the unconscious conflicts which created the
extreme anxiety in him.

We could see no stresses in his life now. A most significant change, however, were the plentiful supports.
There was more than adequate financial support, and the
wife was particularly supportive. She was a mothering,
supporting, encouraging person who, curiously enough, seemed
not to be too bothered by the lack of a sexual relationship. His life was more need-congruent. He had a wife

and, not only that, he had managed to carve out some business possibilities for himself. By the time of termination he had bought some property, was making other investments that turned out well. Opportunities were still plentiful for him.

4. Summary of Situational Variables at the Time of Follow-
   up Study

     During the follow-up period the patient continued at
about the same level of adjustment for a while but then
appears to have improved considerably. He remained married
but was unable to enter into a mature relationship with his
wife. He related more like a son to a mother. She apparently was content to function in this role. He denied
perversions or promiscuity. He carried on his business
dealings and continued to drink and take enormous doses of
tranquilizers. He apparently had a heart attack; this
experience frightened him so much that he gave up all tranquilizers. His former therapist was called in upon the
advice of the internist and the two of them withdrew him
from the heavy doses of tranquilizers. He slowly started
drinking wine and whiskey. He became assaultive to his
wife who apparently felt physically menaced the night she
called the former therapist. As a consequence of this
call, both the patient and his wife entered into family
therapy with the former therapist.

     The patient claimed to have quit drinking. There
had been a marked improvement in his agrophobia and he had
also continued to manage his business interests rather well.
In addition, he purchased a farm and was able to be there
alone and at other times he could be away from his wife.
He felt that he had made a marked improvement and his wife
agreed. He had developed a renewed interest in farming
and often spent many hours pouring over reading material
related to farming and animal husbandry. There were no
stresses in his life. Supports continued to be abundant
in the form of finances and also his wife, who stuck by
him faithfully. Therapy was highly supportive to him.
Opportunities continued to be good and need-congruence was
at a pretty high level although the fact that the wife was
willing not to have children and coitus reflects some aspects of her own personality that might tend to impede
continued maturation in the patient.

5. Summary

     This patient appears to have developed conflicts at

every psychosexual level. The perversions of childhood
presumably were never really repressed, while the phallic-
oedipal attachment to the mother seems to have been repressed.
Some of the perverse practices that are noted shade into
the normal phallic activities of young children but there
was an obviously perverse element in them. Other practices
are clearly perverse. The patient did not become overtly
ill until he began to study seriously in the university for
a life's work. At the same time he was making his first
efforts to establish heterosexual contacts.

It would appear, then, that these attempts to be a
responsible and mature person triggered all of the unconscious conflicts which initially erupted in the form of
Don Juanism and perverse fantasies and eventually acts.
As he progressed in life and as he attempted to increase
his responsibilities in military service and also through
marriage, his conflicts erupted all the more and his symptoms worsened. In addition to perversions, he was unable
to have intercourse with his wife except on rare occasions,
and he also became quite agrophobic.

In time he lost most of his meaningful interpersonal
contacts and gave up all of his responsibilities. This is
a pattern that has appeared over and over again in the patients in this study. After having given up all of his
close interpersonal contacts he attained, at times, a fairly
good adjustment while he was in treatment in Topeka. He
began to develop an investment program for himself and, if
we can believe his story, he made money at it. He worked
on accasion and he developed an ambivalent but apparently
lasting attachment to a therapist. He remarried, a sign
of improved health but, like the first time he married, his
behavior worsened. After his first marriage he went progressively downhill and eventually lost his wife and children. With the second marriage he felt quite trapped, and
had he not had a therapist to run to it seems likely that
he eventually would have lost this wife, too. For a time
his behavior deteriorated to the point of physical assault-
iveness and heavy ingestion of chemicals, and it was partly
this that led to his resumption of treatment.

This case, complicated as it was, and interesting in
so many different respects, shows how, among other things,
the effort to commit himself to life starting in college
coincided with the eruption of the manifest illness. As
he shed his responsibilities, his behavior improved, and
then as he took on responsibilities again his behavior
degenerated some. Fortunately, however, after having

married the second time he was able, because of his previous experience with treatment, to look up his old therapist (upon his wife's initiative) and apparently was launched
in a new and healthy direction. It should be noted that
he still could not have intercourse, and the thought of
having children made him remember the fact that his drinking worsened when his children were born in the first marriage. It seems quite obvious that the continued warm
support of his wife without a concomitant insistence on her
part for heterosexual contact had been a most significant
factor in his improvement. It should be noted also in this
respect that there was something quite boyish about this
woman. She, on the one hand, claimed to want children but,
on the other hand, had been willing to marry a man so sick
and so obviously impotent that one cannot overlook the fact
that, need-congruent as she was in the sense of offering
him the opportunity for growth and maturation, at the same
time she must have played into his neurosis.

SYNTHESIS OF SITUATIONAL VARIABLES - CASE #37

1. Brief History

This patient was the elder of two boys born into a
Kansas farm family. His earliest memory was seeing his
brother for the first time. Very little is known about the
patient's father except that the patient saw him as a stern,
forbidding person while the mother was considered to be
rather domineering, overprotective and oversolicitous. The
brother was the more successful of the two, had been able
to marry and was doing well in his life work.

The patient enrolled in college in the late thirties
and entered the service as an enlisted man in the early
forties. He saw duty in the Pacific theatre, and upon his
discharge from the service enrolled at a university and
remained there until the spring term of the late forties.
He was married in the mid-forties, primarily for sexual
reasons, to a woman with whom he had little in common. The
marriage lasted only a few months. He attended another
college for a while, but finally began working. Because
he was feeling lonely, depressed, and was extremely isolated
socially, he came to the Menninger Foundation and was evaluated. He had previously seen a private psychiatrist in
Topeka but came to an impasse with him and finally assaulted
the doctor when the doctor suggested the therapy should
terminate if the patient couldn't cooperate better.

2. Summary of Situational Variables at the Time of Initial
   Study

This was an extremely paranoid, constricted, and inhibited man. His passivity and suppressed hostility were
much in evidence, as was his stubbornness. Based on the
material from the psychological tests, in which he is seen
as a tender animal being hunted down by a killer, it appears
that oedipal conflicts were at the center of his conflicts
along with oral and anal conflicts. It is likely that he
must have experienced his mother as a very hostile,

321

poisonous woman. Nearly all of life had been conflict-
triggering for him. His way of managing was to avoid significant contact anywhere in life. Women were conflict-
triggering and although he was able to marry, he soon
divorced. Similarly, his parents had been conflict-triggering, most notably the father. It is noted that for no
apparent reason he severed relationships with his father
about a year prior to coming to treatment. He had had little
contact with either of his parents for the prior ten years.

Thus, women, sex, parents, people in general, were all
conflict-triggering. Stresses were minimal if not absent.
About the only human support this patient had were the co-
workers and the one brother with whom he maintained some
contact. Very little was need-congruent except for his
work. Opportunities were not lacking; he was fairly handsome, and if his illness could be worked out it seems likely
that he could have more from life. Nothing was immutable.

3. Summary of Situational Variables at the Time of Termination Study

The patient began treatment but was unable to make
any significant progress with his first therapist, although
for a time he became more involved with his environment in
a variety of ways. He enlarged his social contacts, joined
a club or two, and was carrying on an affair with a woman
in another city. A transference resistance jam developed,
however, which was overtly hostile and paranoid and his
treatment ultimately bogged down despite the gains that had
been made. Not all of these gains were sustained for he
tended to withdraw some from the contacts he had made. He
had continued to date and to go hunting, something he did,
however, before he ever came to treatment.

The second treatment also ended in an impasse. The
patient had, however, built a house during this period of
treatment without telling his therapist.

Progress continued to be slow with a third therapist,
but interestingly enough he got married during the third
period of psychotherapy. He married without the doctor
knowing about it.

At first glance it would seem that the treatment of
this man failed; looked at from a distance it appears that
during the many years of therapy he slowly but progressively
improved. The first therapist helped him overcome some of
his social isolation. He was able to build a house during

the second period of treatment, and he put a woman in that house during the period with the third therapist. In the meantime he continued to do well at his work.

Symptoms were about the same; for instance, anxiety has been rated as moderate both initially and at termination. The loneliness was somewhat less severe, social isolation was a little less severe but his paranoid view of life was essentially unchanged. Core conflicts at termination were unchanged. At what level of psychosexual development his conflicts were formed is unclear. It seems likely that his view of the world as a hostile place must have come from the early experiences with the mother. The domination-submission conflict may have developed at the anal period although the hostility towards the severe father and the characterologic passivity with its associated unyielding qualities point to oedipal difficulties.

Conflict triggers continued to be involvement with people and, in particular, heterosexual involvements. Supports were largely gained from his work, from a few social contacts in a couple of organizations, and from the one brother. Very little was need-congruent in his life save for his work and the home he had purchased for himself.

4. Summary of Situational Variables at the Time of Follow-up Study

During the follow-up period the patient remained in treatment with the third therapist (termination was arbitrarily set at the end of his second period of treatment). During this period he got married without telling his doctor and then told him when he asked the doctor to arrange for professional help for his wife. Marital difficulties did not seem to be too serious; apparently he was somewhat jealous of his wife giving attention to others. There were a few open quarrels when his dependent needs weren't satisfied by her.

Core conflicts were essentially unchanged. Parents were still conflict-triggering although he avoided them most of the time. Work seemed to be minimally conflict-triggering. The wife was somewhat conflict-triggering. Supports and need-congruent environmental factors were now considerably increased by virtue of the marriage. He had a home and a wife.

5. Summary

This is a heavily conflicted man, frightened by life and angry for having been treated the way he was as a child. The anger has been woven into a paranoid system which has caused him to view the world as a hostile, rejecting place. It seems quite likely that in addition to these preoedipal conflicts, he never resolved his Oedipus complex so that by the time he did attempt to marry he chose a woman for sex only. He frankly admitted to the first therapist that he had no relationship whatsoever with this woman. He was extremely hostile toward all of his therapists; he wanted to make them fail, no doubt, as he wanted to make his father fail, and yet despite these efforts something moved forward in him. Slowly but surely he made commitments and finally, after having run through three therapists and settling with the fourth, he was able to marry. To what extent this was a function of the therapy is unclear. His ability to move forward and intensify his commitment to life had not been due to resolution of intrapsychic core conflict. It would seem, rather, to have been assisted by some kind of corrective emotional experience with the four different psychotherapists.

SYNTHESIS OF SITUATIONAL VARIABLES - CASE #38

1. Brief History

     At the time of admission to the hospital the patient,
daughter of a professional man, was an unemployed single
girl in her early twenties. There was one brother, four
years older than she, who was a professional student at
the time.

     The patient was born after a normal pregnancy and
delivery and was breast-fed. After weaning she was left
in the care of a young hired girl a good deal of the time
because of the mother's preoccupation with social events.
At age four she was going to the bathroom alone at night
in the dark. Until age seven she slept in a bedroom ad-
joing her parents and in order to go to the bathroom she
had to go through their room.

     She was described as a sweet child with no emotional
problems, who dressed in pretty clothes which the mother
was proud of making. She seemed doll-like, a fact which
gave her mother much satisfaction.

     When the patient was four her father became severely
ill and suffered a severe weight loss. This illness sometimes caused him to weep at the table because he was unable
to eat. At age five the patient developed a febrile illness and soon thereafter obesity became a problem.

     She was usually a very outgoing girl, popular with
friends, the buffoon at the party and, in general, very
sociable. She sucked her thumb until she was eight years
old. Excessive sex play occurred around age six. This
consisted mainly of undressing, mutual fondling of genitalia and so on (with other children). She seemed unper-
turbed by the onset of menses at age 12 and masturbation
at age 14 which she had continued ever since. She had her
first sexual intercourse when she was a junior in high
school and since that time had been quite promiscuous. Her

illness is believed to have been most noticeable at age ten
when she developed a fear of the dark and had nightmares
following a tonsillectomy. Mother had to comfort her a
great deal by being in the bed with her for several hours
each night. Between the ages of 10 and 11 she developed a
fear of being caught in some place in which there was no
toilet. The patient herself dated the onset of her illness
to age 12 when she saw a drunk, became panicked, telephoned
her mother who came to take her home.

Her promiscuous pattern included various kinds of perversions, including being beaten and finding pleasure in
watching the boy masturbate. Sometime before coming to the
hospital the patient's father had a severe illness. It was
a cloudy day when the patient was informed of this and she
subsequently developed a phobia for dark skies. Two attempts
at psychotherapy failed to bring any progress. With regard
to the phobia, therapy subsequently revealed the fact that
she claimed to have witnessed the primal scene on a cloudy
day, and in this connection it should be noted that the
patient used to rub her father's back when he requested it.
She would become nauseated when she did this.

2. Summary of Situational Variables at the Time of Initial
   Study

At the time of initial study this patient had come to
the hospital from her parental home where she was living
and where she had become increasingly phobic. She had also
been extremely promiscuous during this time. She was placed
in the hospital for about eight months. She subsequently
was discharged to a family care home because of lack of
money.

The core conflicts at the time of the initial study
were primarily at two levels. There was the oral dependency which seemed to have grown out of the distrubed early
mother-infant relationship, and the later conflict was very
clearly oedipal. It seems that the obesity was a direct
expression of her oral cravings but was also a regressive
defense against incestuous wishes towards her father. The
promiscuous acting out undoubtedly was overdetermined but
it certainly was an alloplastic symptomatic expression of
oedipal wishes. It is significant that she usually took
another female with her on her sexual escapades.

The relationship to the mother had been a highly complicated one and for this reason the most obvious conflict
trigger was the mother herself. However, the father was

also conflict-triggering by his mere presence, but this
was aggravated by the fact that as a child she was asked
to massage him, an activity which caused her to become nauseated. The patient reported that she felt consciously
that her father was sexually stimulated by this. It was
clear that puberty and young adulthood with its implicit
demands for establishing relationships was itself conflict-
triggering. Promiscuous behavior broke out under these
conditions.

There were few stresses of much significance other
than perhaps the high expectations of the mother. The mother
was a very dominant, controlling person. Supports were
plentiful. The parents had, despite their stressful and
conflict-triggering aspects, always supported her well.
The hospital was supportive, and later the family care home.
Opportunities for the future were quite good for this girl.
She was, despite her obesity, a rather attractive girl.
She could have, had she not been ill, married or gone into
some form of work without too much difficulty.

In addition to being conflict-triggering, the parents
were also need-incongruent. The mother was a dominant
woman who had many narcissistic expectations of the patient.
The father, with his overt seductiveness and oscillation
between extreme passivity and extreme temper, was also need-
incongruent. On the other hand, the patient more or less
had the world at her feet and could have had about what she
wanted in terms of heterosexual relationships, college or
work. Therefore the many need-congruent aspects of the
environment were available to her. Her sexual escapades
were, of course, highly need-incongruent. Nothing was
immutable as such.

3. Summary of Situational Variables at the Time of Termi-
    nation Study

The patient was in the hospital for over six months
and then transferred to a foster home. She was in expressive psychotherapy three times a week. At the time of termination she had been seen over 700 hours. She began psychotherapy in the late fifties, worked the next spring,
and then entered college in the fall. She began dating
her husband in the early sixties; her father died the same
year, and she was married the next spring.

By the end of treatment some change had taken place
in her symptom picture. Her phobias had diminished from
severe to moderate. Promiscuity disappeared. Obesity had

been somewhat reduced. She was able to work. Sexual perversions were sharply diminished if not absent and frigidity
was only moderate. The phobias were somewhat less, although
the patient was still anxious. The Treatment Variables
team did not believe that this woman's core neurotic conflicts had been resolved. While this may be true, the facts
are that the patient had changed considerably. Much of
her alloplasticity had diminished; phobias were less; she
had been able to marry.

The Patient Variables team felt that this was due to
the fact that the powerful sexual urges of adolescence had
abated some. This is no doubt true. However, the fact
that her behavior improved so much suggests that some internal changes had taken place and that possibly some resolution of core conflict had occurred. The rest of her improved behavior could be attributed to the strengthened
ego and the diminished intensity of the drives.

That she was still obese, still phobic, etc., testi-
fies to the fact that there was a remaining illness in her.
The patient's self-esteem had increased considerably, however, and she saw a future for herself. A significant
change had also taken place in her environment. The father
had died, and it was not too many months after this that
she was able to marry. One must note, however, that she
knew her husband-to-be before the father's death and,
indeed, was on her way to announce plans for marriage when
the father became ill and died. It is significant to note
also that the mother's behavior towards the patient changed.
She was less dominating, and in this sense was less of a
conflict trigger. It seems reasonable to say that some
change in the core conflicts had taken place, but certainly the ego had been strengthened. The drives may have been
somewhat diminished, but some conflict triggers had been
removed also. Since she had taken a man into her life
a potential conflict trigger had been added.

There were no stresses. Supports again were plentiful in that the Foundation was still a part of her life.
She, in fact, was still in therapy despite the termination
cut-off date, and she now had a husband and friends.
Opportunities were plentiful. The patient's life had become markedly more need-congruent by her having gotten
married. She was now committed to a heterosexual relationship. Nothing was immutable.

4. Summary of Situational Variables at the Time of Follow-
   up Study

During the two-year period between termination and
follow-up the patient's adjustment continued to improve.
Her marriage was stormy at first but it smoothed out with
a definitely clear delineation of roles within the marriage.
It was quite evident that the patient saw herself as a
woman in this relationship and it was also clear that the
husband saw himself as the man. They had a baby a few
months old at follow-up and the whole family seemed to be
doing rather well. The patient's behavior was markedly
improved. The promiscuity was gone, anxiety was considerably less, the phobias were still present but markedly
diminished. She had been able to travel with the help of
her husband and a little medication. She could go about
the city by herself. She still had fear of dark places
and elevators, but by and large was much more comfortable
than she once was. This diminution in symptomatology, both
autoplastic and alloplastic, the fact that she had become
a mother and seemed to be thriving on it, suggests that
some significant internal changes had taken place. That
her father was no longer present, of course, was a loss of
a factor that was once a conflict trigger, but the fact
that she had been able to take a man into her life suggests
that those conflicts which a husband might activate must be
diminished. Therefore, it seems that the core conflicts
had been somewhat resolved. The fact that symptoms remained, including obesity, of course suggests that all of
her unconscious conflicts had not been completely resolved.

Supports were good. The patient still saw her mother.
Her husband stood by her and made a good home for her. She
had friends. One of the most significant changes in her
life by the follow-up period, in contrast to the time of
initial study, was the very need-congruent aspect of her
life. This pertains mostly to the fact that she was married and making a home, and had become a mother. Opportunities for the future seemed quite bright.

5. Summary

This patient was an alloplastically-inclined hysterical character disorder who showed signs of illness from
early childhood onward. The first evidence of symptomatology was her overeating during the oedipal period. This
suggests that at that time she chose a regressive, defensive
mode in the face of oedipal threats. Rather than have a
clear latency, there was sex play with older children

between the ages of 6 and 14. Thumbsucking did not stop until age eight. Following a tonsillectomy the patient developed a fear of the dark and had nightmares for a time. Upon seeing a drunk on the street she developed panics at age 12. At the onset of puberty the patient developed marked promiscuity. In her mid-teens she failed in an educational endeavor; a year later she failed to follow her mother's footsteps in college. Soon thereafter she developed a phobia for cloudy days when she was notified of her father's death, and from then on became progressively worse and eventually had to be hospitalized.

The challenge of establishing heterosexual relationships at puberty, coupled with the intensification of her sexual drives during this period, led to a marked promiscuity. The actual relationship with the parents continued to trigger the infantile neurosis, thus adding fuel to the fire of puberty so that she had to be hospitalized.

The doctor describes his treatment of this patient as very supportive, and attributes some of the change to the patient's having introjected him in a way which strengthened her ego. She modeled much of her view of life after his and thus she acquired a stabilizing force within herself. At the same time it must not be presumed that no resolution of conflict occurred. That all core conflicts were not resolved is very evident, but the evidence points strongly to the possibility of some resolution. This patient, after a long period of treatment, had been able to marry and have a child. Her promiscuity had disappeared, her phobias persisted to some extent, but by and large she was much more a woman in appearance and by her own assessment of herself. It seems that the confluence of natural maturational forces, some resolution of core conflicts, some diminution of conflict triggers, and the strengthening of her ego through the therapeutic process can account for these changes.

SYNTHESIS OF SITUATIONAL VARIABLES - CASE #39

1. Brief History

   The patient was a white, unmarried male in his mid-
thirties who was admitted directly to the hospital. He
had wanted to come for treatment for a long time, and his
father finally agreed to his coming and also to paying the
expenses. He came because of alcoholism and homosexuality
and an inability to decide what to do with his life.

   The patient was the elder of two boys. He was a very
bright boy, and is said by his mother to have had many
friends. He was not good at sports, however, and never
joined in this kind of activity. At age six or seven he
read extensively. By age 10 he attended adult movies and
was reading high level literature rather than playing with
peers. He was engaged in mutual masturbation by age 11 and
from that time on had been consciously aware of homosexual
feelings. From age 14 on he had noticed that he was able
to work very well for a period of time but during other
periods he would become depressed and could not function
adequately. There was an intense homosexual affair in high
school, but he claimed to have begun having normal satisfying heterosexual relationships by his mid-teens.

   He attended a university and did very well academically but tended to associate with only a few people; with
some of them he had sexual relations. On graduation from
the university he saw service overseas. He had a homosexual
relationship in the service and developed gonorrhea, an
illness which seemed to prey on him heavily for he felt he
was being destroyed.

   After discharge from the service he worked as a clerk
in a large city, then as a leg man for a writer. He finally returned home to work in his father's store, a position
he filled until coming to the hospital. After leaving the
service he had been involved in repeated homosexual relationships. These were transient affairs which consisted

331

of mutual masturbation and mutual fellatio. He once suffered a subdural hematoma as a result of a fight with a
homosexual partner.

The patient felt that he was a complete failure in
life. A few years prior to his coming into the hospital
his brother committed suicide. He reacted with a "high
period" which eventually led to his being hospitalized but
he was discharged with a nonpsychotic diagnosis. He was
alcoholic, obese, and characterologically passive and unable to succeed at a vocation in addition to being homosexual.

2.   Summary of Situational Variables at the Time of Initial
     Study

The core conflict at the time of initial study was
largely a profound dependency, which appears to have found
expression in his alcoholism, obesity and passivity. The
self-destructive masochistic element in him appeared to be
coupled with his homosexuality in which he experienced
great delight in destroying powerful males. This behavior,
and his strained adult relationship with his father, points
to unresolved oedipal problems. Thus the two main levels
of difficulty seemed to be on the one hand the oral fixation and, on the other hand, a phallic-oedipal conflict which
manifested itself by a profound, generally self-destructive
life pattern and homosexuality. It was quite evident that
working in his father's store was highly conflict-triggering.
He consumed great quantities of alcohol and continued his
homosexual contacts. That he had been out to destroy the
father is manifested by the fact that the father had spent
nearly all his capital, somewhat over $100,000, for the
patient's treatment. That his brother's suicide triggered
core conflicts in him is evidenced by the fact that his
behavior worsened markedly after this death.

Homosexuality appeared at around age 11, the very time
when heterosexual attachments are usually established. It
would appear, therefore, that his homosexuality had a defensive significance against the clearly unresolved oedipal
conflicts. Any kind of real success with a woman or at a
vocation was impossible for him. It is interesting to note
that he once had sexual relations with a married couple -
first with the man and then with the woman.

Stresses were rather minimal, the main one being alcohol
which was, of course, of a feedback variety. Supports were
moderate to good; despite the conflict-triggering impact of
the parents, they stood behind him, made a job for him,

gave him a home, and spent quite a large sum of money on
him in the name of treatment. Opportunities were excellent.
He was very bright, well educated and talented. His illness, unfortunately, stood in the way. Little was need-
congruent at the time of initial study. His homosexual
contacts were highly need-incongruent. His parents fostered
his dependency, they were not congruent; however, his father
made a job for him and supported his treatment.

3. Summary of Situational Variables at the Time of Termi-
    nation Study

     The patient began a psychoanalysis on a five times a
week basis. He was a hospital patient at that time. After
a few months he was discharged from the hospital and began
working for a Kansas publication. Within two years he had
improved enough to go home for a visit, and a little less
than a year later was having a heterosexual affair, his
first since the mid-forties, but within a few months he
began drinking quite heavily. The patient was then hospitalized after he broke up with this girl and remained in
the hospital for another two years. After five years of
treatment his hours were reduced to two times a week. The
patient lost his job and began working for another magazine
but he was jailed for drunken driving and lost that job. He
finally had his last hour with his therapist after seven years
of treatment. After this the patient flew to another country for a vacation and then returned two years later to
work in his father's store. Soon thereafter his mother
died of a heart attack, following which the patient drank
for five months and gained 35 pounds.

     By the time of the termination interview the patient
had begun working for a university writing textbooks. At
the time of termination it seems that the core conflicts
were essentially unresolved or even unchanged to any significant extent. The patient appears to have gotten into
an unresolvable transference jam and took flight from treatment with the unconscious motivation to destroy the analyst
just as he wanted to seduce and destroy other men as well
as his own father. Despite all of the insights that the
patient apparently gained from his analyst, nothing really
changed with him. His drinking continued, his homosexuality
continued, and he was as self-destructive as ever.

     It is evident that the conflict triggers at the time
of termination continued to be the parents, work in general,
and most certainly any attempt at heterosexuality. It
should be noted, for instance, that treatment apparently

caused him to improve enough at one point that he attempted
to establish a relationship with a woman. As soon as he
became involved, he promptly became worse symptomatically.
By the time of termination there were no heterosexual conflict triggers; he did not involve himself with women. The
mother had died by the time of the termination study, thus
removing a conflict trigger in one sense; however, the loss
of the mother was itself quite illness-triggering as manifested by his marked increase in drinking and weight gain
after her death.

Supports continued to be good in that the father provided a home for him and made a job for him. The work situation was supportive both at the store and, more impor-
tantly, at a university. His work can be considered need-
congruent. The father had become more need-congruent because
he stood up to his son and refused to let him bleed him to
death financially. His homosexual partners were need-
incongruent. Opportunities were quite excellent at work.

4. Summary of Situational Variables at the Time of Follow-
   up Study

The patient continued to live in the same city during
the follow-up period and was able to hold onto his job at
the university. Aside from this fact there were no changes
in him other than some diminution of homosexuality, or perhaps more precisely a narrowing of the range of his homosexual contacts. Whereas he used to be quite promiscuous,
he now confined his activities to one young male whom he
saw a couple of times a week and with whom he lived for a
period of about three months. There were no women in his
life whatsoever, and while he had acquaintances, he had
very few friends. Drinking continued to be heavy; so heavy,
in fact, that he stated the only time that he was really
conscious during the 24 hours was when he was at work.
After work he drank heavily, had dinner, fell asleep, woke
up and read for a time and then slept again. Somewhere in
this schedule he managed to have some contact with his homosexual partner. These activities constituted his living
pattern. It is significant that he had been able to hold
his job.

Conflict triggers were absent insofar as heterosexuality was concerned. That work was conflict-triggering
is made clear by the fact that when he received a promotion
he promptly got worse symptomatically; he drank more, there
was some absenteeism for a period. He had avoided another
conflict trigger in the person of the father and only rarely

saw him. During the last year of the follow-up period he
saw his father only once and this by accident. There was
only one conflict trigger in his life and this had to do
with being responsible enough to hold down a job.

There were no stresses other than the alcohol. Supports centered largely around the homosexual partner and
the job. Opportunities were still good. In fact, his boss
told him that they would have good advances for him if he
would improve. His work was need-congruent, but this is
all that was need-congruent in his life. His homosexual
partner was highly need-incongruent in the sense that he
served to obstruct any maturation toward the direction of
manliness and heterosexuality.

5. Summary

This patient appears to have become fixated at the
oral level and as a consequence developed a marked dependence
and passivity. This fixation may have been partially
accounted for by the fact that he was a colicky baby and
to the fact that during the early months of his nursing
experience the mother had a chronic breast abscess. She
did not stop nursing, but it can be surmised that the
nursing was uncomfortable for her and an unsoothing experience for him. Mother was a more dominant, aggressive
person than the father, who was more of a passive, meek man.

The patient and his father had little contact with
each other and he saw his father as an aggressive person
against whom he could never win. It appears, then, that
the distance between the father and the patient, a distance
which undoubtedly was contributed to by the father because
of his own conflicts and passivity, and the nature of his
relationship with his mother, never allowed the patient to
resolve his dependent nor his oedipal conflicts. As a consequence, when he approached puberty and was faced with the
challenge of establishing a heterosexual relationship he
fled defensively into homosexuality. This incapacity to
succeed in a heterosexual way spread and became a pervasive
life pattern which prevented him from succeeding anywhere.

His life pattern was characterized by alcoholism, job
failure, depression, obesity, passivity, and homosexuality.
Significantly, his prime joy during his homosexual contacts
was to weaken the other male, who undoubtedly was a symbol
for his father whom he wished to destroy. The patient
nearly did destroy his father financially. Homosexuality
made its first appearance at around age 11 and never

disappeared for any length of time. From puberty on the
patient was unable to establish himself successfully as a
male with a woman, nor was he able to live out a nonself-
destructive life pattern.

Two attempts at psychoanalysis failed; the second
analysis lasted over five years. The patient got into an
insoluable transference jam and fled treatment as sick as
ever. There had been some slight improvement in the patient
during the follow-up period in the sense that he was more
restrictive in his homosexuality. He had been able to hold
a job and be reasonably productive at it. This suggests
something had changed slightly. Since there is little
evidence that the treatment produced intrapsychic change,
one must look into his environment for the basis for this
slight change. Here it is immediately evident that the
mother was now gone and that the patient had maintained a
considerable distance from his father. These two changes
may have permitted the unconscious problems to recede
sufficiently so that he could make a marginal vocational
adjustment.

SYNTHESIS OF SITUATIONAL VARIABLES - CASE #40

1. Brief History

The patient came for an evaluation when he was in his
early thirties and an instructor at a university. He was
divorced and the father of a small child who lived with her
mother. He had been going with a girl whom he wished to
marry but he noted that he was developing the same kinds
of difficulties with her that he had had with his former
wife. He recognized the problems were his own and he was
determined to do something about them.

The patient was the third of four children and the
only son. All of his sisters were married and had children.
The patient's father was a successful man and apparently a
rather substantial person but he was passive in relation to
his wife and rather distant from his children, although
he obviously had an interest in them. He was such a conscientious man that he personally made good the losses that
the depositors in his bank had incurred during the depression; for a time he worked for almost no salary to help
pay off these deficits. The father was rather distant from
the mother and instead of discussing things with her he
usually found solitude and spent his time reading. The
mother can be presumed to have been a rather distant person
who was unable to supply the kind of warmth and nurturance
that an infant requires. Some of the data suggest that
the patient found an aunt to be more of a good mother figure
than his own mother.

It is noteworthy that as a child the patient never
felt much internal push towards success and therefore never
tried hard to amount to anything, nor did he remember his
family urging him on to achievement. Despite having come
from an upper socioeconomic level, he spent a great deal
of time with lower classes. It can be inferred that he
found human warmth there and felt that he could be himself
with these people, something he could not experience at
home and probably never with his own mother. He participated

337

some in sports.

After high school he went into the service, a period
about which not too much is known. This was a lonely period
in his life. He met a young woman, and at age 23 he had
one of the long but infrequent talks with his father. His
father said that if he was interested in this girl he, the
father, would provide adequate funds so that he could get
married and go to college at the same time. The patient
married and about nine months later their baby was born.
The marriage never was very happy but after the birth of
the baby serious difficulties developed and the marriage
eventually ended in divorce. The wife had become interested in another man, and rather than stand up and keep
his woman for himself he let another man have her even
though he found giving her up very difficult. While an
instructor at a university he met another woman but found
that he was having the same kind of difficulties with her
as he had with his wife. This concerned him deeply and he
sought psychiatric treatment.

2.   Summary of Situational Variables at the Time of Initial
     Study

The patient's life at the time of initial study was a
rather simple one. He was teaching economics at a university and his main concern was his dissatisfaction and discomfort in relation to women. He feared that he would not
be able to make a marital commitment and he sought help
for this problem.

The core conflicts were at two levels. First, there
was a marked dependence manifested by his search for the
giving, gratifying mother. The second conflict was oedipal.
A characterologic passivity developed from this phallic-
oedipal conflict which reinforced his own deeper dependency.
Associated with these conflictual constellations was an
intense hostility toward women.

The main conflict triggers were women. He had found
sufficient courage to attempt marriage but there is not
much information about the kind of woman she was. The closeness and the degree of commitment that he achieved with
this woman proved to be conflict-triggering, as did parenthood, so severely so that he fled from that situation by
means of divorce. This situation had become history at
the time of initial study; however, he was approaching
another such commitment with a second woman. It is clear,
therefore, that the prospects of an intimate relationship

with a woman and the memory of his previous failure were
the main conflict triggers. Both parents were conflict
triggers and it is, of course, significant to note that
his father's field of endeavor was potentially conflict-
triggering. The patient could not follow his father's
footsteps to become a businessman but instead chose to
teach business administration.

The stresses in his life were minimal. The main stress
might have been a certain amount of loneliness. There was
some stress of the broken marriage; however, this wasn't
much of a burden on him because he had adequate finances
to provide for the ex-wife and child. Material supports
were abundant. Father always gave him substantial gifts.
Father tended to make decisions for him and often gave him
advice. Opportunities were, of course, abundant. He
could have become a businessman or he could become a teacher,
it all hinged on the extent to which he could resolve his
conflicts. Need-congruence was minimal at the time of
initial study. His work was certainly the most, if not the
only, need-congruent aspect of his existence. He lived in
rather spartan conditions and avoided women. While it was
supportive to have his parents watching over him, this
solicitude tended to infantilize him. In fact, it seemed
as if his father was somewhat bent on keeping this patient
a child. The patient tended to search out aggressive,
domineering women to mother him, but these relationships
were hardly need-congruent for they merely reinforced his
illness.

3.   Summary of Situational Variables at the Time of Termi-
     nation Study

The patient entered psychoanalysis and remained in
treatment six years, for something under 1500 hours. His
treatment was then switched to supportive-expressive therapy and at the arbitrary cutoff point of the termination
study he had accrued slightly less than 250 additional hours.
Analysis had been five times a week, psychotherapy three
times a week. The patient regressed rather profoundly
during his psychoanalysis and at one point he believed that
the analyst was having an affair with his (the patient's)
mother. The analyst had met the patient's mother once, at
the insistence of the patient. Because he had seen the
analyst shake the mother's hand, when parting, the next day
the patient accused the analyst of having seduced his mother
in the office.

It is beyond the scope of this brief summary to describe

the treatment; however, these kinds of profound regressive phenomena punctuated the treatment throughout. The
therapist frequently had to introduce various parameters
such as giving advice, counseling, etc., in order to maintain a stable foundation upon which the interpretive work
might be based. During this period the patient progressed
some in his work by taking steps towards his doctorate.
Much of the progress towards his degree can be attributed
to the supportive-expressive psychotherapy which was necessary to pull the patient out of a rather profound transference regression. This supportive-expressive work dealt
with many reality problems and skillfully guided the patient
towards his goals. It should be mentioned that in the
midst of his treatment his father died, and almost immediately his relationship to the rest of his family improved.
He was able to play an active part in managing the family
estate and became friendlier with his mother. Near the end
of his treatment the patient transferred to a large university in another state where he eventually received his
doctorate after termination treatment; however, he kept in
touch with his therapist during this time.

An assessment of the treatment suggests that the patient achieved some intrapsychic structural changes and
that these changes were to some degree associated with insight. It was noted, however, that the patient was overly
psychologically-minded and had too ready an accessibility
to the unconscious forces at work within him but at the
same time was unable to change his behavior as a consequence
of this knowledge. This, of course, speaks to his basic
ego weakness, a fact which eventually necessitated a supportive psychotherapeutic approach.

At the time of termination some slight change had
occurred in his core conflicts. His dependency had ameliorated some but his oedipal problem with its associated
characterologic passivity and tendency to remain detached
from life, and in particular from women, had not been
altered to any significant degree. It seemed clear that
work was less conflict-triggering for him than before.
Women were still unattainable and he avoided them. Some
of his conflicts and feelings about his sisters changed,
as witnessed by the improved relationships with them. The
father's death removed a major conflict trigger from his
life, a fact which, along with some resolution of the intrapsychic problem, made it possible for him to be a significant and helpful influence in the management of the family
estate. Many of his old symptoms seemed to have disappeared.
These symptoms were a severe fear which had required him

to carry a gun, have stomach cramps and headaches. Not
all of these symptoms had completely disappeared but they
were considerably less severe. It seems correct to say that
the treatment with its slight conflict-resolving and ego
strengthening aspects, and the loss of a major conflict
trigger (the father) and his avoidance of women, which
kept him away from the most important conflict trigger of
all, accounted for the improved symptom picture. As mentioned earlier, however, the basic characterologic passivity
was not significantly altered.

There were no stresses in his life. The supports continued to be rather plentiful. His work was the main support and, significantly, the therapist continued to be an
active supporting factor in his life. His work was the
most need-congruent aspect of his life. Contributing to
the management of the family estate was also need-congruent;
however, highly need-incongruent was the absence of a commitment to a woman. Opportunities were plentiful.

4. Summary of Situational Variables at the Time of Follow-
    up Study

During the period between the termination study and
the follow-up study the patient completed his thesis and
obtained a Ph.D. degree. His academic appointment was
immediately upgraded and opened up opportunities in other
schools. He accepted one of these in a nearby university
and his salary was doubled. He was awarded a full professorship. His social life was still rather bleak, and by
and large there were no women in his life at all although
he still hoped to find a woman. He still experienced considerable restlessness, occasional irritability, and he
still tended to be attracted to the more domineering kind
of woman. None of his symptoms had returned except occasional stomach cramps. Since he avoided women there was no
way of knowing whether he was still impotent. He had developed quite an interest in art and moved around the country a great deal more than he did at the time of initial
study. He was planning to take a trip to Europe soon and
he hoped to find social contacts on the boat trip.

The core conflicts at the time of follow-up were presumed to be about the same as at the time of termination.
Some of his dependence and separation anxiety seemed to
have been resolved. He was somewhat less afraid of success,
and he had been able to be considerably more successful,
having achieved a Ph.D. degree and an appointment as a
full professor. He had not been able to achieve a

relationship to women, a fact which suggests that women
were still quite pronouncedly conflict-triggering. He had
developed an interest in his daughter and financed her
college education, but this was a distant relationship and
one which placed little demand on him. There was nothing
stressful in his life. Supports were about the same; he
gained most from his work, and some from not too frequent
contacts with his family. He continued to see his psychotherapist off and on. The most need-congruent aspect of
his life was his work and the least need-congruent was the
absence of heterosexual involvement.

5.   Summary

   This patient was born to a couple who were not able
to meet the needs of a developing child adequately. The
mother was a distant, cold woman who had a terrible temper
and sometimes shook the child to the point that his teeth
rattled (this latter description is a memory of the patient).
His father was a conscientious and well-intentioned man,
but one who was never able to develop a good ongoing relationship with his son. As a consequence of these parental
influences the patient became a very frightened person
whose core conflicts were profound dependence and separation and castration anxiety.

   He developed symptoms early in life; these included
enuresis, stuttering, stealing from his father; later he
developed compulsive symptoms such as stepping on cracks,
driving down prescribed routes, lying, manipulations, and
cheating. His paranoid fears of being attacked caused him
to carry weapons with him. Despite these struggles he
managed to establish a heterosexual relationship, eventually
marry and father a child. Although the patient accepted
his father's offer of financial support so that he could be
married and go to college he, at the same time, resented
the father's help because it "forced" him into something
he felt unready and unable to handle.   It is small wonder
that his marriage went badly from the first and took a
severe downward turn after the wife's pregnancy and the
birth of their daughter because of the conflict-triggering
impact of these events. The marriage ended in divorce,
and by this event the patient escaped the conflict triggers
which had mobilized the infantile conflicts which were so
tenuously held in check by his characterological and other
defenses. However, despite this reversal in his life he
pushed on towards a degree in business administration and
in so doing seemingly was trying to identify to some extent
with his father who was a successful businessman. He made

slow but steady progress in this venture. After his divorce he found that he was repeating with another woman
the kind of difficulties he had had with his wife. He was
also unable to write his thesis. The conflict-triggering
effect of becoming successful at his chosen field of work
and the wish to involve himself seriously with a woman produced enough discomfort in him to cause him to seek treatment.

His treatment was long and sometimes stormy, and the
psychoanalytic aspect of it produced a marked regression
which was characterized by periods of transference psychosis.
By introducing supportive parameters the analyst managed
to bring the patient out of his regressions successfully,
and by later replacing the psychoanalytic approach with a
supportive approach he managed to steer the patient into a
reasonably successful life adjustment. He eventually was
awarded a Ph.D. degree and sought and acquired teaching
positions, the last of which was a full professorship.

The patient's basic character makeup was unchanged
for he still showed considerable passivity and a somewhat
detached, avoidant way of life. He longed for but was unable to find a woman and establish a relationship with her.
The positive changes suggest that some intrapsychic change
took place during his long psychoanalysis despite, or possibly because of, the severe regressions and that these
changes, along with the supportive, guiding, stabilizing
techniques during the supportive phase were the bases for
these changes. It cannot be overlooked that the patient's
father died during his treatment and that soon thereafter
he was able to step in and play a significant part in the
management of the family estate.

Despite the preseumed-to-exist intrapsychic changes
which appear to be related to insight, and despite the
good effects of the supportive phase of the treatment, a
stark fact must be acknowledged. This patient came to
treatment because he could not establish and maintain nor
succeed in a relationship with a woman. His one effort at
marriage had failed dismally. At the conclusion of treatment, and two years later at follow-up, the only women in
his life were his sisters and mother with whom he had rather
distant relationships. There were no women towards whom
he felt love or was sexually interested in. This fact
strongly suggests that some of his symptomatic and behavioral improvement was also due to the fact that there was no
woman (for him the major conflict trigger) in his life.

1. Brief History

     This patient, a divorcee, came to the Menninger Foun-
dation in her late thirties. She was the second of three
siblings, born and reared in the northern Midwest where
her father was a successful businessman. His professional
development grew steadily and at the time of his death he
was the top administrator for a large development program
in the Northeast. Little is known of the mother except
that she underwent some marked personality changes when
the patient was about 12. The patient's father believed
the patient's mother was sweet and affectionate.

     The patient had no serious love affairs during her
youth according to her father although she was frequently
involved in mixed groups. Her mother died in the late
thirties when the patient was approximately 20. She went
to a music school for a year after her mother's death, but
then returned home upon the father's request and managed
the home for one year. Either during the time she was at
home with her father or shortly thereafter she began taking
drugs in large doses. After returning home, and against
her father's advice, she married a severely incapacitated
man who was an alcoholic. This was a very unhappy experience from the beginning and ended in a divorce after two
and a half years. After that she lived in relative
seclusion.

     After a number of years she had an affair with a man
who was approximately 20 years her senior and whose wife
was psychotic. The patient had not done any productive
work for many years and had been on drugs more or less continuously since the early forties. The inheritance from
her mother and supplemental funds supplied by her father
sustained her financially. She finally became so incapacitated that she was brought to the hospital. She had lived
with the man she married for three years prior to actually
marrying him. It is evident that the mother's death and

then having to live with the father are significant events
which triggered the breakthrough of the illness.

2. Summary of Situational Variables at the Time of Initial
    Study

    This woman had a marked dependency conflict and, in
addition to this, was very strikingly masculinely identified. She was unable to meet her father's high expectations.
That she was conflicted at the phallic-oedipal level is
supported by the fact that she had very few heterosexual
contacts early in her life and then when she did attempt to
establish herself heterosexually her attachment took a pathological form. The first conflict trigger, of course, was
the loss of the mother, and then came the close association
with the father. Thus it would seem that in terms of her
unconscious fantasies her oedipal wishes were realized
through this loss and through her closer association with
her father, and it is significant that soon after this
living arrangement was established she fled from the home
and within a short time began taking drugs. It is evident
that all aspects of heterosexuality were most conflict-
triggering for her.

    The main stress in her life was of a feedback variety
due to her drugs. The supports were plentiful in terms of
finances. For a while she had her father supporting her when
she lived in the home and then her two heterosexual relationships had some supportive aspects in them. Her life
was highly need-incongruent at this point. In her marriage
she was able to live out her castrating, dominant characteristics. It is noteworthy that her father believed that
she was able to live our her "maternal instincts" with this
invalided man.

    Opportunities at the time of initial study were not
great. The relationship to the father, while supportive,
was also need-incongruent in that it tended to infantilize
her. Most of her living arrangements in her marriage,
while living alone, or in the affair with the older man,
were highly need-incongruent. While living alone she was
in a kind of Bohemian colony, isolated, buried in book,
food, TV and drugs.

3. Summary of Situational Variables at the Time of Termi-
    nation Study

    After the outpatient evaluation the patient was ad-
mitted to the hospital and began psychoanalysis. She was

discharged from the hospital, the Day Hospital, and finally the family care home, and then moved into an apartment. Her father died in the early sixties and her therapist died two years later. Therapy with a second therapist began immediately.

By the time of termination the patient was no longer taking drugs nor was she drinking. Her panic attacks and phobias had been reduced some. The core conflicts were unresolved. It was noted that the patient's bitterness about the difference between the sexes remained quite pronounced. The objective of analyzing this woman was abandoned.

It should be mentioned that the first therapist noticed that after the father's death the patient became more determined to work, she had begun taking bus rides, she could get along better with women, and she was able to discuss sex more openly. After her father's death she could put up a picture of him. About this she said that before his death having a picture of him in view was like incest. Thus it seems that the removal of a significant conflict trigger, the father, had permitted some symptomatic improvement. However, heterosexuality was still very conflict-triggering.

There were no stresses in her life at this time. Supports were relatively meager because her finances had run out, her father was dead, and the one brother had little contact with her. Her life was not very need-congruent because of her relative isolation. Work was need-congruent, however. Her friends and her home were all need-congruent, but in terms of significant relationships which would help her mature as a woman she was in a relatively need-incongruent environment. Opportunities for her were fewer at termination than at initial study because of her increasing age and the lack of change in her character makeup or her neurosis.

4. Summary of Situational Variables at the Time of Follow-up Study

While this was a follow-up study, the patient was, in fact, still in psychotherapy with the therapist who took over when the first therapist died.

The phobias had slowly begun to disappear so that the patient could now drive where she wanted to although there were still certain areas that she avoided. She was taking

better care of herself; she had not provoked her superiors
at work and had been able to keep her job. She had a few
friends but her association with men was nil. She had a
few dates with a man, which seems to reflect a change in
feeling towards men. Her description of this experience,
however, sounded like an idealized, living out, symptomatic
romance with a man of relatively low socioeconomic class.
It may well be that menopausal changes in her provided the
primary impetus for this brief affair. There were no conflict triggers at the time of follow-up. There were no
stresses other than having to support herself and support
the treatment. Supports were minimal, the main ones being
treatment, her work and her few friends at work. Need-
congruence was quite low because of the isolation her illness had forced upon her. Opportunities for the future
were less plentiful than at the time of initial study.

5. Summary

    This patient was her father's favorite, and while we
do not have a clear developmental history it seems apparent
that she never overcame a strong dependence and developed a
phallic masculine identity. The first signs of disturbance
appeared during latency when she apparently had some kind
of altered state of consciousness, presumably petit mal
epilepsy.

    Being kissed by a boy at age 12 caused her to believe
she was pregnant for about three months. After having
observed parental intercourse she made a prompt weight gain
at age 12. During her early teens she and a girl friend
masturbated men in movie houses. She was possessed by homosexual fears during her midteens and she had her first
attacks of panicky feelings which eventually disappeared.
Her illness seems to have reappeared in gross form sometime
after the mother's death when she was approximately 20 years
of age.

    After her mother's death she went away to school for
a year, then returned home for surgery. It was during this
period of the mother's death, living with the father and
having two major surgeries that she decompensated. She
developed phobias and began taking drugs and alcohol. Upon
the encouragement of her father she went to the West Coast
where she finally decompensated even more and entered into
various kinds of unsavory relationships, and finally had to
be brought to the hospital. While she had some altered
states of consciousness during her latency period, the main
illness did not appear until prepuberty and puberty.

This case beautifully illustrates the conflict-trigger-ing and illness-provoking effect of environmental circum-stances. With the loss of the mother the patient, in essence, realized her oedipal dreams by being able to live alone with her father. It is significant that this object loss was followed shortly afterwards by a flare-up of thyrotox-icosis. She was living with her father, who seemed clearly to have triggered off and mobilized the oedipal wishes in her. In an effort to protect herself she left home and found encouragement from her father, who may have uncon-sciously recognized that it wasn't good for his daughter to live at home with him. Moving away from home was another loss, another separation and, therefore, a conflict trigger. She desperately entered into a relationship with a very sick man from whom she must have found some comfort in the sense of having her dependency and object loss soothed. With this weak man she could live out her dominant "masculine" characteristics.

SYNTHESIS OF SITUATIONAL VARIABLES - CASE #42

1. Brief History

When this patient came to the Menninger Foundation for
evaluation she was a 50-year-old married housewife. Her
presenting complaint, which necessitated her being hospitalized, was depression.

The patient's father was a hard working man who had
grown up in a sod house and who never went to professional
school but who studied on his own and eventually passed the
bar and became a successful attorney. He was civic-minded,
a Sunday school superintendent, and a prohibitionist. The
patient said that he had no vices, and that she worshipped
him. The patient's mother was six years older than her
husband; this was a point about which she was so sensitive
that she denied her age. The mother was said to have been
very nervous inwardly but appeared calm outwardly. Both
parents developed hypertension and both apparently had
cerebral hemorrhages prior to their deaths.

The patient was an only child. From early childhood
on the mother taught her to be afraid of the dark and to
watch for males. She had many somatic illnesses early in
life, and even after her marriage her parents paid some of
her medical bills. Because of her illnesses the patient
had maids to help with the housework and her husband helped
take care of the children. Both the husband and daughter
stated that everyone in the family had been conditioned to
the patient having been sick so much, and that when she
was not sick she tended to be tired. The daughter said she
felt that the patient would have been happier to have been
a man, and that she did not seem to enjoy doing work around
the home. She also said that while the patient enjoyed
participating with the children in intellectual things, she
did not especially enjoy being a mother.

After the patient's mother died the father seemed lost.
The patient did not seem particularly upset by the death

349

of her mother, but she eventually became quite upset at the death of her father. For many months prior to his death, however, she commuted back and forth between her home and the parents' home and she spent most of the week with her father and only part of the weekend with her family.

The precipitating factor for the onset of her illness leading to her severe depression was the prospect of her son leaving hom after he graduated from high school. As the time approached for her son to leave home she became progressively more depressed and finally was given subcoma insulin by her internist. She ultimately became so depressed that she even thought of suicide. The patient had always had high expectations of herself and it is the husband's belief (he seemed to know her very well) that as her powers began failing due to her somatic illness and advancing age she was no longer able to do the many things she expected of herself. These failures, he believed, contributed to the onset of depression.

2. Summary of Situational Variables at the Time of Initial Study

The core conflict seemed to center around her dependency and a marked competitiveness and a need to excel, which in turn seemed to be based on her masculine aspirations and identifications. These, in turn, would seem to be based upon the phallic-oedipal conflict. It seems rather evident that this person devalued women and overvalued men and was herself dissatisfied with her role as a woman. This conflict manifested itself in many ways; for instance, the open competitiveness with the husband in later life; the choice of the same profession as her father's, her difficulties being a mother, and her extreme devotion to her father during the last years of his life. The conflict triggers for this woman seem to have been, first and foremost, the demands of womanhood. These were simply the demands her husband and children and home responsibilities placed upon her. She managed to prevent these conflict triggers from being too intense, however, by avoiding her numerous responsibilities one way or another. Two conflict triggers, however, from which she could not escape were the death of her father and the loss of her son who left for college. Add to these the subtle losses due to advancing age and it seems clear that loss was a major conflict trigger for her. It would appear that the son was a narcissistic extension of herself, and that losing him was like losing part of herself and clearly a loss of narcissistic supply.

Supports at the time of initial study were rather good.
The husband was a supportive man who provided adequately,
who was steady, and who kept their lives on course despite
her instability. The patient had a very good internist who
likewise added a great deal of stability and support to her
life. The children seemed to understand their mother well
and did not withdraw their affection from her. There were
women's clubs and a good social circle. The patient's parents left her considerable wealth. The opportunities were
rather plentiful. She could have worked if she had wanted
to, and certainly she had a fairly good relationship with
her children, who were beginning to give her grandchildren.
There was very little that was need-incongruent in her life.
She had a home, children, a good strong husband who, despite her oppositionalism, never gave up insofar as their
love life was concerned, nor in his devotion to her.

3. Summary of Situational Variables at the Time of Termi-
    nation Study

This patient was seen three times a week by her first
psychotherapist for over 600 hours, and once a week by her
second psychotherapist for over 100 hours at the termination cutoff point. Records show that she went home on a
trial visit, and that she was finally discharged from the
hospital within a few months. She returned to her home and
at that point her psychotherapy was reduced to one hour a
week. After the patient went into Day Hospital she enrolled in law classes. She had been visiting her home
rather frequently during this time.

After returning to her home she worked for five years
as an executive secretary for a large organization. She
got into difficulties with her supervisor. The tension
between them caused her somatic illness to exacerbate and
she stopped working. Apparently the marriage had changed
somewhat in that the patient was working very hard at establishing a closer relationship with her husband. She admitted that for four years she had grown rather distant
from him. The patient seemed to have accepted her husband's
prominence more gracefully, and was able to travel with him
and derive some enjoyment and even be present when he was
receiving honors.

By the time of termination she was by no means relieved
of her psychic disturbances, not to mention her somatic
ones. There was still some depressive quality to her, and
her somatic illness was rather severe. The competitiveness with her husband was still there. It was evident that

she was still dissatisfied with being a woman, that she could not get along with her daughter too well, and that her attachment to her son was quite intense. Competitiveness with men in general seemed apparent still, and while she went through the motions of being a homemaker her heart really wasn't in it. On the other hand, the patient was dissatisfied that there were other attorneys who had more prominence and more money than her husband.

The data suggest that the core neurosis in this patient was not resolved at the time of termination. Despite the fact that the first therapist thought this was an expressive psychotherapy, the treatment team quite correctly, we believe, assessed the first therapy as not being expressive.

It was quite evident that the husband's masculinity still triggered her own competitive phallic conflict. The primary conflict, however, at the time of initial study was the departure of the son. This was no longer a central issue with her, and in that sense one of the major conflict triggers was removed. The patient and her daughter tended to argue a great deal (in the words of the patient's husband, "those two women - the wife and the daughter - know just what to say to infuriate each other"). That the patient gave up working and was back in the home suggests that the home environment was again more of a conflict trigger for her. The only stress was the physical illness.

The supports had been remarkable throughout. Her husband had remained loyal to her; there was adequate financial support; there was a good social circle. The children were good to her even though the patient and her daughter squabbled a good deal. Her life had always been need-congruent. The husband had provided her with a home, with a prominent place in society, and with children. He had been a strong man who had been able to hold her neurosis in check rather well. Working for a time as an executive secretary was need-congruent. Opportunities had always been rather good for this woman.

4. Summary of Situational Variables at the Time of Follow-up Study

At the time of follow-up the patient's son was a practicing attorney in a distant city and the daughter was a wife and homemaker in another distant city. The daughter had a severely alcoholic husband. The patient's husband was still a prominent practicing attorney. The patient picked up with many of her old friends and had taken on a

number of civic activities as well as some volunteer work
for some psychological research. She was on the board of
governors or directors of a hospital.

The core conflicts had not been resolved. There is no
evidence to show that any essential intrapsychic change had
taken place. Her defense structure was considerably more
consolidated. Most notably, however, many of the old conflict triggers were gone. The loss problem which triggered
her illness had been accepted and perhaps even worked
through. The husband was probably still somewhat of a conflict trigger because of his insistent masculine demands
upon her. She managed her home, but it was with considerable effort that she did so. The most outstanding conflict
trigger was the husband. The more general, less specific,
kind of conflict trigger was the role of a woman. In this
role the demands upon her were much less than they used to
be.

We saw no stresses except the continuing somatic illness. The husband had been undaunted by her competitive
obstructionistic makeup, and he persisted in his masculine
demands upon her. This was a most need-congruent aspect
of her life. She had managed somehow to adapt to these
qualities in him and, indeed, respected them. The patient
claimed to love her husband. She found a good deal of satisfaction from pursuits outside the home. She had become
quite a successful investor.

5. Summary

This woman was described as having a dependent core
and also marked phallic-oedipal conflicts. She never fully
accepted her femininity, but despite this was able to marry
and have two children. She had been continually at odds
with herself, thus developing much tension which probably
contributed to the onset of her physical illness. She
herself was an attorney but never practiced after she married. She respected her husband, loved him, but at the
same time was very competitive with him. She was deeply
attached to her father and his death, while it did not
trigger the overt illness, made quite an impact on her.
The final straw seems to have been the imminent departure
of her son from home, and the fact that she never seemed
satisfied with her life and never felt that she fulfilled
herself. She developed a deep depression, was hospitalized briefly, and was treated by supportive expressive
psychotherapy for a long period of time. She slowly recon-
stituted. During this period, however, the major conflict

trigger had been removed by virtue of the fact that she had come to accept the loss of her children (by their leaving home), and during the follow-up period had picked up again with the way of life that was not too different from the way she started out. That is to say, the major part of her energies were expended in pursuits which were outside of the home.

This was a woman who tried her best to fulfill her feminine role in life but who was never at peace with herself in doing so. When her children, particularly her son, left home she developed an acute sense of loss and became depressed. This loss came to be accepted in time, and she gradually established a busy routine which kept her away from her home a good deal of the time. At the same time, she respected her strong husband very much, and without him it is likely that she would have been quite lost for, in fact, there seemed to be a very dependent attachment to him even though she was also competitive with him. It should be noted that the husband thought that she would be very happy if he became an invalid so that she could care for him. She took care of her ailing father for six years, traveling many miles between his home and her own, thus escaping from responsibilities in her own home. Her husband said he believed she would have been happier as a man.